Hellenic Studies 63

POETRY AS INITIATION

Recent Titles in the Hellenic Studies Series

Divine Yet Human Epics
Reflections of Poetic Rulers from Ancient Greece and India

The Web of Athenaeus

Eusebius of Caesarea
Tradition and Innovations

The Theology of Arithmetic
Number Symbolism in Platonism and Early Christianity

Homeric Durability
Telling Time in the Iliad

Paideia and Cult
Christian Initiation in Theodore of Mopsuestia

Imperial Geographies in Byzantine and Ottoman Space

Loving Humanity, Learning, and Being Honored
The Foundations of Leadership in Xenophon's Education of Cyrus

The Theory and Practice of Life
Isocrates and the Philosophers

From Listeners to Viewers
Space in the Iliad

Aspects of History and Epic in Ancient Iran
From Gaumāta to Wahnām

Homer's Versicolored Fabric
The Evocative Power of Ancient Greek Epic Word-Making

Christianity and Hellenism in the Fifth-Century Greek East
Theodoret's Apologetics against the Greeks in Context

The Master of Signs
Signs and the Interpretation of Signs in Herodotus' Histories

The Epic Rhapsode and His Craft
Homeric Performance in a Diachronic Perspective

Eve of the Festival
Making Myth in Odyssey 19

Kleos in a Minor Key
The Homeric Education of a Little Prince

Plato's Counterfeit Sophists

Multitextuality in the Homeric Iliad
The Witness of the Ptolemaic Papyri

POETRY AS INITIATION

The Center for Hellenic Studies Symposium on the Derveni Papyrus

edited by
Ioanna Papadopoulou and Leonard Muellner

Center for Hellenic Studies
Trustees for Harvard University
Washington, DC
Distributed by Harvard University Press
Cambridge, Massachusetts, and London, England
2014

Poetry as Initiation: The Center for Hellenic Studies Symposium on the Derveni Papyrus
Edited by Ioanna Papadopoulou and Leonard Muellner

Published by Center for Hellenic Studies, Trustees for Harvard University, Washington, D.C.
Distributed by Harvard University Press, Cambridge, Massachusetts and London, England

LIBRARY OF CONGRESS CATALOGING-IN-PUBLICATION DATA

Poetry as initiation : the Center for Hellenic Studies symposium on the Derveni papyrus / edited by Ioanna Papadopoulou and Leonard Muellner.
pages cm — (Hellenic studies ; 63)
Includes bibliographical references and index.
ISBN 978-0-674-72676-5 (alk. paper)

1. Derveni papyrus—Congresses. 2. Greece—Religion—Congresses. 3. Greek literature—History and criticism—Congresses. I. Papadopoulou, Ioanna. II. Muellner, Leonard Charles. III. Center for Hellenic Studies (Washington, D.C.) IV. Series: Hellenic studies ; 63.

BL782.P58 2014
292.8—dc23 013049499

Contents

Foreword

Leonard Muellner
Brandeis University
Center for Hellenic Studies

THIS VOLUME HAS BOTH A HISTORY AND A FUTURE. The conference in July 2008 that produced the papers appearing here was a consequence of the permission granted to the Center for Hellenic Studies in 2006 by Leo S. Olschki Editore in Florence to publish online the text of the Derveni Papyrus as presented in its *editio princeps* by Kouremenos, Parássoglou, and Tsantsanoglou and published in that same year. The online publication of this edition was the result of the good offices of several institutions, including the Università degli Studi di Genova, the Aristotle University of Thessaloniki, and the Archaeological Museum of Thessaloniki.

Since 2006, the Center has developed a new digital form for the text within the framework of the CHS–iMouseion Project, which offers the possibility of a "multiversion Derveni Papyrus." Because of the number of unplaced fragments, this exceptionally challenging document is still in the process of being pieced together. New reconstructions can be displayed side by side, offering a simultaneous view of the different proposed versions of each column. We have thus updated the presentation of the papyrus on the Derveni Project site to include Franco Ferrari's edition of the papyrus (cols. I–VI) and to enable comparison between it and the *editio princeps*. The two versions can be viewed at http://nrs.harvard.edu/urn-3:hul.eresource:Derveni_Papyrus_FerrariF_ed_2012.

The conference papers were published in earlier versions as Issue 5 of the Center's online journal, *Classics@*, where they are still accessible; that edition includes video supplements (see http://nrs.harvard.edu/urn-3:hul.ebook:CHS_Classicsat). Many of these papers have been significantly updated for the present publication.

In the spring of 2014, the Center will publish the current volume online on a new website that allows for moderated interaction and response. The study of the Derveni Papyrus is a vital, ongoing process that we wish to foster. That process may well result in new online-only editions of the research published here.

INTRODUCTION

Testing Our Tools

Open Questions on the Derveni Papyrus

Ioanna Papadopoulou
Université Libre de Bruxelles
Center for Hellenic Studies

THE DERVENI PAPYRUS[1] SHOULD NEVER HAVE REACHED US. This text, the oldest European book in our possession, was meant to accompany forever the cremated body buried in Derveni Tomb A. It is our great luck that this roll, with its extraordinary text, did not burn thoroughly but awaited its accidental discovery, during public works, in an uninhabited area about 10 km from Thessaloniki; the tomb is located near the ruins of a small ancient town called Lete, although not in Lete's cemetery but in a graveyard about 2 km away. The carbonized papyrus was discovered on the slabs covering Tomb A, along with other remains from the cremation of the deceased.[2] We owe to the mastery of Petros Themelis, who was supervising the excavation, and to the skills of the Austrian conservator Anton Fackelmann the rescue of this rare (for a modern audience) piece of ancient thought.

There is no need to repeat here in detail the history of this extraordinary discovery, of the process of conservation, and of the edition of the text.[3] A first, unauthorized, transcription of the *P.Derv.* text appeared in 1982 in the *Zeitschrift für Papyrologie und Epigraphik* (*ZPE*), and was followed by R. Janko's "Interim text."[4] In his contribution to the current volume, Burkert, whose uninterrupted interest in the papyrus over a period of more than forty-five years has opened most paths of research on the subject, offers for the first time the "true

1 Henceforth *P.Derv.*

2 See the photos in the article by Tzifopoulos in this volume, pp. 140–141.

3 See the introduction in Th. Kouremenos, G. Parássoglou, and K. Tsantsanoglou, eds., *The Derveni Papyrus, Edited with Introduction and Commentary* (Studi e testi per il "Corpus dei papiri filosofici greci e latini" 13) (Florence, 2006). This is the *editio princeps*, hereafter cited as KPT.

4 *ZPE* 141 (2002): 1–62.

story" about the anonymous publication. The *editio princeps,* by Kouremenos, Parássoglou, and Tsantsanoglou (KPT), appeared in 2006. It presents 26 columns of text and 113 unplaced fragments, precious photographs of the papyrus, a translation, and a commentary. The digital version of the text is available at the Center for Hellenic Studies (CHS) Derveni Papyrus site (http://nrs.harvard.edu/urn-3:hul.eresource:CHS_Derveni_Papyrus).

More progress has been made since the appearance of the *editio princeps.* Janko has published several articles offering new arrangements of the first columns and new readings, which are discussed in this volume, mainly by Tsantsanoglou, Bernabé, and Ferrari, who provides an important critical overview of the initial reconstitution and other papyrological issues relevant to the edition of the papyrus, as well as new arrangements of the first columns.[5] Bernabé, who published a critical edition and commentary on the papyrus in 2007,[6] presents in his paper important new readings and discusses new proposals from Janko and Ferrari that affect the first six columns.

Papers in this volume address a wide range of open questions. Graf, Bernabé, Tsantsanoglou, and Tzifopoulos focus mainly on ritual, whereas Burkert, Calame, Sistakou, and Rusten revisit the problem of authorship, authorial procedures, and literary strategies. Bernabé and Graf offer a new and detailed analysis of possible contexts relative to the *magoi.* Tsantsanoglou revisits the question of Persian influences on the theological system of the *P.Derv.* author, suggesting a possible affinity between Nous and Ahura Mazdā (pp. 16–17). New arrangements and readings presented by Ferrari, namely for columns IV and VI, bring into the discussion new elements about the relation of the *P.Derv.* text to Persian religion, on the one hand, and to Democritus, on the other. Tzifopoulos provides a most instructive parallelism between Bacchic-Orphic *epistomia* and the *P.Derv.* papyrus roll as *entaphia* objects. Furthermore, in Rusten's and Tzifopoulos's papers we find an interesting overview of the "semantics" of burials with books: can a papyrus included amid grave goods be considered a valid proof regarding the religious faith of the deceased? Tsantsanoglou considers the book to be an equivalent of Orphic gold leaves, a more intellectual kind of authoritative passport to the underworld. Johnston shifts the meaning of Ἅιδου δεινά from "horrors of Hades" to "miseries inflicted on the living by the dead" and studies related oracular practices. Calame shows in his paper that by attributing a

5 See F. Ferrari, "Frustoli erranti: Per una ricostruzione delle colonne 1–3 del Papiro di Derveni," in *Papiri filosofici: Miscellanea di studi* VI, ed. M. S. Funghi (Florence, 2011) 39–54. To help readers keep apace with new material, the CHS–iMouseion Derveni Papyrus Project has developed a digital text of the papyrus which features the Ferrari 2012 edition of the first six columns in a "multiversion" structure, enabling comparison with the KPT edition.

6 *Musaeus · Linus · Epimenides · Papyrus Derveni · Indices* (*Poetae epici Graeci: Testimonia et fragmenta,* part II, fasc. 3) (Berlin, 2007).

quasi-oracular process to the poem, the *P.Derv.* author conforms to the traditions concerning the prophetic qualities of the voice of the immortalized Orpheus, who reveals by signs the supreme sacred truth ([μεγ]άλα̣ ἱερ[ολογ]-ε̣ῖ̣ται, VII 8). Using Hippolytus' prayer (Euripides *Hippolytus* 73–87) as a departure point, Hunter examines poetry as coded speech for the few and analyzes related poetological ideas in the scholia. Burkert puts in perspective the interest in souls manifested by the author and shows that it is perfectly compatible with Presocratic philosophy, and especially with what we know about Democritus.[7]

Dating the Derveni Papyrus is a complex issue. It contains a multilayered text: a description of a ritual, verses of a poem of Orpheus, and exegesis by the author. As Burkert, Calame, and Tzifopoulos stress in this volume, one must keep in mind three different chronological issues: the date of the poem of Orpheus (always conjectural; sixth century, according to Burkert); the date of the exegesis (possibly end of fifth century); and the date of the papyrus roll itself (mid-fourth century[8]). Up to now there was no certainty about the original number of papyrus rolls containing the *P.Derv.* text. Tsantsanoglou's hypothesis that the work comprised at least three rolls is confirmed in his present article by an important new discovery: "the papyrus seems to provide column numbering ... if our column V is numbered 35 and the numbering started from column I, the preceding roll should contain thirty columns ... two more columns are missing from the beginning of the preserved roll" (pp. 14–15).

The contents of the surviving roll present a particular thematic and structural division, which makes this work a *unicum* among what we possess of the literary production of the period. Naturally, one of the main efforts of scholars was and is to classify this highly particular text. The first six columns (three are badly damaged by fire, as they were written on what became the outer part of the roll) refer to propitiatory rituals aimed at appeasing souls. Column VII forms the transition to the other thematic unit, in which the author adduces verses of a poem of Orpheus and offers an interpretation, in the form of what most scholars call by anachronism a "commentary." Orpheus's name appears clearly in the papyrus—twice in column XVIII—and also is conjectured in column VII.

Our understanding of the text is progressing steadily. New and important points arise as a result of the reconstruction of column I presented by Bernabé and Ferrari in this volume: a religious authority (probably Orpheus) constructs a ritual whose meaning is revealed by *semeia*. The central addressees here are the

7 We are particularly indebted to Walter Burkert and to Kyriakos Tsantsanoglou, who, not being able to attend the conference, each accepted our invitation to give a video performance of his paper; these are available on the CHS website together with transcripts and handouts (in *Classics@*, Issue 5).

8 KPT, 9.

Erinyes. Erinyes/Eumenides are of utmost importance in the *P.Derv.* text: they are mentioned in all surviving columns related to ritual, except column V. The *exegesis* of the chthonic ritual is of a most peculiar kind compared to what we know. Supernatural entities receive well-known traditional names—*daimones*, Erinyes, Eumenides—but as description and explanation of the ritual merge, the relation of those entities to souls is not clear. It is as if the author describes the ritual acts only to subordinate them to his *hermeneia*, and this is extremely rare in the period under consideration. For instance, when he says that Eumenides are souls (VI 9), it is not clear if he is voicing his own opinion or that of a larger group, religious/spiritual or intellectual or both. As Tsantsanoglou puts it, the author corrects the popular concept of Erinyes—as avengers only of perjury and homicide—by upgrading their jurisdiction from social to cosmic. The ritual acts described are sacrifice, libation, incantation, singing, prayer. Bernabé's reading, ọ[ρ]ṿị́θ̣[ε]ιομ ... [χρὴ λύειν instead of καίειν, in column VI, line 11 ("liberate a bird" instead of "burn a bird") removes a major difficulty regarding the classification of the ritual as Orphic, given that Orphics do not sacrifice living beings. While stressing, as Henrichs did in 1984, that ritual acts themselves seem "native," Johnston believes that the *P.Derv.* author's ritual definitions are mostly innovations. In fact, there is nothing to allow us to define ritual space and time, as Sistakou stresses in her paper.

Furthermore, the absence of gods in this first part, especially the infernal ones, is a paradox which Bernabé explains as a rationalizing effort, probably linked to the monistic tendency of the author, to suppress multiple gods as addressees of the ritual (one can as well think of the unspeakable *orgia* related to the death of Dionysus and compare the reluctance of Herodotus to recount such myths). Nevertheless, following Martín-Hernández, Bernabé considers that the myth of the titanic crime against Dionysos is "the very ground of the ritual" and that ποινὴṿ ἀποδιδόντες in column VI 5 refers to the ritual atonement of this act.

Who then are the performers of ritual in the Derveni Papyrus? The author, the *magoi*, the *mystai*? Is the author referring to a specific occasion, or is he giving a general overview of ritual practices suiting his complex arguments? We can say for sure that the author pictures two types of officiants—*mystai* and *magoi*—linked in an interesting manner, which makes the *magoi* the prototype of the action of the *mystai*. *Mystai*, says the author, address to the Eumenides a preliminary sacrifice in the manner of the *magoi*. Column VI, the best-preserved one in the first part, contains eight lines presenting the *magoi* as "able" (ἐπ̣[ωιδὴ δ]ὲ̣ μάγων δύν[α]ται) to "push away" or "make change" (depending on the translation chosen for μεθιστάṿαι), by their incantations, the *daimones* who are "enemies" of souls or "avengers." Janko's new rearrangements of columns II and

III (accepted by Tsantsanoglou) have produced another mention of the *magoi* in column III, where they are quoted as the authority asserting that the *daimones* who observe the honors of the gods are their servants. In both cases, column III and column VI, the *magoi* appear as prestigious authorities in religious matters, as Bernabé and Graf show in their papers.

Who the *magi* are is one of the major *zetemata* in *P.Derv.* scholarship: Persian priests or Greek sorcerers? According to Graf, who evokes possible Eastern contexts, the Derveni *magi* are religious specialists claiming the Persian title for themselves. "It might be that after the Persian conquest of Lydia in 547 BCE ... enterprising Persian μάγοι began to serve the needs of Greeks and even adapted their ritual repertoire to Greek demands for mystery cults" (p. 83). An overview of divergent opinions (Persian *magoi*, Orphic priests, charlatans?) can be found in Bernabé's paper, where he opts finally, as Calame and Bierl do, for Orphic officiants, "*orpheotelestai*"; this term is attested outside "Orphic" literature in Greece, thus representing probably the "external," sometimes hostile perspective found in historians of religion, for instance, while "*magos*" could be used within Orphic circles positively for the same type of officiant. Tsantsanoglou maintains his position: the *P.Derv.* text refers to Persian *magoi*. Important information on this topic has appeared following a new arrangement by Ferrari and an ingenious supplement by Piano: the word Πέρσαι appears in column V, line 11. Furthermore, by a rearrangement of column VI, Ferrari replaces ψυχαί (souls), in line 1, with ἀρτάδας (the Greek "transliteration" of *artavan*, the Persian word for "the Just, the Heroes"), thus adding one more Persian reference to the debate—which is nevertheless still open, as other contributions in this volume show.

Is the author himself a ritual practitioner? Is he, as some believe, a *magos*, Greek or Persian? Opinions are divided and wildly divergent: is he an atheist, an Orphic, an anti-Orphic, an orpheotelest? Or a *mantis*? Or an enlightened intellectual who mocks, partly at least, divinatory practices (this last hypothesis is based mainly on col. V)?[9] Trying to define better the author's profession as well as his philosophical and religious position, even if the authorship remains an open question, continues to be a most interesting exercise. The fact that the *P.Derv.* author explains ritual doesn't necessarily make a *telestes* out of him, as the editors stated in their introduction to the *editio princeps* (KPT, 52). Our proceedings reopen the question of the authorship. Burkert and Tsantsanoglou revisit the question and discuss possible candidates: the latter sides with Kahn, considering Euthyphro a good candidate. Comparing the views about souls in the Derveni Papyrus with the scraps of information we have about

9 If we side with Janko (*ZPE* 166 [2008]).

Democritus' interest in souls, Burkert plays with the idea of Democritus' authorship, but dismisses it finally because the *Nous* in the Derveni Papyrus is more Anaxagorean than Democritean. Burkert concludes by dismissing as well any ritual competence of the *P.Derv*. author by denying that he or his group is the subject of *parimen* in column V (which he takes for an infinitive): "he is writing on *tà eónta*" and is "an interesting writer among those earlier, pre-Platonic thinkers of Greece" (p. 112). Most scholars in this volume believe, however, that the author is a ritual practitioner.

Unfortunately, the fragmentary state of the document deprives us of a fully structured text and does not always allow for proper connections between agents, actions, and concepts. Nevertheless we can say for sure that justice is a central theme. In column IV, for instance, Erinyes are Dike's *epikouroi*; this is the same column where we find the famous quotation of Heraclitus about Sun having to face the Erinyes if he does not respect his own limits. In this Heraclitean quotation the Erinyes act as guardians of cosmic equilibrium, as assistants of Dike.

Most scholars believe that after he has quoted the authority of Heraclitus on the relation between the Erinyes and Justice, the author refers in the following column (V) to his own mantic craft while addressing a critique to those who do not believe in the horrors of Hades and in signs such as those transmitted by dreams: "On behalf of those persons we go to the oracle to ask if it is permitted not to believe...." Column V (together with col. XX) is crucial in the scholarly debate on the profession and beliefs of the author. Janko, for instance, challenges the *opinio communis* by arguing that the author is an atheist (possibly Diagoras of Melos), and that in column V[10] he is attacking those who believe in the horrors of Hades.

On the meaning of Ἅιδου δεινά, Johnston introduces important clarifications by examining the possible associations between the horrors of Hades and divination and by showing that the author refers not to punishments experienced during the afterlife but to miseries inflicted upon the living by the dead, a theme consistent with the previous ones (the theme of appeasement). Souls can ask the living, via dreams and oracles, to take care of neglected duties, such as funerary rites and the like. As to the author being a *mantis*, Johnston admits the possibility of understanding *parimen* (V 4) as a first-person plural referring not to the author and his fellow practitioners specifically but to the general practice of the divinatory effort "wasted" by the attitude of the nonbelievers (p. 91).

It seems difficult to reach an agreement on the question of whether the *P.Derv.* author is a ritual practitioner. A closer look at column XX might help. Up to now, scholarly analysis of this column has focused mostly on the possibility

10 Following his new reading of lines 5–6 (*ZPE* 166 [2008]: 50).

of a different authorial voice in the text marked by *paragraphoi* (after lines 10 and 13) and on the critique of private initiations expressed in those lines. In this volume, Rusten's paper confirms his 1985 analysis (extensively explained on pp. 127–132), whereas Graf is opposed to the idea of these *paragraphoi* marking a quotation of a different author: "these *paragraphoi* ... function as marginal signs to catch the attention of a reader who was browsing through the text" (p. 74).

Column XX also contains another very important theme. Interrupting his lesson on gods and the universe, our author criticizes the way religious acts are performed in both public and private spheres. In doing so, not only does he "normalize" the scandalous incest stories that follow, as Graf underlines, but he also analyzes laconically the very mechanics of oral performance and its reception:[11] οὐ γὰρ οἷόν τε ἀκοῦσαι ὁμοῦ καὶ μαθεῖν τὰ λ̣εγόμενα, "one cannot hear and understand at the same time the *legomena*" (XX 3). This extraordinary information expresses a fundamental authorial principle operating throughout the *P.Derv.* text, a principle which gives the very *raison d'être* of the whole *exegesis.* By criticizing the formality of performance in ritual, uttering words without *exegesis*, the author brings to the forefront the very moment—mystic or not—of the *hymnos* performance and its mimetic enchantment, much criticized by the intellectuals. The author criticizes the oral reception of Orpheus' poem during solemn occasions. In the second part of column XX (lines 4–12), private initiations—which should respond better to specific needs, as described by Adeimantos in his ironic discourse on *magoi* and *agyrtai* (*Republic* 364b–365a)—are characterized as equally inefficient. If we follow the *P.Derv.* author, *exegesis* should be part of the ritual as initiation should be part of the *mathesis.*

Graf deals at length with the relation of *legomena* to initiation and opts for a religious entrepreneur interested in physics. I think, however, that the *exegesis* allows a different perspective about the profile of the author and his audience. A secret circle of *gignōskontes* and a restricted audience interested primarily in physics seem to me a plausible option. The key passage is not only column XX but the interpretation Air = Zeus in column XXIII (2–7); the two *loci,* read together, reveal the nature of what is mystic and what the interests of the *gignōskontes* might be. These theories are mystical, and they belong to the field of knowledge of the *physiologoi*, of the *Peri physeos* literature. In column XXIII mystic knowledge attached to theogony and ritual is physics, which might mean that the author is trying to initiate his audience into the theories of his time while preserving the prestige of the poetic *lexis.*

This brings us to the second thematic unit of the *P.Derv.* text. Its first part describes a ritual space with no time or place, using the present of the ritual

11 If we admit that a poem is meant here, as Graf suggests.

repetition (a dramatic present, as Sistakou underlines). In column VII the authorial voice continues in its role of teaching and explaining the deeper sense, this time of Orpheus's poem.[12] Bernabé insists upon the symmetry between the two parts of the *P.Derv.* text: description and explanation are interwoven. No specific association is mentioned between *drômena* and *legomena*, however. No certainty about the ritual occasion can be established. Graf considers that the poem was the *legomena* in some Bacchic ritual, but not the *exegesis*, which was meant to follow initiation (p. 70).

Pleading for the necessity of the *onomatōn lusis*, the author develops an exegesis "word by word," on a poetry that he qualifies as "strange" and "enigmatic," commenting upon the intentions of Orpheus, who expresses "great things" in a coded language (*ainigma, ainizomai*; studied in detail in this volume by Bierl). Twenty columns, better preserved than the first six, deal with the *exegesis* of verses quoted from the Orphic poem. These verses recount a version or an episode of the theogonic myth of succession focused on Zeus' power and predominance, whereas their *exegesis* deals mainly with the theme of violence and aims at underplaying it. The tendency is monistic; the world of today is Zeus' creation. The narrative stops abruptly at column XXVI with the theme of incest. It is possible, as Bernabé says, that the missing part, consumed by the funerary pyre, referred to the most mystic theme—Dionysos, the Titans, and the birth of Persephone—according to the principle of symmetry between the two parts (especially if ποινὴ̣ν ἀποδιδόντες in col. VI is an elliptic reference to the Titans' crime).

Combining theology with physics, the author reveals the hidden correspondence between the Orphic lexis and the history of the universe. From column IX on, divine succession becomes a process of *onomatothesia* representing the evolution of the different cosmic phases, following the principles of what we call Presocratic physics in an eclectic blend that resists classification even today. The author unravels the *ainos* (in fact, what we translate as "allegorizing" is *ainizomai* in the text):[13] there is no violence and no succession in divine genealogy. The different stages of the cosmogony receive distinct divine names, but there is only one god and one, evolving, universe. The Heraclitean image about the sun exceeding its limits in column IV, for instance, is probably meant to announce the primordial state of excessive heat referred to later in the text (col. IX and following). According to the *P.Derv.* exegetic vocabulary, where names carry hidden meanings, this cosmic phase corresponds to the divine name of

12 There is no doubt about the existence of Orpheus' name in the *P.Derv.*; as mentioned above, it is clearly discernible twice in col. XVIII.

13 On *ainos* in Greek literature, G. Nagy, "Mythe et prose en Grèce archaïque," in *Métamorphoses du mythe en Grèce ancienne*, ed. C. Calame (Geneva, 1988) 229–242.

"Kronos" and is prior to our universe, which receives the name "Zeus," and owes its stability to the fact that Sun/heat is under control (cols. XIV–XV).

Physics attached to poetics alters radically the "signifié" of gods' names and their "biography": for instance, Kronos is νοῦς and κρούω, the *Nous* who makes the particles collide in a cosmos subdued by excessive heat (col. XIV). Zeus is the creator of the *nun metastasis* because he symbolically represents control over excessive heat, thus allowing the universe to take its stable form—to become, as Hesiod says about Gaia, ἕδος ἀσφαλὲς αἰεί. Words can be pronounced, says the author, but they will not be understood just because they are spoken. It is this very point about mere utterance versus exegesis of sacred or mystic meanings related to physics which seems to me decisive as regards the "professional" profile of the author, who insists upon the importance of *manthanein*, of comprehending tradition and science, both mystic, both demanding knowledge and teaching.[14]

In column XXIII the author comments upon Okeanos, which is not a river, despite the expression εὐρὺ ῥέοντα, which has other meanings than "flow." According to the author the expression signifies "he who has great force." So Okeanos, continues the author, is not a river but rather a mystic name for air.[15] Furthermore, in the same column, the expression ἐν τοῖς λεγομέν[ο]ις καὶ νομιζομένοις ῥήμασι in line 8 can be read as a formula that does not mean only "everyday and conventional language" (KPT translation), as both words are technical terms relating to poetry and ritual. In modern terms we would formulate the meaning as follows: Orpheus uses the "traditional religious language," which is part of the civic religious conventions. In other words, we can say that the *rhemata* he uses are *legomena* and *nomizomena*; he does not opt for a neoteric arrangement such as the Parmenidean poem *Peri physeos*. While choosing the traditional conventions familiar to all, Orpheus intends to dissimulate the truth in the form of poetic *ainigmata*. The *P.Derv.* author respects these *legomena kai nomizomena*, but in Socratic language these would be the "ugly lies" of the great poets (*Republic* 377e).

What are the implications of such a distinction between exoteric *hermeneia*, like that of the Ephesian rhapsode in Plato's *Ion*, and esoteric exegesis for the "few" *gignōskontes*? In order to reconsider the question on a new basis, we should not just oppose public celebrations and private or public initiations. Rusten in this volume formulates nicely the paradox; public and private initiations are both unsatisfactory: "The reader is left to wonder, is there any way

14 Burkert is the only author in the volume who states clearly that "our author is not ... a priest" (p. 112).

15 Following the lines about Achelôos and reflecting the ancient debate about primeval waters—on which Sider adduces interesting quotations.

to be initiated *successfully*?" (p. 129). I think that the Derveni Papyrus, namely its column XXIII, contains a possible answer, while offering a new perspective for understanding the relation between mystic and nonmystic in poetic performances.

At this point a comparison of the *P.Derv.* hermeneutic practices with the Hellenistic commentaries on Homer proves useful, but not for the reasons usually evoked. Let's recall the controversy on the edition of Homer between Alexandria and Pergamon, between Crates and Aristarchus.[16] Most important in this regard is the Okeanos theme, on which I will focus once again for the purposes of the present argument, taking the example of *Iliad* XIV 246 and 246a: the double-verse variant was adopted by Crates but not by Aristarchos (265). Behind this apparently trivial philological matter lie fundamentally different cosmological conceptions. This will not surprise us if we pay due attention to the fact that the cosmos's poetic "geography" is divine and that for the *polloi* Okeanos is a river encircling the earth. For Crates thought the earth was spherical, and this was the criterion of authenticity for the plus verses, conveying the image of water *on* the surface the earth. The editorial vision of Crates reflects an Orphic phase in the evolution of the Homeric tradition, as Nagy shows (267).

It seems to me that the Derveni Papyrus offers another way of understanding the deep roots of such a controversy, a kind of precious missing link in the long chain where poetry, science, and philosophy evolve in close dialogue. The key *locus* is column XXIII, lines 1–7:

> The verse is composed as to be misleading; it is unclear to the many, but quite clear to those who have correct understanding, that "Oceanus" is the air and that air is Zeus. Therefore it was not another Zeus who contrived Zeus, but the same one contrived for himself "great might." But the ignorant ones think that Oceanus is a river, because he adds "wide-flowing. He, however, indicates his own opinion in everyday and conventional language [KPT translation of *legomena kai nomizomena*].

These lines show the mystical nature of the *Peri physeos exegesis*, or, as Bierl puts it, the "two-tier riddling": the Orphic verse is obscure but not secret,[17] whereas the *hermeneia* (what we call "commentary") is for the few. The moment where Okeanos is equated with Air/Zeus belongs to the sphere of knowledge not open to everybody, as this phrasing is in itself "a hidden meaning." Science

[16] On what follows I rely on the more lengthy analysis made by G. Nagy in *Homer the Classic* (Washington, DC, 2010) ch. 2. Relevant page numbers will appear in parentheses.

[17] See R. Martin's arguments on the public character of Orphic poetry, in "Rhapsodizing Orpheus," *Kernos* 14 (2001): 23–33.

here is not exoteric. We are reminded of the Hippocratic law (section 5): "Sacred things are to be shown to sacred persons: to the profane this is not permitted before they are initiated to the *orgia epistemes*."[18] We can also recall Socrates in the *Phaedrus* defending oral speech against writing: [λόγον] ... ὃς μετ' ἐπιστήμης γράφεται ἐν τῇ τοῦ μανθάνοντος ψυχῇ, δυνατὸς μὲν ἀμῦναι ἑαυτῷ, ἐπιστήμων δὲ λέγειν τε καὶ σιγᾶν πρὸς οὓς δεῖ: "the word, which is written with *episteme* in the soul of the learner, which is able to defend itself and knows precisely to whom it should speak, and before whom to be silent." "Pay without learning," "hear without understanding": the author's criticism is radical. He seems to deplore recitations of poetry and rituals which are dissociated from places and occasions of a specific kind of knowledge. We cannot say if the *P.Derv.* author describes a phase synchronic with himself or if he refers, through a historic perspective, to restricted circles of the past, who practiced ritual, poetry, and "philosophy" in a way attested in *testimonia* about Pythagoras' teaching.

We can now revisit briefly the much-debated issue of the generic classification of the work contained in the papyrus, an open question relevant as well to the professional profile of the author. Although difficult to classify, is this text as unusual as it is claimed to be? Further progress on this subject could be made, though only if we suspended for a moment anachronisms, such as the term "commentary," and tried to reconstruct a synchronic model of similar practices using terminology internal to our ancient sources.

As we saw, both parts of the *P.Derv.* treatise, *drômena* and *legomena*, including the author's *exegesis*, link in a clearly didactic manner both traditional poetry and eschatological ritual with the theme of justice. Following this thread, we can spot decisive clues about "genre" in column V. The *P.Derv.* author's critical stance in this column suggests that the Ἄιδου δεινά must have been a subject of vivid debate in that period and that the controversy must have been far-reaching, as δεινά coming from chthonic forces were traditionally considered to be crucial for the survival of the polis (cult of the ancestors, plagues, famines, etc.). As Johnston shows, sometimes the advice of an oracle was needed in order to remove the miseries that the dead were supposed to inflict upon the living, with Oedipus as the most famous literary example. Burkert offers important insights on the issue of "genre" with his article on Democritus' interest in ghosts, souls, and afterlife. Protagoras and Democritus are said to have written treatises about Hades, but we have only indirect and scanty information about them. In a totally different setting, Aristophanes' *Frogs* mirrors, in a superbly comic way, contemporary interests in otherworldly matters.

[18] M. L. West, "Hocus-pocus in East and West," in *Studies on the Derveni Papyrus*, ed. A. Laks and G. Most (Princeton, 1997), 89.

Can we then imagine possible settings for such debates or treatises? The fact is that we do not even need to try very hard: the *Republic* of Plato offers a remarkable literary *paradeigma* of an extensive "treatise in the treatise" on Ἅιδου δεινά, which presents some "ingredients" shared with the Derveni Papyrus. Placed in its wider context within the same dialogue, the famous "critique of poetry" is in fact a detailed discussion of Homeric verses principally referring to gods, *daimones*, and heroes, and to death, lamentation, and the underworld. The "author" is Socrates himself. The time has come, I think, to reconsider the statement about an un-Platonic *P.Derv.* author, and consequently the relation between the Platonic dialogues and the Derveni text: the *P.Derv.* author can be "un-Platonic," but he is not "un-Socratic." The parallels prove interesting if we keep firmly in mind the distinction between what we moderns mean by "Platonic" and what Plato stages as clearly "Socratic."

In books II and III of the *Republic*, Socrates promotes his idea about happiness in death by reciting and commenting on Homeric verses related to the μῦθοι περὶ τῶν ἐν Ἅιδου. The main Socratic message is that Hades is not a dreadful place and that death should not be a source of lamentation and despair for the living. Books II, III, and X are part of an apparently crucial debate on the religious impact of traditional poetry and on how Greeks perceived the afterlife. The fact that these "books" belong to a famous Platonic dialogue[19] should not impede us from experimentally classifying them as a kind of subgenre in the same category as Protagoras', Democritus', and the *P.Derv.* author's treatises on the horrors of Hades.

What Socrates does here is to criticize the ritual representations of traditional poetry during public festivals of the polis, rejecting as false the canonical image of Hades as staged in ritual enactments of traditional poetry or any other type of recitation or storytelling. Hence my first point: The terrors of Hades are not only ghosts, *empousai,* and all other forms of everyday superstition. The main target of Socrates is the canonical poetic image of the underworld endorsed by the civic religious authorities and by the average Athenian, as pictured in Aristophanes' *Clouds*.

I do not intend to minimize the differences between Platonic and Dervenian approaches. Derveni scholarship quite frequently uses material from Plato in a fragmentary way (especially *Republic* 364b–365a, about *magoi* and *agyrtai*), albeit always in agreement with the verdict of an un-Platonic *P.Derv.* author. In this volume Tsantsanoglou, Bernabé, Graf, Rusten, and Tzifopoulos offer interesting thoughts on the topic, either stressing divergences, like the difference in

19 *Non obstat* the debate about the authenticity of book X.

attitude towards ritual, or highlighting convergences, such as the moralizing tendencies of both thinkers. But as I have already said, going a step further and experimenting with a more systematic approach[20] might really deepen our understanding of the work and its context. As we all know, the *Republic* is about justice. If we take a closer look at the thematic structure of the dialogue, however, it becomes clear that death and the underworld frame the discussion in a decisive way. The myths on Hades are present from the very first scene. Furthermore, the *Republic* ends in a similar setting, a Socratic *Nekyia* (distinguished *expressis verbis* from the Odyssean one by Socrates: "I will not recite the *Alkinou apologous*" [614b]), a story meant to correct traditional poetry's image of Hades. In the meantime the "*deina Aidou*" (386b) theme doesn't disappear: it forms the nuclear theme of "the Platonic critique of poetry" in books II and III.

The very first scene of the *Republic* is focused on the theme of the old man close to death, represented here by Kephalos. He is the one who mentions the myths of Hades and relates them to Justice as part of an important and controversial subject in people's lives:

> εὖ γὰρ ἴσθι, ἔφη, ὦ Σώκρατες, ὅτι, ἐπειδάν τις ἐγγὺς ᾖ τοῦ οἴεσθαι τελευτήσειν, εἰσέρχεται αὐτῷ δέος καὶ φροντὶς περὶ ὧν ἔμπροσθεν οὐκ εἰσῄει. οἵ τε γὰρ λεγόμενοι μῦθοι περὶ τῶν ἐν Ἅιδου, ὡς τὸν ἐνθάδε ἀδικήσαντα δεῖ ἐκεῖ διδόναι δίκην, καταγελώμενοι τέως, τότε δὴ στρέφουσιν αὐτοῦ τὴν ψυχὴν μὴ ἀληθεῖς ὦσιν: καὶ αὐτός—ἤτοι ὑπὸ τῆς τοῦ γήρως ἀσθενείας ἢ καὶ ὥσπερ ἤδη ἐγγυτέρω ὢν τῶν ἐκεῖ μᾶλλόν τι καθορᾷ αὐτά—ὑποψίας δ᾽ οὖν καὶ δείματος μεστὸς γίγνεται καὶ ἀναλογίζεται ἤδη καὶ σκοπεῖ εἴ τινά τι ἠδίκησεν. ὁ μὲν οὖν εὑρίσκων ἑαυτοῦ ἐν τῷ βίῳ πολλὰ ἀδικήματα καὶ ἐκ τῶν ὕπνων, ὥσπερ οἱ παῖδες, θαμὰ ἐγειρόμενος δειμαίνει.
>
> "For let me tell you, Socrates," he said, "that whenever someone gets close to thinking he will die, fear and worry come upon him about things which didn't occur to him before. The stories told about what goes on in Hades, how the wrongdoer here must suffer punishment there, which he earlier laughed at, now torment his soul in case they are true. Furthermore, either through the feebleness of old age, or because he is indeed now nearer to the beyond as it where, and so perceives it somewhat more clearly, he himself becomes filled with suspicion and

[20] Such an approach would show that Homer is already referred to as a theologian in the Platonic works, *pace* Tzifopoulos in this volume.

> fear and now begins to reckon up and consider if there is anyone he has wronged in any way. What is more, the one who finds he has committed many injustices in his life and, like children is frequently woken by his dreams, is afraid and lives in fear of the worst."[21]

Of particular interest to the reader of the Derveni Papyrus is the fact that Kephalos mentions explicitly the existence of a frequently ironic attitude towards this kind of myth (I [333e]), as the *P.Derv.* author does in column V. Later on, Socrates will come back to this important issue in the section featuring his close reading of poetry, even if Kephalos is not there, having left a *klēronomos logōn* (331d–e) to replace him in the discussion. Let's add to this Graf's comments on old Axiochus (p. 85), tormented by the fear of postmortem punishments and receiving comfort from Socrates, who tells a story he himself has heard from an ἀνὴρ μάγος.

Leaving for another occasion a closer look at Socrates' poetic quotations, I would like to refer briefly to two more fundamental themes in the *Republic*, which allow a closer comparison between Socrates' "treatise" on Poetry, gods, and the terrors of Hades and the *P.Derv.* treatise, making the latter less "unusual" than generally claimed. First, let me recall that theogonic myths are part of the debate in books II and III: Socrates' critical attitude to poetry focuses on theology, namely on gods and heroes in performance. He shows that *mimesis* as impersonation results in bringing gods on the scene who do not resemble what divine beings really are, says Socrates (ἀνομοὶως).[22] Reenacting in performance their epic presence and uttering what is supposed to be their own words is taken at face value by the *polloi*. As in the Derveni Papyrus, gods cannot be subjected to human faults and passions.

Even if their solutions diverge, Socrates and the *P.Derv.* author share a concern about poetic language not conveying the truth and about the need to handle in one way or another its provocative—literal—content. Nevertheless, even Socrates gives a last chance to the "ugly lies" of Homer and Hesiod on the *megista*.

> οὐδ' ἂν εἰ ἦν ἀληθῆ ᾤμην δεῖν ῥᾳδίως οὕτως λέγεσθαι πρὸς ἄφρονάς τε καὶ νέους, ἀλλὰ μάλιστα μὲν σιγᾶσθαι, εἰ δὲ ἀνάγκη τις ἦν λέγειν, δι'

[21] Translation by Chris Emlyn-Jones and William Preddy, Plato, *Republic*, Loeb Classical Library (Cambridge, MA, 2013).

[22] G. Nagy, *Poetry as Performance: Homer and Beyond* (Washington, DC, 1996) 39–86. I. Papadopoulou, "Poètes et (philo)sophoi: Pour une archéologie de la *mimesis*," *Revue de philosophie ancienne* 24.1 (2006): 3–16.

ἀπορρήτων ἀκούειν ὡς ὀλιγίστους, θυσαμένους οὐ χοῖρον ἀλλά τι μέγα καὶ ἄπορον θῦμα, ὅπως ὅτι ἐλαχίστοις συνέβη ἀκοῦσαι.

"I would not think they should be told to fools and youngsters in this lighthearted way, but should be kept strictly quiet. And if there were any need to tell the story, then as few as possible should hear it in secret, after sacrificing not a pig, but some huge victim, so hard to get hold of that as few as possible hear the story."

(*Republic* 378a)

Public performances of traditional poetry open to "all publics" should not be allowed, as the deeper meaning of such ceremonies is unaccessible to *aphronas* and *neous*, who accept literal meaning at face value. The violent myth of succession is for the ears of the *oligistoi* and demands a mystic setting and a costly sacrifice. Socrates asserts that for this type of *legomenon* a special ritual occasion should be created and a special public should be allowed to attend. The *P.Derv.* text could be the description of such an alternative setting.

If we use ancient categories and terms, the *P.Derv.* author's "commentary" can be said to belong to the discourses *peri physeos*. Even if this field of interest is not characteristic of Plato's Socrates, the Okeanos theme offers one more important connection with the Platonic dialogues. The way the *P.Derv.* author builds his argument—somewhere between theogonic poetry and physics—doesn't differ much from the procedures used by Socrates when he interweaves physics with Homeric and Orphic verses about Okeanos and Tethys in the *Theaetetus* (180d): "We have on the one hand a tradition that derives from the ancient ones, who hid their meaning by way of poetry—a tradition that says that the genesis of all things, Okeanos and Tethys, happen to be flowing streams [*rheumata*] and that nothing is static." In the *Cratylus* (402d), Hermogenes asks Socrates to explain his etymology of the name Tethys after having commented on the famous Iliadic verse XIV 201 and 302 about Okeanos and Tethys, fathers of gods. Socrates answers: "Well, this name comes very close to saying what it is. It is a mystical name [*epikekrummenon*] of a spring since that which is strained and filtered sounds like a spring, and the name Tethys is composed by these two words" (translations: G. Nagy).[23]

23 On the Derveni Papyrus and Socrates' analysis of the Homeric and Orphic verses on Okeanos, see G. Nagy, *Homer the Classic* (Washington, DC, 2009) 253ff.; see also G. Nagy, "Comments on OF 22," in *Tracing Orpheus*, ed. M. Herrero de Jáuregui et al. (Berlin, 2011) 49–53. On a possible connection between the Derveni Papyrus and the *Cratylus*: T. Baxter, *The Cratylus: Plato's Critique of Naming* (Leiden, 1992) 130–139. See recently, P. S. Horky, *Plato and Pythagoreanism* (Oxford, 2013) 125–174.

Understanding divine names and their physical explanation is the second level of access to the meaning of the poetic *hierologein*. Plato in the *Theaetetus* stages a Socratic discourse interweaving poetry and physics, by detecting Heraclitean principles in the deeper meaning of the poetic divine names that relate to the concept of fluidity. The method differs, but some important topics are common: the *P.Derv.* author could be Socrates' interlocutor, but we cannot locate him in time and space, any more than we can locate the rituals and the poetic performance he describes. His work, though, contributes greatly in testing the tools modern scholarship has used up to now to reconstruct ancient Greek religious and intellectual life.

1

Some Desiderata in the Study of the Derveni Papyrus

Kyriakos Tsantsanoglou
Aristotle University of Thessaloniki

IN THE PRESENT PAPER, which I hope will be my last on this subject, I do not intend to deal with the reconstruction of the first three columns of the papyrus, the joining of whose fragments has provoked so many rows among scholars. I accept some of the proposals made—naturally not all—and I readily admit that some of our suggestions should be revised. I prefer, however, that any future debate be undertaken between younger scholars, whose patience has not yet been tested as much as mine. Thus, I shall limit myself only to some proposals in two columns indisputably reconstructed, before I proceed to other, more general desiderata.

Throughout this investigation, "we" refers to the three editors of the *editio princeps* (Kouremenos, Parássoglou, and Tsantsanoglou [= KPT]), while "I" refers only to Tsantsanoglou. The authors of the other proposals are specified by name.

Column IV

3 σ̣ίνεται̣ [..].[: Janko (2008) is right that some traces are visible at a distance of two letters after σ̣ίνεται. He describes these traces as the feet of two vertical strokes. But these feet of verticals appear on the edges of the cuts, left and right, like two thin black strokes. They cannot be relics of letters, or their low ends would be irregularly close to the next line. They are obviously traces of the edge of the carbonized papyrus at the cuts, as is usually discernible in the whole roll. However, there is another trace, which escaped both our and Janko's notice: a waved horizontal curve somewhat lower than the base line, which cannot but belong to Σ. Following σίνεται, one expects an object, which would usually be preceded by the article. And the only accusative articles that fit the space are τάς (τούς is long) and τὸ σ-, τὰ σ-. Speaking of cosmic justice and of handing over its offenders to the Erinyes, I would venture a synonym of κόσμος: possibly, τὸ σύμπαν (Isocrates 11.12) or τὰ σύμπαντα (Plato *Philebus* 28d), "the universe." The Plato passage is especially relevant, since the question in this passage of *Philebus* concerns former wise men who taught that cosmic order is ordained by νοῦς, king of heaven and earth, and not by the power of chance, or ἀτάκτως. In fact, it is νοῦς that governs τὰ σύμπαντα καὶ τόδε τὸ καλούμενον ὅλον, being in charge of καὶ τῆς ὄψεως τοῦ κόσμου καὶ ἡλίου καὶ σελήνης καὶ ἀστέρων καὶ πάσης τῆς περιφορᾶς.

τ̣ὰ τῆς τύχης γά̣[ρ KPT, τ̣ὰ τῆς τύχης π̣ά̣[θη Janko: We took a tiny trace of ink at the base line as the left-hand foot of alpha. The last two letters can be either ΓΑ̣ or Π, but by no means Π̣Α̣, because the left-hand oblique of the alpha would then overlap the right-hand vertical of Π, no matter how short the latter might be. By enhancing the image, I now see that the end of the horizontal of Γ is visible. It is followed by a high, tiny trace of ink that corresponds to the low trace of ink that we took as belonging to alpha. Apparently, the high and the low traces are the two ends of a slightly curving vertical, whose midpart is cut off at the edge of the piece. Certainly, we should take into account that the letters at the end of the line are usually more crowded than elsewhere in the line. If so, I would read γῆ̣[ν. It would then follow that the god in question did not allow τὰ τῆς τύχης, "fortuitous circumstances," to seize or take hold of the earth. In other words, the god did not allow earth to be regulated by fortuity, but administered order instead. Socrates, in the *Philebus* passage, puts it in his usual aporetic fashion:

> πότερον ... τὰ σύμπαντα καὶ τόδε τὸ καλούμενον ὅλον ἐπιτροπεύειν φῶμεν τὴν τοῦ ἀλόγου καὶ εἰκῇ δύναμιν καὶ τὸ ὅπῃ ἔτυχεν, ἢ τἀναντία, καθάπερ οἱ πρόσθεν ἡμῶν ἔλεγον, νοῦν καὶ φρόνησίν τινα θαυμαστὴν συντάττουσαν διακυβερνᾶν;

In sum, I am making a rough *exempli gratia* restoration proposal for the text of lines 1–4:

> ... θ]ε̣ῶν
> ὁ κείμ[ενα] μετ̣α̣θ̣[έσθαι οὐκ ἐῶν, οὗ δ' ἔργον] ἐ̣κ̣δ̣ο̣ῦναι
> μᾶλλ[ον ἃ] σ̣ίνεται̣ [τὰ] σ̣[ύμπαντα, οὗτος οὖν] τ̣ὰ τῆς τύχης γῆ̣[ν]
> οὐκ εἴ̣[α λα]μβάνει̣ν̣.

> ... this one of the gods who does not allow what is stable to be altered and whose duty is to hand over (to the Erinyes) rather what are harmful to the universe, this god then did not allow chance to take hold of the earth.

A stronger punctuation after σύμπαντα is also possible, so that οὗτος οὖν *vel sim.* might start a new sentence.

There can be no doubt that the discussion continues to be about the Erinyes, as in the previous columns and in the ensuing Heraclitus quotation. It is then clear that it is they who constitute the authority to which the offenders are handed over. Why μᾶλλον? Obviously, the distinction is between the universe and the earth. The god's duty is to hand over to the Erinyes ἃ σίνεται τὰ σύμπαντα, μᾶλλον ἢ ἃ σίνεται τὴν γῆν. In other words, the author corrects the popular concept of Erinyes as avengers only of perjury and homicide, by upgrading their jurisdiction from social to cosmic. We are not told who this god is, but he is in charge of the world's stability and does not allow fortuity to control earth. Doubtless he is νοῦς. But the author has not yet exposed his system of cosmogony, nor has he made a hint about his henotheistic inclinations and the supremacy of Nous. So he leaves him unnamed among a number of gods in an indefinite partitive genitive.

7 ἥλι̣[ος ...] .ου κατὰ φ̣ύσιν KPT (]δ̣ου *praeferentes*), ἑωυ]τ̣οῦ, ἑαυ]τ̣οῦ *vel* θνη]τ̣οῦ *olim* KPT, σκύ]φ̣ου Livrea, μεθό]δ̣ου Janko: I would now prefer]λ̣ου or]α̣ου, because a loose bottom end of an oblique is visible in the otherwise muddled area—though I admit that δ has often a similar loose end projecting below its horizontal. If so, I would propose a simple ἥλι̣[ος, ἀλλ]ᾳ̣ οὐ κατὰ φ̣ύσιν, with a parenthetic prolepsis on the part of Heraclitus warning the reader that the breadth of the sun he is referring to should not be taken at face value. He has no problem with accepting his ignorance of the real size, inasmuch as his statement about the immutability of the sun's size holds true with the apparent size as well. I doubt that ἀλλὰ οὐ is a simple case of *scriptio plena*, as we find sometimes in *P.Derv.* in verse quotations (VIII.5, XVI.9, XXIV.3). I believe it is a deliberate authorial avoidance of elision for emphasizing two words of substance (ἀλλὰ οὐ); ἀλλὰ οὐ κατὰ φύσιν = NB not in its actual nature. Janko's μεθό]δ̣ου is too long to fit the size of the gap (M is one of the widest letters of the scribe), and, though later thinkers might well call the system of Heraclitus μέθοδος, I would very much doubt if Heraclitus himself would have used a patently sophistic metaphorical term for describing his epistemology. Our previous ἑωυ]τ̣οῦ, ἑαυ]τ̣οῦ, θνη]τ̣οῦ, and Livrea's σκύ]φου are palaeographically impossible.—I do not know why the scribe writes at line 9 the Doric νιν instead of the Ionic μιν, which is attested also by Plutarch 370d and 604a, the other sources of Heraclitus fr. B 94 D-K, but the fact is that he writes very clearly νιν. (Janko erroneously: "μιν *imago* [...]: νιν *perperam ed.*, Ts.[3]")

I restore the whole passage as follows, at times returning to some old proposals of ours:

ἥλι̣[ος, ἀλλ]ᾲ οὐ κατὰ φύσιν, ἀ̣νθρω[πηΐου] ε̣ὖρος ποδός [ἐστι,] τὸ μ̣[έγεθο]ς̣ οὐχ ὑπ̣ερβάλλων· εἰ γά̣[ρ τι εὔ]ρους ἑ̣[ωυτοῦ ἐκβήσετα]ι̣, Ἐρινύε̣ς νιν ἐξευρήσου̣[σι, Δίκης ἐπίκουροι.

The sun, but not in its actual innate dimensions, is a human foot in width, not exceeding (its) size; for if it steps somewhat out of its width, the Erinyes will discover it.

One might question: "So what if they discover it?" It is in response to this question that I prefer εὔ]ρους to οὔ]ρους, because the first elucidates the word-play that is typical of the style of Heraclitus: "If the sun exceeds its width, the Erinyes will de-widen it."

Column V

2].ο̣ι̣.ε̣[KPT :]δοιγε[Janko *recte*. At the end, the left-hand foot of an oblique suggests λ, therefore]δοιγελ̣[. Then, since this is the column where the author replies to those disbelieving him, εἰσὶν] δ' οἳ γελ̣[ῶσι *vel sim*. Cf. Plato *Euthyphro* 3c καὶ ἐμοῦ γάρ τοι, ὅταν τι λέγω ἐν τῇ ἐκκλησίᾳ περὶ τῶν θείων, προλέγων αὐτοῖς τὰ μέλλοντα, καταγελῶσιν ὡς μαινομένου.

3]......[..]ι KPT :].....[....]ι Janko: I would now propose reading τε]τ̣α̣γμ̣έ[νο]ι. The result cannot be considered certain, due to the almost complete abrasion of the surface, but some faint traces are compatible with each letter in particular. Of τ only the right-hand tip of the horizontal survives. The other letters are more or less complete, but extremely faint. Naturally, προστε]τ̣α̣γμ̣έ̣[νο]ι *vel sim.* is equally possible.

4 ἐπερ̣[ω]τ̣ήσ̣[οντες] KPT, Janko: I write now ἐπερ[ω]τήσο̣ν̣τ̣ε̣[ς]. The formerly dotted letters are now better visible, and the rest faintly discernible.

5 εἰ θεμι[...]..ηδα̣[KPT : εἰ θέμι[ς ἀπιστ]ῆσ̣α̣[ι] Janko: I believe I can see now εἰ θέμι[ς ταῦτ]α̣ δ̣ρᾶ̣ν̣[. The letters in G 10 are abraded, and so faint. The first α and the ν are half-preserved, but δρα is very likely.

6 ἆ̣ρ̣' KPT : ἆ̣ν̣ Janko, ἐ̣ξ Ferrari: By eliminating two dark horizontal fibers that obscured the image and had led us in the past to read τὰ | ἐν (suggested by West), alpha and rho are clearly visible, and should perhaps be published undotted.

The new reading of lines 3–6 dictates different punctuation, syntax, and translation for the whole passage. Taking αὐτοῖς as dative of the agent with the perfect participle, deleting the comma at the end of line 4, and placing a full stop after [ἕν]εκεν, we gain a different meaning:

... (προσ)τε]ṭạγμ̣ẹ́[νο]ι
αὐ̣τοῖς πάριμεṿ [εἰς τὸ μα]ṿτεῖον ἐπερ[ω]τήσọṿτẹ[ς]
τῶν μαντευομένῳṿ [ἕν]εκεν. εἰ θέμι[ς ταῦτ]ạ ḍρᾶṿ,
ἆ̣ρ' Ἅιδου δεινὰ τί ἀπ̣ιστοῦσι;

... appointed by them we enter the oracle, in order to inquire on behalf of those seeking a divination. If it is right [for us] to do these things, why do they disbelieve in the horrors of Hades? [in other words, "Why do they trust us in one occasion of supernatural significance, but not in the other?"]

It is true that πάριμεν in Herodotus has a future value, so Janko translates "we will enter," and Ferrari describes it as an ironic, even sarcastic, future: "we'll end up entering ...". We are lacking the context, and so we cannot know if the sense was something like: "Whenever we shall enter the oracle, it will always be on their command." But in the fourth century παρίασι (πάριμεν does not occur) already has a clearly present force (as do εἶμι and its compounds in poetry since Homer): Plato *Republic* (early fourth century BC) 560c–d οὔτε αὐτὴν τὴν συμμαχίαν παρίασιν, οὔτε πρέσβεις πρεσβυτέρων λόγους ἰδιωτῶν εἰσδέχονται, αὐτοί τε κρατοῦσι μαχόμενοι; Demosthenes 21 (*Against Meidias*, 348 BC) 213 πλούσιοι πολλοὶ συνεστηκότες, ὦ ἄνδρες Ἀθηναῖοι, τὸ δοκεῖν τινὲς εἶναι δι' εὐπορίαν προσειληφότες, ὑμῶν παρίασι δεησόμενοι; Aeschines 1 (*Against Timarchus*, 346 BC) 194 τούτῳ γὰρ παρίασιν ἐκ τριῶν εἰδῶν συνήγοροι.

Other minor points of difference between the text of KPT and that of Janko:

5 μαντευομένῳṿ KPT : μαντευομέν[ων Janko
6 ἀπ̣ιστοῦσι KPT : ἀ[πισ]τοῦσι Janko
7 πρ̣αγμάτων KPT : πρ̣[α]γμάτων Janko.

In all these cases Janko notes "Ts.[1] *haud recte*" and follows "ed." [Ts.[1] = "readings and conjectures by K. Tsantsanoglou in Laks and Most 1997:9–22, with his edition of columns 1–7 (93–128)"; ed. = Parássoglou's and Tsantsanoglou's readings as they appeared in the unauthorized edition of the *P.Derv.* in *ZPE* 47 (1982)]. What happened is simply that between "ed." and "Ts.[1]" (and, naturally, Ts.[3] = KPT), in other words some time between 1982 (date of the unauthorized edition) and 1993 (date of the Princeton colloquium), we joined a small piece (F 5a) to the top of F 12, which contained the letters in question: 5 ῳṿ, 6 π̣ις, 7 αγ. The fragment figures in its right place in plate 5 of our edition.—The distance between the group F 5a + 12 + 13 + 11 and G 10, as accepted by KPT and Janko, even if an adjustment of a millimeter might be necessary, does not allow the supplements 7 ἕκαστ[α], 8 ὑπὸ ṭ[ῆς] proposed by Janko, especially if one accepts, as Janko does, the supplement 9 νενικημέν[οι, οὐ] μανθ[άνο]υσιν. In order to attain perfect alignment, we proposed 7 ἕκαστ[ον], 8 ὑπό [τε γὰρ]. Janko is correct that we should have published τ̣[ε and not [τε. Janko is also right that an ι is added *supra lineam* in 8 ἁ̣μαρτης.

Now, leaving aside the contested readings, which will likely only prove to be more and more so, let us turn to another topic: trying to find out who the author of the book is. I have repeatedly made the same attempt, not observing the advice of my good friend, colleague, and co-author Theokritos Kouremenos: "attempting to identify the Derveni author in the light of the available evidence seems to be an exercise of rather low epistemic value" (in KPT 2006:59). No doubt, he is technically right, but I hope it will not constitute a mortal sin to apply guesswork and conjecture in exploring so important a question.

It is this belief that led me to consider Charles Kahn's suggestion about Euthyphro as a very likely possibility.[1] Whoever reads Plato's *Cratylus* and *Euthyphro* cannot fail to perceive the similarities between the Euthyphro described and presumed in these dialogues and the author of the Derveni book. This does not involve precise affinities in his philosophical theories or his religious creeds, because it is clear that Plato does not take seriously these features of Euthyphro and, when he does not caricature them, he speaks of them with a flippant attitude. The question is rather of the image of the author that comes into sight after the subtle ironies or the grotesque exaggerations are removed. And the impression is of a rather whimsical personage, coming from Prospalta, an Attic deme in Mesogaia, but whose family had connections, possibly as cleruchs, with Naxos; who was a contemporary of but younger than Socrates; who was a religious practitioner professing to be an expert authority in sacrifices and prayers; who distinguished himself from the many and the ignorant; who was a soothsayer, whose fellow citizens did not believe his prophecies and derided him as a lunatic;[2] who was a follower of the then-trendy practice of etymologizing divine names, according to which several thinkers claimed not only to have decoded the deeper sense (ὑπόνοια) of time-honored texts, but also to have figured out fundamental truths about creation, reality, and existence. This description is a faithful reproduction from Plato's dialogues, with only one exception. It was arbitrary on my part to employ the term "author" for Euthyphro. Yet it was Wilamowitz who observed, long before the discovery of the Derveni Papyrus, that Socrates' hints about Euthyphro

1 Kahn 1973:156nn5–6, 158n9. Extensively, Kahn 1997.

2 Cf. Numenius, fr. 23, who, depending on the *Euthyphro*, describes the mantis as ἄνδρα ἀλαζόνα (charlatan, quack) καὶ κοάλεμον (stupid fellow, booby).

would have been unintelligible in the year of the writing of the *Cratylus*, some forty years after the incident described in the dialogue, had the latter not put down on paper his idiosyncratic teachings.[3]

Now, it seems that this etymological perversion was widely spread. Philodemus, *On Piety* (part 1, 19.518–541, in Dirk Obbink's 1996 edition), in an interesting passage mentioned also by Richard Janko,[4] refers to the attack of Epicurus against those individuals who, by changing some letters in the names of gods, would throw away the divine from the world. They are named: Prodicus, Diagoras, Critias, and others (καὶ ἄλλοι). There follows a special reference to Antisthenes. While there is hardly any evidence about Prodicus, Diagoras, and Critias with regard to etymology, Plato's *Cratylus* offers ample information about Euthyphro.

> 396d–e ΣΩ. Καὶ αἰτιῶμαί γε, ὦ Ἑρμόγενες, μάλιστα αὐτὴν [*sc.* τὴν σοφίαν] ἀπὸ Εὐθύφρονος τοῦ Προσπαλτίου προσπεπτωκέναι μοι· ἕωθεν γὰρ πολλὰ αὐτῷ συνῆ καὶ παρεῖχον τὰ ὦτα. κινδυνεύει οὖν ἐνθουσιῶν οὐ μόνον τὰ ὦτά μου ἐμπλῆσαι τῆς δαιμονίας σοφίας, ἀλλὰ καὶ τῆς ψυχῆς ἐπειλῆφθαι. δοκεῖ οὖν μοι χρῆναι οὑτωσὶ ἡμᾶς ποιῆσαι· τὸ μὲν τήμερον εἶναι χρήσασθαι αὐτῇ καὶ τὰ λοιπὰ περὶ τῶν ὀνομάτων ἐπισκέψασθαι, αὔριον δέ, ἂν καὶ ὑμῖν συνδοκῇ, ἀποδιοπομπησόμεθά τε αὐτὴν καὶ καθαρούμεθα ἐξευρόντες ὅστις τὰ τοιαῦτα δεινὸς καθαίρειν, εἴτε τῶν ἱερέων τις εἴτε τῶν σοφιστῶν.

Etymology—or rather, weird etymology—is the δαιμονία σοφία that, emanating from Euthyphro of Prospalta, overtook Socrates. The latter decides to contemplate names and/or nouns (περὶ τῶν ὀνομάτων ἐπισκέψασθαι) by making use of this wisdom today, but to conjure it away tomorrow and find some priest or sophist to purify him and his collocutors. Of the thinkers named by Epicurus, it is to Antisthenes that the saying ἀρχὴ παιδεύσεως ὀνομάτων ἐπίσκεψις is attributed (fr. 38 Decleva Caizzi), no matter what meaning modern pedagogy attaches to it. As for the purification that Socrates feels he is in need of, it does not seem unrelated to the description of the etymologists by Epicurus as "deranged," "madmen," and "frenzy-stricken" (παρακόπτειν καὶ μαίνεσθαι, καὶ βακχεύουσιν αὐτοὺς εἰκάζει)—as well as to the initial impression of numerous modern scholars, who saw the Derveni author as a raving lunatic.

Even so, however, Euthyphro is but one out of several possible authors who practiced etymology. The difference from the other thinkers, if we continue

3 Wilamowitz 1920: i.204f., ii.76f.

4 Janko 1997:89–90.

employing the Philodemus passage, is that the Derveni author (as well as Euthyphro of Plato's dialogues) does not eliminate the divine element from nature—as we know from other sources too that the aforementioned did (τοῖς τὸ θεῖον ἐκ τῶν ὄντων ἀναιροῦσιν)—but does exactly the opposite: he puts forward arguments that support the role of the divine in cosmogony and cosmology.

Antisthenes—always according to Epicurus—stands also in opposition to this group of thinkers. The sentence that mentions him is important, though considerably obscure. Some trifling changes, without much altering the image as a whole, may possibly illuminate the passage. The text, as published by Dirk Obbink and accepted by Janko, is:

Column XIX
κα[ὶ γὰρ] παραγραμ̣μίζ[ουσι]
τὰ τ̣[ῶ]ν̣ θεῶν [ὀνόμα-]
τα, [κα]θάπερ Ἀν̣[τισ-]
θέ[νης] τὸ κοινό[τατον]
ὑποτ<ε>ίνων ἀν̣[αφέρει]
τὰ κατὰ μέρος [τῆι θέ-]
σει καὶ διά τι̣[νος ἀπά-]
της ἔτι πρότ[ερον·]

For indeed they explain the names of the gods by changing letters, just as Antisthenes, substituting the most common, ascribes the particular to imposition and even earlier through some act of deceit.

My proposals, no more than trivial παραγραμματισμοί, are 537 τὸ κοινὸ[ν ὄνομ'], 538 ἀν̣[αιρεῖ] (*iam* Obbink *olim*), 539 [συνέ]|σει (*etiam* Obbink *olim*), 541 ἔτι πρότ[εροι.]:

κα[ὶ γὰρ] παραγραμ̣μίζ[ουσι]
τὰ τ̣[ῶ]ν̣ θεῶν [ὀνόμα-]
τα, [κα]θάπερ Ἀν̣[τισ-]
θέ[νης] τὸ κοινὸ[ν ὄνομ']
ὑποτ<ε>ίνων ἀν̣[αιρεῖ]
τὰ κατὰ μέρος [συνέ-]
σει καὶ διά τι̣[νος ἀπά-]
της ἔτι πρότ[εροι.]

For they change letters in the names of the gods, just as Antisthenes, who, proposing the common noun, eliminates sagaciously the particular ones, and through some trickery others even earlier.

ἔτι πρότεροι is the subject of the second part of the comparative clause—καὶ (καθάπερ) διά τινος ἀπάτης ἔτι πρότεροι. What Antisthenes proposes by implication (ὑποτείνω) is the employment of the common noun, that is θεός, but rejects and discards τὰ κατὰ μέρος, the particular proper names, say Cronus, Zeus, Hera, Demeter, and so forth. He makes this rejection in a shrewd manner. Others before him had done the same thing through some kind of trickery. Epicurus is not completely hostile to Antisthenes. While he disapproves of his use of etymology and the elimination of the particular gods, he recognizes that his proposal is made prudently. The word συνέσει, if correctly restored, has to do with Antisthenes' sagacity and not with the craft of those who, in the myth, forced the different gods on humankind. The sentence proceeds by antitheses: τὸ κοινὸν ὄνομα vs. τὰ κατὰ μέρος, ὑποτείνων vs. ἀναιρεῖ, συνέσει vs. διά τινος ἀπάτης.

If then we are to place Euthyphro and/or the Derveni author within the climate described by Epicurus, we must dissociate him or them from the group of outright atheists—Prodicus, Diagoras, Critias, and others—and connect him with Antisthenes, who taught that the oneness of the divine exists by nature (κατὰ φύσιν), but the plurality of gods by convention (κατὰ νόμον) (fr. 39a Decleva Caizzi, again from Philodemus *On Piety*). And if Antisthenes is partly commended by Epicurus, despite his refusal of the multiplicity of gods and his use of etymology, Euthyphro and/or the Derveni author must belong to the ἔτι πρότεροι, who reached the same conclusion by using the same stratagem, but some more trickery as well. I dare propose that this further trickery is the employment of allegory, as used by the Derveni author. No matter how important his religious or cosmogonic teachings may be, the claim that they derive from an allegoric interpretation of an Orphic poem can only be described as "fraud," or ἀπάτη.

It is true that the attitude of the Platonic Socrates towards Euthyphro is somewhat different in the homonymous dialogue from what is in the *Cratylus*. In the latter, the derision is explicit and unambiguous, whereas in the *Euthyphro* the ironic discussion touches on the subject in which the *mantis* was supposed to be an authority. Yet the playful attitude and the mockery are plain. Plutarch 580d (*De genio Socratis*) describes a fictional meeting with Socrates (with most of its elements deriving from the *Euthyphro*) in which the philosopher is strolling with the *mantis* ἅμα τι διερωτῶν (asking continually) καὶ διασείων (throwing into confusion) τὸν Εὐθύφρονα μετὰ παιδιᾶς. In both dialogues, though the main subjects are different, at the bottom there is the problem of the multiplicity of the gods. In both, the Platonic Socrates appears to have an implicit critical position on the problem, whereas the *mantis*, present in the *Euthyphro*, and implied in the *Cratylus*, appears as a supporter of the multiplicity. The difference lies in the fact that the "Euthyphro-inspired" etymologies in the *Cratylus*, which are supposed to lead to an allegorical/physical explanation of the particular multiple divine names, are ridiculed; in the *Euthyphro* the problems arising from the myths that depend on the multiplicity of the gods, such as the battles among them, are accepted by Euthyphro as undisputed dogma (Plato *Euthyphro* 7b5 εἴρηται γάρ), though the allegoric interpretation—for instance, of book 20 of the *Iliad* (θεῶν μάχη)—as the battle of the elements in the process of cosmogony, must already have been widely known. No doubt, in the *Euthyphro*, the allegoric interpretation would not serve the arguments of the *mantis* and would lead the discussion to alien paths, whereas etymology is the main topic in the *Cratylus*. Therefore, it would be futile to look for a significant development in Plato's thought on this subject between his early (*Euthyphro*) and middle (*Cratylus*) periods.[5]

Apart from Plato's references or hints, no other direct mention of Euthyphro seems to have survived.[6] Similarly, no certain mention of the Derveni book appears to have come down to us. I must say that I strongly doubt if the reference to the hymns of Orpheus by Philochorus or the quotation of an Orphic verse in the Homeric *scholia*, both quoted also in the Derveni book (XXII.11 and XXIII.11), can be considered citations from the latter. The Orphic hymns and theogonies must have enjoyed some circulation in antiquity, not only as literary works but also as liturgical texts. Certainly, Philochorus, himself a seer and diviner and a prolific writer on religious topics, would have had no need of the Derveni book for citing an Orphic verse.

The only reference that may be associated with the Derveni book with some likelihood is Syncellus *Chronography* 140c, i.282.19 Dind. = Cedrenus *Historia compendaria* i.144.16 Bekk. ἑρμηνεύουσι δὲ οἱ Ἀναξαγόρειοι τοὺς μυθώδεις θεοὺς νοῦν μὲν τὸν Δία, τὴν δὲ Ἀθηνᾶν τέχνην, ὅθεν καὶ τὸ 'χειρῶν ὀλλυμένων ἔρρει πολύμητις Ἀθήνη'.[7] The passage, with the reference to Zeus = Nous omitted and the first two words of the verse inverted (ὀλλυμένων χειρῶν), occurs also in Ioannes Antiochenus, a Byzantine chronicler who is older than Syncellus (*FHG* iv.1.21 [2]); the verse in Meletius medicus (*De natura hominis*, Cramer, *Anecdota graeca ... Oxoniensium* 118) is possibly contemporary with Ioannes.[8] The combination of Anaxagoreans with allegorizing an Orphic poem is really in-

5 The inconsistency between the *Euthyphro* and the *Cratylus* was noticed already by Proclus (*Platonic Theology* 5.18), who does not recognize the derision in Plato's etymologies.

6 The title, *Πρὸς τὸν Εὐθύφρονα*, of a book by Metrodorus the younger is but a shortening of the full title *Πρὸς τὸν Πλάτωνος Εὐθύφρονα vel sim.*—in other words, a treatise that criticizes Plato's dialogue or possibly the famous *Euthyphro* dilemma about the nature of piety; extensively discussed by Obbink (1996) on 25.701–708.

7 Burkert 1970:443n1; Sider 1997:138.

8 The verse is attributed to Orpheus, fr. 856 Bernabé, by Orion *Etymologicum* 163.23 (where πολύεργος Ἀθήνη is transmitted).

triguing, even though the particular allegory (πολύμητις, or rather, πολύεργος, Ἀθήνη = τέχνη) seems too transparent for the deliberately obscure author of the Derveni book.[9]

The lack of reference to the book may, of course, be coincidental. But the lack of reference to the author may possibly mean something—for instance, that he was not taken seriously enough by his contemporaries, just as the situation between Socrates and Euthyphro in Plato's dialogues seems to be. Understandably, it is not my intention to underestimate the Derveni author as regards the invaluable information he conveys about Presocratic philosophy and mystery religion. But I cannot believe that anyone of his contemporary intellectuals, even if he agreed with his theological conclusions, would regard his interpretations of the Orphic hymn as worthy of attention.

Apart from the character of the author, scholars have occupied themselves with detecting the character of the book. Without further ado, I must say that I am convinced that, in spite of the personal touches here and there, the book is intended as a handbook, or rather an instruction book, or even better a *vade mecum* for prospective μύσται. That word is mentioned only once (VI.8), but the author does employ synonymous expressions. In many ways it is obvious that the sacrificial instructions and the allegorical interpretations are addressed to them. And it is in their τελεταί that the hymn in question was sung. In which mystery cult, however, the initiates were involved, I do not know. I have the inclination to locate it in eastern Attica, at the mysteries of Phlya, at modern Khalandri, where Orphic hymns constituted a part of the λεγόμενα, but also for which, as tradition has it, Orpheus and Musaeus, his pupil, had written their hymns.[10] I also have considered identifying the oracle mentioned in the Derveni book as the Amphiaraeion at Oropus. But I fear that in both instances I am influenced by Euthyphro's origin, Prospalta in the Mesogaia area.

On the other hand, if the book is really an initiate's *vade mecum*, this satisfactorily explains why the roll was burned. The usual passports certifying that the traveling soul was καθαρά and ἄποινος, purified and not owing a punishment, were the well-known Orphic gold leaves. But those leaves, with their text usually corrupt, full of errors and misspellings, attest to a popular production. The relatives of the deceased might easily order one or possibly buy a ready-made one outside the cemetery, thus cheating the immortals—ἡ τῶν θεῶν ὑπ' ἀνθρώπων παραγωγή, deceit of gods by humans, in the words of Plato (*Republic* 364d), was an activity as usual in antiquity as it is today. But the

9 In D-K ii.50, the fragment is ascribed to Metrodorus of Lampsacus (61 fr. 6), whose other allegories are, however, referred to Homer, not Orpheus. Hussey (1999:315) specifies the source as Philochorus.

10 Plutarch *Themistocles* 1.4; Pausanias 1.22.7, 1.31.4, 4.1.6, 9.27.2, 9.30.12.

personal *vade mecum* of the deceased, a book circulating in a small and closed circle of initiates, was no doubt the most authoritative passport that, burned together with the holder, could accompany him to the access gates of Hades.

Speaking of the character of the book, we might possibly speculate about its missing portions. In the *editio princeps*, I conjectured that the surviving papyrus fragments speak for a twenty-sheet roll, the standard size, according to Pliny the Elder: *Natural History* 13.77 *numquam plures scapo quam vicenae*, "never more sheets than twenty to a roll."[11] In any case, the reality is that we possess, damaged or fragmented, a ten-foot-long roll, almost the whole of it. But though the end of the roll is intact, it does not coincide with the end of the book. In 1983 Martin West showed, beyond a doubt, I believe, that "in all probability the text continued in another roll, or several, which perhaps perished on the funeral pyre."[12] His study, however, concerned the Orphic poems, and so he limited his investigation to restoring the narrative of the Orphic theogony. It was beyond the scope of his book to reconstruct the rest of the physical theory, something that would anyway be much too risky. Because, whereas the narrative of the Orphic theogony is presented in the Derveni book in the order of the verses inside the poem, the unfolding of the cosmological system does not follow a logical sequence—but rather is made with leaps and backward movements, depending on what allegory each quoted Orphic verse would recall to the author.

As regards the constituents of the Derveni book, let me remind you that the first six columns deal with cultic particulars connected only or mainly with souls, Erinyes and Eumenides (who, according to the author, are also souls), Dike, and Hades. A better look shows, however, that we are not dealing simply with cultic instructions, but with a system of eschatology or soteriology that, among other things, details some cultic practices necessary for salvation. Recall that although cultic practices may, in the popular religious conception, be thought to be sufficient, an intellectual preacher of soul salvation cannot content himself with them. The second chapter of soteriology, or the second prerequisite for salvation, is no doubt the "special knowledge." Special knowledge in the area of soteriology is usually tantamount to mystic knowledge addressed to selected people, the μύσται. Here, however, it is not a mystic object, but a mystic method of approaching and interpreting a religious, probably a liturgical text, the Orphic theogonical hymn. The physical theory of cosmogony, set forth in the second part of the papyrus, would have nothing mystic or mysterious, if it came from the mouth of, say, Anaxagoras or Diogenes of Apollonia. It is the

11 A statement refuted by preserved rolls that consist of more sheets. Turner (1968:4) describes the twenty-sheet roll as a common but not exclusive size.

12 West 1983:94.

allegorical interpretation that elevates the theory to higher levels than science and philosophy.

Is there a third prerequisite in the same context? As far as I know, every religious teaching on the salvation of souls presupposes a righteous life in this world. The surviving text mentions ἁμαρτίη and ἡδονή, but only *en passant*, within the context of the other soteriological references. We used to read also ἄνδρες ἄδικοι, but Janko does away with it, perhaps correctly. Nowhere is a lifestyle system described—what would constitute an Ὀρφικὸς βίος—such as is expressly mentioned by Plato, but also alluded to by Herodotus and Euripides; a chapter on pragmatic anthropology or practical ethics is missing. I propose that this chapter, whose size and contents cannot be estimated by any means, is missing from the beginning of the book. If these speculations prove true, the book must thus have consisted of at least three papyrus rolls. Why must it come from the beginning? I imagine that a soteriological teaching must proceed by elimination. A religious functionary should regularly start by demanding of his entire flock that they follow in their life an inviolable ethical code of commandments. A first selection from the whole congregation would be those who perform certain cultic practices, rites, ceremonies, prayers, sacrifices. The last stage of selection would be the clearly mystical selection, the instruction in some sort of special and profound knowledge, the analogue of an Eleusinian *epopteia*. Here, it would coincide with the allegoric physical interpretation of the Orphic hymn.

I am well aware that all this is much too speculative, and impossible to prove. Further, the placement of the supposedly missing chapter depends, at least, on the meaning of the sentence found in column XXV.10–12: "The god made the sun of such a form and size as is related at the beginning of the λόγος." If *logos* is the present treatise, as we suggested based on the common usage of the word in Herodotus, Plato, and Aristotle, the reference may have been to column IV, the Heraclitus column, where there is mention of the stability in the size of the sun as security for the preservation of cosmic order. If, however, *logos* is the Orphic poem, often referred to as Ἱερὸς λόγος, as Gábor Betegh suggested,[13] the reference may have been to columns VIII and IX, where god or air/Mind is said to have turned a sufficiently large amount of fire into the sun, for enabling the rest of the ἐόντα to condense and form the present world. At first sight, Betegh's approach seems to allow a further roll before the surviving one, while ours does not. At any rate, λόγος is used technically not only for the whole of a literary composition, but often for a part of it, as usually in Herodotus (1.140.3, 7.137.3 ἐπὶ τὸν πρότερον λόγον; 4.82, 5.62.1 τὸν κατ' ἀρχὰς ἤια λέξων λόγον, and

13 Betegh 2004:327–329.

elsewhere). So, whether the beginning of the λόγος is the opening of the Ἱερὸς λόγος or of the chapter that poses the problem to be faced with the physical interpretation of the Ἱερὸς λόγος, a previous chapter may well have existed.

Now, some breaking news. Only while preparing the written version of this paper did I notice that the papyrus seems to provide column numbering.[14] This numbering appears 0.25–0.30 cm above the first line, near the left-hand edge of the column and at uneven distances from it. The problem is not only that the top margin is missing in most of the columns, but also that even where the margin is preserved, it often happens that the particular point is torn away. The number-letters are conspicuously larger than the letters of the text and are written with a different calamus in paler or more dilute ink, a fact that may explain why we missed them before now.

Though the letters surviving are no more than seven, it is easy to discern that the script is somewhat different from that of the rest of the text, as it exhibits a more formal calligraphic style. Gamma, delta, lambda, and what is preserved of nu are more or less common, slightly curvilinear, but not more so than the letters of the text. Distinctive are the epsilon, rounded, almost in a complete circle; the mu, three-stroked, low, and very flat; and the alpha, with a downward curved crossbar. The uncommon alpha and mu are identical to those of the oldest dated Greek papyrus, the Peukestas order (331–323 BC; *P.Saqqara* inv. 1972 GP 3).

The only letter that may affect the dating proposed for the writing of the Derveni Papyrus (ca. 340–320 BC) is the rounded epsilon. Such epsilons are found in a few papyri dated to the end of the fourth or the beginning of the third century—dated so, perhaps precisely because of the rounded epsilon. From the third century on, rounded epsilons are regular.[15] Examples include the Berlin Scolia and Elegiacs of *P.Berol.* 13270 and the Epicharmus or Pseudo-Epicharmea of *P.Saqqara* inv. 5673 GP 6 (both dated by their editors ca. 300 BC). Important here are the papyri that present both the square and the rounded form: the musical Orestes fragment of *P.Vind.* G 2315 (ca. 300 BC), where the square form is presented in the notes, but the rounded one in the Orestes text, and the accounts of *P.Saqqara* inv. 5676 GP 9 (late fourth century BC), where the particular entries use the square epsilon, but the contemporary sum totals the rounded one. I doubt if the evidence is strong enough to allow us to date the Derveni Papyrus one or two decades later than what we did, thus approaching the dating of the burial by the archaeologists (end of the fourth or beginning of the third century BC)

14 Parallels are mentioned by Turner (1987:16).

15 Larfeld (1914: Schrifttafel) records two inscriptions, of 378/7 and of 313 BC, with rounded epsilons.

or the original dating of the papyrus by E. G. Turner (325–275 BC), before he settled for the fourth century.

The numbering appears as follows:

In column V (G 1)]λε[16]
In column XIII (I 26)]μγ̣[
In column XIV (C 10)]μ̣δ̇
In column XX (D 4) ν̣
In column XXI (D 6)]ν̣α
In column XXVI (A 6)]ν̣

In column XXIV some random traces conspire to give the impression of letters, H being the most conspicuous; however, not only are the letters more than what are needed for a number, but they are also written lower than the other number-letters; some traces at the usual height are inscrutable to me. At XXVI (A 6) the lower part of a ν is clear, but I am not sure if the low trace of a curve that follows is compatible with the digamma as written in the fourth/third century (like a c with its high and low ends extended horizontally). If μγ̣ (=43) is correctly read at XIII, being eight columns after λε (=35) at V, this would verify that the letters are really column numbering. The same holds for]μ̣δ (=44) at XIV, for ν̣ (=50) at XX, for]ν̣α (=51) at XXI, if ν were confirmed, and for]ν̣ at XXVI, if we might read]νϝ̣. Of these, the number ν̣ of XX is suspicious, as its size is smaller than the rest. Column XXIV does not help.

It now becomes clear that the numbering was continued from roll to roll and that one roll had preceded ours. If our column V is numbered 35 and the numbering started from column I, the preceding roll should contain thirty columns. To have two rolls absolutely equal in length, one should divide fifty-six by two and have two rolls of twenty-eight columns each. This should mean that two more columns (and possibly one papyrus sheet?) are missing from the beginning of the preserved roll—more, that is, than what we had initially calculated. This would actually verify the proposal of Janko.[17] With the evidence available, it is impossible to decide. Even if both rolls were of twenty equal sheets each, the width of the columns and so their number might have differed from roll to roll, if, for instance, no hexameters were cited in the first part of the book, and thus the columns were able to be narrower. In any case, the existence

16 The photograph of G 1 taken by Ch. Makaronas when the sheets of the roll were still stuck together shows the]λε very faintly; it is much clearer after the treatment of Anton Fackelmann, which also produced, however, a large hole in the area.

17 Janko 2008:38.

of a further roll and possibly a further chapter that preceded our text is now verified.

Another issue for further investigation is the question of the *magi*. When we initially detected their presence, we were thrilled at finding Iranian priests involved in Greek religious affairs. But when we ventured to make any proposal about them, we were faced with suspicion. Was the reading correct? Were they Iranians, or rather Greek μάγοι, crooks, quacks, impostors, magicians? But how on earth could the author recommend and advertise a mystic worship that, in *his own words*, followed the practices of crooks and magicians? More influential voices than ours were needed to reinforce the view that the author really referred to the priestly caste of Persia. Now Janko has detected one more mention of them. The references to the *magi* have to do with souls: their reception in the Hereafter, the prayers and the offerings that secure a favorable treatment, their relation with certain *daimones*, who impede their entrance into the domain of eternal bliss.

Now, is it prudent to limit the influence of Iranian religion on the mysteries promoted by the Derveni author only to some concepts about souls and the cultic details accompanying these concepts (hymns, libations, *popana*)? The last mention of the *magi* is found in column VI, with the libations and the offerings of the initiates, which we are told are made in the same way the *magi* do. Column VII starts with a reference to the Orphic theogonic hymn apparently sung by the initiates. I have already attempted to associate the singing of the hymn with the information provided by Herodotus (1.132), that Persian sacrifices had to be accompanied by an ἐπαοιδή sung by a *magus*, and that this ἐπαοιδή was called "theogony."[18] The similarity is striking, but again, is it prudent to limit ourselves to the outward resemblance of the cultic elements? From column VII on, the book deals with the allegoric interpretation of the Orphic hymn, and *this* is the focal point from here on in. In the author's words, the intention of Orpheus was to say not riddles but rather great things in riddles. What if these "great things" were influenced by the teachings of the *magi*? There is a vast literature on the possible Eastern philosophical and religious influences primarily in Ionia, the westernmost satrapy of the Persian state, and from there, through Ionian teachers of rhetoric and philosophy to the rest of the Greek world, but mainly to Athens.[19]

The gist of the physical system the Derveni author exhibits, irrespective of whether it is his own or not, is a compromise between materialism and religion. The agent at the basis of this compromise is Nous, the center of the Anaxagorean

[18] Tsantsanoglou 1997:111.
[19] Tsantsanoglou 2008:31–39.

system, which was popular at the time. Nous in Anaxagoras is corporeal, yet the finest and purest of all things; he is also infinite and self-ruled. In the Derveni book Nous is aerial, like everything in the world; he prevails over all ἐόντα, as he is equivalent with the whole of them, but is also characterized as φρόνησις τοῦ θεοῦ, the thought or the wisdom of god, which is also described as air. Elsewhere he is named "mightiest" and is also compared to a king. It is he who decided and effected the creation—the turn, that is, from the πρὶν ἐόντα to the νῦν ἐόντα—by giving a principal role in the creative process to the sun. Is then this compromise between the Anaxagorean "Mind" or "Wit" and the ancestral "almighty God"—the meeting and fusion of religion and cosmology—unrelated to the Iranian omniscient creator Ahura Mazdā, which means no more than "Lord Wisdom"? I admit that this is much too speculative, because the concept of the creative Mind or Wisdom, a thinking principle in cosmogony and cosmology, extends throughout the history of religions, from Hesiod's Metis down to the Intelligent Demiurge of modern theoreticians. In between, we may spot lots of stages, from the γνῶσις of the Gnostics, to the λόγος of the Gospel of John, to the Holy Spirit of the Christian Trinity. I pose the question to my philosophically minded colleagues. It is not for me to answer.

References

Betegh, G. 2004. *The Derveni Papyrus: Theology, Cosmology, and Interpretation*. Cambridge.

Burkert, W. 1970. "La genèse des choses et des mots: Le papyrus de Derveni entre Anaxagore et Cratyle." *Études Philosophiques* 25:443–455.

Ferrari, F. 2007. "Note al testo delle colonne II–VII del papiro di Derveni." *Zeitschrift für Papyrologie und Epigraphik* 162:203–211.

Hussey, E. 1999. "The Enigmas of Derveni: A Review of A. Laks & G. W. Most (eds.), *Studies on the Derveni Papyrus*." *Oxford Studies in Ancient Philosophy* 17:303–324.

Janko, R. 1997. "The Physicist as Hierophant: Aristophanes, Socrates, and the Authorship of the Derveni Papyrus." *Zeitschrift für Papyrologie und Epigraphik* 118:61–94.

———. 2008. "Reconstructing (Again) the Opening of the Derveni Papyrus." *Zeitschrift für Papyrologie und Epigraphik* 166:37–51.

Kahn, Ch. 1973. "Language and Ontology in the *Cratylus*." In *Exegesis and Argument: Studies in Greek Philosophy Presented to G. Vlastos* (ed. E. N. Lee, A. P. D. Mourelatos, and R. M. Rorty) 152–176. *Phronesis* Suppl. 1. Assen.

———. 1997. "Was Euthyphro the Author of the Derveni Papyrus?" In Laks and Most 1997:55–63.

Kouremenos, Th., G. Parássoglou, and K. Tsantsanoglou. 2006. *The Derveni Papyrus, Edited with Introduction and Commentary*. Florence.

Laks, A., and G. W. Most, eds. 1997. *Studies on the Derveni Papyrus*. Oxford.

Larfeld, W. 1914. *Griechische Epigraphik*. 3rd ed. Munich.

Livrea, E. 2008. "Eraclito nel papiro del Derveni." *Zeitschrift für Papyrologie und Epigraphik* 164:8–9.

Obbink, D. 1996. *Philodemus On Piety*, part 1: *Critical Text with Commentary.* Oxford.

Sider, D. 1997. "Heraclitus in the Derveni Papyrus." In Laks and Most 1997:129–148.

Tsantsanoglou, K. 1997. "The First Columns of the Derveni Papyrus and Their Religious Significance." In Laks and Most 1997:93–128.

———. 2008. "Magi in Athens in the Fifth Century BC?" In *Ancient Greece and Ancient Iran: Cross-Cultural Encounters. Transactions of the 1st International Conference, Athens, 11-13 November 2006* (ed. S. M. R. Darbandi and A. Zournatzi) 31–39. Athens.

Turner, E. G. 1968. *Greek Papyri: An Introduction*. Oxford.

———. 1987. *Greek Manuscripts of the Ancient World*. Bulletin of the Institute of Classical Studies, Suppl. 46. 2nd ed., ed. P. J. Parsons. London.

West, M. L. 1983. *The Orphic Poems*. Oxford.

Wilamowitz-Moellendorff, U. von. 1920. *Platon*. 2nd ed. Berlin.

2

On the Rites Described and Commented Upon in the Derveni Papyrus, Columns I–VI

Alberto Bernabé
Universidad Complutense

1. Introduction

IN THIS PAPER, I INTEND TO DISCUSS A NUMBER OF ISSUES concerning the rituals described and commented upon in the first six columns of the Derveni Papyrus, and to propose a few suggestions regarding two specific aspects: first, the nature of the rituals described in the document; and second, the interpretation of these rituals offered by the text's author.[1] Several seminal studies have already made significant progress in this field,[2] but it is possible, in my opinion, to advance a few steps forward.

Nevertheless, an obstacle to such progress is the fact that the text of the first columns has undergone continuous and significant changes in the last years. In the first draft of this paper for the CHS Conference I used the text of the six first columns in the form it has in my edition of the papyrus,[3] analyzing the remains of these, taking into account recent interpretations of this text, and trying to situate the isolated and incomplete statements within a context that will plausibly serve to explain them. But Janko proposed many changes in the arrangement of the fragments of columns I–III and joined fragments unplaced in the edition by Kouremenos, Parássoglou, and Tsantsanoglou (henceforth KPT);[4] during the conference itself, Tsantsanoglou made new proposals based on

1 The Spanish Ministry of Economy and Innovation has given financial support for the research for this paper (FFI2010-17047).

2 Henrichs 1984; Obbink 1997; Tsantsanoglou 1997; Johnston 1999; Betegh 2004:74–91; Kouremenos, in Kouremenos, Parássoglou, and Tsantsanoglou 2006; Ferrari 2011a, 2011b, 2011c. See also Chiarabini 2006; Martín Hernández 2010.

3 Bernabé 2007a.

4 Janko 2008.

Janko's text of the third column;[5] and since then, Ferrari and Piano have made successive efforts to place some scraps in the first columns and rearrange the fragments.[6] So, after reading my paper at the CHS Conference I have reworked it four or five times, accepting and rejecting statements according to the successive rearrangements of the text.

Now, following the texts of Ferrari and Piano, I present my proposals with some variations.

2. Text Analysis

2.1 Column I[7]

2.1.1 The text

The text of column I 2–11 and its translation are as follows:[8]

. .] . ιδ[ ]κ̣ε.̣ . [
. δ̣α̣ρα . [ ]επιτα[ ] ἕκαστον
. . α̣ν̣ταν . [ ].οις καὶ κα[ ]ας
ἐλ̣[π]ίδι νεῖμ̣[αι κ]αὶ τὰ σημε[ῖ(α) δ]ι̣ὰ̣ θ̣έ̣α̣ν̣
ὧδ̣' ἐ̣π̣έθηκ' ἐ[ντα]ῦθ̣' εὐχῆ̣ς ἵν' ἀμφὶ̣ ['Ερι]ν̣ύ̣ων
κ̣α̣τασημαι[. .] . . . . ρ̣αι ἐᾶμ̣ μ[αν]τ̣ε̣ί̣α̣ς
μ̣[υ̣]σ̣τῶν κατ̣[ο]χῆς . . . . λ[. .] . . . [. . .]α̣ν̣ εἰ̣ ἔ̣σ̣[τιν
ὁ]μ̣ῶς ἐ̣π[ὶ π]υρὸς ὕδατος δι̣[ ] . . [. . . .]εια
]ιν ἕκαστα σημεῖα [
ἀχ]λὺς καὶ̣ τ̣ἆ̣λ̣λ' ὅσα̣ [

... each ... to entrust with hope ... and [to decipher] ... the signs through observation, he added the following instruction in that passage of the prayer about the Erinyes ... to dismiss the prophecies [resulting from] a state of mental possession of the *mystai* ... if it is equally possible .... according to fire and water ... each sign ... the mist and all things that ...

2.1.2 ἐλπίδι

It is not clear whether it is Orpheus who recommends "to entrust with hope" or if this recommendation is part of the author's explanatory method on the correct attitude toward the rites, to which we shall return in §2.1.3. In the first

5 Tsantsanoglou, in this volume. Also Scermino 2008–2009:70.

6 Ferrari has published the new arrangement of col. IV (Ferrari 2010), cols. I–III (Ferrari 2011c), and col. VI (Ferrari 2011a); cf. also Ferrari 2012 and Piano 2011.

7 Col. 0 is in a very bad state. No full words are discernable.

8 A critical apparatus can be seen in Ferrari 2011c:42 and 2012. Translation by Ferrari (2012).

case, this might refer to the belief in the afterlife; in the second, to the conviction that it is possible to understand the meaning of the rites through observation (δ]ι̣ὰ̣ θ̣έ̣α̣ν̣).[9] The reference to hope recurs in column XX 12, when the commentator states that those who are with an incompetent initiator expect to acquire knowledge but, after performing the rites, go away devoid even of expectation.

2.1.3 τὰ σημε[ῖ(α) … δ]ι̣ὰ̣ θ̣έ̣α̣ν̣

The commentator's references to σημεῖα and to the verb κατασημαίνω indicate that he is describing particular ritual practices with the intention of attributing to them some specific meaning. It seems that he takes for granted that the meaning of the ritual is not evident (i.e. it is not what it seems to be) and must be attained through observation ([δ]ι̣ὰ̣ θ̣έ̣α̣ν̣, I 5).[10] The commentator does this in precisely the same way in which he later cites verses from an Orphic text verbatim in order to ascribe to them an interpretation from philosophical points of view. In other words, in the same way in which the literary text contains two distinct levels—the first being the ancient poem and the other its subsequent commentary—so also does the ritual description. The first level describes the performance of the ancient ritual. On another level, the commentator's interpretation of the performance is provided, following the idea that rituals, like Orpheus' verses, contain an undisclosed meaning. The commentator, therefore, considers himself able to explain what lies beneath the surface of the text—its hidden truth and final significance.[11] He differs from other practitioners in positioning his explanations within a cosmic framework much vaster in extent than that of others.[12]

Furthermore, as we shall see, the text contains linguistic markers indicative of this hermeneutic activity. In brief, these are:

9 Ferrari 2011c:42–43.

10 According to KPT 114 σημε[ῖα can be supernatural signs. Janko (2008:44) thinks that the text deals with divination from signs, apparently using lots. Probably the word means "signals" in rites that allow the wise (i.e. the commentator) to interpret rightly their meaning.

11 Cf. Bernabé 2010a. Henrichs (1984:261) writes: "the author of the papyrus speculates about the underlying meaning of the ritual which he is describing," thus highlighting the fact that, except for Plato, this type of theological speculation is somewhat uncommon in authors writing in the fourth century. He also distinguishes (Henrichs 1998:45) two methodologies of ritual explanation: "the traditional form provides an etiological explanation via the mythical paradigm, whereas the 'historical' rationale explains the efficacy of action." Obbink (1997) also emphasizes this point. Betegh (2004:84) takes the "explanatory account" a step further when he outlines the following formula: "the interpretation or ritual action can be described in the general form 'Actor *a* performs ritual action *R* because *E*.'" He develops this theory on p. 350, but these remarks have generally failed to attract the attention of other scholars.

12 Betegh 2004:354.

(a) the use of the verb "to be" in expressions of the form "A is B" in which A frequently corresponds to what is done during the ritual and B to its interpretation;

(b) a variant of (a), whereby "A and B" are identified as "the same [thing]" (τὸ αὐτό);

(c) the use of the verb δηλόω, indicating that Orpheus "makes clear" something that is a part of the commentator's explanation;

(d) rhetorical questions used as argumentative resources (ἆρα, τί);

(e) the use of the optative to refer to alternative possibilities (e.g. "if we interpret *a* in some way, then *b* might occur, so we must interpret *a* in a different way");

(f) references to the ignorance of others (οὐ γινώσκοντες);

(g) comparative particles like ὅπωσπερ; and

(h) causal expressions such as ὅτι, γάρ, or τούτου ἕνεκα, used to introduce an explanation of ritual performance by the commentator.

The ritual does not supply its own interpretation as such; only an etiological myth can explain its *raison d'être*.[13] Thus, if the text includes an explicitly causal explanation, one clearly arises from the commentator's intervention. The words ἕκαστα σημεῖα suggest an accurate observation of individual phenomena, similar to those in column XIII 6 about the text that is considered allegorical; for this reason "it is necessary to speak about each word/verse in turn" (κ̣[α]τ̣' ἔπος ἕκαστον ἀνάγκη λέγειν).

2.1.4 ἐπέθηκ'

The subject of the verb ἐπέθηκ' should be the person who transmitted the ritual. If we are here dealing with Orphic rites, as everything seems to indicate, this person cannot be anyone other than Orpheus himself, who at several points is mentioned either by name or using the third-person pronoun as the author of the poem which is to be discussed in following columns; Orpheus is always considered to be responsible for introducing the τελεταί into Greece.[14]

13 Cf. Henrichs 1984.

14 Ferrari 2011c:42. Cf. Orpheus fr. 546–562 Bernabé 2004–2005 (henceforth *OF*) and Bernabé 2008a. On the other hand, Kouremenos (KPT 145) believes that the person in question is Orpheus and he quotes *OF* 547, 549–554, though he does not exclude the possibility of ὁ τέχνην ποιούμενος τὰ ἱερά. The later proposal is, however, difficult to accept since the performer does not create the ritual, but only performs it.

2.1.5 εὐχῆς ... ἀμφὶ' [Ἐρι]νύων

The commentator refers to a prayer addressed to the Erinyes as part of the ritual. It must be stressed that, after he lists the component parts of the ritual in column VI 1 (χοαὶ ... εὐ]χαὶ καὶ θυσ[ί]αι, "libations, pra]yers, and sacrifices"), both χοαί and θυσίαι recur in the column, but εὐχαί does not.[15] Instead, we find in column VI 2 ἐπ[ωιδή "spell," a term that most likely refers to the same reality, which may be evidence of connections to magical practice.[16]

2.1.6 μ[αν]τείας

A mantic practice was also part of the rite.[17] With regard to this issue, it seems that the commentator rejects divination practices based on the possession of *mystai* (col. I 7–8 ἐᾶμ μ[αν]τείας μ[υ]στῶν κατ[ο]χῆς); rather, he prefers to use water and fire as means of divination,[18] although he thinks it is necessary to draw a rational knowledge after observing the sacred action.[19] On the eventual relationship between the Erinyes and divination, Johnston reconsiders Harrison's idea that the prophecy of Xanthus in *Iliad* 19.408–417 was inspired by the Erinyes:[20] when the prophecy had been completed, the Erinyes would have stopped the horse's voice.

2.1.7 ἀχ]λύς

In line 11 we read the sequence]λὺς καὶ τἆλλ' ὅσα [. KPT 114 suggest the reading πο]λὺς, which would not seem to tie in very well with the following καὶ τ' ἆλλ' ὅσα. Conversely, ἀχ]λὺς, as proposed by Janko, provides a wonderful reading. It would refer to a "shroud of mist," a clouded frame of mind that can hinder the proper comprehension of things.[21] The commentator would be referring to the fact that most people do not understand the meaning of ritual (cf. σημαίνει, σημεῖα) due to certain mental clouding. The expression is very similar to the

15 χοαὶ in col. VI 1 is a conjecture by Tsantsanoglou (see §3.1.1). The word recurs in col. VI 7 χοὰς (cf. ἐπισπένδουσιν in col. VI 6); θυσία reappears in col. VI 4 θυσ[ία]ν (cf. θύουσιν in col. VI 8, προθύουσι in col. VI 9, and θύειν in col. VI 10).

16 Pfister 1924; Furley 1933. In Plutarch *Quaestiones convivales* 706D (ὥσπερ γὰρ οἱ μάγοι τοὺς δαιμονιζομένους κελεύουσι τὰ Ἐφέσια γράμματα πρὸς αὑτοὺς καταλέγειν καὶ ὀνομάζειν), the μάγοι—the term naturally being understood with the sense it had in the time of Plutarch—use a form of ἐπωιδή (the *Ephesia grammata*) to act upon *daimones*, in this case those who were possessing an unfortunate victim. On the *Ephesia grammata* see Bernabé 2003 and forthcoming.

17 On divination in the Derveni papyrus see Johnston in this volume.

18 Cf. KPT 114.

19 Ferrari 2011c:44.

20 Johnston 1992:95; cf. Ferrari 1911c:45–46.

21 As in Archilochus 191.2 West (here due to love), or in Critias 6.10 West.

one we find in column V 8–9 (ὑπὸ τ̣[ῆς τε] ἁμαρτ<ί>ης / κ̣αὶ [τ]ῆς ἄλλης ἡδον[ῆ]ς νενικημέν̣[οι, οὐ] μ̣α̣ν̣θ̣[άνο]υ̣σιν οὐδὲ] π̣ιστεύουσι, “overcome both by error and pleasure as well, they neither learn nor believe”) and is consistent with the numerous references in the poem to the ignorance of others.

2.1.8 In sum

In column I the commentator is making references to a purificatory ritual to honor the Erinyes, in which prayers, the burning of pure offerings, and some divinatory practices were included; here he rejects divination practices based on the possession of *mystai* and prefers a thoughtful analysis of water and fire. The commentator advises that the ritual has a meaning and that there are signs in it (σήματα) that could be (philosophically) interpreted one by one. People, however, are unable to either notice this meaning or interpret the signs due to their obfuscated minds. Hope also takes an important part in this process.[22]

2.2 Column II

2.2.1 Text

The text and translation of column II 3–8 are as follows:[23]

]᾿Ε̣ριν[υ
]τιμῶσιν[
α̣υ̣[χ]ο̣αὶ στα̣γόσιν̣ [χ]έον̣[ται
[ν]ε̣κ̣ροὺς τιμὰς [χ]ρὴ
.[ ]σ̣ι̣ [δ᾿] ἑκάστοις ὀρν̣ί̣θ̣ειόν τι
κλ̣ε̣[ισθὲν ἁρμ]οστο[ὺ]ς τῆ[ι] μ̣ουσ̣[ι]κῆι

7 ἐπιτελοῦ]σ̣ι̣ *vel* ἐπιτελέσου]σ̣ι̣ *temptaverit* Bernabé : δαίμο]σ̣ι̣ Ferrari || **8** κλ̣ε̣[ισθὲν Bernabé (*temptaverit* κλ̣ε̣[ισθὲν οἴκημα) : κ̣ά̣ε̣[ται Ferrari

... the Erinyes ... they honor ... the libations are poured down in drops... the dead ought [to be given] honors ... [and] to each [of the participants (?) in the rite they give] a little bird in a cage[24] ... [hymns] adapted to music ...

[22] Cf. in contrast col. XX 11–12, concerning bad performers of the rites: πρὶμ μὲν τὰ [ἱ]ε̣ρὰ ἐπιτελέσαι, ἐλπίζον̣[τε]ς εἰδήσειν, ἐπ̣[ιτελέσ]α̣ντ̣[ες] δ̣έ, στερηθέντες κα̣[ὶ τῆ]ς ἐλπί[δος] ἀπέρχονται̣, “before they perform the rites expecting to acquire knowledge, but after performing them they go away devoid even of expectation” (translation from KPT).

[23] Text and translation by Ferrari, unless otherwise indicated. For a complete critical apparatus cf. Ferrari 2011c:46, CHS.

[24] “[of the performers? of the rites they give] some little bird in a cage” (my translation); “[and] for each [of the daimons] a ... of bird is burnt” (Ferrari CHS).

2.2.2 Some impressions

This is the second time that the Erinyes, who will be analyzed by the commentator in the following columns, are mentioned, probably as addressees of a ritual performed by the *magoi* (col. VI) and as objects of the verb τιμῶσι. Libations are poured[25] and some ritual duty is stated, consisting of honoring the dead. It seems that each of the participants in the rite is given a little bird in a cage.[26] There is also a reference to music (]μ̣ουσ̣[ι]κῆι), a usual part of Orphic rituals.[27]

2.3 Column III

2.3.1 Text and translation

The text and translation of column III 3–11 are as follows:[28]

. . . . . .] . . α̣ιω̣σ . [. . . .]σ̣ι̣ κ̣ά̣τ̣ω̣[
δαίμ]ω̣γ γίνετα[ι ἑκά]σ̣τωι ἵλ̣ε̣[ως θε]ήλ̣α̣τ̣[ος· οὐ γὰ]ρ̣ ἡ̣
θείη τύ]χη ἐξώλεα σ̣[ίνεται] ε̣ἰ̣ ἔ̣τεισ’ ἕκ̣α̣[στ’] Ἐρινύσ̣[ι, οἱ] δ̣ὲ
δ]α̣ίμονες οἱ κατὰ̣ [γῆς ο]ὐδέ̣κ̣οτ̣’ [ἐλευθ]ε̣ρ̣ο̣ῦσι, ὡ[ς δὲ
θ̣εῶν ὑπηρέται δ̣[εινο]ὶ̣ π̣ά̣ν̣τ̣ας υ̣[ ]ι
εἰσὶν ὅπωσπερ ἄ[νδρες] ἄ̣δικο̣ι θ̣α̣[νάτωι ζημιούμε]νοι
αἰτίην [τ’ ἔ]χουσι̣[
οἵους .[. .] . [
. .]υστ[

8 θ̣α̣[νάτωι ζημιούμε]νοι West *ap.* Tsantsanoglou 1997:96 : θ̣ω̣[ὴν τίνωσι ἐπιμελόμεν]οι Ferrari

... down there ... [at the moment] of his birth[29] every human being is given a benevolent *daimon* sent [by the gods, for] the [heavenly] fate [does not harm] a noxious man who has paid all his faults to the Erinyes. On the contrary, [the] under[world] *daimones* never release, [but, as] servants of the gods [are quite capable of persecuting] all [the culprits. ...] They [*i.e. the culprits*] are in exactly the same way as unjust [punished by death],[30] and they are responsible ... just as ...

[25] See §3.1.1.

[26] See §3.1.5.

[27] On music in Orphic rituals see Molina 2008.

[28] Text and translation by Ferrari, unless otherwise indicated. For a complete critical apparatus see Ferrari 2011c:50, CHS.

[29] Cf. Menander fr. 500.1–3 KA: ἅπαντι δαίμων ἀνδρὶ συμπαρίσταται / εὐθὺς γενομένῳ, μυσταγωγὸς τοῦ βίου / ἀγαθός; Ferrari 2011c:51.

[30] "[but, as] servants of the gods, [they are quite capable of persecuting] all [the culprits....] They [*i.e. the culprits*] are in exactly the same way as unjust [punished by death]" (my translation):

The statements in column III are not a description of the rite, but clearly a commentator's explanation, as indicated by the use of the causal conjunction γάρ as well as the two comparisons (ὅπωσπερ line 8, and οἵους line 10), for clarifying the exposition. This leads me to posit that West's integration is more convenient than the one proposed by Ferrari, since it implies a comparison between the punishment of *daimones* and the punishments of human justice.

The commentator provides a theory about two kinds of *daimones*. In the first place are those who are sent by the gods[31] and who, according to Tsantsanoglou,[32] "reflect the widespread concept of a *daimon* who accompanies every person either as a 'guardian angel' or as his or her fate, from the moment of birth until death"; second are the *daimones* from the underworld, who chase the culprits. Later on we shall return to the commentator's daimonological theory.[33]

The proposal of θείη τύχη is also interesting. Apart from the significant parallels presented by Ferrari,[34] it should be noted that Τύχη has a relevant role in some of the Orphic texts.[35] Certainly the expression has a strong eschatological meaning. The culprit of a given fault can be freed from it by making offerings to the Erinyes; this is the religious context that explains the ritual, described and commented on in the papyrus.

2.4 Column IV

The text of the first five lines of column IV has been improved by the integration of two scraps (F 14 and F 17) by Ferrari,[36] but these lines are not important for our purposes.

In lines 6ff., the function of the Erinyes in their role as auxiliaries of Justice is connected to the cosmic order as a whole. The commentator insists that the punishment of the Erinyes is not solely related to bloodshed; in fact, the text by Heraclitus cited in support does not concern itself with the topic of violent crime within the family. "It is unlikely that he (Heraclitus) completely ignored the roles and characteristics that common opinion had assigned to them (the Erinyes), but it is likely that he adapted them probably by extending

"[but, as] servants of the gods [quite capable of persecuting] all [the culprits,] they [take care that] the unjust [men will pay] the penalty for their crimes" (Ferrari).

31 On the link δαίμ]ω̣ν ... θε]ή̣λ̣α̣τ̣[ος, Ferrari (2011c:52) provides the parallel with Plutarch *De vitando aere alieno* 830F: οἱ θεήλατοι καὶ οὐρανοπετεῖς ἐκεῖνοι τοῦ Ἐμπεδοκλέους δαίμονες; cf. Empedocles B 115 DK.

32 Tsantsanoglou 1997:105.

33 See §4.5.

34 Ferrari 2011:52n52.

35 Just like the Orphic tablet from Thurii *OF* 492, the *Orphic Hymn* 72, and two lead tablets from Selinous; cf. Martín Hernández 2011.

36 Ferrari 2010. For the following lines see Bernabé 2007a:188–195.

the jurisdiction in which the Erinys operated,"[37] and so they persecute unjust celestial bodies. The commentator quotes Heraclitus because he ascribes to the Erinyes the role of guarantors of natural order and justice in the universe.[38]

On the contrary, his insistence on the link between the Erinyes and Justice leads us to postulate that good destiny in the afterlife is connected to justice, a theory that seems strange in the context of the Orphic leaves, but not in that of Apulian pottery (where Orpheus and Dike appear on the same vase and in the same explanatory context) or of Plato.[39]

2.5 Column V[40]

In column V, the commentator mentions, most likely in relation to the punishments just discussed, that "the terrors coming from Hades"[41] should be taken seriously. These terrors are connected to the consultation of oracles. Janko[42] has suggested a reading for line 5 that makes this connection explicit: εἰ θέμι[ς ἀπιστ]ῆ̣σ̣α̣[ι, "whether it is right if one were to disbelieve."

The first-person πάριμεν̣ (line 4) and χρη[στη]ριαζόμ[εθα in line 2 seem to present the very author of the papyrus as a specialist in oracular consultation.[43] If there is no punctuation after αὐ̣τοῖς (line 3) we should understand that the consultation is on behalf of others.[44] One parallel that immediately suggests itself if this is the case is Tiresias' consultation of the Delphic Oracle at the request of Oedipus in the *Oedipus the King* of Sophocles.[45]

The mention of dreams appears to indicate that, if correctly interpreted—an act of which common people are incapable—they provide, as παραδείγματα of reality, testimony of the existence of horrific scenes in Hades.[46] The commen-

37 Rightly Johnston 1999:266.

38 Obbink 1997:51. As Tsantsanoglou (1997:109) points out, it is not the size of the sun that worries the exegete but rather the theological problem of the role played by the Erinyes.

39 Cf. Bernabé 2010b:201–204. About δίκη among Orphics see Jiménez San Cristóbal 2005.

40 Cf. the deep analysis of this column in Johnston in this volume.

41 Ferrari reads ἐ̣ξ (ἐ̣ν̣ Tsantsanoglou; ἆ̣ρ̣' KPT; ἂ̣ν̣ Janko).

42 Janko 2008:50–51.

43 Johnston (in this volume), however, considers that our author is not talking only about himself and people just like him when he uses the first-person plural.

44 Cf. the interpretative possibilities offered by Kouremenos (KPT 162) and by Johnston (in this volume).

45 Edmonds 2008:25 and 34. Kouremenos (KPT 162) asserts that "there is no reason to assume that the speaker here is the Derveni author," but his text does not offer any alternative explanation of the first-person plural. Cf. also Santamaría 2012.

46 Col. V 6–8: οὐ γινώσ̣[κοντες ἐ]ν̣ύ̣πνια ο̣ὐδὲ τῶν ἄλλωμ πρ̣αγμάτων ἕκασ̣[τον], δ̣ιὰ ποίω̣ν ἂν π̣α̣ρ̣α̣δειγμάτωμ π̣[ι]στεύοιεν; "without knowing (the meaning of) dreams or any of the other things, by what kind of evidence would they believe?" (trans. KPT). Johnston in this volume considers that the commentator means "miseries that *those already dead* are suffering, which causes

tator censures people because they are ignorant and because, as they do not wish to restrict their pleasures with just behavior, they take no notice of this testimony. He argues that dream-visions (and perhaps also oracles, given the reference to their consultation) are παραδείγματα, in which correct faith and learning should be rooted. Because people ignore these models, however, they neither learn nor believe. In this way the commentator equates lack of faith with ignorance. It is worthwhile to recall at this point that, according to the Pythagorean text I will quote in §4.5, *daimones* are responsible for dream-visions and for oracles.[47] In any case, the author intends to convince these people that they are endangering their own salvation.

2.6 Column VI

2.6.1 New readings

Janko has integrated fr. I 70 in this column, affecting the reading of lines 8–10; I have also modified a former suggestion of mine for lines 11–12,[48] because Ferrari has offered a better alternative,[49] and I have accepted it with some different readings. The text is as follows:[50]

[χοαὶ γάρ, εὐ]χ̣α̣ὶ καὶ θυσ[ί]αι μ[ειλ]ί̣σ̣σ̣ουσι τ̣ὰ̣[ς ψυχάς.]
ἐπ̣[ωιδὴ δ]ὲ̣ μάγων δύν[α]ται δ̣αίμονας ἐμ[ποδὼν]
γι̣[νομένο]υ̣ς μεθιστάν̣αι· δαίμον̣ες ἐμπο[δὼν ὄντες εἰσὶ]
ψ[υχαὶ τιμω]ροί. τὴν θυσ[ία]ν̣ τούτου̣ ἕνεκε[μ] π̣[οιοῦσ]ι̣[ν]
οἱ μά̣[γο]ι̣, ὡ̣σ̣περεὶ ποινὴ̣ν̣ ἀποδιδόντες. τοῖ<ς> δὲ
ἱεροῖ[ς] ἐπισπένδουσιν ὕ[δω]ρ καὶ γάλα, ἐξ ὧμπερ καὶ τὰς
χοὰς ποιοῦσι, ἀνάριθμα̣ [κα]ὶ̣ πολυόμφαλα τὰ πόπανα
θύουσιν, ὅτι καὶ αἱ ψυχα[ὶ ἀν]ά̣ριθμοί̣ εἰσι. μύσται
Εὐμεν̣ίσι προθύουσι κ[ατὰ τὰ] α̣ὐτὰ μάγοις· Εὐμενίδες γὰρ
ψυχαί ε̣ἰσιν. ὧν ἕνεκ̣[εν ὁ μέλλων ἱ]ερὰ θεοῖς θύειν
ὀ̣ρ̣ν̣ί̣θιον πρότερον [λύει, ἵνα φίλος αὐτ]α̣ῖ̣ς̣ τ̣ό̣τ̣' ἔ̣[ρχη]ται
[κάτ]ω, [ὅ]τε καὶ τὸ κα̣[κὸν]ου . . . [. .]οι̣,
εἰσὶ δὲ [ψυχα]ὶ...[.].τουτο.[
ὅσαι δὲ [ ]ων ἀλλ̣[
φ̣ο̣ρ̣ου[ ]...[

them, in turn, to inflict miseries on the living." If this is so, ritual described in the papyrus could mainly concern the correct manner to avoid such a situation.

47 καὶ ὑπὸ τούτων (sc. δαιμόνων) πέμπεσθαι ἀνθρώποις τούς τ' ὀνείρους καὶ τὰ σημεῖα νόσους τε.

48 Bernabé 2007b, 2007c.

49 Ferrari 2011a:75, reproduced in Ferrari CHS.

50 Janko 2008. In the critical apparatus I present only the new proposals. Cf. Bernabé 2007a and Ferrari 2011a:75 for more complete critical apparatus.

1 χοαὶ Tsantsanoglou : χοαὶ γάρ Bernabé : *nihil rest.* Ferrari | εὐ]χ̣α̣ὶ Tsantsanoglou 1997:95 : χ̣ο̣ὴ Tsantsanoglou 2008, *prob.* Ferrari | τ̣ὰ̣[ς ψυχάς Tsantsanoglou 1997: 95 : τ̣ὰ̣[ς ἀ]ρτά̣δ̣[ας Ferrari || **3** ἐμπο[δὼν ὄντες εἰσὶ Janko 2001 : ἐμπο[δίζειν τὰς Ferrari || **4** ψ[υχαὶ τιμω]ροί Tsantsanoglou 1997:113 : ψ[υχὰς δει]ν̣οί Ferrari || **10** ὁ μέλλων ἱ]ερὰ Janko 2008 : τὸμ μέλλοντ]α Tsantsanoglou || **11** ὀ̣ρ̣ν̣ί̣θ̣ιον Ferrari : `ὀ̣´[[θ̣]][ρ]ν̣ίθ̣[ε]ιον Janko 2008 | λύει Bernabé, *prob.* Ferrari : θύει Janko 2008 | εἰ σὺν ψυχ]α̣ῖ̣ς π̣ο̣τ̣ε̣ [ἔσ]ται Ferrari : ὅτι σὺν αὐτ]ο̣ῖ̣ς π̣ο̣τ̣έ̣[ον]ται Bernabé :]α̣ι̣σ̣π̣ο̣τ̣ε̣[. .]ται Janko 2008 || **12** κάτ]ω Bernabé : [ὅ]τε καὶ τὸ κα̣[κὸν Ferrari : . . .] ὥ[σ]τε (*iam* Janko) καὶ τὸ κα̣[(κα̣[κὸν *dub. in ap. crit.*) Bernabé

[For libations, pra]yers, and sacrifices placate [souls]. An in[cantation] by *magoi* can dislodge *daimones* that [have become] a hindrance; *daimones* that [are a hindrance] are vengeful so[uls]. This is why the *magoi* per[form] the sacrifice, as they are paying a blood-price. Onto the offerings they make libations of wa[ter] and milk, with both of which they also made drink-offerings. They sacrifice cakes which are countless and many-humped, because the souls too are countless. Initiates make a first sacrifice to the Eumenides in the same way as *magoi* do; for the Eumenides are souls. For these reasons [a person who intends] to make offerings to the gods, first [frees] a bird, [so that he will come welcome] to them in the [netherw]orld, when the e[vil (?)] also ... but they are [souls] ... this (?), but as many (souls) as ... of ... but (?) they wear ...

The reason I prefer these readings in lines 1–4, instead of following Ferrari, is partially that ἀρτάδας is based on very scarce evidence but mostly because, in my opinion, the commentator's argument can be more easily followed this way: first, he announces that certain practices placate the souls (which will be mentioned again in a later explanation; otherwise, if we read ἀρτάδας, it seems strange that no further explanation of the term is introduced, as if it was completely familiar to him) so, given that the rite intends to placate the Eumenides, the initial statement must be explained, something that the commentator does in subsequent steps:

(a) the ἐπωιδή dislodge *daimones* that are souls;

(b) the sacrifice is equivalent to a ποινή;

(c) the cakes are many-humped since the souls are countless;

(d) sacrifices are made to the Eumenides because they are souls.

2.6.2 Description and explanation

In column VI the commentator returns to the ritual and its explanation; as a result, the two levels I pointed out in §2.1.3 necessarily reappear. Following the above-explained methodology, I will analyze first the descriptive level (§3), trying to place this ritual within a Greek religious context. Afterwards, I will focus on the commentator's interpretation (§4), aiming at placing it in a philosophical framework.

3. Ritual's Reconstruction[51]

3.1 Δρώμενα and Λεγόμενα

3.1.1 χοαί

References to libations appear in column VI 6 (ἐπισπένδουσιν) and 7 (χοὰς), and in column II 5. As Tsantsanoglou has already noted, it is likely that among the six to eight letters missing in column VI 1 we should read χοαὶ, which are usually associated with funerary rituals.[52] I propose χοαὶ γάρ, εὐ]χαὶ κτλ. In column II 5, the commentator specifies that they are made in drops (στᾳγόσιν). Yet such a libation was in fact uncommon, since scholars define the χοή as a libation in which the content of the entire vessel was poured out, a practice common in the ritual dedicated to the dead. On the other hand, σπονδή consists of a moderate pouring over the altar.[53] However, sequences such as Aeschylus *Choephoroi* 149 (τάσδ' ἐπισπένδω χοάς)[54] call into question the existence of a categorical difference between the two types of libation.

We must pay attention to a small fragment of the papyrus (fr. I 78, KPT 124):

]σ[
]νηφ[

where νηφ[could be read as a form of νηφάλιος "lacking in wine, sober, abstemious."[55] In fact, many texts mention wineless libations for the Erinyes,[56] and in almost all cases their purpose is to appease these vengeful divinities. The most interesting is a passage of the Orphic *Argonautica* in which there are many striking coincidences with the Derveni text:

[51] About Orphic rituals, see Jiménez San Cristóbal 2002. The reconstruction will be easier when we have a better text.

[52] Tsantsanoglou 1997:110; cf. Graf 1980:217–218; Henrichs 1984:260; Betegh 2004:76. Ferrari reads] χọὴ instead of εὐ]χạὶ.

[53] Rudhardt 1958:240–248; Casabona 1966:231–297; Graf 1980:217–218; Henrichs 1984; Tsantsanoglou 1997:102–103; Jourdan 2003:2n2; Betegh 2004:76.

[54] Which Henrichs (1984:260n18) underscores as "exceptional," even though he adds "and similar phrases in Euripides." See further Martín Hernández's inspiring appraisals (2010:237–241).

[55] Cf. Bernabé 2007a. Ferrari (2007:203) suggested the inclusion of ᾳὐ[ταῖς] δ̣' ἄ̣ρ̣ᾳ ν̣[ηφαλίοις χ]οαὶ in col. II 5.

[56] Aeschylus *Eumenides* 107–109, Sophocles *Oedipus Coloneus* 100, 159, and schol. *ad loc.* (16.1 di Marco), Apollonius Rhodius 4.712–715. Cf. Henrichs 1983, 1984.

αὐτὰρ ἔγωγε
ψυχὴν ἱλασάμην, σπένδων μειλίγματα χύτλων
ὕδατί τ᾽ ἠδὲ γάλακτι, μελισσορύτων ἀπὸ νασμῶν
λοιβαῖς συμπροχέων, καὶ ἐμοῖς ὕμνοισι γεραίρων.[57]

That such libations are made without wine seems to arise from the fact that in sacrificial contexts wine is normally considered a substitute for blood. The ritual described by the commentator appears to be similar in this respect to those mentioned elsewhere.

3.1.2 θυσίαι

As the second component of the ritual, the author mentions sacrifices (θυσίαι) in column VI 1 and 4; the verbs θύουσιν (col. VI 8), θύειν (col. VI 10), and προθύουσι (col. VI 9) also appear. Usually, the sacrifice in question is a burnt offering.

It is therein specified (as one might expect, given Orphic beliefs) that this offering does not involve bloodshed, its main components being some cakes (col. VI 7 πόπανα). Other texts give evidence of cake offerings in similar ritual contexts, in particular the mysteries celebrated in honor of the chthonic deities Demeter and Dionysus[58] or in funeral rites.[59]

3.1.3 εὐ]χ̣α̣ί/ἐπ̣[ωιδή

The third component of the ritual, according to column VI 1, consists of invocations εὐ]χ̣α̣ί.[60] εὐχῆς also appears in column I 6, but in column VI 2 we find ἐπ̣[ωιδή instead of εὐχή.[61] In the ritual context, the most likely purpose of the ἐπωιδή is to appease the Erinyes. Yet the commentator hastens to explain, in the course of discussing the Erinyes and Eumenides, that the addressees are the

57 *Orphei Argonautica* 572–575.

58 Clemens Alexandrinus *Protrepticus* 2.22.4 (*OF* 590): πόπανα πολυόμφαλα (with regard to the mysteries related to Orpheus); Aristophanes Plutus 660: πόπανα καὶ προθύματα; *Thesmophoriazusae* 284–289: τὴν κίστην κάθελε, κᾆιτ᾽ ἔξελε / τὸ πόπανον, ὅπως λαβοῦσα θύσω τοῖν θεοῖν (Demeter and Kore); Polybius 6.25.7: τοῖς ὀμφαλωτοῖς ποπάνοις παραπλήσιον (a shield) τοῖς ἐπὶ τὰς θυσίας ἐπιτιθεμένοις; Menander Dyscolos 449–451: ὁ λιβανωτὸς εὐσεβὲς / καὶ τὸ πόπανον· τοῦτ᾽ ἔλαβεν ὁ θεὸς ἐπὶ τὸ πῦρ / ἅπαν ἐπιτεθέν (from a pious sacrifice, as opposed to the sacrifice with extravagant expenditure); Epiphanius *Expositio fidei* 10 (*OF* 592): τύμπανά τε καὶ πόπανα, ῥόμβος τε καὶ κάλαθος amongst the elements of the Eleusinian mysteries; Callimachus fr. 681 Pf.: νηφάλιαι καὶ τῇσιν ἀεὶ μελιηδέας ὄμπας / λήιτειραι καίειν ἔλλαχον Ἡσυχίδες; Sokolowski, *Lois sacrées* 52.9: π[ό]πανον χιονικιαῖον ὀρθόμφαλον δωδεκόνφαλον. Cf. Henrichs 1984:260–261nn22–24, Kearns 1994, Martín Hernández 2010:248–252.

59 In Lucian *Cataplus* 2 Charon says: παρ᾽ ἡμῖν μὲν γὰρ ἀσφόδελος μόνον καὶ χοαὶ καὶ πόπανα καὶ ἐναγίσματα.

60 *Contra* Ferrari 2011a.

61 See §2.1.5.

souls of the dead, rather than the Erinyes—here identified, as always, with the Eumenides, a point to which I shall return (§3.2.1).

3.1.4 ἔπη

Another component of the ritual is the hexameter text the author comments upon in columns VII–XXVI, which might form part of τὰ λεγόμενα, though the issue is not the primary focus of our current discussion.

3.1.5 ὀρνίθειον/ὀρνίθιον

In column II 7 we read ὀρνίθειον and in column VI 11 ὀρνίθιον. I have dealt with this topic in a prior paper.[62] Here I will restate the main conclusions along with some new proposals following the new readings:

(a) ὀρνίθειον is attested in ancient authors as a noun meaning "a little bird."[63] An alternative possibility would be to consider it an adjective in column II 7, and to reconstruct a neuter term for "cage" in the gap (e.g. οἴκημα)[64]; cf. *infra* (d).

(b) Since the Orphics did not use living beings (ἔμψυχα) in their sacrifices, I think that this ὀρνίθ(ε)ιον cannot be destined for sacrifice.

(c) I suggested reconstructing λύει instead of Janko's θύει in column VI 11. Liberation of a bird can be understood as a soul's liberation from injustice by some sort of sympathetic magic. The *mystai* probably received (or took) a caged bird. We have parallels to the bird metaphor,[65] and the motif of the cage of the soul-bird stands in clear relation to the Orphic theory of the body as prison of the soul, quoted by Plato,[66] and thus to the doctrine of metempsychosis. The Orphics held the belief that, once

[62] Bernabé 2007b. Although this paper was based on the former readings of cols. II–III, I think that the main arguments are still valid. Details and criticism of other interpretations can be read in it.

[63] Clytus fr. 1: σκέλη δὲ ἄκεντρα, ὅμοια τοῖς ὀρνιθείοις, "their legs lack spurs, just like chickens"; Pherecrates 50.5–6 KA: ὀρνίθεια πλήθει πολλά, "a vast number of birds" (trans. Gulick); Aristophanes *Aves* 1590: καὶ μὴν τά γ' ὀρνίθεια λιπάρ' εἶναι πρέπει, where Del Corno translates "*gli uccelli.*"

[64] Cf. Herodotus 7.109: ἔτρεφόν τε ὄρνιθας χερσαίους καὶ λιμναίους ἔν τε οἰκήμασι; Hippolitus *Haereses* 6.8.2: τότε ἀνοίξας τὸ οἴκημα εἴασεν ἄλλον ἀλλαχόσε τοὺς ψιττακούς; Hsch.: κουμάσιον· τὸ τῶν ὀρνίθων; Suda: οἴκημα ὀρνιθοκομεῖον· τὸ τὰς ὄρνιθας ἔχον οἴκημα. Cf. Aristophanes fr. 446 KA and note *ad loc:* ὀρνίθειον οἰκίσκον. Nevertheless, οἰκίσκος is masculine and cannot be restored here since τι requires a neuter noun.

[65] Plutarch *Consolatio ad uxorem* 611D (*OF* 595 I), cf. Bernabé 2001 (there is a similar statement in *Non posse suaviter vivi secundum Epicurum* 1105D), an Orphic gold tablet found in Thurii (*OF* 488.5). See also Turcan 1959; Casadio 1991:135–136; Bernabé and Jiménez San Cristóbal 2008:120.

[66] Plato Cratylus 400c, cf. Bernabé 1995 and 2010b:115–143; see also Méautis 1932:582, Nilsson 1957:123n15, Turcan 1959:38.

freed from the cycle of reincarnation, the soul would fly like a bird. If we are to imagine caged birds that later fly away as part of the ritual, their release would be an imitative act serving as a preliminary part of the ritual.

(d) I had proposed a reconstruction of the text based on the reading π̣ọτ̣ẹ́[ον]ται "they fly" in line 11. Ferrari's reconstruction seems to be more acceptable (since ποτέονται is a poetic term), but this does not change the interpretation of the ritual act: it consists in the liberation of a bird in order to please the Eumenides. Besides, Ferrari[67] mentions two images in tombstones, where releasing a little bird from a cage seems to hint at a soul departing from its body.

3.2 Addressees of the Ritual

3.2.1 The Eumenides/Erinyes

The addressees of the ritual performed by the *magoi* are the Erinyes/Eumenides. Given the frequency with which this euphemism is employed in cult worship,[68] it seems likely that the Eumenides are being also identified here with the Erinyes.[69] The type of the offering described is, in fact, the same as that usually offered to the Eumenides in the parallels given above (§3.1.1).

Martín Hernández[70] points out that outside of Orphic circles the ritual for the Erinyes would carry significance in eschatological terms only if the deceased or some of his ancestors had committed a blood crime or made a slanderous allegation against the family.[71] It would be nonsensical, however, to suppose that the ritual described in the papyrus would be aimed at a large group of *mystai* who were all guilty of a crime of this type. Martín Hernández furthermore turns her attention to the role that these divinities play in the afterlife as depicted on Apulian vase paintings.[72] As in the Orphic texts, in these paintings we find the Erinyes punishing dead individuals who were presumably uninitiated, unjust,

67 Ferrari 2011a:80.

68 Johnston 2004:35, with additional bibliography; see also Johnston 1999:267–273.

69 Henrichs (1994) points out that "Erinyes" was a term that could be used, from the middle of the fifth century at the latest, to express negative aspects of the Eumenides. Betegh (2004:86) points also to a close link between the Erinyes and Bacchic initiates—especially in tragedy, where the Erinyes frequently show maenadic or Bacchant-like characteristics, or are explicitly described using such terms.

70 Martín Hernández 2010:271.

71 In relation thereto he quotes *Iliad* 9.571; *Odyssey* 11.280; Pindar *Olympian* 2.41; Aeschylus *Septem* 70, 700, 723, 1055, *Choephoroi* 283, *Eumenides* 950; Sophocles *Electra* 112, *Antigone* 1075. See also Johnston 1999:252.

72 Martín Hernández 2010:272. Cf. also Schmidt 1975; Pensa 1977; Tsantsanoglou 1997:112n23; Bernabé 2009.

or those who did not manage entirely to atone for guilt incurred during their lifetime.[73]

Henrichs believes that the "preliminary sacrifice" to the Eumenides cannot be anything like that dedicated to them in the woods near Athens because the cult of the Eumenides is not of a mystic nature and because if it were a preliminary sacrifice, the principal one would then be dedicated to other gods.[74] Both assumptions would be correct within the context of the Attic cult of the Erinyes/Eumenides, but nothing prevents mystic rituals from embracing elements drawn from other Greek rituals and adapting them to their own "liturgy."

3.2.2 The *daimones*

There are two different types of *daimones* in column III. Some of them are benevolent *daimones* sent by the gods at the moment of birth, one for each human, as a sort of "guardian angels"; the others come from the underworld and chase the culprits. These are probably the same entities as the hindering *daimones* of column VI 2–3.[75] They most likely hinder the passage of the soul to the afterlife by demanding a penalty for the guilt of each individual.[76]

Tsantsanoglou rightly rejects any supposed relationship between these *daimones* and the reference Patroclus makes in the *Iliad* to the souls that will not let him cross to the afterlife because he is unburied.[77] Instead he notes parallels to the μακραίωνες δαίμονες of Empedocles, who keep sinful souls away from those of the just.[78]

These hindering (ἐμ[ποδῶν) *daimones* are also related to the Ἔμπουσα that Aristophanes introduces in *The Frogs*.[79] Brown believes that the appearance of Empusa in this role should be linked to the presentation of the φάσματα in the Eleusinian Mysteries.[80] He furthermore suggests that this scene should be interpreted as comic imitation of the dramatization of the afterlife carried out by the *mystai* and priests in their concoction of their great mysteries. Martín Hernández, however,[81] argues that we should not reject the possibility that one or more similar beings might in fact appear in the panoply of Orphic ritual.

73 Cf. Schmidt 1975; Bianchi 1976:32–34; Aellen 1994; Bernabé 2009. Cf. also Aristophanes *The Frogs* 144f–161; Pseudo-Plato *Axiochus* 371d; *Papyrus Bononiensis* 4.24.

74 Henrichs 1984:266.

75 See §4.5.

76 It cannot be ruled out that, in the framework of a ritual or the analysis of the commentator, they might be identified with the Erinyes. Cf. Betegh 2004:88 as well as Martín Hernández 2010: 258–270.

77 *Iliad* 23.71–74; Tsantsanoglou 1997:112.

78 Empedocles B 115 DK.

79 Aristophanes *The Frogs* 292–305; cf. Johnston 1999:130–139, Betegh 2004:89n45.

80 Brown 1991.

81 Martín Hernández 2010:261–264.

3.3 Ritual Performers: *Mystai* and *Magoi*

In column VI, two types of ritual performers are mentioned: the μύσται (8) and the μάγοι (2, 5, and 9).

The μύσται are assistants to the μάγοι, who direct the initiation rituals. Obbink calls attention to the fact that μύσται can be associated with both Eleusinian initiates and the Bacchic mysteries.[82] Earlier, Henrichs had suggested the possibility of linking this cult with that of Eleusis,[83] based on the fact that in this period μύσται refers above all to Eleusis. However, Tsantsanoglou rightly refuses to credit this inference.[84] Moreover, Henrichs himself shows that μύσται can be found in the Heraclitus fragment already cited, and in the Orphic gold tablet from Hipponium,[85] where the word μύσται is paired with βάκχοι. Tsantsanoglou adds the testimony of the tablet from Pherai[86] that confirms that the mystai are freed from any punishment after death. Given that the *magoi* are not to be identified at all with the hierophants of Eleusis, it is clear that these *mystai* participate in an Orphic-Bacchic ritual.

Tsantsanoglou outlines clearly and precisely the conditions that a *mystes* should fulfill, always as seen through the eyes of our commentator:[87] he should live a righteous life, avoid injustice, acquire a certain degree of knowledge, eschew the pleasure and distrust that might hinder him from doing so,[88] and celebrate the rite. Dream-visions also provide a source of information for the men, and their exegesis is a part of the process. The *mystai* probably believed that they could be liberated from their own injustice through the ritual.

On the other hand, the identity of the *magoi* is a controversial issue. Tsantsanoglou, Burkert, and Ferrari insist that the *magoi* are professionals of foreign origin, perhaps Persian; Jourdan sees them as charlatans; Most and Betegh see them as Orphic priests.[89] I agree with Betegh's explanation that, despite the

82 Obbink 1997:51.

83 Henrichs 1984:266–267.

84 Tsantsanoglou 1997:115.

85 Heraclitus fr. 87 Marcovich (= B 14 DK and *OF* 474), cf. Bernabé and Jiménez San Cristóbal 2008: 52–53.

86 *OF* 493, cf. Bernabé and Jiménez San Cristóbal 2008:151.

87 Tsantsanoglou 1997:101.

88 Cf. Tsantsanoglou 1997:102, quoting the parallels in vocabulary in the *Bacchae* 473–474 (εἰδέναι), 480 (ἀμαθής), and 490 (ἀσέβεια).

89 Most 1997; Tsantsanoglou 1997:110–115; Jourdan 2003:XIV and 37–38; Burkert 2004:117; Ferrari 2011a, 2011b; Betegh 2004:78. West remarks, in less explicit form, that the Babylonian or Assyrian priests, then subdued by the Persians, can serve as a role model of exegesis and that the exegete bridges the ritual of the Orphic initiates with the *magoi* "speaking as if the wisdom of the μάγοι guaranteed the validity of Orphic ritual" (West 1997:89–90). The expression "as if" does not make it clear whether he believes that the authentic Babylonian *magoi* participated in the rituals or that they are a model for the Greek officiants; cf. Bernabé 2006.

Persian origin of the word, the *magoi* mentioned here are Orphic officiants. It seems likely, furthermore, that the Persian *magoi* were considered experts in ritual acts and that Orphic officiants were accordingly compared with them. I have dealt with *magoi* in the Derveni Papyrus in another paper,[90] whose main conclusions are that *magoi* were neither charlatans nor Persian *magoi*, but Orphic officiants identical to those who in some sources are referred to as "Orpheotelests." This name has never been documented in any Orphic source, yet it appears in works of "external" authors, including those with an openly hostile attitude toward Orphism; it almost seems as though the word Ὀρφεοτελεστής is virtually a technical term used by authors with an "external perspective" upon Orphism.[91] If this is the case, the designation "Orpheotelest" might best be understood as a term of art used by erudite ancient "historians of religions," whilst the term *magoi* is that current with those who share the "internal perspective." If we compare the activities attributed to the Orpheotelests (or to the same professionals called by other names) with the ones quoted in the Derveni Papyrus, we can see that they are the same. In the table that follows, I compare the information given in the quoted texts regarding the Orpheotelests with the information about the *magoi* offered in column VI. This comparative view clearly indicates that the sources refer to the same type of person.

INFORMATION ABOUT THE ORPHEOTELESTS IN OTHER SOURCES	INFORMATION ABOUT THE μάγοι IN *P.DERV.*
Their rituals are mystic[92]	VI 8 μύσται
They perform sacrifices[93]	VI 1 εὐ]χ̣α̣ὶ καὶ θυσ[ί]αι
They promise happiness in Hades[94]	VI 2 δύν[α]ται δ̣αίμονας ἐμ[ποδὼν γι̣[νομένο]υ̣ς μεθιστάν̣αι[95]
...and terrors to those who were not initiated[96]	V 6 ἐξ Ἅιδου δεινά

90 Bernabé 2006.

91 Plutarch *Apophthegmata Laconica* 224D (*OF* 653), Theophrastus *Characteres* 16.11 (*OF* 654), Philodemus *De poematis Papyrus Herculanensis* 1074 fr. 30 (181.1 Janko = *OF* 655); see also Hippocrates *De morbo sacro* 18.6 (90 Grensemann = *OF* 657), Plato *Respublica* 364b (*OF* 573 I) and 364e (*OF* 573 I), Strabo 7 fr. 10a Radt (*OF* 659), about Orpheus himself described as an Orpheotelest (cf. Livy 39.8.3, and Bernabé 2002a).

92 μυηθέντες: Plutarch *Apophthegmata Laconica* 224D; τελετάς: Plato *Respublica* 364b, Strabo 7 fr. 10a Radt; τελεσθησόμενος: Theophrastus *Characteres* 16.11.

93 θυσίαις and θυηπολοῦσιν: Plato *Respublica* 364b.

94 εὐδαιμονοῦσι: Plutarch *Apophthegmata Laconica* 224D; τελευτήσουσι: Plato *Respublica* 364b.

95 I understand that liberation from δαίμονες ἐμποδών that are ψ[υχαὶ τιμω]ροί allows the initiate to be free from punishment in the netherworld.

96 μὴ θύσαντας δὲ δεινὰ περιμένει: Plato *Respublica* 364b.

They use incantation[97]	VI 2 ἐπ̣[ωιδή
and also divination[98]	V 3 χρησ̣[τ]ηριάζον[ται, V 4 μ̣ά]ν̣τεῖον̣
They base their knowledge on Orpheus' books[99]	The text of Orpheus is commented on in *P.Derv.*
They purify from injustice[100]	VI 4–5 τὴν θυσ[ία]ν̣ ... π̣[οιοῦσ]ι̣[ν οἱ μά̣[γο]ι̣, ὡ̣σ̣περεὶ ποινὴν̣ ἀποδιδόντες.
Dream-visions play a specific role[101]	V 6 ἐ]ν̣ύ̣πνια

Edmonds offers an insightful approach to this topic when he points out "the Derveni author's use of the text of Orpheus and mention of the *magoi* as part of his definition of himself as an extra-ordinary ritual specialist" and that "one of the aims of the text was to establish the credentials of the Derveni author as an authority on religious matters, one who was able to give an explanation in support of his ritual practices."[102] Furthermore, he highlights the fact that "the fundamental ambivalence of the term *magos* admits a sense of both a positive and a negative abnormality, and the shift from positive to negative is not a chronological, but a situational shift, dependent upon who is labeling whom and for what reasons."[103] It is likely that criticism cast by competitors upon the *magoi* in their capacity as religious or healing practitioners eventually infected the word with the negative connotations it acquires in other texts. The positive or strictly technical associations of the word thus came to be overshadowed by the "negative aspect" that Edmonds recognizes within its ambivalent designation of what he calls "extra-ordinary people."

The analysis of the given data leads us to conclude that the *magos*, a term of Persian origin referring to certain specific ritual performers, was accepted in Greece, most likely because of the professional prestige such performers enjoyed. More importantly, this expression refers to performers of non-civic rites related to mystic and initiatory rituals. It is crucial to understand that

97 ἐπωιδαῖς: Plato *Respublica* 364b.

98 μαντικῆς: Strabo 7 fr. 10a Radt; μάντεις: Plato *Respublica* 364b.

99 βίβλων Ὀρφέως: Plato *Respublica* 364b.

100 λύσεις τε καὶ καθαρμοὶ ἀδικημάτων διὰ θυσιῶν: Plato *Respublica* 364b.

101 Probably it is not a coincidence that Theophrastus *Characteres* 16.11 refers to the Orpheotelests just after talking about ἐνύπνια. Cf. Tsantsanoglou (1997:98–99), who rightly argues that the professional referred to consults the oracles—he is a μάντις—interprets dreams (ὀνειροκρίτης), and might even be a τερατοσκόπος as well. In *Leges* 933d, Plato jointly quotes the μάντις and the τερατοσκόπος when he most likely refers to these Greek professionals (Bernabé 2010b:222).

102 Edmonds 2008:31–32. See also Burkert 1962.

103 Edmonds 2008:35. On the contrary, KPT's argumentation (53) is based on a false dilemma: "the term μάγος is used pejoratively ... unless it refers to a member of the priestly Persian caste."

these rituals are Greek, in the Greek language, and intended for Greek participants. The λεγόμενα refer almost certainly to explanations of the mythical significance of the mysteries, and also to ἐπῳδαί, which brings them closer to the world of magic. The professionals designated as *magoi* undertook diverse duties, such as sacrifice (apparently bloodless), divination, healing, purification, preparation for death, funerary rituals—all of them containing a strong magical component. Those who participated in the rituals were called *mystai*, and they acted in the way indicated by the *magoi*.

Other types of priests, physicians, official diviners, and other "professionals" must have seen in their performances a dangerous competition, or an intolerable intrusion. They accordingly denounced their practices as being ill-intentioned or simply deceptive and useless. The *magoi* thus became more and more discredited, and gradually the use of the term became restricted to what we now call "magicians."

3.4 Conclusions: Concerning Elements of the Ritual

Let us briefly review, then, what elements of the ritual described in the first columns of the papyrus can be asserted.

The first libation is carried out by pouring droplets, as homage paid to the Erinyes/Eumenides. Every *mystes* takes a little bird, probably caged. The ritual act involves, in addition to the burning of many-lobed cakes, new libations made of water and milk being poured over offerings, accompanied by the recitation of an ἐπῳδή or Orphic poem. Every mystes then releases his caged bird.

It seems clear that the goal of such a ritual act is to propitiate the Erinyes in a funerary ceremony, or better in a τελετή that involves an *imitatio mortis* by means of sacrifices, prayers/incantations, and libations.[104] Releasing the bird is *prima facie* an act in accordance with the principles of sympathetic magic, performed to free the soul from its corporal imprisonment or as a metaphor of this liberation. In a previous paper I have underscored the significance of a series of Buddhist rituals linked with *karma* in which releasing caged birds forms a part of the ritual act.[105] Casadesús[106] provides an interesting alternative when he interprets the bird in a context of ornithomancy and supports this theory by a quotation of a Stoic passage.[107] However, he fails to offer any specific reading for filling the gap.

[104] Martín Hernández 2005.

[105] Bernabé 2007b.

[106] Casadesús 2010.

[107] SVF II 1213: *eademque efficit in avibus divina mens, ut tum huc tum illuc volent alites tum in hac tum in illa parte se occultent, tum a dextra tum a sinistra parte canant oscines*, etc.

4. Ritual as Interpreted by Commentator

4.1 Premises

The commentator, as I have pointed out (§2.1.3), not only describes the rite, but also proceeds to explain its meaning. At this point it is important to scrutinize the principles upon which his explanation is based, as well as the linguistic markers that indicate his interpretation, which separate the roles of the μάγοι and the μύσται.

4.2 The Function of *Magoi*

The interpreter concludes the following about the rite performed by the *magoi*:

(a) The effect he attributes to the χοαί, εὐχαί, and θυσίαι (col. VI 1) is to appease the dead souls: μ[ειλ]ί̣σ̣σ̣ουσι is an almost certain reading. The reconstruction τ̣ὰ̣[ς ψυχάς relies on the commentator's following statements: *daimones* must be moved away, and they are souls (col. VI 3–4); it is said in lines 7–8 that πόπανα of countless "nombrils" are sacrificed because the souls of the departed are themselves countless.[108] The commentator thus understands that those who are appeased are the souls. The marker could be γὰρ if, as I believe, this should be read in the lost initial part of line 1.

(b) The effect he attributes to the ἐπωιδή is μεθιστάναι (col. VI 3) to the *daimones* that hinder (δέ coordinates the sentence with the first one introduced by γάρ). The problem is that the word μεθιστάναι has a double sense in Greek; it may refer to a "change of place" or "displacement," but it has also the sense "to change in spirits or mood."[109] I have discussed this problem in another paper,[110] concluding that if the Eumenides are appeased they maintain their distance and do not attack, or, as Henrichs[111] rightly puts it, "they are kept at a safe distance by proper rites of appeasement." To use a phrase our commentator might have endorsed, "to appease" and "to maintain distance" τὸ αὐτό ἐστι.

108 Instead of offering analogous or symbolic interpretations of the ritual, Betegh believes the passage is intended to have the sense "to give each of the angry souls its share" (see Betegh 2004:84).

109 Laks and Most (1997a:11) translate it as "to change," but they add in n7 "or 'keep away.'" Tsantsanoglou (1997:98) takes it as "change (or drive away?)," Janko (2002:13), as "to dislodge," while Betegh (2004:15) prints "remove" and Jourdan (2003:6) opts for "*change de voie*," attempting to maintain both meanings, "*déplacement*" and "*transformation*."

110 Bernabé 2008b.

111 Henrichs 1984:257.

(c) Impeding *daimones* are vengeful souls (the linguistic marker being εἰσί).[112]

(d) This is why the *magoi* perform the sacrifice precisely as though they were paying a blood-price (the linguistic markers are τούτου ἕνεκε[μ] and ὡσπερεὶ).[113]

(e) The cakes have multiple lobes because the souls are likewise multiple (marker: ὅτι).

4.3 The Function of *Mystai*

Regarding what the *mystai* do, the commentator concludes:

(a) The *mystai* perform the same acts as the *magoi* (col. VI 8–9; the marker κατὰ τὰ αὐτά indicates the identification of apparently distinct phenomena).

(b) The Eumenides are the souls of the dead.

(c) προθύουσι is interpreted in etymological terms not as "to sacrifice in the foremost position" in honor of the Eumenides, but rather as "to do prior to the sacrificial act" (θύειν ... πρότερον col. VI 10–11; marker: ὧν ἕνεκ[εν).

(d) The bird's liberation implies that the soul of the μύστης will be welcomed by the Erinyes in the netherworld.

4.4 The Erinyes/Eumenides

The commentator identifies the Erinyes/Eumenides as the souls of the dead, which confirms the theory of Rohde to that effect.[114] This scholar, however, takes his hypothesis even further when he states that they are the souls of the dead who passed away in a violent fashion. Nothing in the text seems to indicate this conclusion. Tsantsanoglou suggests that they are the souls of the pious instead, the ἀγαθοί.[115]

Nevertheless, in my opinion, it is important to nuance this picture considerably. Johnston points out that "there is no good indication that the Erinyes were considered to *be* souls of the dead in popular belief,"[116] and I believe she is absolutely right. More attention should be paid to the fact that the identification

112 On *daimones* see §4.5.

113 Cf. Jourdan's (2003) interpretation of ὡσπερεὶ and my criticisms in Bernabé 2007b.

114 Rohde 1901:229, 1925:269; cf. Henrichs 1984, Tsantsanoglou 1997:99–100.

115 Tsantsanoglou 1997:100. Betegh (2004:86) considers the Erinyes to be "principally positive agents."

116 Johnston 1999:274.

of the Erinyes/Eumenides with the souls of the deceased is not depicted in the text as being the belief of ritual performers; rather, as the linguistic marker γάρ in line 9 indicates, it is an explanation offered by the commentator. The Derveni commentator can thus be said to have arrived at Rohde's idea many centuries earlier, but this is not to say his explanation reflects ancient beliefs. On the other hand, there is no indication that they are "principally positive agents," given the necessity of performing a ritual act in order to appease them.

4.5 The Demonological Theory

The commentator seems to support a rather complex demonological theory, but it is difficult to derive its exact formulation because it is for the most part revealed in the first columns, whose text is not yet sound. I will summarize what we can currently read in the papyrus about *daimones*:

(a) *Daimones* are souls (col. VI 3–4).

(b) They are countless and must be propitiated with offerings (col. VI 8).

(c) The Eumenides are also souls, that is, *daimones* (col. VI 9).

(d) They are sent by the gods and they act as their assistants (col. III 2 δαί-μ]ω̣γ ... [θε]ή̣λ̣α̣τ̣[ος; col. III 6–7 ὡ̣[ς δὲ θ̣εῶν ὑπηρέται δ̣[εινο]ί̣).

(e) The commentator makes mention of diverse types of *daimones*, but it is not easy to determine whether some of these groups can be distinguished from others.[117]

(e_1) First are the *daimones* that, according to Tsantsanoglou,[118] "reflect the widespread concept of a *daimon* who accompanies every person either as a 'guardian angel' or as his or her fate, from the moment of birth until death" (col. III 4 δαίμ]ω̣γ γίνετα[ι ἑκά]σ̣τωι ἵλ̣ε̣[ως θε]ή̣λ̣α̣τ̣[ος).

(e_2) Second are the ones who come from the underworld and chase the culprits. The statement in column III 4–5 οὐ γὰ]ρ̣ ἡ̣ θείη τύ]χη ἐξώλεα σ̣[ίνεται] ε̣ἰ̣ ἔ̣τεισ' ἕκ̣α̣[στ'] Ἐρινύσ̣[ι seems to indicate that it is the function of these *daimones* from the underworld to punish those who have not propitiated the Erinyes.

(e_3) Some of them are a hindrance and are vengeful souls (col. VI 3–4). It is highly probable that they are the same *daimones* of the previous group.

117 Cf. Betegh 2004:88.

118 Tsantsanoglou 1997:105.

Many points of contact with the commentator's ideas can be found in a text by Alexander Polyhistor in which Pythagoras identifies the *daimones* with the souls of the dead and portrays the Erinyes, who put shackles on those who enter the afterlife without being ritually pure (ἀκαθάρτους), as divinities in charge of punishing such souls:

> Hermes is the controller of the souls ... he brings upwards the purified souls, but impure souls were not allowed to approach each other, much less to come close to pure souls, since they were fettered in unbreakable bonds by the Erinyes. And all the air is full of souls and they are called *daimones* and heroes; and they carry to men dreams, portents, diseases, and purification, averting by expiatory sacrifices, all divination and omens are related to them.[119]

Although it seems clear that Pythagorean eschatology is celestial (the righteous being is brought upwards) whereas Orphic eschatology is chthonic, there are a number of significant points of contact between the two, most notably the presence of the Erinyes as guardians and punishers of impure souls, references to dreams, portents, and prophecies, and the relationship of these to *daimones*.

Martín Hernández also draws attention to a very clear parallel in Plutarch.[120]

On the other hand, δαίμων ἵλεως does not lack parallels: there are references in Marcus Aurelius to a similar entity;[121] additionally, Socrates alludes to a personal *daimon* (τι/τὸ δαιμόνιον), to whom he attributes discouraging functions, above all.[122] Plato presents *daimones* as intermediaries between gods and men in *Symposium*; in *Republic* the philosopher refers "to gods, *daimones*, heroes, and Hades' things."[123] Even Menedemos' jokes indicate that the relationship between Erinyes and *daimones* was a widespread belief.[124]

119 Diogenes Laertius 8.31 (FGH 273 F 93 = Phythagorici B 1a DK): τὸν δ' Ἑρμῆν ταμίαν εἶναι τῶν ψυχῶν ... καὶ ἄγεσθαι μὲν τὰς καθαρὰς ἐπὶ τὸν ὕψιστον, τὰς δ' ἀκαθάρτους μήτ' ἐκείναις πελάζειν μήτ' ἀλλήλαις, δεῖσθαι δ' ἐν ἀρρήκτοις δεσμοῖς ὑπ' Ἐρινύων. εἶναί τε πάντα τὸν ἀέρα ψυχῶν ἔμπλεων· καὶ ταύτας δαίμονάς τε καὶ ἥρωας ὀνομάζεσθαι· καὶ ὑπὸ τούτων πέμπεσθαι ἀνθρώποις τούς τ' ὀνείρους καὶ τὰ σημεῖα νόσους τε, ... εἴς τε τούτους γίνεσθαι τούς τε καθαρμοὺς καὶ ἀποτροπιασμοὺς μαντικήν τε πᾶσαν καὶ κληδόνας καὶ τὰ ὅμοια.

120 Plutarch *De defectu oraculorum* 417C: (περὶ μὲν οὖν τῶν μυστικῶν) θεῶν μὲν οὐδενὶ δαιμόνων δὲ φαύλων ἀποτροπῆς ἕνεκα φήσαιμ' ἂν τελεῖσθαι μειλίχια. "I will never believe that this [*sc.* mysteria] is done for any of the gods: but will say rather, it is to appease the fury of some malign *daimones*." See Martín Hernández 2010:261.

121 Marcus Aurelius 3.16: τὸν δὲ ἔνδον ἐν τῷ στήθει ἱδρυμένον δαίμονα μὴ ... θορυβεῖν ... ἀλλὰ ἵλεων διατηρεῖν; 8.45: τὸν ἐμὸν δαίμονα ἵλεων, cf. 12.3.

122 Plato *Apologia* 31d; *Phaedrus* 242b; *Euthydemos* 272e; *Alcibiades* 1.103a.

123 Plato *Symposium* 202e; *Respublica* 392a, cf. 427b.

124 Hippobotus *ap.* Diogenes Laertius 6.102.

Although the issue can be only sketched here, this doctrine can be traced to Hesiod, who speaks about the golden race that become *daimones*, guardians of mortal human beings.[125] Some philosophers speak about a world that is ἔμψυχον and full of souls or *daimones*.[126] An enigmatic fragment by Heraclitus talks about certain beings who transform themselves into guardians watching over the living and the dead.[127] The Ephesian philosopher seems to allude to this doctrine as well when claiming that the δαίμων (that is, the individual one) is the character.[128]

On the other hand, Sara Macías[129] points out an interesting parallel in a fragment of Euripides,[130] where reference is made to a bloodless sacrifice accompanied by a libation to Zeus, here identified with Hades. Subsequently, they ask a god, whom Macías interprets as Dionysus, to wield the scepter of Zeus, share power over the underworld with Hades, and send the souls of the dead to the light in order to increase the ritual knowledge of the participants in the rite.

Also we find in Chrysippos evil *daimones* used by gods as executioners and avengers upon unholy and unjust men. Plutarch says that, while others go about as avengers of arrogant and grievous cases of injustice, *daimones* are guardians of sacred rites of the gods and prompters of the Mysteries.[131] Plutarch also asserts that it is ridiculous that Apollo "should offer some libations and perform those ceremonies which men perform in the effort to placate and mollify the wrath of *daimones* whom men call the 'unforgetting avengers,' as if they followed up the memories of some unforgotten foul deeds of earlier days."[132]

125 Hesiod *Opera et dies* 122–123: τοὶ μὲν δαίμονες ἁγνοὶ ἐπιχθόνιοι τελέθουσιν / ἐσθλοί, ἀλεξίκακοι, φύλακες θνητῶν ἀνθρώπων.

126 Aëtius *Placita* 1.7.11 (Thales A 23 DK): Θαλῆς ... τὸ δὲ πᾶν ἔμψυχον ἅμα καὶ δαιμόνων πλῆρες; Diogenes Laertius 9.7 (Heraclitus A 1 DK): ἐδόκει δὲ αὐτῶι ... πάντα ψυχῶν εἶναι καὶ δαιμόνων πλήρη.

127 Heraclitus B 63 DK: φύλακας γίνεσθαι ἐγερτὶ ζώντων καὶ νεκρῶν.

128 Heraclitus B 119 DK: ἦθος ἀνθρώπωι δαίμων. Cf. Schibli 1993; Tsantsanoglou 1997:105; Betegh 2004:76; Kouremenos in KPT 146–147; and Bernabé 2007a:185–186.

129 Macías Otero 2007 and 2010.

130 Euripides fr. 912 Kannich; Macías Otero proposes some different readings: σοὶ τῶι πάντων μεδέοντι χλόην / πέλανόν τε φέρω, Ζεὺς εἴτ' Ἀίδης / ὀνομαζόμενος στέργεις· σὺ δέ μοι / θυσίαν ἄπυρον παγκαρπείας / δέξαι πλήρη προχυταῖαν. / *** / σὺ γὰρ ἔν τε θεοῖς τοῖς οὐρανίδαις / σκῆπτρον τὸ Διὸς μεταχειρίζεις / χθονίων θ' Ἅιδηι μετέχεις ἀρχῆς. / πέμψον μὲν φῶς ψυχὰς ἐνέρων / τοῖς βουλομένοις ἄθλους προμαθεῖν / πόθεν ἔβλαστον, τίς ῥίζα κακῶν, / τίνα δεῖ μακάρων ἐκθυσαμένους / εὑρεῖν μόχθων ἀνάπαυλαν.

131 Chrysippus *ap.* Plutarch *Aetia Romana et Graeca* 277A (deest in SVF), *De defectu oraculorum* 417A (cf. 417B, *De facie in orbis lunae* 944C).

132 Plutarch *De defectu oraculorum* 418B, whose last words (ὡς ἀλήστων τινῶν καὶ παλαιῶν μιασμάτων μνήμαις ἐπεξιόντας) can be easily applied to the Titanic crime.

To sum up, the commentator's interpretation does not seem to be utterly idiosyncratic. Rather, it is situated within a deep, and widely understood, cultural context.

4.6 The Absence of the Gods

In the above-mentioned passages, we met Hermes in the text by Pythagoras (Diogenes Laertius 8.31) and Zeus/Hades and Dionysus in the text by Euripides (fr. 192 Kannicht). We can also find gods situated within an Orphic eschatological context in the gold tablets. A gold tablet from Thurii mentions that the soul of an initiate addresses a declaration of purity to Persephone (the queen of the subterranean world), Hades (Eucles), and Dionysus (Eubouleus).[133]

However, in the papyrus no god is mentioned in the context of the rituals related to the netherworld. Tsantsanoglou offers a useful explanation when he notes: "He would contradict himself if he spoke of the worship of Hades and Persephone, since he goes on subsequently to deny the existence of distinct deities, claiming that their different names represent successive stages in the creative process of the world."[134] Probably for this reason he prefers to refer to the divine with general designations, such as θε]ή̣λ̣α̣τ̣[ος (col. III 4) or θείη τύ]χη (col. III 5).

4.7 Conclusions Concerning Commentator's Interpretation

The commentator understands that the goal of the ritual act is to propitiate not the Erinyes or the *daimones*, but rather—given that the *daimones*, Eumenides, and Erinyes are merely souls of the dead—souls who may potentially seek to obstruct the liberation of the deceased after death. The *mystai* perform their preliminary sacrifice in the same way that the *magoi* do. He considers their acts to be parallel: the sacrifices to the Eumenides are identical to appeasing the souls of the dead, and liberating birds from their cages serves to remove impeding *daimones*.

133 Gold tablet from Thurii (4th cent. BC), *OF* 489–490: "I come from among the pure, pure, queen of the subterranean beings, / Eucles, Eubouleus, and the other gods and *daimones*"; cf. Bernabé and Jiménez San Cristóbal 2008:100–105.

134 Tsantsanoglou 1997:99.

5. Coda. Some Concluding Remarks

5.1 About the Described Ritual

Columns I–VI of the Derveni Papyrus describe a ritual that the *magoi* (in other words, Orphic priests) perform in the presence of initiates (*mystai*) who also participate. A first libation is carried out by pouring droplets. The rest of the ritual involves simple elements well known in the Greek world, including some divinatory practices, "abstemious" libations, the burning of πόπανα, and magical rites (ἐπωιδαί and probably the liberation of caged birds) performed to ward off the hindering *daimones* and liberate the souls, as well as to propitiate the Erinyes/Eumenides, as they are the ones who punish the non-initiates in the Beyond. A poem is also recited that explains a "history of the world" in which the ritual acquires its mythical foundation. The ritual probably also refers to gods such as Persephone, Dionysus, and Zeus-Hades, in accordance with the mythological and ritual practice elsewhere, but the commentator seems to have deliberately muted this aspect of the rite. In the commentary of the poem, the commentator proclaims an absolute supremacy of Zeus, though it is impossible to say if this reflects the first part of the papyrus.

It seems clear that, in a ritual such as this, the purpose is to propitiate the Erinyes in a funerary ceremony, or τελετή, which involves an *imitatio mortis* by means of sacrifices, enchanting songs, and libations.[135] The ritual is therefore performed on two levels, both initiatory and eschatological, for the τελετή anticipates in the ritual the soul's journey into the afterlife. The act of releasing a bird follows the principle of sympathetic magic performed in order to liberate the soul from its bodily imprisonment, or alternatively serves as a metaphor for this liberation.

Betegh[136] recognizes two different kinds of rite: "one, rites that should secure the safe passage of the soul of the dead to the underworld and to the most blissful part of it; the other, initiation rites." He does not forget to add, however, that "these two ritual contexts are closely connected." His assumptions are entirely correct, but we may add another consideration to complete them. Martín Hernández[137] has postulated that what is described in the papyrus is a ritual intended to purify its participants of μίασμα, the stain caused by the rebellion of the Titans—the precedent sin which humanity must bear throughout its existence.[138] The new readings can be easily placed within this

135 Martín Hernández 2005.

136 Betegh 2004:88–89.

137 Martín Hernández 2010:267.

138 Cf. Plutarch *De defectu oraculorum* 418B: παλαιῶν μιασμάτων μνήμαις ἐπεξιόντας, also quoted in n132.

paradigm. The soul of the participant, united with the body, is in a state of pollution due to the ancient blood crime committed against the son of Persephone. In this respect, the Erinyes would play a distinctive role since they are, as noted above, in charge of avenging crimes committed against blood relations—in this case, the blood of the child Dionysus that must be atoned for by all men, who are polluted by this crime. The *magoi* would try to appease the Erinyes by means of the sacrifices and prayers described in the papyrus, and would purify the souls of the *mystai*. The rite could liberate them from the μίασμα of the Titan's crime and from the cycle of reincarnations. The ποινή quoted in column VI 5 should be taken as a reference to the wrongdoings of ancestors—the Titans—committed against the son of the goddess of the netherworld, before whom the dead must appear in the afterlife. We may find similar expressions in some gold tablets from Thurii,[139] in the *Papyrus from Gurôb*,[140] in two passages by Pindar,[141] and in one by Plato.[142] One gold tablet from Pherai confirms that the *mystai* are freed from any penalty in the afterlife.[143] These texts describe the wrongdoings of the ancestors and their subsequent liberation in various ways, but the recurrence of vocabulary indicates their relation to common religious antecedents.[144]

Thus it is more than likely that the myth of the Titans provides the very grounds of the ritual. In fact, column XX 13ff. of the papyrus seems to allude to Demeter and Persephone, while column XXVI makes clear reference to Zeus and the incestuous act that would lead to the birth of Persephone.

In this way, the *mystai* are liberated from the terror of Hades in a triple sense: first, they will be free from hindering *daimones*; second, because they are initiates, they have taken steps to ensure that they do not suffer punishment in the afterlife, because they have paid all his faults to the Erinyes; and, third, they are liberated from having to fear these punishments in this world.

139 *OF* 489.4 (cf. 490.4): ποινὰν δ' ἀνταπέτεισ' ἔργων ἕνεκ' οὔτι δικαίων; see Bernabé and Jiménez San Cristóbal 2008:105–114.

140 *Papyrus Gurôb* (in an Orphic τελετή): δῶρον δέξ]ατ' ἐμὸν ποινὰς πατ[έρων ἀθεμίστων, 1 (*OF* 578 col. I 4, with bibliography).

141 Pindar fr. 133 Maehl. (*OF* 443): οἷσι δὲ Φερσεφόνα ποινὰν παλαιοῦ πένθεος / δέξεται, which refers to a moment in which a mortal has paid for the original wrongdoings of his ancestors, the Titans (see Bernabé 1999); and in Pindar *Olympian* 2.57f. (*OF* 445): ὅτι θανόντων μὲν ἐνθάδ' αὐτίκ' ἀπάλαμνοι φρένες / ποινὰς ἔτεισαν (also in an Orphic context) (see Santamaría 2005).

142 Plato *Cratylus* 400c (*OF* 430 I): ὡς δίκην διδούσης τῆς ψυχῆς ὧν δὴ ἕνεκα δίδωσιν, (see Bernabé 2010b:115–118).

143 Gold tablet from Pherai (fourth cent. BC) (*OF* 493): εἴσιθ<ι> ἱερὸν λειμῶνα. ἄποινος γὰρ ὁ μύστης (see Bernabé and Jiménez San Cristóbal 2008:157–158).

144 See also Bernabé 2002b; Martín Hernández 2010:268.

5.2 About the Commentator's Interpretation of the Ritual

The commentator, furthermore, attempts to confer a profound value upon the ritual act—a moral perspective—which it did not have before. He causes the gods to disappear from rites of magic propitiation. He also sketches a complex demonological theory with different types of *daimones*/souls, good and evil, and makes the Erinyes guarantors of justice. He considers the purpose of the ritual to be to the warding off and/or propitiating of the Eumenides and the δαίμονες who hinder the souls' progress after death, and that both the Eumenides and the δαίμονες are in fact the souls of the deceased. The *magoi* perform the sacrifice as if they were paying a blood-price. So, in the commentator's interpretation, the ritual acts, in a way, like criminal compensation, which individuals condemned for an offense are expected to pay; sacrifice plays the same role as ποινή in human justice. The poem contains an explanation of the world that is philosophical in tone and conceptualized within a framework of natural philosophy. That the commentator mentions neither Dionysus nor the myth of the Titans may reflect the scientific and quasi-monotheistic hermeneutic tendencies of the interpreter, who in fact strives to eliminate the infernal gods as the addressees of the ritual.

The most interesting point regarding the commentator's contribution is, according to Betegh, the ethical perspective[145] with which he interprets the ritual. Betegh writes: "col. IV indicates that the discussion is still within the sphere of improper behaviour-justice-punishment." He then further indicates that "the precondition both for piety and gain in knowledge about the divine can be taken as an intellectualized interpretation of the need for purification before initiation."[146]

Instead of the quasi-automatic nature of the ritual, the commentator introduces a more intense conceptualization of the idea of justice and transgression. References to Justice permeate the text. In column IV, the author's reference to a fragment by Heraclitus suggests that he considers the Erinyes to watch over transgressions of natural law, which allows him to contextualize the injustice-penalty pattern within the cosmic order. In column V he alludes to the terrors of Hades. In defending their existence, the commentator outlines a vision whereby wrongdoings, rather than any lack of initiation, constitute the faults that are atoned for with terrible punishments in the afterlife. In the next column, he offers an explanation of the ritual as a form of atonement, comparable to the

145 Betegh 2004:89.
146 Betegh 2004:90.

role played by ποινή—the mandated compensation for a crime (almost always involving blood) in human justice.[147]

On the other hand, the Erinyes had already broadened their function[148] within the Orphic rite so that they might serve also as the guardians of the ritual order. In the commentator's interpretation this role is defined even more broadly, so that they become guardians of the moral order.

The commentator thus shares with Plato a moralizing tendency, as well as the notion that ritual elements are not the sole or fundamental factor in affecting the punishments one can expect in the afterlife. Such an idea, in fact, would in this conception be an offense against justice and ethics. The difference between the commentator and the Athenian philosopher lies in the fact that, whereas the former attempts to include a new moralized and philosophical vision in ritual practice, Plato goes a step further as he denies the ritual act any kind of value, instead developing a system in which the true τελετή is philosophy.[149]

Bibliography

Aellen, Ch. 1994. *À la recherche de l'ordre cosmique*. Zurich.

Alvar Ezquerra, A., and J. F. González Castro, eds. 2005. *Actas del XI Congreso Español de Estudios Clásicos*. Madrid.

Bernabé, A. 1995. "Una etimología platónica: σῶμα-σῆμα." *Philologus* 139:204–237.

———. 1999. "Una cita de Píndaro en Platón *Men*. 81b (Fr. 133 Sn.-M.)." In *Desde los poemas homéricos hasta la prosa griega del siglo IV d. C.: Veintiséis estudios filológicos* (ed. J. A. López Férez) 239–259. Madrid.

———. 2001. "La experiencia iniciática en Plutarco." In *Misticismo y religiones mistéricas en la obra de Plutarco (Actas del VII Simposio Español sobre Plutarco)* (ed. A. Pérez Jiménez and F. Casadesús) 5–22. Madrid.

———. 2002a. "Un 'resumen de historia del orfismo' en Strab. 7 fr. 18." In *Actas del X Congreso Español de Estudios Clásicos*, vol. III, 59–66. Madrid.

———. 2002b. "La toile de Pénélope: A-t-il existé un mythe orphique sur Dionysos et les Titans?" *Revue de l'Histoire des Religions* 219:401–433.

———. 2003. "Las *Ephesia grammata*: Génesis de una fórmula mágica." *MHNH* 3: 5–28.

147 Cf. Johnston 1999:138.

148 Nevertheless, as Casadesús *per litteras* points out, Erinyes have a similar function of maintaining the cosmic order already in *Iliad* 19.418, when they stay the speech (Ἐρινύες ἔσχεθον αὐδήν) of Achilles' horses. See Edwards 1991 *ad loc.* with discussion and further bibliography.

149 Cf. Bernabé 2010b.

———. 2004–2005. *Orphicorum et Orphicis similium testimonia et fragmenta. Poetae epici Graeci: Testimonia et fragmenta*, part II, fasc. 1–2. Munich [cited as OF with fragment number].

———. 2006. "Μάγοι en el Papiro de Derveni: ¿Magos persas, charlatanes u oficiantes órficos?" In *Koinòs lógos. Homenaje al profesor José García López* (ed. E. Calderón, A. Morales, and M. Valverde) 99–109. Murcia.

———. 2007a. *Musaeus · Linus · Epimenides · Papyrus Derveni · Indices. Poetae epici Graeci: Testimonia et fragmenta*, part II, fasc. 3. Berlin.

———. 2007b. "Sur le rite décrit dans les colonnes II et VI du Papyrus de Derveni: Que peut-on faire avec un oiseau?" *Les études classiques* 75:157–170.

———. 2007c. "¿Νηφάλια en el Papiro de Derveni?" *MHNH* 7:285–288.

———. 2008a. "Orfeo y Eleusis." *Synthesis* 15:13–36.

———. 2008b. "'Mudar a los démones que estorban' (Papiro de Derveni col. VI 2–3)." *MHNH* 8:261–264.

———. 2009. "Imago Inferorum Orphica." In *Mystic Cults in Magna Graecia* (ed. G. Casadio and P. Johnston) 95–130. Austin.

———. 2010a. "The Derveni Papyrus: Problems of Edition, Problems of Interpretation." In *Proceedings of the Twenty-Fifth International Congress of Papyrology, Ann Arbor 2007*, 77–84. Ann Arbor.

———. 2010b. *Platón y el orfismo: Diálogos entre religión y filosofía.* Madrid.

———. Forthcoming. "The *Ephesia grammata*: Genesis of a Magical Formula." In *The Getty Hexameters: Poetry, Magic, and Mystery in Ancient Selinous* (ed. Ch. A. Faraone and D. Obbink) 69–93. Oxford.

Bernabé, A., and F. Casadesús, eds. 2008. *Orfeo y la tradición órfica: Un reencuentro.* Madrid.

Bernabé, A., F. Casadesús, and M. A. Santamaría, eds. 2010. *Orfeo y el Orfismo: Nuevas perspectivas.* http://www.cervantesvirtual.com/FichaObra.html?Ref=35069.

Bernabé, A., and A. I. Jiménez San Cristóbal 2008. *Instructions for the Netherworld: The Orphic Gold Tablets.* Leiden.

Betegh, G. 2004. *The Derveni Payrus: Cosmology, Theology, and Interpretation.* Cambridge.

Bianchi, U. 1976. *Prometeo, Orfeo, Adamo: Tematiche religiose sul destino, il male, la salvezza.* Rome.

Borgeaud, Ph., ed. 1991. *Orphisme et Orphée, en l'honneur de Jean Rudhardt.* Geneva.

Bremmer, J. 1999. "The Birth of the Term 'Magic.'" *Zeitschrift für Papyrologie und Epigraphik* 126:1–12.

Brown, C. G. 1991. "Empousa, Dionysus, and the Mysteries: Aristophanes, *Frogs* 285ff." *Classical Quarterly* 41:41–50.

Burkert, W. 1962. "ΓΟΗΣ: Zum griechischen 'Schamanismus.'" *Rheinisches Museum* 105:36–55.

———. 2004. *Babylon, Memphis, Persepolis*. Cambridge, MA.

Casabona, J. 1966. *Recherches sur le vocabulaire des sacrifices en grec, des origines à la fin de l'époque classique*. Aix-en-Provence.

Casadesús, F. 2010. "Similitudes entre el Papiro de Derveni y los primeros filósofos estoicos." In Bernabé, Casadesús, and Santamaría 2010:192–239.

Casadio, G. 1991. "La metempsicosi tra Orfeo e Pitagora." In Borgeaud 1991:119–155.

Chiarabini, Ch. 2006. *Ricerche sul papiro di Derveni*. Tesi di laurea. Bologna.

Edmonds, R. 2008. "Extra-ordinary People: *Mystai* and *Magoi*, Magicians and Orphics in the Derveni Papyrus." *Classical Philology* 103:16–39.

Edwards, M. W. 1991. *The Iliad: A Commentary*, vol. 5: *Books 17-20*. Cambridge.

Ferrari, F. 2007. "Note al testo della colonne II–VII del Papiro di Derveni." *Zeitschrift für Papyrologie und Epigraphik* 162:203–211.

———. 2010. "Democrito a Derveni? PDerv. col. 4, 1–6." *La Parola del Passato* 65:137–148.

———. 2011a. "Rites without Frontiers: *Magi* and *Mystai* in the Derveni Papyrus." *Zeitschrift für Papyrologie und Epigraphik* 179:71–83.

———. 2011b. "Eraclito e i Persiani nel Papiro di Derveni (col. IV 10–14)." In Herrero et al. 2011:365–370.

———. 2011c. "Frustoli erranti: Per una ricostruzione di P. Derveni coll. I–III." In *Papiri filosofici: Miscellanea di studi* 6:39–54. Florence.

———. 2012. "Derveni Papyrus. F. Ferrari Edition." CHS-iMouseion Project. http://nrs.harvard.edu/urn-3:hul.eresource:Derveni_Papyrus_FerrariF_ed_2012.

Furley, W. D. 1933. "Besprechung und Behandlung: Zur Form und Funktion von ΕΠΩΙΔΑΙ in der griechischen Zaubermedizin." In *Philanthropia kai Eusebeia. Festschrift für Albrecht Dihle zum 70. Geburtstag* (ed. G. W. Most, H. Petersmann, and A. M. Ritter) 80–104. Göttingen.

Graf, F. 1980. "Milch, Hönig und Wein: Zum Verständnis der Libation im griechischen Ritual." In *Perennitas. Studi in onore di Angelo Brelich*, 209–221. Rome.

Henrichs, A. 1983. "The 'Sobriety' of Oedipus: Sophocles OC 100 Misunderstood." *Harvard Studies in Classical Philology* 87:87–100.

———. 1984. "The Eumenides and Wineless Libations in the Derveni Papyrus." In *Atti del XVII Congresso Internazionale di Papirologia*, II, 255–268. Naples.

———. 1994. "Anonymity and Polarity: Unknown Gods and Nameless Altars at the Areopagus." *Illinois Classical Studies* 19:27–58.

———. 1998. "Dromena und Legomena: Zum rituellen Selbstverständnis der Griechen." In *Ansichten griechischer Rituale* (ed. F. Graf) 33–71. Stuttgart.

Herrero de Jáuregui, M., A. I. Jiménez San Cristóbal, E. Luján Martinez, R. Martín Hernández, M. A. Santamaría Álvarez, and S. Torallas Tovar, eds. 2011. *Tracing Orpheus. Studies of Orphic Fragments In Honour of Alberto Bernabé.* Berlin.

Janko, R. 2002. "The Derveni Papyrus: An Interim Text." *Zeitschrift für Papyrologie und Epigraphik* 141:1–62.

———. 2008. "Reconstructing (Again) the Opening of the Derveni Papyrus." *Zeitschrift für Papyrologie und Epigraphik* 166:37–51.

Jiménez San Cristóbal, A. I. 2002. *Rituales órficos.* PhD diss., Universidad Complutense. Madrid.

———. 2005. "El concepto de dike en el orfismo." In Alvar Ezquerra and González Castro 2005:351–361.

Johnston, S. I. 1992. "Xanthus, Hera, and the Erinyes." *Transactions of the American Philological Association* 122:85–98.

———. 1999. *Restless Dead: Encounters between the Living and the Dead in Ancient Greece.* Berkeley.

———. 2004. "Erinys." *Brill's New Pauly* 5:34–35. Leiden.

Jourdan, F. 2003. *Le Papyrus de Derveni: Texte présenté, traduit et annoté.* Paris.

Kearns, E. 1994. "Cakes in Greek Sacrifice Regulations." In *Ancient Greek Cult Practice from the Epigraphical Evidence. Proceedings of the Second International Seminar on Ancient Greek Cult, Organized by the Swedish Institute at Athens, 22-24 November 1991* (ed. R. Hägg) 65–70. Stockholm.

Kouremenos, T., G. M. Parássoglou, and K. Tsantsanoglou, eds. 2006. *The Derveni Papyrus, Edited with Introduction and Commentary.* Florence. [Cited as KPT.]

Laks, A., and G. W. Most. 1977a. "A Provisional Translation of the Derveni Papyrus." In Laks and Most 1997b:9–22.

———, eds. 1997b. *Studies on the Derveni Papyrus.* Oxford.

Macías Otero, S. 2007. "Las ψυχὰς ἐνέρων del fr. 912 Kannicht de Eurípides y la columna VI del Papiro de Derveni." *Cuadernos de Filología Clásica (EGI-E)* 17:145–161.

———. 2010. "Eurípides fr. 912 Kannicht (OF 458)." In Bernabé, Casadesús, and Santamaría 2010:405–420.

Martín Hernández, R. 2005. "La muerte como experiencia mistérica: Estudio sobre la posibilidad de una experiencia de muerte ficticia en las iniciaciones griegas." *'Ilu Revista de ciencias de las religiones* 10:85–105.

———. 2010. *Orfeo y los magos.* Madrid.

———. 2011. "Τύχα in Two Lead Tablets from Selinous (OF 830)." In Herrero et al. 2011:311–315.

Méautis, G. 1932. "Plutarque et l'orphisme." In *Mélanges G. Glotz*, 575–585. Paris.

Molina Moreno, F. 2008. "La música de Orfeo." In Bernabé and Casadesús 2008: 33–58.

Most, G. W. 1997. "The Fire Next Time: Cosmology, Allegoresis, and Salvation in the Derveni Papyrus." *Journal of Hellenic Studies* 117:117–135.

Nilsson, M. P. 1957. *The Dionysiac Mysteries of the Hellenistic and Roman Age.* Lund (repr. New York, 1975).

Obbink, D. 1997. "Cosmology as Initiation vs. the Critique of Orphic Mysteries." In Laks and Most 1997b:39–54.

Pensa, M. 1977. *Rappresentazioni dell'oltretomba nella ceramica apula*. Rome.

Pfister, F. 1924. "Epode." In *Realencyclopädie der Classischen Altertumswissenschaft,* Suppl. 4, 323–344. Stuttgart.

Piano, V. 2011. "Ricostruendo il rotolo di Derveni: Per una revisione papirologica di P Derveni I–III." In *Papiri filosofici: Miscellanea di studi* 6:5–37. Florence.

Rohde, E. 1901. *Kleine Schriften*, II. Tübingen.

———. 1925. *Psyche*. Tübingen.

Rudhardt, J. 1958. *Notions fondamentales de la pensée religieuse et actes constitutifs du culte dans la Grèce classique*. Geneva.

Santamaría Álvarez, M. A. 2005. "Poinas tinein: Culpa y expiación en el orfismo." In Alvar Ezquerra and González Castro 2005:397–405.

———. 2012. "Tiresias in Euripides' Bacchae and the Author of the Derveni Papyrus." In *Actes du 26e Congrès international de payrologie (Genève 2010)* (ed. P. Schubert) 677–684. Geneva.

Sarian, H. 1986. "Erinys." *Lexicon Iconographicum Mythologiae Classicae* III 1, 825–843. Zurich.

Scermino, M. 2008-2009. *Orfeo interpretato: Testo e contesto della Teogonia di Derveni e del suo esegeta*. PhD diss., Pisa.

Schibli, H. S. 1993. "Xenocrates' Daemons and the Irrational Soul." *Classical Quarterly* 43:143–167.

Schmidt, M. 1975. "Orfeo e orfismo nella pittura vascolare italiota." In *Orfismo in Magna Grecia,* 105–137. Naples.

Tsantsanoglou, K. 1997. "The First Columns of the Derveni Papyrus and Their Religious Significance." In Laks and Most 1997b:93–128.

Turcan, R. 1959. "L'âme-oiseau et l'eschatologie orphique." *Revue de l'histoire des religions* 155:33–40.

West, M. L. 1997. "Hocus-pocus in East and West: Theogony, Ritual, and the Tradition of Esoteric Commentary." In Laks and Most 1997b:81–90.

3

Democritus, Heraclitus, and the Dead Souls

Reconstructing Columns I–VI of the Derveni Papyrus*

Franco Ferrari
Università dell'Aquila

On January 15, 1962, the remains of the Derveni Papyrus were unearthed from a cist grave in northern Greece. Anton Fackelmann, curator of the papyrus collection of the Österreichische Nationalbibliothek in Vienna and the world's leading expert in the handling of carbonized papyri, began work on the find. During the summer of that year, Fackelmann, working alone, succeeded in unrolling the fragments of the papyrus.

First he cut the scroll apart lengthwise, producing two symmetrical hemicylinders. Then he detached each of the layers of the two halves, placing them under seven pieces of glass (A–G). Beneath two additional pieces of glass (H and I), he arranged many fragments that he described in his report to the museum of Thessaloniki as "countless small pieces (down to a postage stamp) lying all around haphazardly" (see KPT, 5). These fragments consisted of about eighty bits of papyrus that had been labeled as "unplaced" on plates 28–30 of the *editio princeps*, in addition to the pieces placed by the first editors throughout the first twenty-six columns.

The outer parts of the roll—those that match the present columns I–VI, referring to prophecy and rites (prayers, offerings and libations)—had been reassembled on the basis of fragments from hemicylinders F and G, with occasional additions of pieces from the H and I groups. In turn, hemicylinder G consisted of two minor sections: "great G" and "small G" (Gg and Gp, respectively, in Figure 1).

In this configuration, each alternation of an F and a G section recomposes one circumference, or volute, of the roll, decreasing in size as we move from the outer (with a width of 9.8 cm) to the inner sections of the scroll and down to its

* The author's own edition of the papyrus may be found at http://nrs.harvard.edu/urn-3:hul.eresource:Derveni_Papyrus_FerrariF_ed_2012.

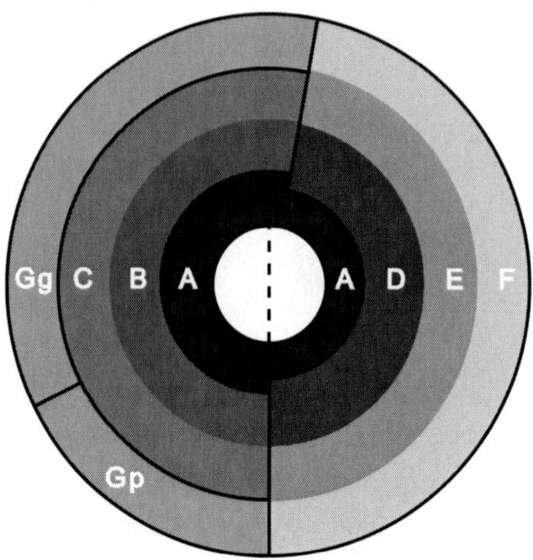

Figure 1. Lettered volutes of the Derveni Papyrus.

midollo, or marrow. It is specifically on this basis that Tsantsanoglou (1997) reassembled these columns for the first time. His arrangement has been repeated in the *editio princeps* (KPT) with the exception of a change concerning G 7, which we will examine presently.

Therefore, one cannot say, as Janko (2008) has claimed, that Tsantsanoglou and Parássoglou ignored the procedures applied to the unrolling of burnt scrolls, wherein, as with the Herculaneum papyri, the bark must be cut into halves before the layers can be separated. Janko rightly noted, however, that the Greek editors made an unfortunate error in their edition, putting the piece G 7 in column II between two other fragments of the G type. In this way they mistakenly placed three sections of the G type in direct sequence.

This mistake did not derive from a disregard of the "alternation principle" regarding the F and G sections. It arose from the suspicion, clearly stated on page 64, that Fackelmann had wrongly classed G 7 as a fragment of the G, rather than the F, type. In fact, G 7 can be perfectly inscribed within the bottle-like surface of a "Great G," which we see in its entirety (that of G 1) in a photograph taken before the separation of the G layers. This image, reproduced in the first plate of the *editio princeps,* shows the intact stalk with no overflowing under G 1. This means that all the pieces of the "Great G" type were inscribed within the perimeter of G 1.[1]

Moreover, the fact that G 7 belongs to the "Great G" series is corroborated by its formal congruence with a piece from the "small G" series, namely G 20, in that G 20 and G 7 create a "small G/great G" set (gG): hence, the possibility

1 See Piano 2011:18–19.

Figure 2. The reunification of G 20 and G 7 as parts of a "small G/great G" whole.

of reading, as I did in Ferrari 2011a:42–43, ἐλ̣[π]ίδι "to the hope" at line 4, ὧδ̣' ἐ̣π̣έθηκε "he added in this way" at line 5, and μ̣[υ]σ̣τῶν "of the mystae" at line 7 (Figure 2). The actual fiber congruence between G 7 and the G 17/G 8 complex at the end of the first column can be explained at least as well as in the *editio princeps* if, with Janko (2008), we place G 7 at the beginning of the first rather than the second column (but at the height established by the first editors).

Another criticism of the Greek editors by Janko (2008) is that they ignored the *kollesis* that he claims is visible along the right edge of G 6. Solely on the basis of this alleged adhesion of two papyrus sheets, Janko disrupted the *editio princeps'* arrangement of columns I–III, shifting G 11 from column III to column II and G 15/G 6 from column II to column III. Yet the *kollesis* Janko identifies would require, between this join within Janko's column III and the undenia-ble *kollesis* recognized by the first editors at the end of column IV, a papyrus sheet (*kollema*) with the odd width of 12.85 cm. The widths of the other sheets in the first ten columns range from 14.6 to 16.25 cm. Also, in the photograph of G 6 taken through a microscope, a *sottoposto* (a scrap coming from a preceding volute and stuck under the higher level of the following one), rather than a *kollesis*, is visible along the right edge of the sheet. This observation is supported by the fact[2] that,

[2] Highlighted by G. Del Mastro *ap.* Piano 2011:34–35.

Figure 3. G 6 upper layer, revealing some extensions along the right edge.

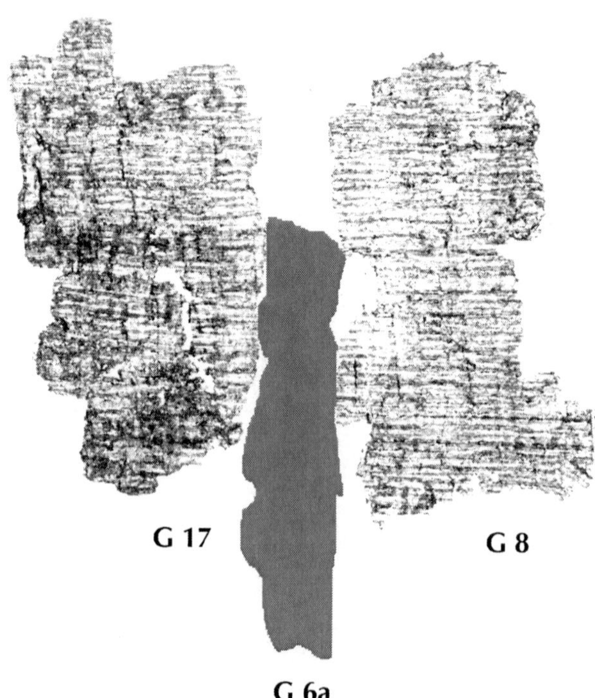

Figure 4. The shape of G 6 fits between G 17 and G 8 (col. I).

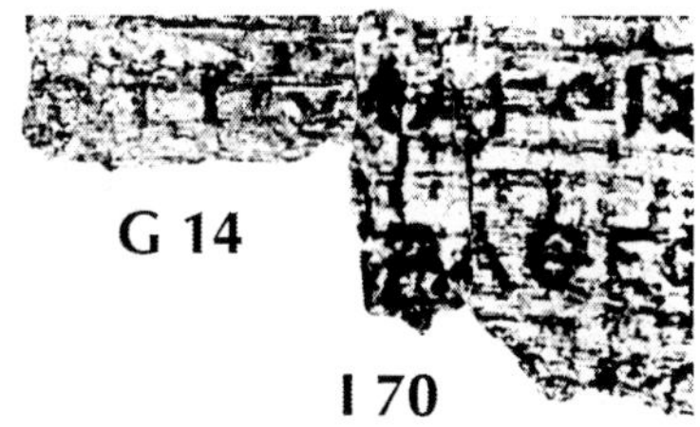

Figure 5. I 70 as placed by Janko along the left edge of G 2.

in G 6, the upper layer reveals some extensions crossing the border of the edge (Figure 3). Furthermore, one can observe that the contour (G 6a) of G 6, which presumably (and, along its right edge, demonstrably) repeated that of its *sotto-posto*, fits between G 17 and G 8 (Figure 4).

Another change to the arrangement established by the first editors concerns the upper margin. In a comparison of plates 5 and 6 of the *editio princeps*, it is clear that the first line of G 1 in KPT is in fact the second line of the column (additionally, some ink traces can perhaps be identified in the photograph of the untouched stalk in KPT, plate 1). Therefore, if for practical reasons one would prefer to keep KPT's numbering, one should add a line "0" at the beginning of each column.

In short, except for the unavoidable transfer of G 7 from the second to the first column and the insertion of a new line on the beginning of every column, the arrangement laid out by the first editors is trustworthy. As I hope to have proved in a new edition of columns I–VI, it allows a plausible re-creation of the argument developed by the anonymous Derveni author (henceforth D).

On the other hand, as I have already mentioned, some fragments belonging to the H and I groups might be assigned to the first columns. According to the first editors, these pieces include H 7 in column II, H 46 and H 8 in column IV, H 2 in column V, and H 18 and H 28 in column VI. Janko (2008) also adds I 70 in column VI along the left edge of G 2 (1.10).

Here, however, we should read not τὸν μέλλοντ]α θεοῖς θύειν with KPT, but ὁ μέλλων] ἱ̣ρ̣ὰ θεοῖς θύειν "he who is about to make offerings to the gods." Janko writes ἱ]ε̣ρα, yet *iota* is almost certainly the first letter of I 17.2 (KPT, 124: "ι is very likely"), whereas *epsilon* cannot be read. Thus, the Ionic form ἱ̣ρ̣ὰ (cf. Herodotus 2.47.3 τὰ ἱρὰ θύσωσι) must be read (Figure 5) in spite of ἱεροῖ[ς] in line 6, ἱερά in column XX 4, and ἱερ[ο- in column VII 7. This is another instance of the continuous alternation of Ionic and Attic dialect forms in the text of the Derveni Papyrus.[3]

3 See Tsantsanoglou in KPT, 11–14 and Lulli 2011.

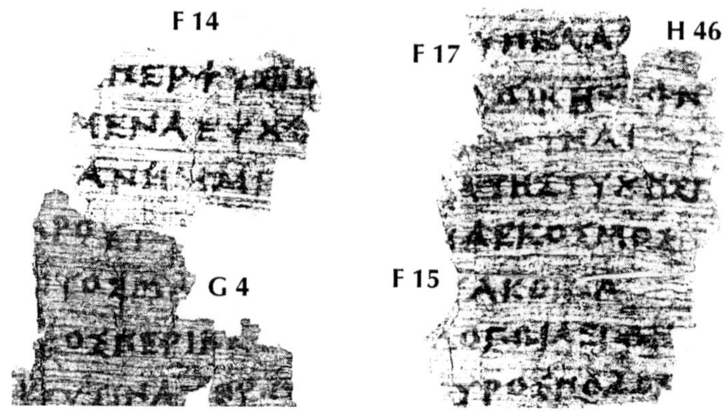

Figure 6. F 14 and F 17 placed at the top of col. IV.

In his review of the *editio princeps*, Janko wrote that "it is astonishing to learn that 113 fragments, or 42% of the total, remain unplaced."[4] Three days later the Greek editors replied in the same electronic journal that such a reproach reminded them "of the farmer whose only possessions were a bull and a frog and who, upon the demise of the latter, exclaimed in agony that he had lost half of his livestock." Indeed, most of the unplaced pieces are very small. Statistically, however, it is very likely that quite a lot of them originally belonged to the first columns. Such probabilities diminish as one moves to the better-preserved columns.

Democritus and the First Lines of Column IV

First I would like to complete what I wrote in Ferrari 2010, where I suggested this reconstruction of column IV 0–4, starting with the fact that in column IV 4 (= fr. G 4.1) the sequence of letters OYT in]μμάνει̣ν̣; ἆρ' οὐ τ.[is shared on the upper-line level by the traces of the first three letters of an unplaced piece, F 14.4. In addition, another unplaced fragment, F 17, matches very well with H 46 and F 15, as well as sharing the epsilon of ἐ̣ὼν in 1.1 (Figure 6):

ὑπελάμ̣μ̣[ανε
[.]ου ε . [. . . . . ὥ]σ̣περ φυσι̣κ̣[ὸς μετ]ὰ̣ δίκης ἐ̣ὼν
ὁ κείμ[ενα] μετα̣θ[εὶς] μὲν ἃ εὐχα̣[ῖς χρὴ] ἐκ̣δο̣ῦναι,
μᾶλλ[ον ἃ] σ̣ίνεται [ἢ ὡ]σ̣ ἀνημμέ[να εἰς] τ̣ὰ τῆς τύχης π̣[ῶς
οὐκ εἴ [α λα]μμάνει̣ν̣; ἆρ' οὐ τα̣ῦ̣[τα κρατεῖ ο]ὐ̣δὲ κόσμος;

[4] *Bryn Mawr Classical Review*, 2006.10.29.

> ... he supposed ... rightly being, like a physicist, ... why, after altering the rudiments that should be given to prayers, did he not allow to consider what damages us more than something depending on chance? Isn't it true that not even the universe is able to control it?

The intellectual D charged with this controversy must have been Democritus of Abdera, born around 460 BC. In D's opinion, Democritus had altered the basic principles of the traditional faith and cult. He had stated which of those principles should govern prayers and had refused to accept any unfortunate aspect of human existence as anything more than a chance accident. Actually, Democritus considered *eidola* and phantoms, perceived by common people as godlike phenomena, to be mental images (cf. Lucretius 5.1173–1174), atom clusters coming from the mind of man or beast and able to move through the air. He did not, however, underrate their impact. As we read in 68 B 166 DK (= Sextus Empiricus *Adversus mathematicos* 9.19), he prayed that he would encounter only benevolent *eidola* in his daily life (εὔχετο εὐλόγχων τυχεῖν εἰδώλων).

According to Democritus, the wise man (the ἀνὴρ εὐλόγιστος of 68 B 236) can hope that the *eidola* disseminated through the air do not interfere with his peace of mind (cf. Epicurus *Letter to Herodotus* 49). If they do, however, he cannot recover his mental or bodily health by entreating the gods (68 B 234). This sole Democritean argument allows D to state that Democritus altered (μεταθείς) religious habits and beliefs by arguing that the harmful aspects of life did not depend on the gods, but on atomic determinism.

My reconstruction entails two facts that seem to be at odds with the general principles established by the first editors:

(1) The first line of the column is actually immediately above the line identified by KPT as the first.

(2) The fragment F 14 in fact belongs within a G section.

The first point presents no problem since, as we saw above, the *editio princeps* fails to recognize that the actual first line of every column is directly above the line it misidentifies as the first.

On the second point, until recently I believed I had overcome the obstacle by acknowledging that, in accordance with Fackelmann's report and Tsantsanoglou's clarifications (KPT, 4–5), the G series includes two different typologies. First are the fragments which allowed Fackelmann to reassemble the outer volutes of the roll: the pieces F 1–9, D 1–11, and E 1–13 (Fackelmann's "third type") alternating with the pieces G 1–21 (Fackelmann's "fourth type"). Second are the fragments F 10–20, H 1–68, and I 1–97, which comprise the "countless small pieces lying all around haphazardly" that we recalled above.

Figure 7. Suggested placement of F 14a within a "Great G" piece such as G 1.

A new communication to M. S. Funghi from the first editors stating that the separation of these two typologies arises only from an oversight of theirs would seem to run against my theory. However, in reexamining F 14, I noticed that this piece is actually made of two smaller bits, rightly put together by Fackelmann before being placed under glass. The left fragment (Fa) fits together very well with G 4, a "great G" piece (Figure 7). Thus, Fackelmann's assignment of F 14 to the F group seems to have been a mistake.[5]

Heraclitus, the Persians, and Column IV 7–14

In column IV, lines 5–9, D names Heraclitus as one who, like Orpheus, spoke as a *hierologos*, giving credence to broadly accepted feelings or opinions (κοινά) at the expense of idiosyncratic ones (ἴδια). The quotation (perhaps a little free, as I have shown in Ferrari 2011b) encompasses what were thought to be two separate Heraclitean fragments (22 B 3 and B 94 DK), as two different authors quote them. Thus we can suppose that these fragments initially belonged to a single statement.

5 For another instance (the erroneous classification of D 12–14), see Piano 2011:10.

In spite of the papyrus gaps, the Heraclitean quote has been adequately recovered through other evidence. The differences between the first editors on one side and Janko (2002) and Bernabé (2007) on the other concern the formal shape of the passage rather than the substance of the argument (col. IV 5–11, with Sider's ἱερο]λόγωι in line 6, my supplement περιό]δ̣ου in line 7, and Lebedev's θύο̣υ̣[σι in line 11; the other supplements are by the first editors).

κατὰ̣ [....]α̣ Ἡρ̣άκλ̣ε̣ιτοσ μα̣[. . . . .] τ̣ὰ κοινά,
κατ̣[αστρέ]φ̣ει τὰ ἴδ[ι]α, ὅσπερ ἴκελ̣α̣ [τῶι ἱερο]λόγωι λέγων [
"ἥλι̣[ος περιό]δ̣ου κατὰ φύσιν ἀν̣θρω[πηΐου] εὖρος ποδός [ἐστι
τὸ μ̣[έγεθου]ς̣ οὐχ ὑπερβάλλων εἰκ̣[ότας οὔ]ρους ε[ὔρους
ἑοῦ· εἰ δὲ μ]ή, Ἐρινύε̣[ς] νιν ἐξευρήσου̣[σι, Δίκης ἐπίκουροι
ὑπερ]βατὸμ ποῆι κ[
]α̣ι̣ θύο̣υ̣[σι

... invoking common truths Heraclitus disrupts the idiosyncratic opinions, he who said, speaking like an author of sacred tales: "The sun, according to the nature of its circumference, is a human foot in width, not exceeding in size the proper limits of its width. Or else the Erinyes, assistants of Dike, will find it out ... so that it makes not passable ... they make sacrifices ...

One gathers from the references to a human foot, its "size" (εὖρος) and its "boundaries" (οὔ]ρους) as terms of comparison, that the issue here is the *real* (κατὰ φύσιν), rather than the apparent, size of the sun.[6] In the next line ὑπερ]βατὸμ ποῆι must be part of a statement by D, rather than Heraclitus, where the subjunctive ποῆι is the core of a final clause connected with a sentence pivoting on θύο̣υ̣[σι.

D himself (rather than Heraclitus) reminds his audience that some people (their identity is lost in the gaps of the papyrus) offer sacrifices to the sun in order to prevent it from defying its own *physis* by changing size. The identity of this people can be recovered through a neglected palaeographic datum: two tiny fragments, so far left unplaced (I 62 and I 80), can be put together using both their shape and the trend of their fibers. The resulting larger piece fits easily between G 4 and H 8 (Figure 8).

Hence, with Piano's ingenious supplement to line 10, the new text of lines 10–13 is:

[6] See Kouremenos in KPT, 156–161.

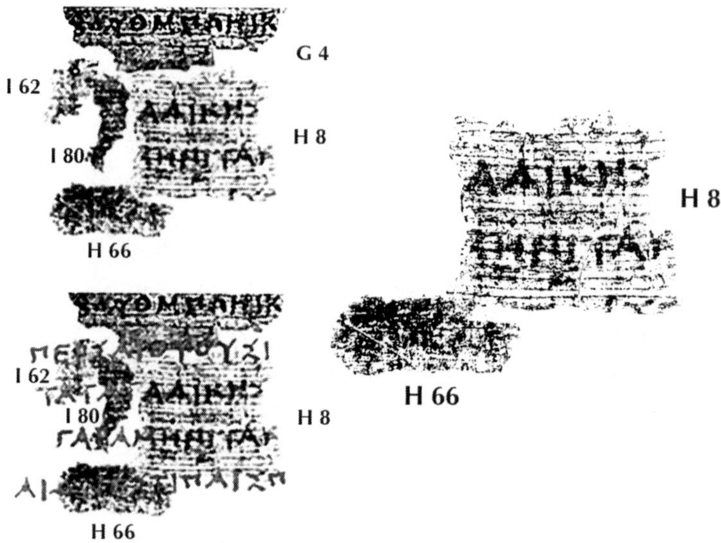

Figure 8. The new placement of I 62, I 80, and H 66 in relation to G 4 + H 8 (col. IV).

μὴ ἑὸμ μέγεθος ὑπερ]βατὸμ ποῆι κ[
Π]ε̣ρ̣σ̣α̣ι̣ θύο̣υ̣[σι(ν)
κ]ατ̣ὰ̣ τ̣ὰ Δίκης [μέτρα (?)
γὰ]ρ̣ [ἀ]μήνιτα κ[

... Persian people make sacrifices ... so that (the sun) does not make surmountable its own size ... according to Dike's rules ... not angry indeed ...

Thus, taking into account the interest in Iranian ritual practices and the entities to whom they were addressed, the sacrificers must be Persian people.[7]

Finally, another quote from Heraclitus (22 B 52):

αἰ]ώ̣ν̣ ἐ̣σ̣τ̣ι̣ π̣α̣ῖ̣ς π̣[αίζων, πεσσεύων· παιδὸς ἡ βασιληίη

Eternity is a child playing at the table: the kingship of a child.

comes to light in line 14 thanks to one more tiny unplaced piece, H 66, that can in fact be placed below I 80 and H 8.[8] The outline of the higher right edge of H 66 matches with that of the lower left edge of H 8. Also, the two pieces share the

7 As testified during the Classical age by the sources (Herodotus 1.131.2; Xenophon *Cyropaedia* 8.7.2). A plain reference to them also comes out in Plato *Laws* 821c–d, where the Athenian urges the reader to honor "the gods of the sky" (see Horky 2009:48).

8 The word order παῖς παίζων occurs in Lucian *Vitarum auctio* 14; see Marcovich 1978:339.

sigma and *tau* of ἐστί. As to the deciphering of the letters of H 66, ες has been already recognized by the first editors (KPT, 120) and can be taken as certain, but the sketch of the preceding ΩΝ also seems retraceable (KPT, pl. VIII, detail).

The meaning of this puzzling passage must be, at least according to D, that αἰών, the ceaseless stream of time in the universe, is like a child playing at *petteia* (a board game of controversial identity). Because the scene is repeated in every daily or annual cycle, it is, paradoxically, forever both old and young. "The everlasting child," as Kahn wrote,[9] "remains forever youthful, even infantile ... playing his endless game and maintaining kingship by a series of births and deaths across the generations" (even the gods play at *petteia* with men's souls as their pieces in Plato *Laws* 903d.)

The Souls of the Right Ones and the Beginning of Column VI

My last issue concerns the beginning of column VI, which deals with rituals (spells, offers, libations) undertaken both by *magi* and by *mystae*.

Here is the text of lines 1–3 as it was established by the first editors:

> [*ca. 8* εὐ]χαὶ καὶ θυσ[ί]αι μ[ειλ]ίσσουσι τὰ[ς ψυχάς,
> ἐπ[ωιδὴ δ]ὲ μάγων δύν[α]ται δαίμονας ἐμ[πο]δὼν
> γι[νομ]ένους μεθιστάναι...

> ... prayers and sacrifices appease the souls, while the incantation of the *magi* is able to drive away the *daimones* who are hindering ...
>
> (Translation in KPT)

The initial point to be noted here is that the first, partly legible word is not εὐ]χαί but, as Tsantsanoglou (2008) has recognized, χ]οή "libation." This reading establishes a connection between χοή and θυσίαι, one closely paralleled on the Persian side in Xenophon's *Cyropaedia*, where Cyrus the Great, just after crossing the Assyrian frontier, offers libations to appease the land and its gods and "heroes" (3.3.22). Herodotus (7.43) had already mentioned libations offered by Xerxes to the "heroes" of the Troad.[10]

A more subtle issue is the supplement to be adopted at the end of line 1. Tsantsanoglou[11] rightly remarked that Persian sacrifices in the presence of a *magos* were addressed to ancestors of a family group (cf. Herodotus 7.191; Strabo

9 Kahn 1979:228.

10 See Carastro 2006:17.

11 Tsantsanoglou 1997:111–112 (and 2008:33).

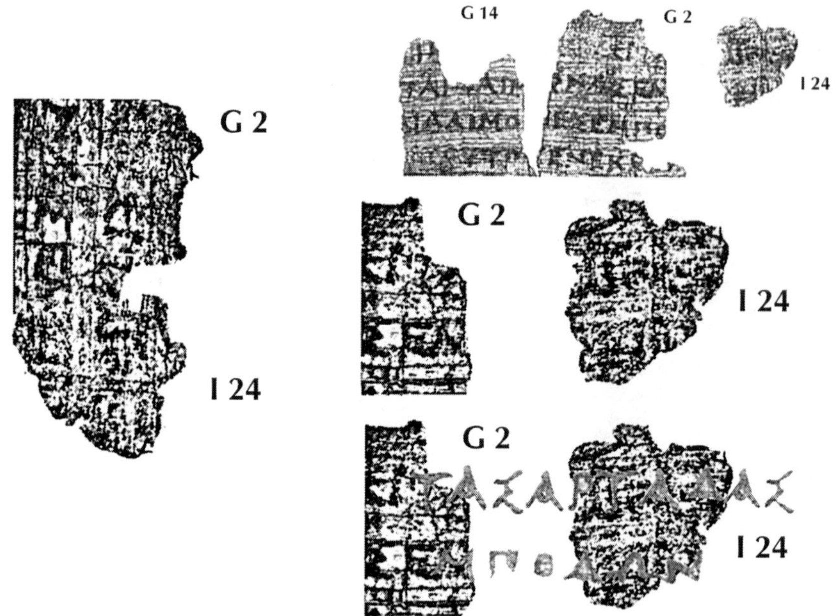

Figure 9. I 24 placed near G 14 + G 2 (col. VI).

15.3.14; Pausanias 5.27.5). He also noted that the Iranian equivalents of Greek ancestors or "heroes" were the *artavan* or *ashavan*, "those who possess truth." These ancestors are mentioned in some Greek sources as *artaioi* or *artades*: Herodotus 7.61; Hesychius α 7472 Schmidt ἀρτάδες· οἱ δίκαιοι, ὑπὸ μάγων and 7473 ἀρταῖοι· οἱ ἥρωες, παρὰ Πέρσαις; Stephanus Byzantinus *Ethnicorum quae supersunt*, p. 127 = Hellanicus *FGrHist* 4 F 60. The feminine ἀρτάδες can depend on the fact that by this word the source of Hesychius probably pointed to the *fravashi* (this Avestic word is grammatically feminine) of the *artaioi*, namely, their souls.

On the other hand, the *daimones* of line 2, beings to be driven back rather than appeased, are opposed to the *artades*. They should be identified not with the *fravashi*, as Tsantsanoglou presumed, but with the *daêvas* (recorded in Hesychius' entry δ 714 Schmidt Δεύας· τοὺς κακοὺς θεούς. Πέρσαι), who were perpetually at war with the *fravashi*. The *daêvas* were to be driven off from the places where they lurked, trying to hinder the deceased on their way toward the afterlife.[12] Against them the *magi* sang their *epoidai*,[13] Avestic texts that were incomprehensible to Greek ears, sung in low voices.

[12] See Panaino 2009:34–36.

[13] See Herodotus 1.132 and, above all, for spells performed *against* numinous beings, 7.191: καταείδοντες βοῇισι.

Thus, if the *daimones* can be identified with the *daêvas* of Persian religion, a supplement such as τ̣ὰ̣[ς ψυχὰς (KPT) is not a suitable name for these beings, who should be designated in a more specific way than with the generic word "souls." But, precisely that, the Iranian loan ἀρτάδες with the explanation in the Hesychius' gloss οἱ δίκαιοι "(the souls of) the Right ones," occurred at the end of line 1 if one places the piece I 24 in the upper right corner of this column (Figure 9). The fiber consistency between G 2 and I 24 is striking, and the reading τ̣ὰ̣[ς ἀ]ρ̣τά̣δ̣α̣[ς is corroborated by the obvious supplement ἐμ[πο]δ̣ώ̣ν in the following line (already suggested by KPT on the basis of ἐμπο[δών in line 3).

Therefore, we may have identified the correct word for the recipients of the libations and sacrifices of the Persian people.

Bibliography

Bernabé, A., ed. 2007. *Musaeus · Linus · Epimenides · Papyrus Derveni · Indices. Poetae epici Graeci: Testimonia et fragmenta,* part II, fasc. 3. Berlin.

Carastro, M. 2006. *La cité des mages: Penser la magie en Grèce ancienne*. Grenoble.

de Jongh, A. 1997. *Traditions of the Magi: Zoroastrianism in Greek and Latin Literature.* Leiden.

Ferrari, F. 2010. "Democrito a Derveni? PDerv. col. 4, 1–6." *Parola del Passato* 65: 137–155.

———. 2011a. "Frustoli erranti: Per una ricostruzione delle colonne 1–3 del Papiro di Derveni." In Funghi 2011:39–54.

———. 2011b. "Rites without Frontiers: Magi and Mystae in the Derveni Papyrus." *Zeitschrift für Papyrologie und Epigraphik* 179:71–83.

Funghi, M. S., ed. 2011. *Papiri filosofici: Miscellanea di Studi* VI. Florence.

Horky, P. S. 2009. "Persian Cosmos and Greek Philosophy: Plato's Associates and the Zoroastrian Magoi." *Oxford Studies in Ancient Philosophy* 37:47–103.

Janko, R. 2002. "The Derveni Papyrus: An Interim Text." *Zeitschrift für Papyrologie und Epigraphik* 141:1–62.

———. 2008. "Reconstructing (Again) the Opening of the Derveni Papyrus." *Zeitschrift für Papyrologie und Epigraphik* 166:37–51.

Kahn, C. H. 1979. *The Art and Thought of Heraclitus*. Cambridge.

KPT = Th. Kouremenos, G. M. Parássoglou, and K. Tsantsanoglou, eds., *The Derveni Papyrus, Edited with Introduction and Commentary* (Florence, 2006).

Lulli, L. 2011. "La lingua del papiro di Derveni: Interrogrativi ancora aperti." In Funghi 2011:91–104.

Marcovich, M., ed. 1978. *Eraclito. Frammenti*. Florence.

Panaino, A. 2009. "Aspetti della complessità degli influssi interculturali fra Grecia e Iran." In *Grecia Maggiore: Intrecci culturali con l'Asia nel periodo arcaico. Atti del 75 anniversario di W. Burkert, Istituto Svizzero di Roma (2 febbraio 2006)* (ed. Ch. Riedweg) 19–53. Basel.

Piano, V. 2011. "Per una revisione papirologica delle prime colonne del papiro di Derveni." In Funghi 2011:5–37.

Tsantsanoglou, K. 1997. "The First Columns of the Derveni Papyrus and Their Religious Significance." In *Studies on the Derveni Papyrus* (ed. A. Laks and G. W. Most) 93–128. Oxford.

———. 2008. "Magi in Athens in the Fifth Century BC." In *Ancient Greece and Ancient Iran: Cross-Cultural Encounters* (ed. S. M. R. Darbandi and A. M. L. Zournatzi) 31–39. Athens.

4

Derveni and Ritual

Fritz Graf
The Ohio State University

In many respects, the Derveni papyrus remains as intriguing as it appeared in 1964 when Stylianos Kapsomenos published the first choice morsels to whet the appetite of the scholarly community, or when, in 1968, Walter Burkert proposed the first thorough interpretation of the text known at the time and anchored the commentary firmly in Presocratic thinking. If I remember correctly, he presented this as a public lecture in Zurich when he applied for the chair in Greek philology which he was to hold and shape until his retirement—little did he know that the text would accompany him through most of his professional career.[1] Over the years, the text has become even more intriguing with the presentation of the very fragmentary first seven columns in the final critical edition, after Kyriakos Tsantsanoglou revealed them first at a Princeton colloquium in 1993, and with the new readings suggested by Richard Janko and Franco Ferrari.[2] What originally was thought to be an allegorical commentary on a theogony of Orpheus has now turned out to be a treatise whose exact character is still to be determined but that is as much about rituals as it is about Orphism or Presocratic physics—so much about rituals that Burkert suggested to identify it with a the treatise *On Rituals* (Περὶ τελετῶν) of Stesimbrotus of Thasus—as good a guess as any, given the little we know about this text and its author.[3]

In what follows I will return to the problem of the Derveni author—not in order to give him a name, but to understand who he could have been, and what his world and his background might have been. To this purpose, I will start from the crucial column xx, and then look at other hints in the text. The picture that

1 Kapsomenos 1964, 1964/65; Burkert 1968, 1980, 1986, 1997, 1998, 2006:95–111.

2 Text and commentary: Tsantsanoglou 1997; *editio princeps:* Kouremenos, Parássoglou, and Tsantsanoglou 2006; new reconstructions: Janko 2008, Ferrari 2011b and 2012.

3 Burkert 1986.

emerges will not be radically new, but I am confident that it will help to situate the text somewhat better.

1. The Interpretative Voice

The one reflection on ritual that has been known almost from the start is found in column xx (formerly col. xvi). It reads:

> ὅσοι μὲν] ἀνθρώπω[ν ἐν] τοῖς πόλεσιν ἐπιτελέσαντες [τὰ ἱ]ε̣ρὰ εἶδον, ἔλασσόν σφας θαυμάζω μὴ γινώσκειν· οὐ γὰρ οἷόν τε ἀκοῦσαι ὁμοῦ καὶ μαθεῖν τὰ λ̣εγόμενα· ὅσοι δὲ παρὰ τοῦ τέχνην ποιουμένου τὰ ἱερά, οὗτοι ἄξιοι θαυμάζεσθαι καὶ οἰκτε[ί]ρεσθαι· θαυμάζεσθαι μὲν ὅτι δ̣οκοῦντες πρότερον ἢ ἐπιτελέσαι εἰδήσειν ἀπέρχονται ἐπιτελέσαντες πρὶν εἰδέναι οὐδ' ἐπανερόμενοι ὥσπερ ὡς εἰδότες τ̣έ̣ων εἶδον ἢ ἤκουσαν ἢ ἔμαθον· [οἰ]κτε<ί>ρεσθαι δὲ ὅτι οὐκ ἀρκεῖ̣ σφιν τὴν δαπάνην προσαναλῶσ̣θαι, ἀλλὰ __καὶ τῆ̣ς γνώμης στερόμενοι πρὸς ἀπέρχονται. πρὶν μὲν τὰ [ἱ]ερὰ ἐπιτελέσαι ἐλπίζον[τε]ς εἰδήσειν, ἐπ̣[ιτελέσ]α̣ντ̣[ες] δὲ στερηθέντες κα[ὶ τῆς] ἐλπίδ[ος] ἀπέρχονται̣ __τω̣[ ].υοντ[...] λ̣όγος ..[...]ται[..].να .[ ]ι τῆι ἑαυ̣τ̣ο̣ῦ ο..[μ]ητρὶ μὲν]δ̣' ἀδελφη[ ]ωσειδε

> [Those] among men[4] who performed and saw the rites in the cities, with regard to those I am not as much surprised that they have no knowledge: it is impossible to hear the ritual words and at the same time to understand them. But those who (received) the rituals from a ritual specialist, those cause deserved surprise and pity. Surprise because before they were initiated, they assumed that they would gain knowledge, but they went away from their initiation before they had this knowledge and they did not ask, as if they would already know what they were seeing or hearing or learning. Pity because it was not enough that they had to pay the fee beforehand, but they also went away deprived of knowledge. Before they performed the rites, they hoped they would know; after the performance, however, they walk away deprived even of their hope.

[4] [ὅσοι μὲν] is an easy supplement to create a functioning syntax.

The passage has often been commented upon, in regard to both its content and its role in the overall text.[5] As the very fragmentary lines 14–15 seem to indicate, its auctorial reflections ends with line 13. This intrusion of the author interrupts the flow of the allegorical interpretation at a strategically important point: after the narration of how Zeus made himself the origin of the entire cosmos, and before the story of his incest (and, as col. xxi seems to indicate, formal marriage[6]) with his mother (another attempt of Zeus at totality, this time genealogical totality[7]).

Already, for purely formal reasons, I think that the speaker of this auctorial voice must be the author of the overall text: the two *paragraphoi* after lines 10 and 13 need not mark off a quotation, as Jeffrey Rustens assumes.[8] In the Derveni Papyrus, *paragraphoi* serve two functions: they mark a quotation, mostly (but not exclusively) from Orpheus' poem and often framing this quotation; and they indicate the beginning of a new paragraph even when the preceding paragraph had ended with a *vacat*.[9] Here, it is easier to understand both *paragraphoi* as marking two new paragraphs: lines 11–13 rephrase and summarize the preceding text, and thus they probably are not quotations;[10] and line 14 moves back to the interpretation at hand.[11] The speaker opposes people who perform rituals (ἐπιτελέω, the proper verb for performing any ritual) in cities to those who get their rituals from a specialist, παρὰ τέχνην ποιουμένου τὰ ἱερά. There is general agreement that we deal not just with any ritual but with the rites of mystery cults: the performers in the cities are described as people who "saw the sacred things," τὰ ἱερὰ εἶδον; seeing the rites is typical for Eleusis from the *Homeric Hymn to Demeter* onwards.[12] But the author must mean more than just the one city mystery cult of Athens, if his plural ἐν ταῖς πόλεσι deserves any credit; I take it that ἐν ταῖς πόλεσι does not necessarily mean what we have learned to call a polis cult, that is, a cult financed and supervised by

5 A (partial) bibliography is provided in Bernabé's edition (2007:238).

6 The column mentions Aphrodite and Peitho, the usual divinities that assist and are invoked in the wedding ritual.

7 I read the presence of Aphrodite Ourania, Peitho, and Harmonia in col. xxi as *aition* of the traditional wedding ritual with its sacrifices to these deities. For another attempt at genealogical totality, written as a joke by a gifted medievalist, see Heimito von Doderer's hilarious novel *Die Merowinger*.

8 Rusten 1985:138–140; see the counterarguments of Obbink (1997:44–45).

9 Quotations: iv 6, viii 1, xii 2, xiii 3/4, xiv 5/6, xv 5/6, xv 12, xvi 2/6, xix 9, xxiii 10/11, xxiv 2/3, xxv 13/14, xxvi 3/4, 11/12; new paragraph: x 10, xi 7, xii 6, xv 10, xxiii 7.

10 Except if we assume that after line 10, the scribe marked a paragraph inside a quotation that would end at 13; but this assumption accepts the double function of the *paragraphoi* and is unnecessarily complex.

11 I will come back to this question below.

12 *Homeric Hymn to Demeter* 480, with the passages collected by Richardson (1974, *ad loc.*).

the polis and concerned with the welfare of the city as well, but simply a cult that is performed in a city sanctuary and with group participation, as were, for example, the rites of Dionysos Bakcheios in Olbia, according to Herodotus.[13] In the later fifth century, the most likely time for the treatise, the one mystery cult that is widespread enough among Greek cities is the Bacchic mysteries, attested in the late sixth and early fifth centuries in cities as far apart as Ephesos, Olbia Pontica, and Cumae in Italy. This then means that the professionals "who make the sacred into their craft" are not the Eleusinian priests such as the Eumolpids (although their activities could be described in this same way) but the religious entrepreneurs that Plato calls μάντεις καὶ ἀγύρται who, in his negative and rather hostile representation, peddle private initiations to the rich. There is no need to separate these specialists whom a few later texts call *Orpheotelestai*, from the initiators in the cities: they might well all have performed Bacchic rituals.[14]

The author regrets that the clients of these private mystery initiators did not obtain the knowledge they could have gained if they only had asked their initiator. He concedes that such a demand would have been out of place during the rites in the cities: "It is impossible to hear the ritual words and at the same time to understand them." In this reading, then, the key to knowledge is not the ritual gestures or the objects shown, despite the focus on seeing (εἶδον), but the words spoken during the ritual, and these words are not immediately understood. In order to obtain the knowledge they are entitled to, the initiates would need not only to hear the *legomena*, but to have them explained: interpretation has to follow initiation. The words uttered during the rituals (prayers, hymns, invocations) have a surface meaning that the participants could easily understand during the ritual and thus think they had gained knowledge; but the deeper meaning has eluded them, because they did not ask for elucidation after the end of the ritual.

There is, of course, a text that immediately qualifies for exactly this sort of *legomenon*: it is the theogony of Orpheus, whose surface meaning of a rather alarming theogony the Derveni author explains in physical terms. In column vii 2, he introduces the text he is interpreting as a "hymn" ([ὕ]μνον). In the following characterization of this text as "a hymn saying things that are sound and sanctioned by divine law" ([ὕ]μνον [ὑγ]ιῆ καὶ θεμιτὰ λέγοντα), the author makes a strong claim that the following surface reading does not justify at all. The author is quick to point this out: the poem appears as "strange and a riddle for humans" (ξ[ένη τις ἡ ποίησις [κ]αὶ ἀνθρώ[ποις] αἰνι[γμ]ατώδης, vii 4): the characterization thus draws attention to the necessity for the allegorical

13 Herodotus 4.79.

14 Plato perseveres in his hostility against the religious entrepreneurs: in *Laws* 909B, he proposes incarceration for them. On the *Orpheotelestai* see Graf and Johnston 2012:145–146.

reading that the author advocates, in a well-established move that takes an apparent scandalous statement in the text as the starting-off point for an allegorical reading. Perhaps he justified this claim in the sentence that immediately followed: one possible way of filling the lacuna at the end of vii 2 is Janko's [ἱερολογεῖ]το γὰρ [τῆ]ι ποιήσει, "he said sacred things in his poem": thus the strange and offending surface meaning must be misleading. But another supplement is more likely.

If we assume (with most editors) that [..ὕ]μνον and not, as also suggested, [..σ]εμνὸν is the correct reading at the beginning of vii 2, this has important consequences for the status of the theogony.[15] At this time and in this sort of text, ὕμνος must be cult poetry as in Plato and other fifth- and fourth-century texts, used as *legomena* during some ritual act, not any poetic composition about the gods, as in Homer and Hesiod.[16] Plato confirms this when he says that the ἀγύρται καὶ μάντεις were using "a din of books," βίβλων ὁμαδόν, by Orpheus and Musaios in their rites, καθ' ἅς θυηπολοῦσιν;[17] so does Euripides' Theseus in the famous passage where he accuses Hippolytos of being a Bacchic sectarian, worshiping "the smoke of books" of Orpheus.[18] This argues strongly for the alternative supplement in vii 2, Tsantsanoglou's [ἱερουργεῖ]το. Even if we read it personally—"he [Orpheus] was performing a ritual by means of this poem"—it still must be the foundational story that justifies its use in later rites; this is obvious when we take it impersonally as "a rite was being performed." The Derveni author anchors his claim in the ritual importance of his text: as a ritual text, it has to be "sound and sanctioned by divine law."

In column xx, the author distinguishes between two groups of people, both initiates: those who, through neglect or ignorance, have deprived themselves of the full benefit of initiation, knowledge, and those who would follow his advice and gain deeper knowledge. A similar dichotomy appears several times throughout the interpretation of Orpheus' poem, between those who take the text literally, and those who, like the author, understand the deeper meaning.[19] In vii 4–8, the author states the principle that Orpheus's poem appears "as strange and a riddle to people" (ξένη [...] καὶ ἀνθρώποις αἰνιγματώδης) and thus needs explanation, with the same opposition he uses in xviii 4, where he

15 See Bernabé 2007:201 on the text.

16 Homer *Odyssey* viii 249 (the Demodokos story); *Homeric Hymn to Aphrodite* 161; Hesiod *Works and Days* 662 (with West's remark) as against e.g. Aeschylus *Persians* 623, *Seven Against Thebes* 866; Plato *Republic* 459e, 607a, *Laws* 700b; Demosthenes 21.5; Philochorus *FGrHist* 328 F 188.

17 Plato *Republic* 2.364e.

18 Euripides *Hippolytos* 953f. = OF 627 Bernabé.

19 The principle (Orpheus "speaks in riddles," ἐν αἰνίγμασιν, vii 4–8); the opposition in ix 2 (οἱ οὐ γινώσκοντες), xii 3–5 (ἁμαρτάνουσι ... οὐ γινώσκοντες), xviii 3–6 (Orpheus versus οἱ ἄλλοι ἄνθρωποι).

opposes the meaning Orpheus gave to a term to the surface understanding of "the other people" (οἱ ἄλλοι ἄνθρωποι). A similar opposition appears in ix 2 between the true understanding of a mythical detail and "those who do not know what is said" (οὐ γινώσκοντες τὰ λεγόμενα), whereas in xii 4–5 the author censors those who identify sky and Olympus because they err on a detail of poetical diction. Although these latter passages generalize, it is a generalization in the service of an interpreter who claims special knowledge that others do not possess; they thus align with the more specific opposition made in column xii, between initiates who hear the poem of Orpheus but think they understand it from their everyday use of language, and the interpreter who knows better and will tell his clients the real meaning. If this is correct, then the book must be addressed to initiates only and not destined for a larger readership. We do not deal with learned allegorization of a traditional poem (as, much later, in the *Homeric Allegories* of Heraclitus), we deal with the correct way to explain the ritual text to those undergoing initiation.

If we understand the poem in this way, the famous and often-remembered introductory line to Orpheus' hymn whose second half the author comments upon in vii 9 serves a double purpose. Its full version is transmitted in two forms, ἀείσω ξυνετοῖσι and φθέγξομαι οἷς θέμις ἐστί, both completing the hexameter with the command θύρας δ' ἐπίθεσθε, βέβηλοι.[20] We do not know which version the Derveni commentator read since in the preserved text he only comments on the common second half of the hexameter, but we can make a reasonable guess. His usual practice is to quote first at least one entire hexameter that fills its own line and is framed by two *paragraphoi*, then to comment on parts of the quotation that he usually cites again, lemma-like, at the beginning of his comments. Column vii 9 is such a lemma, as usual without a *paragraphos*; the entire verse then must have been cited towards the end of column vi, of which we have lost the lower two thirds. When the papyrus text sets in again in column vii, vii 2 describes the poem as a ὕμνος ... θεμιτὰ λέγων. I suspect that this echoes the opening φθέγξομαι οἷς θέμις ἐστί—an opening that fits a ritual situation somewhat better than the second version (ἀείσω ξυνετοῖσι), although Plutarch explicitly connects this second variant with ritual performance, ἐν τελετῆι.[21] When the text was recited in the ritual, either opening kept away the noninitiated; for the allegorist who claimed to be one of those who have understanding, ξυνετοί, it provoked and justified his search for a second level of meaning.

[20] *OF* 1a, 1b, 377 and 378 Bernabé. See five different approaches to this text in Herrero 2011:1–28 (J. N. Bremmer, C. Calame, F. Graf, M. Dolores Lara, and S. Macías Otero).

[21] Plutarch fr. 202 Sandbach. See also Bremmer in Herrero 2011:1–6 (on performance, but without citing Plutarch).

In what we read of column xx, the writer again justifies his own—preceding and following—allegorical explanation. But why in the middle of the interpretation and not at the beginning? To be precise, he had already justified his methodology at the outset of the interpretation, in column vii. Orpheus' text, he said there, is enigmatic for ordinary humans, ἀνθρώποις αἰνιγματώδης (vii 5):[22] this explains the need for allegory. But this not nearly as forceful as what we read in column xx. The key to the renewed justification in column xx, I suspect, lies in the initial assertion that the hymn "tells things that conform to divinely sanctioned standards," θεμιτὰ λέγοντα. Before column xx, we might have some surface events that hardly conformed to this standard, such as the swallowing of Ouranos' genitals (if this is meant in col. xii 4[23]). But the real scandal is yet to come; it is Zeus' marriage and incest with his mother. At about the same time, the Athenians heard on their stage how Jocasta hanged herself and how her son and husband Oedipus dug out his eyes, both to punish themselves for what Oedipus himself terms ἀσέβεια, "lack of respect for the gods" who set these standards[24]—and Zeus' incest is worse, because premeditated and not the result of divine intrigue and human flaw. It makes some rhetorical sense to enter into yet another discussion of the need for allegorization at the very point before the story touches upon this final scandal.

The *paragraphoi* after column xx 10 and 13 have to be seen in this same context. I have argued above that they mark the beginnings of two new paragraphs. The first paragraph, 11–13, is very short. Lines 11–12 rephrase the immediately preceding argument: "Before they performed the rites, they hoped they would know, after the performance; however, they walk away deprived even of their hope"; I suspect that line 13 ended the digression with a final summarizing statement of which we only can read λόγος. I do not think that 11/12 is a textual variant, as the Greek editors understand it[25]—I cannot see the need for offering variant readings in this sort of text, unlike in the scholarly editions or in texts destined for oral performance, where the exact wording was vital for the success of the performance, such as healing and other spells in the Magical Papyri or the manuscripts of Cato's *On Agriculture.*[26] I rather think that this small paragraph highlights the main message of the auctorial digression, efficiently

22 See esp. Calame 2005.

23 See the discussion in Kouremenos, Parássoglou, and Tsantsanoglou 2006:26–28, citing earlier positions.

24 Oedipus as ἀσεβής: Sophocles *Oedipus Rex* 1441, cp. 1382 (the killer of King Laius); in 1360, he calls himself ἄθεος and ἀνοσίων παῖς.

25 Kouremenos, Parássoglou, and Tsantsanoglou 2006:241, with some hesitation.

26 In the magical papyri such textual variations are usually introduced by ἐν ἄλλωι (εὗρον) "I found in another copy" or similar formulae, *PGM* II 50, IV 500, 1277, V 51, VII 204, XII 201, XIII 731. Cato *On Agriculture* 160, with a similar formula (modern editions print one variation—in a rather

put at its very end—the reader should not follow the example of the foolish initiates but listen to the professional explanations that provide knowledge free of charge. These *paragraphoi*, then, function as marginal signs to catch the attention of a reader who was browsing the text; this also helps understand why they mark a new paragraph even after a *vacat*.

The papyrus contains another case of an auctorial digression on methodology that is framed by two *paragraphoi* and thus singled out as interrupting the flow of the allegorization, and important enough to be underlined. It is to be found in column xiii 5 and 6:

> ὅτι μὲν πᾶσαν τὴν πόησιν περὶ τῶν πραγμάτων αἰνίζεται, καθ' ἔπος ἕκαστα ἀνάγκη λέγειν.
>
> Since he composed the entire poem as a riddle about reality, one has to explain word by word.

This is an important hermeneutical precept. The commentator leads his audience verse by verse through the poem, explaining every important word or expression: this precept guarantees that we deal with a rather short text, well suited to be spoken during a ritual. If it were considerably longer, the close reading proposed by the interpreter would take up much more space than the physical text suggests it did.[27] The statement comes at another crucial passage, at the very moment when Orpheus has Zeus swallow his fathers genitals—the genitals from which he earlier masturbated the *aither*, in Burkert's attractive reading.[28] Gods behaving offensively again trigger explicit methodological statements.

All this has an immediate consequence for our understanding of column xx. Interpreters are divided into two camps, those who read the text as being critical of "Orphic" mysteries (whatever they are), and those who take it as a serious admonition to ask for more information when being initiated.[29] If we understand the Derveni theogony as the *legomenon* of such an initiation, to give its full text, "word by word," is tantamount to divulging a text protected by the secrecy of the mysteries. We are accustomed to Greek authors (at least before the Christian polemics), from Herodotus and Plato to Pausanias, respecting this secrecy; no wonder that Janko took the Derveni author to be Diagoras. But

superficial decision, since both variations must be ancient—and ban the other into the critical apparatus).

27 See also the two versions of the so-called *Testament of Orpheus*, OF 377 and 378 Bernabé: both are short, ca. 25 hexameters (F 277) and 41 hexameters respectively (F 378). See Riedweg 1993.

28 Burkert 2006:103.

29 See Kouremenos in Kouremenos, Parássoglou and Tsantsanoglou 2006:53–58, 238–240, who sees the author as rejecting any religious interpretation.

this cannot be. The author's motive for allegorical interpretation is, in his own words, the assumption that the text says "things that are sound and sanctioned by divine law": the need for interpretation is anchored in the author's theology, which is as normative as Xenophanes' or Plato's: Zeus' swallowing all gods or his incest with Hera are not θεμιτά. The need for sound theology stems from the fact that the text is used in a mystery ritual which the author takes very seriously: he is not laughing at the people who undergo initiation without receiving all the benefits, he pities them (οἰκτείρεσθαι xx 5) and promises them help from being defrauded by their own shortsightedness and the incompetence of their initiators. If taken seriously, this leads to the assumption that he himself is τέχνην ποιούμενος τὰ ἱερά, a religious entrepreneur who initiates people for a fee; but the specialty that he advertises in order to stand out from the other competing entrepreneurs is to explain the text he uses in his ritual as a physical allegory. The commentary is addressed to the initiates, in order to help them remember what they learned during the ritual, not unlike the gold tablets, or the Orphic hymn to Mnemosyne that, towards the very end of the ritual *parcours*, prays that the goddess "awake in the initiates the memory of the sacred rite."[30]

The archaeological context confirms this reading. The Macedonian nobleman buried in Derveni grave A most likely is such an initiate, as was the person buried in grave B, which contained the splendid Dionysiac crater. The fact that the charred remains of the book were found not among the grave goods but on top of the stone slab that closed the grave, together with the remains of everything else he had on his body, suggests that the deceased had the scroll on his body, most likely holding it in his hand, as does the deceased on the famous Basel Orpheus vase.[31] It is tempting to assume that the entire small cluster of elite graves, far removed from the main graveyard area of the city of Lete, was a Bacchic graveyard; the existence of such separate graveyards is suggested by an inscription from Italian Cumae dated to before 450 BCE.[32]

2. Theorizing the Mystical Experience

The Derveni commentator claims that it is possible to gain knowledge (μαθεῖν, εἰδέναι) in mystery rites, if only one listens to an allegorist. In a famous fragment from his early *On Philosophy*, Aristotle thinks otherwise:

30 *Orphic Hymn* 77.9–10 (μύσταις μνήμην ἐπέγειρε εὐιέρου τελετῆς); see Ricciardelli 2000:512 and Graf 2009. Analyzing the literary voice of the Derveni author, Calame (2005:166–169) came to a similar conclusion: "the commentary most likely served earlier in this intellectual initiation."

31 This might even explain the way the scroll burned: the part that was protected by the deceased person's hand was the only part that survived the flames.

32 Arena 1994: no. 15.

> Aristotle thinks that those who undergo initiation should not learn but experience and be brought into a certain condition [τοὺς τελουμένους οὐ μαθεῖν τι δεῖν ἀλλὰ παθεῖν καὶ διατεθῆναι].[33]

The fragment inserts itself into a very specific Platonic context, as Synesius (who cites it) makes clear. The Neoplatonic bishop of Cyrene juxtaposes two groups of extraordinary men who open up to divine inspiration: the very few who have immediate access to the divine, such as Egyptian ascetic monks, and the many religiously minded who need rational arguments to be brought to the jumping-off point of revelation. Bacchic mysteries are a reference point throughout this discussion. Synesius refers to Plato's quotation of the famous verse of Orpheus, πολλοὶ μὲν ναρθηκοφόροι, παῦροι δέ τε βάκχοι: "for there are many that carry the thyrsus, but few are the Bacchi": this Bacchic dichotomy already used by Plato reflects the two ways of attaining inspiration.[34] But even the most extraordinary people have to be conscious of their human nature, as Synesius shows in an allegorical interpretation of a Bacchic ritual, handling the basket with the phallus; his source for this is unclear.

The dichotomy Synesius uses goes back to Plato himself. Plato, however, used it differently, to describe in mystery language how a philosopher could arrive at truth. As Christoph Riedweg showed long ago, the Platonic tradition uses a three-step access to divine revelation as performed in the mystery cults as a metaphor for the philosopher's trajectory to truth: after an initial purification rite, the second step consists of teaching and learning (παράδοσις, *traditio*), and the final step is pure vision, ἐποπτεία. This is never explicitly spelled out in Plato's extant writings, but it is present in later Platonists, starting with his close student, Aristotle: it might well be a part of Plato's oral teachings that did not surface in his own written dialogues, but only in the writings of his students and followers.

If Riedweg's analysis is correct, we perceive a Platonic doctrine that resonates in an intricate way with what the Derveni author says. Mystery initiation contains an element of μαθεῖν, (intellectual) learning; it is central to the Derveni author, but preliminary only in the Platonic tradition. Both sides agree that an important part of what was taught in the mystery cults involved mythical stories. If we take Plato seriously, these myths were theogonical and eschatological. In *Republic* 377e, Socrates thinks that the story of Cronus' castration should be only told secretly and to very few, after a sacrifice that is much more expensive than a piglet; the "piglet" might refer to the Eleusinian preliminary sacrifice,

33 Fr. 15 Rose from Synesius *Dio* 10. See also Psellos, *Scholia on John Climacus* 6.171, who seems to know the same Aristotelian text.

34 Plato *Phaedo* 69c = OF 576 Bernabé.

but more important is the mostly overlooked fact that Plato can imagine traditional theogonical poetry in a mystery context. In Laws 870d, Plato talks about a λόγος ἐν ταῖς τελεταῖς that tells of punishment after death. Isocrates informs us that it was the Demeter myth that was told to the initiates in Eleusis.[35] Both Plato and the Derveni author agree that these myths were the *legomena* of the mystery rituals, and that they were only preliminary to the acquisition of truth. They split on the way to acquire this final truth. For the Derveni author, it can be acquired from the initiator, who should be able to explain the *legomena*: the truth consists in a final discursive rationalization and allegorization of the ritual texts. Plato disagrees radically: the final truth is available only through mystical experience, during which the philosopher experiences a direct vision that transcends any rationality.

We can understand these two positions as two different reactions to the same ritual facts: an initiation ritual contained both *dromena* and *legomena*, and it claimed a very special insight as its final goal; it is worth while recalling that in Greek to see, ἰδεῖν, and to know, εἰδέναι, are closely connected. The Platonic tradition understood this special knowledge as created by an emotional experience (παθεῖν καὶ διατεθῆναι, in Aristotle's terms[36]), and the Derveni author as the result of individual discursive rationalization. This sounds not unlike the difference between Plato and the Sophists, who stress their technical, rational approach: I cannot help thinking that Plato was aware of such a practice and refuted its importance; he had, after all, some knowledge of the doings of ἀγύρται καὶ μάντεις. It does not necessarily follow that he knew the Derveni text; as Burkert had noted already in 1968, the philosophical horizon of the Derveni author is decidedly un-Platonic and thus most likely pre-Platonic. But it means that there existed a late fifth-/early fourth-century discourse on the experience gained in mystery cults that was important enough that Plato felt compelled to state his own position.

The same discourse resonates in yet another late fifth-century Athenian text, Aristophanes's *Clouds*. Socrates is about to initiate the reluctant Strepsiades, and he lures him with a question:

> Βούλει τὰ θεῖα πράγματ' εἰδέναι σαφῶς
> ἅττ'ἐστὶν ὀρθῶς; ...
>
> Do you want to know divine matters clearly, how they are truly?

The means to obtain this knowledge, at least in Socrates' promise, is a meeting and discussion with the divinities themselves:

35 Isocrates *Panegyric* 28.

36 Aristotle fr. 15 Rose.

> καὶ ξυγγενέσθαι ταῖς Νεφέλαισι εἰς λόγους
> ταῖς ἡμετέραισιν δαίμοσι;
>
> .... and to meet and talk with the Clouds, our divinities?

Whatever the mystery cult is that resonates with this scene, Aristophanes' Socrates proposes a private initiation by a philosophical entrepreneur (ἱερεύς 359) that will lead to superior knowledge—not, as in the Derveni text, through the later explanations given by the initiator, but through the direct epiphanic communication provided by the ritual.[37]

3. Μάγοι and the Derveni Author

If the Derveni author is an Orpheotelest (to use the term as a shortcut to the complex of religious entrepreneurship that manifested itself in divination, purification, initiation, and binding spells and in the creation of texts that were needed for these ritual and pretended to be written by Orpheus and Musaios[38]), and if his allegorical explanation of the theogonical hymn of Orpheus explains a ritual text used in the Bacchic mysteries, how does this tie into the ritual discourse that we can glimpse in columns i–vi, especially in columns v and vi? More precisely: what does this mean for the rituals discussed in column vi as rituals performed by μάγοι, and for the μάγοι themselves? Are they Persian priests or Greek sorcerers?[39]

In a paper published well after the original conference published in this volume, Franco Ferrari proposed an interesting answer.[40] He combined two hitherto unplaced fragments (162 and 180) and placed them at the beginning of column iv 11, as part either of the preceding citation from Heraclitus or of the Derveni author's own discussion; since we miss the left margin, the *paragraphos* that would mark the end of the citation (possibly as early as after line

37 Aristophanes *Clouds* 250–330. Scholars usually have stressed the echoes of Eleusinian ritual, see e.g. Christiane Sourvinou Inwood, "Reconstructing Change: Ideology and the Eleusinian Mysteries," in *Inventing Ancient Culture: Historicism, Periodization, and the Ancient World*, ed. M. Golden and P. Toohey (London, 1997) 132–164; P. Bonnechère, however—and more problematically—argued for the cult of Trophonios at Lebadeia, "La scène d'initiation des *Nuées* d'Aristophane et Trophonios: nouvelles lumières sur le culte lébadéen," *Revue des Études Grecques* 111 (1998): 436–480.

38 Thus, I use the term in a much wider sense than Ferrari (2011a:71), who understands the "Orpheotelestae"—i.e. initiators who do not explain—as the target of the criticism of the Derveni author: but Ferrari's understanding, based on the three passages that mention an Ὀρφεοτελεστής (Theophrastus *Characters* 16 = OF 654; Philodemus *On Poems* 1.181.1 Janko = OF 655 Bernabé; and Plutarch *Apophthegmata Laconica* 22 = OF 653 Bernabé), presupposes that we know whether they did more than just the ritual: but we don't know.

39 Resolutely Persian according to Russell (2001), but he overlooks the Greek side.

40 Ferrari 2011a.

9) is lost. The recovered text talks of Persians sacrificing, Πέρσαι θύουσιν, to the sun, and Ferrari derived from this the certainty that the μάγοι of vi 2 were Persian priests. But nothing in the text suggests that the rites were Persian as opposed to Greek.[41] Libations of milk and water are common for the Eumenides, but water libations at least are impossible in Persian cult,[42] and sacrificial cakes are a widespread although underresearched ingredient of many Greek sacrificial rites, without necessarily an equivalent in Persian ritual: in a Greek text, this remains firmly inside a Greek ritual horizon. Although one could imagine (unattested) sacrificial cakes among the Persians, and although Herodotus tells us that Xerxes' *magoi* performed libations to the heroes at Troy (perhaps imitating Greek customs),[43] nothing forces us to assume that in vi 2 we are dealing with Persian rituals, and with Persian specialists performing them. Ferrari solved the ensuing quandary with the assumption that the Derveni author presented "neither a faithful account of Iranian ideas nor a sketch of Greek mysticism disguised with some Persian names and references, but a cross-cultural accommodation worked out by him and his sources to make Persian rites available to people already accustomed [...] to cathartic practices and chthonian cult."[44]

But this disregards the first occurrence of μάγοι ever, Heraclitus' famous (and disputed) fragment cited by Clement of Alexandria:[45]

> Τίσι δὴ μαντεύεται Ἡράκλειτος ὁ Ἐφέσιος; Νυκτιπόλοις, μάγοις, βάκχοις, λήναις, μύσταις, τούτοις ἀπειλεῖ τὰ μετὰ θάνατον, τούτοις μαντεύεται τὸ πῦρ· τὰ γὰρ νομιζόμενα κατὰ ἀνθρώπους μυστήρια ἀνιερωστὶ μυοῦνται.
>
> To whom prophesies Heraclitus of Ephesus: to the dwellers in the night, the *magi*, Bacchi, maenads, initiates: those he threatens with what will come after death, to those he prophesies the fire: what the people call mysteries is performed in an ungodly way.

There can be little doubt that the entire list that I have highlighted, from νυκτιπόλοις to μύσταις, is Heraclitean, and that the rest is Clement's summary of the Heraclitean passage. In addition, νυκτιπόλοι is, in all likelihood, not a noun but an adjective that is applied to the following nouns: thus, four groups of people are active during the night, three groups of performers of Bacchic mystery rites (the βάκχοι being perhaps a special group among the initiates

41 See the contribution of Sarah Iles Johnston in this volume.

42 Eumenides: Henrichs 1984:255–268, Graf 1980:209–221; water: Bremmer 1999:8.

43 Herodotus 7.43.

44 Ferrari 2011a:82.

45 Heraclitus 21 B 14 DK.

of Dionysus, more exalted than the simple "bearers of narthex," the λῆναι and μύσται), and a group of religious specialists, the μάγοι, who must belong to the same contemporary Ionian world and, more narrowly, to the same religious background as the three Bacchic groups. Like them, the term μάγος is not intrinsically negative, but is as descriptive as the other three are, despite its Persian origin—but unlike those the term is not Greek but Persian. We thus learn (and I confess my own surprise) of priests in Bacchic mystery cults in Heraclitus' world during the Persian occupation who were called or called themselves μάγοι.

This forces me to rethink the semantics of the three occurrences of μάγος in the fifth century outside Herodotus' ethnographical text. Two cases come from tragedy, Sophocles *Oedipus Rex* 384–386 and Euripides *Orestes* 1494. In the *Orestes*, a servant describes the sudden disappearance of Helen, "through sorcery, the art of the *magoi*, or the secret attack of the gods" (ἤτοι φαρμάκοις | ἢ μάγων τέχναις ἢ θεῶν κλοπαῖς). This passage is fully descriptive; the μάγοι wield supernatural power which humans cannot resist; there is nothing intrinsically negative in the term. The Sophoclean passage is less easy to gauge. Oedipus is angry at Tiresias and abuses him as a false prophet, bought by Creon—"this wizard hatcher of plots, this crafty beggar who has sight only when it comes to profit, but in his art is blind" (μάγον τοιόνδε μηχανορράφον, | δόλιον ἀγύρτην, ὅστις ἐν τοῖς κέρδεσιν | μόνον δέδορκε, τὴν τέχνην δ' ἔφυ τυφλός). Hugh Lloyd-Jones' translation "wizard" begs the question: it might well be that the term is descriptive only and gets is negative force from the adjectives. At any rate, even if negative in itself, the English "wizard" is somewhat beyond the point: Tiresias is a seer, and it is his divinatory profession that is expressed by μάγος. Ἀγύρτης, the second noun, is in itself descriptive as well: he is the priest who "collects contributions." Such priests, however, never belonged to established polis cults but to marginal and often foreign cults; unlike the polis priest, they were itinerant professionals, not citizens serving their community. The contrast with the citizen priesthood must have been enough to give the term a somewhat negative connotation. But again, as with the μάγος, it is the adjective that carries the main weight of Oedipus' revilement.

Finally, there is the attack of the Hippocratic doctor on the people who proposed a religious explanation and a ritual cure for epilepsy, people "like the magicians, purifiers, begging priests and quacks of our own time, men who claim great piety and superior knowledge," ἄνθρωποι οἷοι καὶ νῦν εἰσι μάγοι τε καὶ καθάρται καὶ ἀγύρται καὶ ἀλαζόνες, ὁκόσοι δὴ προσποιέονται σφόδρα θεοσεβέες εἶναι καὶ πλέον τι εἰδέναι.[46] Some of the nouns are derogatory (ἀλαζόνες and, much less if at all negative, ἀγύρται); the others are descriptive:

[46] Hippocrates *On the Sacred Disease* 2.

overall, it is again the context and the following relative clause that convey most of the negativity, not the term in itself. On the other hand, if we disregard the polemical tone and take the claim of religiosity (θεοσεβέες εἶναι) and superior knowledge as defining characteristics of these specialists, we arrive again at a description of religious entrepreneurs that is close to what we can perceive in column xx of the Derveni text.

Thus, these four passages present the μάγος as an itinerant religious specialist who concerned himself with Bacchic initiations that had an eschatological component (Heraclitus), with divination (Sophocles), healing and purification (*On the Sacred Disease*), and with strange supernatural acts (Euripides). With the Derveni μάγοι, these specialists share the concern with the afterlife (col. vi) and, if we assume that the speaker is not very different from the *magoi*, divination (col. v) and initiation into mystery cults (col. xx). We hear at least of one historical seer who combined similar activities with his own: two passages from Old Comedy describe the seer and *chresmologos* Diopeithes as an ecstatic performer (παραμαινόμενος) whose performances comprised dance and the music of tympana;[47] if Diopeithes were not an outspoken enemy of Anaxagoras, he would easily qualify as my candidate for the title of Derveni author.[48] Diopeithes' portrait in Old Comedy recalls both Plato's description of the ἀγύρται καὶ μάντεις and the use which Bacchic initiators and Orpheotelests made of the *tympanon*.[49] We can see a similar constellation inside an Athenian family, with an interesting sociological twist that belies Plato's dismissive description: whereas Aeschines' mother Glaukothea was the high priestess of the ecstatic and cathartic mysteries of a divinity closely related to Dionysus, her brother Kleioboulos was a famous seer rich enough to serve as Athenian general and leave an impressive grave stele.[50]

The healing and cathartic power of the μάγος, by the way, seems to have been fully established in the fourth century: Theophrastus does not hesitate to talk of healing μαγεία,[51] and later Atticist lexica derive the word μάγος from ἀπομάσσειν, "to cleanse ritually"—the very ritual performed by young Aeschines for the clients of his mother; the lexica might reproduce an etymology that goes back to the fourth century BCE. If this is at best ambivalent, it is worthwhile to point out that it was only in this same century that the term μάγος

47 Ameipsias fr. 10 Kock: ὥστε ποιοῦντες χρησμοὺς αὐτοὶ διδόασ' ᾄδειν Διοπείθει τῷ παραμαινομένῳ.; Phrynichos fr. 9: ἀνὴρ χορεύει καὶ τὰ τοῦ θεοῦ καλά.| βούλει Διοπείθη μεταδράμω καὶ τύμπανα;.

48 The sources on Diopeithes appear in Kett 1966: 33 no. 21.

49 See the *Orpheotelestai* in Philodemus *On Poems* 1.181 Janko, and King Ptolemy IV Philopator in Plutarch *Agis and Cleomenes* 54.2 (820D) (τελετὰς τελεῖν καὶ τύμπανον ἔχων ἐν τοῖς βασιλείοις ἀγείρειν); see also Plutarch *Moralia* 60A.

50 See Kett 1966:52 no. 42; the epigram *SEG* 16,193.

51 Theophrastus *Inquiry into Plants* 15.7: the plant moly, used πρὸς τὰ ἀλεξιφάρμακα καὶ τὰς μαγείας.

became negative. The negativity is fully established when the writer of the Pseudo-Aristotelian *Magikos*, presumably a Hellenistic ethnographer, stressed that "the Persians do not practice wizardry," τὴν δὲ γοητικὴν μαγείαν οὐδ' ἔγνωσαν (sc. οἱ μάγοι).[52]

But the Greek conceptualization of the Persian *mágoi* was rather more ambiguous than is suggested by the protest of whoever wrote the Pseudo-Aristotelian *Magikos*. For some, they were indeed priests of another culture, either seen as authoritative, as in Herodotus and Xenophon, or as somewhat uncanny, as in the historian Theopompus, who tells of their power to resuscitate the dead.[53] To philosophers such as Aristotle, they represented an alien but acceptable philosophy whose doctrines could be cited in the same breath as those of early Greek philosophers.[54] To others again, they were simply weird and sexually ambiguous figures; to think that they were not really Greek helped to save one's own identity. On stage, Greeks could relish actors that were called *magōidoi* ("singers in the style of the *mágoi*"). Aristoxenos of Tarentum, a student of Aristotle, describes them as comic actors that performed both male and female parts; Athenaeus, who cites Aristoxenus, describes them thus:

> ὁ δὲ μαγῳδὸς καλούμενος τύμπανα ἔχει καὶ κύμβαλα καὶ πάντα τὰ περὶ αὐτὸν ἐνδύματα γυναικεῖα· σχινίζεται δὲ καὶ πάντα ποιεῖ τὰ ἔξω κόσμου, ὑποκρινόμενος ποτὲ μὲν γυναῖκας [καὶ] μοιχοὺς καὶ μαστροπούς, ποτὲ δὲ ἄνδρα μεθύοντα καὶ ἐπὶ κῶμον παραγινόμενον πρὸς τὴν ἐρωμένην.

> The so-called *magōidós* has hand drums and cymbals and his entire dress is that of a woman. He makes exotic movements and behaves entirely without order, playing either adulterous women and procuresses, or drunken men who during their revelries encounter their paramours.[55]

52 Aristotle fr. 36; the late source, Diogenes Laertius 1.8, ascribes the same distinction to Deinon and Hermodorus, the former a little-known Hellenistic historian from Rhodes, and the latter perhaps a student of Plato.

53 Theopompus *FGrHist* 115 F 64a; he cites the satyr play *Harpalos* (performed ca. 324 BCE at the Dionysia on the river Hydaspes), where this art is ascribed to the βαρβάρων μάγοι (Athenaeus 13.68 [595 D]).

54 Aristotle *Metaphysics* 1091a30 cites the *mágoi* alongside Empedocles, Pherecydes of Syros, and Anaxagoras; in his lost *On Philosophy* fr. 6, he accurately reported on Zoroastrian dualism and regarded the *mágoi* as older than the Egyptians. The *Alcibiades Maior* 122ab (presumably spurious) contains an equally positive opinion on Zoroastrian *mágoi*: they teach the king "the worship of the gods," θεῶν θεραπεία. In his *Republic*, however, Plato has a much poorer opinion of the *mágoi*: in 572e, he talks about the lawless seducers of a morally healthy youth as δεινοὶ μάγοι τε καὶ τυραννοποιοὶ, "dire magicians and tyrant-makers," who encourage his irrational passions. The reference here is either again to the Persian *mágoi* as royal advisers, or to the powerful but evil rhetorical power of the seducers, in a reaction to Gorgias, or to both.

55 Athenaeus 14.14 (621C).

There is more in this description than just ambiguous sexuality. Hand drums and cymbals are the stock instruments of ecstatic cults; no Persian *mágoi* used them, as far as we know, but they were the standard outfit of the Orpheotelests.[56] An average fifth-century Greek met a *mágos* not in the Persian empire, but in a Greek town, as the itinerant priest of Bacchic mysteries who also offered an array of other ritual services, and projected this image on faraway Persia.

In the light of all this, and especially of Heraclitus' testimony, I understand the Derveni μάγοι against Ferrari as religious specialists who might have been first active in the Greek East and who claimed the title of the Persian specialist for themselves.[57] The dialect of the Derveni treatise itself might point to the Greek East as place of composition, although I subscribe to Tsantsanoglou's careful admonition that "some prose authors employed Ionic or mixed Ionic as a literary dialect irrespective of their provenance."[58] Still, as Herodotus shows, the Persian μάγοι were exactly this: independent religious specialists who claimed special knowledge in sacrificial technique and on the interpretation of dreams and omens. It might be that after the Persian conquest of Lydia in 547 BCE enterprising Persian μάγοι began to serve the needs of Greeks and even adapted their ritual repertoire to Greek demands for mystery cults; it might also be that enterprising Greeks claimed the prestige of the Persians for themselves, as Tsantsanoglou has suggested.

We can perceive a similar development among the Etruscan *haruspici*, as a result of the cultural contact between Etruria and Rome. Whereas the Roman state employed only professional *haruspices* who belonged to the established families of Etruria, itinerant *haruspices* from other backgrounds offered their services to whoever wanted them, and incurred the contempt and scorn of upper-class Romans such as the Elder Cato. There is no guarantee whatsoever that these lesser *haruspices* were Etruscans at all, as there is no guarantee that Heraclitus' μάγοι or those of the Derveni Papyrus were Persians.[59]

We can go one step further. In his most exhaustive description of a Persian sacrifice and the role of the μάγοι in it, Herodotus regales us with an unusual detail. Once the victim is slaughtered and its meat (all the meat: the gods get nothing) is cooked and laid out on a bed of herbs, "a μάγος ἀνὴρ who stands nearby sings a theogony, as they call the ritual chant; there are no sacrifices without the *magos*."[60] Herodotus hesitates when it comes to the term θεογονίη

56 Philodemus *On Poems* 1.181 Janko; Plutarch *Agis and Cleomenes* 54.2 (820D); see above n49.

57 This contradicts not just my earlier assumptions but also the construction of Bremmer (2008).

58 Kouremenos, Parássoglou, and Tsantsanoglou 2006:11.

59 See the overview in Briquel 1997:9–50.

60 Herodotus 1.132: παρεστεὼς ἐπαείδει θεογονίην, οἵην δὴ ἐκεῖνοι λέγουσι εἶναι τὴν ἐπαοιδήν· ἄνευ γὰρ δὴ μάγου οὔ σφι νόμος ἐστὶ θυσίας ποιέεσθαι.

and he treats is as if it were a translation from Persian; his hesitation seems to be based on the fact that a ritual chant, ἐπαοιδή—the term also used to designate a healing spell as early as the *Odyssey*—should not have the form of a narrative theogony: the Persians seem to mix literary categories. But of course this is exactly what the Derveni theogony does: it is a theogonical hymn, a ritual song, performed in the course of an initiatory ritual.

Appendix: Heraclitus, Fire, and Persia

Let me end with a final suggestion. Once again, Heraclitus has cropped up, this time as the main witness to the μάγοι as they appear in column vi. Furthermore, Heraclitus's νυκτιπόλοι μάγοι, βάκχοι, λῆναι and μύσται—Bacchic initiates and their initiation priests—must have taken a lively interest in the afterlife: if Heraclitus predicts to them fire after their death, he must somehow turn the tables on them. Clement's patchwork quote seems to make at least this clear, despite its opaqueness: Heraclitus does not just attack mystery rites, he connects them with eschatological beliefs that he himself rejects. Fire must either have been significantly absent from their *post-mortem* hopes, or (much more likely) it must have played a negative and punitive role in their eschatology.

References to fire as a *post-mortem* punishment in Greek or Roman eschatological thinking are relatively rare. (Pyri-)Phlegethon, the underworld river, is mostly a boundary marker, not a place of punishment, although in the *Phaedo* parricides and matricides are annually swept out from Tartaros κατὰ τὸν Πυριφλεγέθοντα, "in the region of the Pyriphlegeton."[61] Diels read the name in a passage from Philodemus' first book *On the Gods* where Philodemus, in good Lucretian manner, talks about human fear as a reason for belief in gods: humans fear gods as the ones who are responsible for the bad things they expect in Hades (δραστικοὺς τῶν κακῶν τῶν ἐν Ἅιδου), because they lead them to the punishing fire (ἐν τούτωι πυρωθησομένους).[62] The crucial word is mostly restored, π̣[υρω]-θησ[ομέν]ους, although the following comparison with Phalaris and his fiery bull makes the restoration highly attractive. The punishment itself is so rare in Greek sources that Diels thought this to be its first attestation in extant Greek literature; "der Syrer Philodem," he speculated in the spirit of his time, might have learned it from "orientalische Gehennavorstellungen."

But there is at least one other, presumably earlier, and certainly very Greek attestation. It appears in a strangely suggestive context:

61 Plato *Phaedo* 114a.

62 Philodemus *On the Gods* I, col. 19, 19–23; see the edition and commentary by Diels (1926).

> Those who have spent their life in evil deeds are brought by the Erinyes through Tartaros to Erebos and Chaos: there is the place of the Unholy Ones [ἀσεβῶν χῶρος] [...] There they are consumed by eternal punishments, gnawed by wild animals, burnt by the torches of the Poinai, suffered every abominable thing.

Thus the final eschatology in the Pseudo-Platonic *Axiochus*, a Platonic or Academic dialogue of disputed but most plausibly Hellenistic date.[63] The eschatology has strong ties to the mystery cults: in the nice part of the underworld, the εὐσεβῶν χῶρος, there is eternal spring, sources of fresh water and flowery meadows, details known from Aristophanes *Frogs* and the Bacchic gold tablets, and "the initiated have some sort of special place," τοῖς μεμυημένοις ἐστίν τις προεδρία. All this, the writer tells us, has been inscribed on two bronze tablets, brought by the Hyperborean maidens to Delos; there, they were read by Gobryes, ἀνὴρ μάγος who visited the island under Xerxes, to protect it from the Persian invasion and who is Socrates' witness for this eschatological narrative.[64] That is: we are dealing with yet another text that is connected, if not with Orpheus, at least with an Apolline background, and told by a μάγος. Moreover, the situation of the entire small dialogue is suggestive: Socrates talks to old Axiochos, who is on the brink of death and needs some comfort, since he is tormented by fear. Comfort comes to him from a philosopher who tells a mystery tale revealed to him by a μάγος.

One cannot but wonder, on several levels. Since the Derveni Papyrus did not simply serve to kindle the pyre, its text was supposed to bring some comfort to the nobleman burnt and buried there. Sarah Iles Johnston treats some of the fears he might have had in her contribution to this volume. There might have been others: I wonder whether the dead Macedonian was as afraid of the fire in the beyond as was the Athenian Axiochus, Alcibiades' uncle and thus his social equal. If so, he had found comfort in the rites performed by a Bacchic μάγος and a book written by one of them with an ambitious intellectual outlook, destined to convey this sort of comfort through the correct explanation of the rituals and of Orpheus' theogonic hymn.

63 Plato *Axiochus* 371d–e. For a translation with a useful introduction see Hershbell 1981. The dates range from "not long after Plato's life-time" (Wycherley 1961:160) to "nach Karneades" (Müller 1975:296n6, 328); Guthrie (1978:393–394) cautions against a late date and points to the traditional eschatological motives that the dialogue shares with the Orphic gold tablets.

64 On the strange bronze tablets Guthrie 1978:396.

Bibliography

Arena, R. 1994. *Iscrizioni greche arcaiche di Sicilia e Magna Grecia, III: Iscrizioni delle colonie euboiche*. Milan.

Bernabé, A. 2007. *Musaeus, Linus, Epimenides, Papyrus Derveni · Indices. Poetae epici Graeci: Testimonia et fragmenta*, pars II, fasc. 3. Berlin.

Bremmer, J. N. "Paradise: From Persia, via Greece, into the *Septuagint*." In *Paradise Interpreted: Representations of Biblical Paradise in Judaism and Early Christianity* (ed. Gerard P. Luttikhuizen) 1–20. Leiden.

———. 2008. "Persian Magoi and the Birth of the Term *Magic*." In *Greek Religion, the Bible, and the Ancient Near East*, 235–247. Leiden.

Briquel, D. 1997. *Chrétiens et haruspices: La religion étrusque, dernier rempart du paganisme romain*. Paris.

Burkert, W. 1968. "Orpheus und die Vorsokratiker: Bemerkungen zum Derveni-Papyrus und zur pythagoreischen Zahlenlehre." *Antike und Abendland* 14: 93–114 [= Burkert 2006: 62-88].

———. 1980. "Neue Funde zur Orphik." *Informationen zum Altsprachlichen Unterricht* 2/2:27–42.

———. 1986. "Der Autor von Derveni: Stesimbrotos Περὶ Τελετῶν." *Zeitschrift für Papyrologie und Epigraphik* 62:1–5 [= Burkert 2006:89–94].

———. 1997. "Star Wars or One Stable World? A Problem of Presocratic Cosmogony (PDerv Col. XXV)." In Laks and Most 1997:167–174 [= Burkert 2008: 35–42].

———. 1998. "Die neuen orphischen Texte: Fragmente, Varianten, Sitz im Leben." In *Fragmentsammlungen philosophischer Texte der Antike* (ed. W. Burkert and L. Gemelli Marciano) 378–400. Göttingen [= Burkert 2006:47–61].

———. 2006. *Kleine Schriften*, 3: *Mystica, Orphica, Pythagorica*. Ed. Fritz Graf. Göttingen.

———. 2008. *Kleine Schriften*, 8: *Philosophica*. Ed. Th. A. Szlezák and K.-H. Stanzl. Göttingen.

Calame, C. 2005. *Masques d'autorité: Fiction et pragmatique dans la poétique grecque antique*. Paris.

Diels, H. 1926. *Philodemos, Über die Götter*, Erstes Buch. Abhandlungen der Preussischen Akademie der Wissenschaften 1915, no. 7. Berlin.

Ferrari, F. 2010. "Democrito a Derveni? PDerv. col. 4, 1–6." *Parola del Passato* 371: 137–148.

———. 2011a. "Rites without Frontiers: Magi and Mystae in the Derveni Papyrus." *Zeitschrift für Papyrologie und Epigraphik* 179:71–83.

———. 2011b. "Frustoli erranti: Per una ricostruzione delle colonne 1–3 del Papiro di Derveni." In *Papiri filosofici: Miscellanea di Studi* VI (ed. M. S. Funghi) 39–54. Florence.

———. 2012. "Derveni Papyrus. F. Ferrari Edition." CHS-iMouseion Project. http://nrs.harvard.edu/urn-3:hul.eresource:Derveni_Papyrus_FerrariF_ed_2012.

Graf, F. 1980. "Milch, Honig und Wein: Zum Verständnis der Libation im Griechischen Ritual." In *Perennitas. Studi Angelo Brelich*, 209–221. Rome.

———. 2009. "Serious Singing: The Orphic Hymns as Religious Texts." *Kernos* 22:169–182.

Graf, F., and S. I. Johnston. 2013. *Ritual Texts for the Afterlife*. London.

Guthrie, W. K. C. 1978. *A History of Greek Philosophy*, 5: *The Later Plato and the Academy*. Cambridge.

Henrichs, A. 1984. "The Eumenides and Wineless Libation in the Derveni Papyrus." In *Atti del XVII Congresso Internazionale di Papirologia (Napoli, 19-26 maggio 1983)*, 255–268. Naples.

Herrero di Jáuregi, M., ed. 2011. *Tracing Orpheus. Studies of Orphic Fragments in Honor of Albert Bernabé*. Berlin.

Hershbell, J. P. 1981. *Axiochus*. Chico, CA.

Janko, R. 2008. "Reconstructing (Again) the Opening of the Derveni Papyrus." *Zeitschrift für Papyrologie und Epigraphik* 166:37–51.

Kapsomenos, S. G. 1964. "Ὁ Ὀρφικὸς πάπυρος τῆς Θεσσαλονίκης." *Archaiologikon Deltion* 19:17–25.

———. 1964/65. "The Orphic Papyrus Roll of Thessalonika." *Bulletin of the American Society of Papyrologists* 2:3–12.

Kett, P. 1966. *Prosopographie der historischen griechischen Manteis bis auf die Zeit Alexanders des Grossen*. Erlangen-Nürnberg.

Kouremenos, Th., G. M. Parássoglou, and K. Tsantsanoglou, eds. 2006. *The Derveni Papyrus, Edited with Introduction and Commentary*. Florence.

Laks, A., and G. Most, eds. 1997. *Studies on the Derveni Papyrus*. New York.

Müller, C. W. 1975. *Die Kurzdialoge der Appendix Platonica*. Munich.

Obbink, D. 1997. "Cosmology as Initiation vs. the Critique of Orphic Mysteries." In Laks and Most 1997:39–54.

Ricciardelli, G., ed. 2000. *Inni Orfici*. Milan.

Richardson, N. J. 1974. *The Homeric Hymn to Demeter*. Oxford.

Riedweg, Chr. 1993. *Jüdisch-hellenistische Imitation eines orphischen Hieros Logos: Beobachtungen zu OF 245 und 247 (sog. Testament des Orpheus)*. Tübingen.

Russell, J. R. 2001. "The Magi in the Derveni Papyrus." *Nâme-Ye Irân-e Bâstân: International Journal of Ancient Iranian Studies* 1:46–56.

Rusten, Jeffrey S. 1985. "Interim Notes on the Papyrus from Derveni." *Harvard Studies in Classical Philology* 89:121–140.

Tsantsanoglou. K. 1997. "The First Columns of the Derveni Papyrus and Their Religious Significance." In Laks and Most 1997:93–128.

Wycherley, R. E. 1961. "Peripatos: The Athenian Philosophical Scene I." *Greece and Rome* 8:152–163.

5

Divination in the Derveni Papyrus

Sarah Iles Johnston
The Ohio State University

IN THIS PAPER I WILL LOOK AT COLUMN V OF THE PAPYRUS and then, more briefly, at column VI, in hopes of better understanding two issues. First, in what sorts of divinatory practices did the author of the Derveni Papyrus (hereafter the "Author") engage, and what did he imagine those practices to accomplish? And second, what did he mean when he complained that other people disbelieved in (ἀπ̣ιστοῦσι) or misunderstood (ἀμα̣[θίη) what divination had to offer?[1]

Let me clarify one thing at the outset. I will be using the word "divination" in a broad sense here: I define it as the acquisition of knowledge humans would not otherwise have, through a variety of methods. Likewise, I define "diviner" as anyone who practices one of these methods, from enthused mouthpieces such as the Pythia to dream diviners to interpreters of omens and readers of entrails. Later in the paper, I will briefly discuss the question of who the Author of columns V and VI is, in the sense of what sorts of rituals he included in his repertoire, but for the moment I will assume only, as most of us have,[2] that the Author was an independent ritual practitioner who could operate as a diviner, an initiator, and perhaps other things as well, and that in our papyrus, among other things, he was trying to clarify for his audience the significance of some of the rituals that he offered.

The first question we need to ask about column V is: who is the "we" of the phrase "for them *we* enter the *manteion* to enquire" (αὐ̣τοῖς πάριμεν̣[εἰς τὸ

1 Throughout this paper, unless otherwise noted, I will use the text of Kouremenos, Parássoglou, and Tsantsanoglou (2006).

2 Tsantsanoglou (1997); West (1997; 1983); Janko (1997) draws a parallel with Empedocles; Betegh (2004:78–83) leans towards the possibility that he was a *magos*. Henrichs (1984) is against these interpretations; he thinks the author is an anti-Orphic. Obbink (1997) is also cautious on the question although he notes that a firm case against the Author being a practitioner is yet to be made. Kouremenos (2006:45–58) reviews all previous discussions and leans towards the conclusion that he was not a practitioner.

μα]ṿτεῖον ἐπερ̣[ω]ṭήσ̣[οντες]) in line 4? Theokritos Kouremenos, in his commentary to the new edition, has already pointed out that Herodotus uses the phrase πάριμεν εἰς τὸ μαντεῖον of the Pythia entering the Oracle at Delphi, and that Euripides uses a similar phrase. In other authors we find variations such as κάτεισιν εἰς τὸ μαντεῖον.[3] All of these reflect the fact that, before the Pythia became inspired, she entered a physically discrete space that had been dedicated to the purpose. In other words, it seems that the "we" in πάριμεν εἰς τὸ μαντεῖον are people similar to the Pythia insofar as they operate out of one or more institutional oracles.[4]

This brings us to a problem: the Pythia and individuals like her did not also operate, as far as we know, as independent diviners, much less as private initiators, which are two aspects of what most of us assume our Author did. This is not to say that the two types of diviners opposed one another. Myth made independent diviners such as Calchas and Mopsus the founders of oracles, and certain families of *manteis* were historically affiliated with oracles: the Iamids were connected with the oracle of Zeus at Olympia, for instance.[5] Oracles sometimes recommended the services of independent diviners such as Epimenides, who at the advice of Delphi was brought in by the Athenians to solve the problems they suffered after the Cylonian affair. Independent diviners, moreover, sometimes recommended that their clients consult Delphi. Indeed, Plutarch says that it was the local *manteis* who told Athens to enquire at Delphi when they could not solve the Cylonian problem themselves.[6] So, there could be cooperation between institutional oracles and independent diviners but nonetheless, as far as our sources indicate, independent diviners never also served at institutional oracles in the sort of role that the Pythia did.[7]

Our Author goes on to mention two other sorts of divination: divination through dreams, in line 6, and, in line 7, what Tsantanoglou in 1997 and subsequently Kouremenos, in the commentary to the *editio princeps*, have interpreted to mean "omens" or "portents": ἄλλα πράγματα.

3 E.g. Plutarch *The Oracles at Delphi* 397a and *Obsolescence of Oracles* 438b.

4 The verb ἐπερωτάω, found in line 4 of col. V, is also common in descriptions of making enquiries at institutional oracles.

5 For details on these and similar stories, see Johnston 2008:81–82, 94, 128.

6 Epimenides: Parke and Wormell 1956: no. 13 = Fontenrose 1978: no. Q65 = Diogenes Laertius 1.10.110; cf. Plutarch *Solon* 12, Plato *Laws* 642d4–643a1 and Jacoby at *FGrH* 457F4 (esp. 4e: Clement of Alexandria *Protrepticus* 2.26.4). Discussion at Johnston 2008:119–125.

7 The reasons for this are obvious: institutional oracles took care to keep their diviners isolated, away from potentially corrupting influences, for the duration of their terms of service. And at most oracles, official business kept the diviner busy; he or she did not have time to freelance. Even if the Pythia gave forth inspired oracles only one day a month, she participated in divination by lot on other days, for instance.

Both dream interpretation and the reading of omens are techniques characteristic of independent diviners. Putting that observation together with the Author's reference to institutional oracles in lines 3 through 5, I would interpret the fragmentary statements that open column V as what remains of a generalizing statement. Our Author is not talking only about himself and people just like him when he uses the first-person plural. Rather, what he means to express is that humans have available to them a *variety* of methods for learning things that they would not otherwise know—including methods that the Author does not practice himself as well as some that he probably does—but that *all* of this divinatory effort is wasted because people either do not understand completely what divination tries to convey, or do not believe it, in spite of the efforts of experts such as himself.

More specifically in this case, as becomes clear as the column continues, people do not understand or believe what diviners can teach them about the "horrors of Hades" (Ἅιδου δεινά). What are these horrors? And what questions are people asking during divinatory enquiries that leads to their revelation?

Let us start with the second issue. We seem to have the beginning of a question that people would ask an oracle in line 5: that is, whether it is *themis* (εἰ θέμις) to do something—we are missing the rest of the phrase. Kouremenos considered the phrase puzzling in this context because he found virtually no evidence for use of the phrase εἰ θέμις or cognates within our records either of questions that were asked of oracles or of the answers that they received. (The more common way of making an enquiry was to ask whether something was ἄμεινον or λώιον or both.[8]) The only instance that Kouremenos could cite for the use of εἰ θέμις in an oracular context comes from Porphyry's *On Abstinence*: Apollo tells a certain *episkopos* that it is not *themis* to sacrifice sheep unless they first have nodded their heads in assent.[9]

But we can, in fact, add a few more instances in which *themis* or its cognates appear in oracular questions or answers. In a fragment of another Apolline oracle, quoted by Porphyry in his *Philosophy from Oracles*, Apollo tells the listener to sacrifice animals "in the proper way" (ὡς θέμις ἐστί).[10] In a first-century C.E. oracle that may be from Didyma, Apollo instructs his listeners about whom it is proper (θέμις ἐστί) for them to allow to enter the *anaktora* of Athena.[11] Somewhat similarly, in another Didymean oracle from the third century, Apollo says that it is "proper for him to give the enquirer an oracle" ([τῷ χρῆσαί μ']

8 See Plato *Laws* 828a.

9 Parke and Wormell 1956: no. 537 = Fontenrose 1978: no. L147 = Porphyry *On Abstinence* 2.9.

10 Fr. 314 Smith line 24 = Eusebius *Praeparatio evangelica* IV.9.

11 Text at Wörrle 1990:19–58 = *SEG* 40 (1990) no. 956 = *SGOst* I (1998) no. 01/23/02; discussed by Busine (2005:169 and 182–183).

εἰσαῦθις ἀνειρομένῳ θεμι[τόν σοι]).[12] As Busine notes, uses of *themis* and its cognates in these and other Apolline oracles suggest that the words of the god, as conveyed through oracles, are in conformity with established law or custom, or are of parallel significance. This should not be too surprising: the word *themis*, after all, means both "law or custom" and, especially in the plural, "oracular utterance." Themis herself was worshiped at oracular sites and mythologically credited with having run them at early stages of their existence.[13] Oracles, laws, and custom, in other words, shared the important job of informing people how to act properly, as well as to their own benefit.

It must also be remembered that there are numerous instances in which we do not have the exact phrasing of either the question asked of an oracle or the reply that it gave, especially in cases in which the enquiry has been embedded in a narrative source. If we had more examples of exactly what was asked and exactly what was answered, we might find yet other uses of *themis* or its cognates in oracular settings. Certainly, we know that the Delphic Oracle was credited with resolving a number of issues that, like those mentioned above, would be better described as issues of *themis*—that is, of whether something was *proper* to do—than as issues of whether something was *profitable* to do. To exemplify this, two cases can be used, in neither of which our source provides the specific words of the question posed to the oracle.

The first case comes from Herodotus. Cleisthenes wanted to throw the hero Adrastus out of Sicyon—that is, Cleisthenes wanted to abolish Adrastus' long-standing cult within the city. It is possible to imagine that the formal question that Cleisthenes put to the oracle included a phrase built around the word *themis*—something such as "Is it *themis* to abolish Adrastus' cult?" or "Is it *themis* to remove Adrastus' remains beyond the borders of the city?"[14]

My second case also involves Sicyon. Plutarch tells us that in the late third century, the Sicyonians wanted to bury the corpse of their statesman Aratus within their city walls, in spite of a long-standing custom (*nomos*) against intramural burial and also in spite of, Plutarch says, local superstition (*deisidaimonia*) against such a thing. In other words, intramural burial contravened what was understood to be *themis*. We might imagine that the formal question put to

12 *I.Didyma* 277 = Rob. D-56 = Fontenrose 1978:29 = *SGOst* I (1998) no. 01/19/10; text and discussion in Busine 2005:169 and 181–182. Cf. also a second-century oracle from Claros to the citizens of Kaisareia Troketta, which enjoins them to carry out Apollo's orders "in accordance with the law [or custom]": κατὰ τεθμόν: Buresch 1889:8–9 = *IGR* IV 1498 = Rob. C-14 = Merkelbach and Stauber 1996: no. 8 = *SGOst* I (1998) no. 04/01/01.

13 See Johnston 2008:57–60.

14 Parke and Wormell 1956: no. 24 = Fontenrose 1978: no. Q74 = Herodotus 5.67.2. Apollo withheld his approval.

Delphi was something such as "Is it *themis* to bury Aratus' body within the city walls?"[15]

Column V might have discussed something similar. The Author seems to be complaining that divinatory experts know what the horrors of Hades are and that some of these experts, at least, enter *manteia* to ask whether it is proper to do certain things in connection with them, but that ordinary people persist either in disbelieving part or all of what the experts subsequently tell them or in misunderstanding it.

Exactly what it was that was questionably *themis* in this case must remain open, although my own hunch is that whatever followed εἰ θέμις either was very general, expressing the *sorts* of things that the experts might be expected to ask, such as "Is it proper to contravene our burial customs?," or was a specific question that exemplified the larger category, such as "Is it proper to leave bodies unburied?" Not being a papyrologist, I cannot go further in suggesting phrases that would fit the lacuna. But in any case, what I want to emphasize is simply that issues of *themis* are not out of place at oracles—indeed, they are very much at home.

I will return now to a question I posed above: what are the "horrors of Hades" that divination reveals? Scholars have tended to assume that they are the horrors that await the souls of people who have not been initiated: wallowing in mud or carrying water in a sieve, for example. This is understandable, given that the papyrus interprets an Orphic poem and Orpheus was known as a poet who described the fate of the soul in the afterlife and what to do about it.

But as Kouremenos has noted in his commentary, oracles were virtually never asked what the afterlife was like. He found one exception—according to Porphyry, Amelius enquired at an oracle about where the soul of Plotinus had gone after death.[16] There is another exception from Didyma, where a man named Polites enquired in the late second century CE about what happened to souls after death.[17] But both of these oracles are from a late period, when questions of a theological nature were more frequently being asked of oracles. The probability that during the fourth century BCE any of the oracles for which we have good evidence—Delphi, Dodona, Claros, Didyma—provided information about what awaited the souls of people who had not been initiated is virtually

15 Plutarch *Life of Aratus* 53.2 = Parke and Wormell 1956: no. 358 = Fontenrose 1978: no. Q235. Apollo gave his approval.

16 Parke and Wormell 1956: no. 473 = Fontenrose 1978: no. H69 = Porphyry *Life of Plotinus* 22.

17 Polites at Didyma: Lactantius *Divine Institutes* 7.13 = *Theosophia Tubingensis* 37; cf. Fox 1986:192–193; Busine 2005:213–214. Apollo replied, "While the soul is still in the body, it tolerates the pains that cannot hurt it. When the body fades and dies, the soul ranges freely through the air, ageless, forever unwearied. For this is the ordinance of divine providence."

nil. Moreover, to turn to the other divinatory method specifically mentioned by our Author, we have no record of dreams indicating what would happen to souls in the afterlife, or how they should prepare for it, either.[18]

So, we are left with two choices. First, we could choose to imagine that there were divinatory specialists, as represented generally by the first-person-plural subject in column V, who worked out of one or more oracles different from any we now know about, specializing in information about the fate of the individual soul in the afterlife and what could be done about it. The Oracle of Orpheus on Lesbos might be a tempting candidate, were it not that what little we hear about it comes only from Philostratus and that Philostratus tells us it was used as a local alternative for those who did not wish to travel to Delphi, Dodona, or other oracles in mainland Greece. In other words, it marketed itself as offering the same services as these others did.[19]

Our second choice is to assume that the oracles, dreams, and portents concerning Hades to which our Author refers gave information of a different kind from what most scholars have presumed—not about the potentially horrible postmortem fates of the people who were in the Author's audience, but about something else of a horrible nature that was happening in Hades, or something horrible arising *out of* Hades.

And in fact, the institutional oracle for which we have the fullest record, that at Delphi, provided a lot of information about a particular sort of horror connected with Hades. From early times till late, Delphic oracles reported on the anger of souls who were already in Hades, and how that anger could in turn affect the living.[20]

These oracles I am talking about, at least according to the longer narratives in which most of them are embedded, were precipitated by people going to Delphi to find out why terrible things were happening—why their city had been beset by plague or famine, why the local women were sterile, or why some other disaster had struck them—even, in one case, why they kept losing at the Olympic Games. According to the pattern common in these stories, Apollo tells them that the disasters are due to the anger of one or more ghosts. Usually, Apollo goes on to explain *why* the ghosts are angry (they are murder victims, or their bodies have been left unburied, or they feel that they deserve a hero cult that has not yet been given to them). I collected all such Delphic oracles in an article I published several years ago; they comprise just over 10 percent of our corpus.

18 The closest we come is Er's out-of-body experience, but neither Er himself nor Plato calls that a dream, whatever Cicero chose to make of it. The standard way of conveying such information was through the inspired words of poets such as Orpheus.

19 Philostratus *Life of Apollonius* 4.14 and *On Heroes* 28.9.

20 Johnston 2005.

I offer just a few examples here to illustrate the way that most of the stories run.

In a case I have already mentioned, Apollo told the Athenians to end a plague and other disasters by calling in Epimenides to lay the ghosts of those who had been murdered at the altars of the Semnai Theai. In another instance, the inhabitants of Caphyae in Arcadia were told that they could stop a spate of miscarriages by burying the bodies of children whom they had stoned after the children had blasphemed Artemis, and then establishing a cult to the dead children.[21] Similarly, Delphi told the Ephesian tyrant Pythagoras that he could stop a plague in *his* city by burying the corpse of a girl whom he had murdered and establishing a cult to her.[22] Apollo told the people of Delphi to end a plague by propitiating the ghost of Aesop, whom they had murdered.[23] To get back to that case of local pride and sporting disaster: Apollo told the Achaeans that the reason they repeatedly lost at the Olympics was that they had failed to establish a cult for a dead athlete named Oibatas. They erected a statue of him at Olympia and started to win again.[24] And to end with a famous literary instance of the pattern: when the Thebans were beset by plague, famine, and sterility, the oracle told them to seek out the murderer of Laius and set the matter straight.[25]

These cases and many others indicate that the Delphic Oracle repeatedly sent the message that the dead could and would make life miserable for the living until the living made things better for the dead: there were horrible things in Hades and they could make things horrible for those who dwelt above ground as well. Of course, I am relaying the pattern to you in the same way as our sources usually narrate it. That is: first, disaster strikes; then, puzzled people go to Delphi to ask what the cause is; and finally, they are told that certain ghosts are angry and must be propitiated. We must assume that, in reality, the enquirers often already suspected what Delphi's answer would be—that is, we must assume that they went to the oracle with some expectation of being told that a particular local scandal of either the recent or the distant past had precipitated the current problem. It may even be that the enquirer had already been told what the problem was through a local form of divination and wanted Delphi to confirm it. Pindar provides an example of this when he says

21 Children stoned to death in Caphyae: Parke and Wormell 1956:385 = Fontenrose 1978: no. L91 = Pausanias 8.23.7.

22 Pythagoras the Tyrant: Parke and Wormell 1956: no. 27 = Fontenrose 1978: no. Q82ng = Suda s.v. *Pythagoras Ephesios* (Ael. fr. 48 = Baton *FGrH* 268 F 3).

23 Aesop and the people of Delphi: Parke and Wormell 1956: no. 58 = Fontenrose 1978: no. Q107ng = Herodotus 2.134.4.

24 The Achaean losing streak at the Olympics: Parke and Wormell 1956: no. 118 = Fontenrose 1978: no. Q169g = Pausanias 6.3.8.

25 Sophocles *Oedipus Rex* 95–141.

that Pelias first learned that the ghost of Phrixus wanted to be brought home from Colchis, where his body had been buried, when the ghost cried out to him in a dream. Pelias—not being sure whether this was right—sent to Delphi to ask whether the dream should be heeded and Apollo confirmed Phrixus' request—thus precipitating the voyage of the Argo.[26]

In any case, whether it be through knowledge of earlier dreams and portents, knowledge of local affairs, or simple common sense, if the Delphic Oracle operated like most oracles in most cultures do, then its officials probably had a good idea, consciously or subconsciously, of the answers that would be suitable for a given enquiry. They must have known, for example, that the Orchomenians would accept a command to bring home Hesiod's bones if they wanted to end a plague,[27] and that the Tegeans, in turn, would accept a command to establish a hero cult to their ancestor Skephros if they wanted to end a famine.[28]

But having brought up Pelias' dream, let me pause for a moment and consider the broader topic of dreams. Our Author mentioned them in a manner suggesting that they could also make known the discontent of the dead. To give another famous example: we see this in the *Choephoroi*, where professional dream interpreters tell Clytemnestra that her nightmares were caused by Agamemnon's wrath. "Those under the earth hold a grudge and are angry with those who killed them."[29] According to a later passage in the same play, Apollo told Orestes that if he failed to avenge Agamemnon, not only would he get disgusting skin diseases, but the dead would send nocturnal "madness" and "fear" (*lussa* and *phobos*) upon him—really bad dreams, in other words.[30]

Finally, to take up the third type of divination mentioned in column V—ἄλλα πραγμάτα, omens or portents—we can find cases that fit the pattern as well. In the *Antigone*, for instance, Tiresias says that he has been given signs (σημεῖα) that something is awry between the world of the living and the world of the dead. First, he sat at a special place that was dedicated to divining by birds—the παλαιὸν θᾶκον ὀρνιθοσκόπον—and heard bird cries like none he had ever heard before, mad and inarticulate. Then, he tried to sacrifice but the "omens of the rites failed,"[31] as he put it. As he goes on to explain, all of these signs indicate that Creon must "yield to the dead" (εἶκε τῷ θανόντι). A second example comes from Aelian's *Historical Miscellany*: a fountain of blood erupted in the temple to

26 Pindar *Pythian* 4.156–164.

27 The bones of Hesiod: Parke and Wormell 1956: no. 207 = Fontenrose 1978: no. L42 = Pausanias 9.38.3.

28 Hero cult for Skephros: Parke and Wormell 1956: no. 566 = Fontenrose 1978: no. L154 = Pausanias 8.53.3.

29 Aeschylus *Choephoroi* 37ff. The same sequence plays out in Sophocles' version of the story.

30 Aeschylus *Choephoroi* 269ff.

31 Sophocles *Antigone* 998–1022.

Hera in Sybaris. When the Sybarites consulted Delphi, the oracle explained that this reflected the fact that they had murdered a suppliant at Hera's altar.[32]

Let me sum up what I have suggested so far. Drawing on the examples I have just offered and others like them, I suggest that when our Author talks about the "horrors of Hades" that are revealed by oracles or dreams or portents, he means miseries that *those already dead* are suffering, which causes them, in turn, to inflict miseries on the living. But understanding this doesn't solve all of our problems, of course. We need to explore how the Author considered such information about Hades to be relevant to the kinds of rituals that he performed or expected other people to perform, and what disparity might lie between *his* interpretation of the information and that of the ordinary people, who apparently don't heed his advice.

I will start by eliminating some otherwise attractive possible interpretations. Oracles, dreams, and omens about how the already dead were faring in the afterlife could not provide even a rough behavioral model for the living. In stories like those I have been telling you, the dead suffered because of things that were beyond their control: they had been murdered, for example, or had not received the cult they deserved. Nor are we to imagine, I think, that the Author means to suggest to his audience that they all need to assuage *specific* ghosts in the same manner as the oracles and dreams directed: it simply could not have been the case that all of them had committed murder or otherwise offended specific individuals among the dead.

This is not to say that our Author might not have performed, or directed others to perform, rituals that would solve problems such as those the Delphic Oracle described; the sort of practitioner whom most of us envision this Author to be wore more than one hat, and could have been a *psychagôgos* in addition to everything else. Epimenides is an ideal example of such a combination: he was a *mantis*; he visited the Athenians at the Delphic Oracle's recommendation in order to lay troublesome ghosts; while there he established *teletai* for the Athenians and modified their funerary customs; and he even wrote theogonic poetry—the sort of poetry that our Author is interested in.[33] Epimenides, incidentally, shared yet another trait with our Author. According to Clement of Alexandria, Epimenides claimed to be able to purify anyone from any difficulty, whether of the soul or of the body, by means of *teletai, and to identify its cause* (καὶ τὸ αἴτιον εἰπεῖν).[34] Like our Author, Epimenides wasn't content with simply performing

32 The Sybaritic fountain of blood: Parke and Wormell 1956: no. 74 = Fontenrose 1978: no. Q123ng = Aelian *Historical Miscellany* 3.43.

33 Sources for Epimenides above n6.

34 *FGH* 457 4e = Clement of Alexandria *Protrepticus* 2.26.4. Cf. also Plato *Meno* 81a5–c4: "Those who tell it are priests and priestesses of the sort who make it their business to be able to account

rituals; he wanted to understand how the problem they addressed had arisen and why the ritual would work. Another example of the kind of person I am describing is the sort of ritual specialist whom Plato derides at *Republic* 364–365, one who is described as a *mantis*; as being able to erase misdeeds committed by an individual or his ancestors through purification and sacrifices; as being able to deliver those who were already dead from the miseries they suffer as well as to prepare the living for the afterlife; and as crediting his techniques to treatises composed by Musaeus and Orpheus.[35]

But to get back to our Author and his audience of people who didn't understand or believe what they needed to about the horrors of Hades. We start to get an answer as to what they were missing when we look at the next column of the papyrus. There, in the first two and a half lines, we are told that souls can be appeased by prayers and sacrifices and that impeding *daimones* can be fended off by the special songs of the *magoi*. And then perhaps, depending on what reading one accepts for the next bit, we are told that impeding *daimones* and avenging souls (ψυχαὶ τιμωροί) are the same thing. I think that ψυχαὶ τιμωροί is the correct reading here because of what the Author goes on to say in lines 7 and 8: the knobs on the cakes that are offered are innumerable because the souls of the dead are innumerable. The inherent logic is that you must sacrifice enough of something to ensure that everyone who should receive a bit of it does so; ergo, souls of some kind are receiving sacrifice, and the most economical way to understand the whole passage is to assume that the souls to whom the *magoi* offer cakes are the same souls as those mentioned in line 4, in which case ψυχαὶ τιμωροί makes perfect sense.

What did these souls impede? As I discussed in *Restless Dead*, a number of mystery cults, probably including the Dionysiac mysteries, whose promulgation was credited to Orpheus, taught that impeding *daimones* or similarly named creatures could cause two problems. They might show up while someone was being initiated and stop him from completing the ritual successfully, or they might impede an uninitiated soul's safe passage into the Underworld, or the better parts of the Underworld.[36]

For example, in Aristophanes' *Frogs*, Dionysus' passage into the Underworld is threatened by Empousa, a demon whose name is an appellative formed from

---

for the functions which they perform." These priests and priestesses are also credited with the doctrine of metempsychosis and with the idea that one must atone for an "ancient grief" after death in connection with how one's soul returns to the upper world.

35 Betegh (2004:370–372) notes that Empedocles' voice had magical power, he proclaimed oracles, he cured illnesses, he was a *mantis* and a propagator of cathartic and telestic rites, and on one occasion he raised the dead.

36 Johnston 1999:130–139.

the same root as *empodôn*.[37] Demosthenes calls Aeschines' mother an *empousa* when referring to a role she played in a mystery cult dedicated to Sabazius; we can guess that she dressed up as an *empousa* and did something in the course of the rites that threatened to impede initiates.[38] Iamblichus, describing theurgic mysteries, says that initiates who have not properly purified themselves will be confronted by *kaka pneumata* that will be *empodôn* for them.[39] Lucian's satire of a *katabasis* includes a confrontation with the Erinys Tisiphone; one of the characters says that this reminds him of what happens at Eleusis.[40] Threatening *phasmata* appeared during Hecate's mysteries on Aegina—mysteries that were said to have been established by Orpheus, by the way.[41] Plutarch talks about confronting "all kinds of terrible things" (πάντα δεινά) either during initiation into mysteries or after death, if one has not been initiated.[42] Proclus mentions that in the holiest of *teletai*, the initiates are threatened by chthonic *daimones* who attempt to distract them from completing the ritual.[43]

Performing rituals to protect yourself from creatures of the Underworld—who were variously called *empousai, daimones empodôn, kaka pneumata* that were *empodôn, Erinyes,* or *phasmata*—then, was crucial to winning a good afterlife: the kind of afterlife that mystery initiations promised. But *only* within mystery religions was it important, as far as we can tell: we don't hear about it outside of the context of mysteries. It seems to have been one of the innovations that mysteries introduced into eschatology.

One wonders how mysteries justified the idea: as I said above, it simply cannot have been the case that all potential initiates had committed murder or otherwise offended members of the dead. A possible answer is that blood-guilt was contagious. Even if you had committed no murder yourself, you could not be sure that everyone else in your family or town was clean. Given that one might inherit blood-guilt from even distant ancestors, as Plato reminds us in

37 Aristophanes *Frogs* 293.

38 Demosthenes 18.130.

39 Iamblicus *On the Mysteries of Egypt* 3.31, 178.8–16.

40 *Lucian Cataplus* 22.

41 Dio Chrysostom *Orations* 4.90.

42 Fr. 178.

43 Other sources mention more vaguely that something frightening happened to initiates, or was seen by them, during mystery initiations: Aristides 22.3 p. 28 and 41.10 p. 333 (Keil); Demetrius *Elocution* ch. 100; Plutarch fr. 178; Proclis *Theologia Platanica* 3.18 pg. 151 Portus and also *Alcibiades* 340.1. See also the late first-century decree discussed by Clinton (1974:56–57). The words I translate as "frightening" and "shocking" are cognates of *phrikê* and *ekplêksis*. Each is used in several sources. Plutarch refers to *panta deina*, "all sorts of terrible things." On the process as a whole, Clinton 1992:84–87, Graf 1974:126–139, Seaford 1981:254–263, Johnston 1999: 130–139.

the *Phaedrus* and as many myths confirm,[44] a persuasive initiator could present the risk as being high enough to require everyone's attention. In *Restless Dead*, I discussed in some detail the likelihood that contagious blood-guilt was the official reason for requiring participation in the Lesser Mysteries that preceded the Greater Mysteries held at Eleusis.[45]

Not all mysteries were as drawn-out as the Eleusinian, however; only Eleusis, as far as we know, had this two-stage process, and I assume that most mysteries incorporated both purification from blood-guilt and confrontation by an impeding *daimôn*—from which the purified initiate emerged victorious—into the same ritual program. The idea of blood-guilt contagion also underlay many of the stories I mentioned earlier about plagues and famines, of course—it was Oedipus who murdered Laius, for example, but all of Thebes suffered until the score had been settled. Mysteries were taking an old idea and applying it more broadly, and then mysteries were promising to do something about it.

There is a difference, however, between the way that our Author presents these impeding *daimones* and the way that other mysteries present them. Only our Author explicitly identifies them with the souls of the (avenging) dead. This, I suggest, was his own innovation, or the innovation of an exclusive subgroup of initiators amongst whom he counted himself. It was also, I would suggest, what provoked the frustration that the Author expresses in column V. As our Author sees it, the sorts of information about the horrors of the angry dead that people take away from divinatory methods—for example, some ghost is mad and is causing a plague in your city; you must propitiate that ghost to restore the equilibrium—is only part of a larger problem. In his understanding, angry ghosts are much more pervasive sources of trouble; the horrors they can bring go beyond those narrated in the solutions provided by Delphi. The horrors include attacks against not only those who were personally responsible for

44 *Phaedrus* 244d5–245a1: "When grievous maladies and affliction have beset certain families by reason of some ancient sin, madness has appeared among them, and breaking out into prophecy has secure relief by finding the means thereto, namely by recourse to prayer and worship, and in consequence therefore rites [*teletai*] and means of purification were established and the sufferer was brought out of danger, alike for the present and for the future..." Cf. Burkert 1992:66. Cf. Orph. fr. 350 (Bernabé = 232 Kern) = Olympiodorus *On Phaedo* p. 87.13 Norv. where Orpheus describes how Dionysiac initiations bring relief both from the persecutions of "lawless ancestors" (*progonoi athemistoi*) and from the "difficult labors and endless sufferings" that await one in the Underworld.

45 According to myth, these had been established by Demeter for Heracles' sake. He wanted to be initiated at Eleusis, but she was forced to refuse him because he had blood on his hands. Once he had been purified at the Lesser Mysteries, he was free to go on. Representations show Heracles being treated at the Lesser Mysteries with the Fleece of Zeus, which is associated with purification from blood-guilt in other contexts, and it is fairly clear that this object was used on actual initiates during the Lesser Mysteries as well: details at Johnston 1999:132–136.

their miserable situations or people who were closely associated with those who were responsible, but *anyone* who came into striking distance, including people who were being initiated—a process that brought them temporarily closer to the world of the dead—and people who had died without getting initiated. The "horrors of Hades," in other words, include the ψυχαὶ τιμωροί who have become δαίμονες ἐμποδών.

Our Author, then, understands relations between the living and the dead to be in an ongoing state of potential disruption, even when there is no plague or famine or losing streak at the Olympic Games to bring the matter to the immediate attention of the living, and he considers himself a specialist in adjusting those relations. And yet, instead of doing what our Author knows that they should, people are overcome by error—that is, they do not understand or believe what he advocates—or they are overcome by pleasure—and here, I think he is referring to the same sorts of rituals as Plato famously complained of in the passage from the *Republic* that I mentioned earlier, where he said that *agurtai kai manteis* trick not only individuals but whole cities into thinking they are off the hook for both their own sins and those of their dead ancestors once they have participated in what Plato scornfully calls ἡδοναὶ ἑορταί or παιδιᾶς ἡδοναί. Our Author rants against not only ordinary people who refuse to accept the full import of what he thinks divination can teach us about the Underworld but also against fellow initiators who fail to understand matters fully themselves, and therefore pass off simpler, easier rituals than those he advocates and practices himself.

A few words, before I close, about the Eumenides of column VI and the Erinyes of columns I and II. Outside of the Derveni Papyrus, we have only one piece of evidence that equates either the Erinyes or the Eumenides with the souls of the dead. In Aeschylus' *Seven Against Thebes*, the Chorus calls upon the *potnia skia Oidipou, melain' Erinus.*[46] *Pace* Erwin Rohde,[47] this single, poetic passage is not enough on which to build a theory about general Greek notions of the soul, particularly given that all of our other information suggests that both the Erinyes and the Eumenides were normally viewed as independent agents who sometimes interacted with, but were not identical to, the dead. In equating the Eumenides with certain souls of the dead, then, our Author is again innovating both upon popular tradition and upon what other ritual experts said or did. If we were to read into the fragments of column II an equation between souls and Erinyes—which I don't think we can do with certainty, unfortunately—then that would be our Author's innovation as well. Both innovations would fit well with

46 Aeschylus *Seven Against Thebes* 976–977.

47 Rohde 1925:178–180.

the rest of what I have argued our Author does: he explains that the impeding entities that other mysteries talk about are really souls of the dead, and then goes on to explain that entities whom people usually call Eumenides are really the souls of the dead in a happier state.

The sequence of events narrated in column VI, as far as we know it, could be reconstructed as follows, then. The impeding *daimones*, who were liable to cause problems for initiates and who were identified by our Author with the angry souls of the dead, first were approached by ritual experts who assuaged or appeased them with prayers, sacrifices, and incantations that our Author credits to *magoi*.[48] Whether those who performed these rituals identified themselves as *magoi* or merely used techniques they thought had been invented by the *magoi*, I leave an open question.[49] By performing these rituals, the experts paid a penalty (ποινὴν ἀποδιδόντες)—they paid it on behalf of the initiates, I assume—and they thereby changed the impeding *daimones* into something else. (Here I am taking μεθιστάναι of line 3 in the same way as Tsantsanoglou did in his 1997 essay, and as Glenn Most and André Laks did in their translation, rather than adopting the suggestion "remove" that is used by Gábor Betegh, or "drive away" that is used in the newer translation by Tsantsanoglou and Parássoglou.)[50]

We are not explicitly told what the impeding *daimones* changed into, but if the change followed the prayers, sacrifices, and songs, then it was a positive transformation—and thus when we hear a few lines later about "Kindly Ones" or "Eumenides" also being souls, it is most economical to assume that this was the end result. Now the initiates might safely approach these souls on their own, and make additional offerings, as lines 10 and 11 tell us. After this, the papyrus becomes fragmentary, but it may be the case, as Albert Henrichs suggested in 1984, that the initiates went on to make sacrifices to certain unspecified gods.

[48] Notably, the more specific description of offerings in the middle of this column specifies water, milk, and cakes, all of which are found in descriptions of offerings to the dead.

[49] Only one of the many other references to *magoi* in classical sources, so far as I know, suggests any connection to the dead at all: at Herodotus 7.43, the *magoi* help Xerxes make libations and sacrifices to the dead heroes buried at Troy. Herodotus credits the true Persian *magoi* with a variety of functions, including the interpretation of dreams and portents such as eclipses, the propitiation of river gods through sacrifice, and the recitation of sacred theogonies. *Magoi* in Greece similarly had a variety of skills, including the production of drugs and protective amulets and perhaps divination. Xenophon's description of them as "technicians of the divine" (*hoi peri tous theous technitai*) is likely to come close to the common Greek view: they knew a lot about the gods that was hidden from the average individual (Herodotus 1.107–108, 1.132, 7.37, 7.113–114; Euripides *Suppliants* 1108-1110, Plato *Statesman* 280e1–2 and *Laws* 933c6–d1; Xenophon *Cyropaedia* 8.3.11. On the significance of *magos* cf. Graf 1995:32, taking a slightly different approach.)

[50] Tsantsanoglou 1997:110–112. Tsantsanoglou also noted here that the Author uses the noun *metastasis* in col. XV to mean "change."

The pattern makes sense, not only because, as Henrichs noted,[51] it was common practice in many cults to sacrifice to lesser entities before sacrificing to gods, but also because it matches a pattern we know of from other mysteries, where the demons appear and are dealt with before the gods manifest themselves. Iamblichus is most explicit about this point: he says that the arrival of the gods during the mysteries actually helps to vanquish the last traces of the *kaka pneumata* that impede initiates; but it is also hinted at by the fact that in the *Frogs*, Dionysus and Xanthias encounter an *empousa* as soon as they enter the Underworld—before they meet the happy band of initiates or proceed to Hades' palace.

To sum up: like most scholars, I understand the Author of columns V and VI to be a ritual expert who wants to justify the particular techniques that he recommends by explaining what they really mean. In particular, he wants to explain the real identities of the entities to whom he directs his rituals, and why those entities must be given the attention he recommends.

To do so, he draws on a concept that is familiar to everyone: that the angry dead can harm the living. In this sense, our Author is actually preserving, and even valorizing, certain aspects of mainstream religious practices and beliefs. His complaint is only that the average person fails to understand or believe all of the implications, in spite of the fact that those implications are crucial to their postmortem happiness. The Author also draws on knowledge that is specific to mysteries—although it is knowledge that to some degree was shared by non-initiates as well, if Aristophanes and Lucian could satirize it: namely, that some sort of entity is apt to impede initiates during mystery rituals and impede the uninitiated after death.

The Author innovates upon both mainstream tradition and previous mystery practices by combining the two sets of beliefs and practices: that is, by understanding the first group of entities—the angry dead about whom oracles, dreams, and portents inform us—to be the same as the second group—the impeding *daimones* against whom mysteries protect us. And then he innovates again, by arguing that these ghosts who were *daimones* can be transformed—once more, through ritual—into creatures who were traditionally understood to be goddesses, the Eumenides. It is a tightly woven set of connections, each step of which depends not only on the previous step, but also on a highly developed propensity to seek out analogies and relationships that are hidden to others. The final result, here as elsewhere in the Derveni Papyrus, is an idiosyncratic, cerebral religious system that can justify the individual planks of its doctrines with reference to existing beliefs and practices, but which, as a

51 Henrichs 1984.

whole, undoubtedly would have struck someone of average religious disposition as counterintuitive.

We will not see anything quite like it for another five or six hundred years, when the equally cerebral Neoplatonists give birth to the equally idiosyncratic religious system known as "theurgy." And that turn of events, by the way, went hand-in-hand with a huge burgeoning of interest in Orphic theogonies, for alongside their much revered *Timaeus* and *Chaldean Oracles*, the theurgists set the poetry of Orpheus, and then labored intensely to show how these three great sources of theological knowledge were in concord with one another, so that they might better decipher the hidden messages these works contained. What a shame it is that from the most industrious of these interpreters, Proclus, we have inherited a complete *Platonic Theology*, and quite a lot of what he wrote about the *Chaldean Oracles*, but relatively little of what we know to have been his extensive exposition of Orpheus' theogonic poetry. There, if anywhere, we might finally meet the match of our Derveni Author.

Bibliography

Betegh, Gábor. 2004. *The Derveni Papyrus: Cosmology, Theology, and Interpretation.* Cambridge.

Buresch, Karl. 1889. *Klaros: Untersuchungen zum Orakelwesen des späteren Altertums. Nebst einem Anhange, das Anecdoten Χρησμοὶ τῶν Ἑλληνικῶν Θεῶν enthaltend.* Leipzig.

Burkert, Walter. 1992. *The Orientalizing Revolution: Near Eastern Influence on Greek Culture in the Early Archaic Age.* Cambridge, MA.

Busine, Aude. 2005. *Paroles d'Apollon: Pratiques et traditions oraculaires dans l'Antiquité tardive (IIe–VIe siècles).* Religions in the Graeco-Roman World 156. Leiden.

Clinton, Kevin. 1974. *The Sacred Officials of the Eleusinian Mysteries.* Transactions of the American Philosophical Society 64.3. Philadelphia.

———. 1992. *Myth and Cult: The Iconography of the Eleusinian Mysteries.* Skrifter Utgivna av Svenska Institutet I Athen 8, XI. Stockholm.

Fontenrose, Joseph. 1978. *The Delphic Oracle: Its Responses and Operations with a Catalogue of Responses.* Berkeley.

Fox, Robin Lane. 1986. *Pagans and Christians.* New York.

Graf, Fritz. 1974. *Eleusis und die orphische Dichtung Athens in vorhellenisticher Zeit.* Berlin.

———. 1995. *La magie dans l'antiquité gréco-romaine.* Paris.

Henrichs, Albert. 1984. "The Eumenides and Wineless Libation in the Derveni Papyrus." In *Atti del XVII Congresso Internazionale de Papirologia, Napoli, 1983*, 2: 255–268. Naples .

Janko, Richard. 1997. "The Physicist as Hierophant: Aristophanes, Socrates, and the Authorship of the Derveni Papyrus." *Zeitschrift für Papyrologie und Epigraphik* 118:61–94.

Johnston, Sarah Iles. 1999. *Restless Dead: Encounters between the Living and the Dead in Ancient Greece.* Berkeley.

———. 2005. "Delphi and the Dead." In *Mantikê: Studies in Ancient Divination* (ed. S. I. Johnston and P. T. Struck) 283–306. Leiden.

———. 2008. *Ancient Greek Divination.* London.

Kouremenos, Theokritos, George M. Parássoglou, and Kyriakos Tsantsanoglou, eds. 2006. *The Derveni Papyrus, Edited with Introduction and Commentary.* Florence.

Laks, André, and Glenn Most, eds. 1997. *Studies on the Derveni Papyrus.* Oxford.

Merkelbach, R., and J. Stauber. 1996. "Die Orakel des Apollon von Klaros." *Epigraphica Anatolica* 27:1–53.

Obbink, Dirk. 1997. "Cosmology and Initiation vs. the Critique of the Orphic Mysteries." In Laks and Most 1997:39–54.

Parke, H. W., and D. E. W. Wormell. 1956. *The Delphic Oracle, II: The Oracular Responses*. Oxford.

Rohde, Erwin. 1925. *Psyche: The Cult of Souls and Belief in Immortality among the Ancient Greeks*. London.

Seaford, Richard. 1981. "Dionysiac Drama and the Dionysiac Mysteries." *Classical Quarterly* 31:252–275.

Tsantsanoglou, Kyriakos. 1997. "The First Columns of the Derveni Papyrus and Their Religious Significance." In Laks and Most 1997:93–128.

West, Martin. 1983. *The Orphic Poems.* Oxford.

———. 1997. "Hocus-pocus in East and West: Theogony, Ritual, and the Tradition of Esoteric Commentary." In Laks and Most 1997:81–92.

Wörrle, M. 1990. "Inschriften von Herakleia am Latmos, II: Das Priestertum von Athena Latmia." *Chiron* 20:19–58.

6

How to Learn about Souls

The Derveni Papyrus and Democritus

Walter Burkert
University of Zurich

THE DERVENI PAPYRUS HAS BEEN CALLED the most important discovery for Greek philology in the twentieth century: a burned papyrus scroll from the fourth century BC, one-third of which has been preserved in a carbonized state. The discovery was made nearly fifty years ago, and I myself have been working on this fascinating text for forty-five years. Yet it has been only a few years since a real edition appeared (2006)—and not in Thessaloniki, where the papyrus is kept, but in Italy, thanks to the diplomacy of Maria Serena Funghi.

It was clear from the first fragmentary publication of 1964 (or rather 1965) that this is mainly a commentary on the theogony of Orpheus, based on the philosophy of Anaxagoras and Diogenes of Apollonia—in other words, it is Presocratic. The name of Heraclitus turned up later (col. IV 5). My first study appeared in 1968. I stated, and I think this still holds true, that the "Presocratic" author was writing in about 400 BC and dealing with a sixth-century text. The quotations from the Orphic theogony have laid a new foundation for Orphic studies (comprising fr. 2–18 in Bernabé's *Orphicorum fragmenta* [2004]). My interpretation of this strange yet highly interesting text was published in 2006.

The quotations from the theogony start in column VII. Fragments of the first six columns have successively accumulated, but, because they form the outside of the scroll, they are badly damaged and desperately lacunose. No wonder modern judgments as to this part of the text are widely, or wildly, divergent. Suggestive catchwords to be read are *Erinyes* (cols. I, II, III), *Hadou deiná* ("terrors of the Underworld," col. V), *daimones* (cols. III, VI), *oracles* (col. V), *mystai* (col. VI)—but what does the author say about these? Is he preaching, is he criticizing, is he just reporting? Is he an Orphic initiation priest or even a *magos* himself, is he an "Anaxagorean," a "Presocratic" rationalist, is he kind of a historian? Column IV quotes Heraclitus by name in two famous fragments which are now linked together (B 12; B 94); but what is the point?

Let me first sketch the author's position on the basis of the better-preserved, later columns. I find the author has a concept of "reality," *prágmata* (col. XIII 5), *eónta*, which can be adequately transmitted by speech: an *ónoma* can be "adequate," *prospherés*, or even *prospheréstaton* (col. XVIII 8). This "reality" of our world is described in the terms of Anaxagoras/Diogenes/Leucippus: the world of reality always was there; there is no real *génesis*; but things were mixed, in fine particles (*leptomerés*), dominated by air, which can also be called "god" or "Zeus," or "Intelligence" (*Noûs*); thus there has evolved the structure of our world, and corresponding "names," in accordance with the changing interrelations of real things (*eónta*). The author is quite sure as to his own "knowledge" about reality, and he is looking down at those "many" people who do not know, who misunderstand, who suffer from *amathía*; these people do not know even what they are practicing themselves (col. XX), and they do not know the full meaning of their own words (col. XVIII 5). The author will help his reader to "learn" and "recognize" (*manthánein, ginóskein*).

But what about those catchwords hinting at "underworld," "mysteries," and "*mágoi*" in the earlier columns? I start from column V, where I find at least a few consecutive sentences with clear meaning:

> ... they disbelieve, not recognizing dreams nor the single instances of other realities by which examples they might believe. For overcome by gluttonness and other pleasure, they do not learn or believe. Disbelief and ignorance are the same thing. For if they do not learn or recognize, it is impossible that they should believe, even when seeing...

"Disbelief" recurs in the following line, and "it appears" is what is left from the last.

I presume the author is speaking here in his own name. His insistence is on "learning," "knowledge," and "belief," in contrast to "ignorance" and "disbelief" (*amathíe, apistíe*). People—"normal"—people, fail to acquire knowledge on account of disbelief: the fault is theirs, motivated by an unruly life. In contrast to this, there is a chance for knowledge, through dreams, and by other "examples" or "single facts" (*paradeígmata*). In contrast to this, people may use oracles. This has been mentioned before: people go there to ask, and to ask again, about the "terrors of Hades." These people are disregarding the real sources of "belief."

It is helpful to realize that the author is applying, with slight variation, a sentence of Heraclitus (B 86) about "the Divine" (τὸ θεῖον): "on account of disbelief it escapes so that it is not recognized," ἀπιστίηι διαφυγγάνει μὴ γιγνώσκεσθαι. These are nearly the same words, for the same effect: through ἀπιστίη men block their own chances of knowledge; they should just look instead, and pay attention. We may recall the sentence of Heraclitus B 1, the invective against normal people who "prove to be inexperienced while they do experience" reality as Heraclitus is going to describe it. Evidently, for Heraclitus "the Divine" is there, perhaps everywhere; everything is full of gods, according to the saying of Thales (A 22) which Heraclitus quotes in another place (A 9). The Heraclitus parallel suggests a similar understanding even for our author: there are things to be seen and to be learned which escape many people on account of disbelief.

"Disbelief" ἀπιστία also makes its appearance in a famous section of Plato's *Gorgias* (493a–d),[1] an allegorical interpretation of an underworld myth, probably Orphic. Plato, or Socrates, refers to somebody else who "has spoken" to Socrates; the passage describes pouring water from sieves into a leaky vessel (*pithos*), as certain souls are said to do in the underworld; this recalls, the explanation goes, the futile exertions of a "leaky" soul that, dominated by pleasures, cannot "keep" and retain knowledge, on account of ἀπιστία and forgetfulness, λήθη. This allegorizer changes the mythical Beyond into an image of reality. The word *apistia* has been found odd here (Dodds), but seems to recall Heraclitus B 86 once more, and is now supported by the Derveni text.

Heraclitus, the Derveni text, and the Plato passage form a closely connected group in their treatment of "nonbelieving" and "knowledge." I do not claim that Plato is quoting the Derveni book, but the warning against pleasure makes a strong link. Unfortunately, in the Derveni text what could or should be learned in contrast to disbelief has disappeared in the following lacuna. It should be some part of reality, not immediately obvious but attainable through observation, including dreams, and also by other "examples." It is "the divine" in Heraclitus, and "the soul" in Plato. Remembering those catchwords mentioned above, we conclude that it is about souls even in the Derveni text.

The following column (VI) deals with the rites and teachings of *mágoi*. It leaves us at a loss as to whether these *mágoi* are priests of the Medes and Persians, as in Herodotus, or even Zoroastrians, or else *mages hellénisées*, as treated by Cumont, or even—as has been suggested by Betegh—a group of the author himself and his associates. This text concerns rituals and their explanation concerning "souls." The author mentions "prayer and sacrifices" and states: "The incantation of the magoi can make *daimones* who stand in the way to change place; *daimones* are in the way..."; the following words indicate some correlation between *daimones* and souls; unfortunately the lacuna of eight letters can be filled by different supplements.

1 See E. R. Dodds, *The Greeks and the Irrational*, 1951:209n5.

Here the enlightening parallel comes from the account of Diogenes Laertios (1.6) on the *mágoi*: "*Mágoi* are concerned with the cult of gods (and not with magic), with sacrifices and prayers, claiming that they alone are perceived" by the gods. This is the very privilege on which the Derveni text expounds in more detail: *mágoi* have the power to clear the way toward the gods of some blockade wrought by *daimones*. This shows that the *mágoi* of the Derveni text belong in Greek discussions, following Herodotus; the chapter of Diogenes Laertios probably goes back to Aristotle's *Peri philosophias* and/or to the book *Magikos* ascribed to Aristotle or even to Antisthenes (Aristotle fr. 32–36 Rose). Our author goes on: "Innumerable cakes with many knobs [*poluomphaloi*] they—the *mágoi*—sacrifice, because the souls too are innumerable" (VI 7f.). For confirmation, the author adds: "Initiates [*mystai*] make a preliminary sacrifice to the Eumenides in the same sense as the *mágoi*; for the Eumenides are souls" (VI 8f.). Note that these are no longer the *mágoi*, but other Greek sacrificers compared to, and thus distinguished from, the *mágoi*. Our author states that rituals of *mágoi* and rituals of Greek *mystai* follow the same reason: they deal with a plurality of souls. We have no other testimony of such a ritual naming Eumenides, in the context of Greek mysteries; the closest seems to be the cathartic ritual performed in the grove of the Eumenides in Sophocles, *Oedipus at Kolonos* (465–492). At any rate, the rituals described and explained imply a doctrine, imply knowledge about "innumerable souls": innumerable souls, between human prayer and gods—this is taken as unquestioned reality. It seems to have the full approval of the author.

It is here that our own "disbelief" will start: Shall we "believe" in the reality, nay, activity, of *daimones* and "innumerable souls" whom the *mágoi* handle? For the sake of this, should we even believe in dreams? Doesn't this make the author a sectarian Orphic, or a *mágos* himself, rather than a Presocratic philosopher?

It might be the case that we are victims of our own tradition. The great movement of "enlightenment" more than two hundred years ago has cured us of beliefs in demons, spirits, or specters. Science is to replace superstition. We take the Presocratics to have been activists of Greek enlightenment, elaborating the concept of "nature," *physis*. Hence we see a fundamental divide between the "Presocratic" world picture which we read in the main part of our book, the commentary on Orpheus, based on Parmenides and Anaxagoras, and, on the other hand, the religious ritual of *mágoi* and mysteries with their "belief" about souls and warnings against ἀπιστίη.

Yet I now propose to turn to Democritus, the father of atomism, hence apparently the most modern of all Presocratics. It is just Democritus who developed strange theories about souls and specters. Democritus taught that "in the air there is a great number of those things which he calls mind and soul" (*noûs*, *psyché*: A 106 = Aristotle *On the Soul* 472a6); with every breath, he said, they enter the body of the living being, and they prevent the soul inside from flying out. So there is continuous interaction of an individual life-soul with the air around, which is full of souls (cf. Heraclitus A 6 = Sextus Empiricus, *Adversus mathematicos* 7.129). We are of course reminded of Thales (A 22), "everything is full of gods," changed to "everything is full of souls" (Pythagoreans: Diogenes Laertios 8.32 = VS 58B1a).

Diogenes of Apollonia seems to be relevant here. For him Air, thinking and divine, is also to be found in every single being; this air is "soul and thinking" for the individuum; so every living being is a "particle of god" (VS II 56.3). The Derveni author, with his equation of Air, Zeus, and *Noûs*, is quite close to Diogenes. They could even be identical; Diogenes wrote more than one book.

More special is the theory of Democritus that phantoms, *eidola*, are produced constantly; they spontaneously separate themselves from existing things, they move around, they make us see things, but also have certain effects beyond what enters the eye. *Eidola* is a word for the souls of the dead in Homer; in pictures these *eidola* appear as tiny winged humans; but for Democritus *eidola* are not confined to Hades: they are present everywhere, in all kinds of shapes.

Democritus declared that such *eidola* "dive into the bodies through the pores, that they come up and produce appearances in sleep" (A 77); they thus become visible, or audible, they even indicate future events (B 166). So here we have the activities of dream, and at the same time the hypothesis of the reality of the objects which appear in dream. Note there is no place for fantasy in the atomistic system; even visions and spirits do not come from nothing, they must somehow be the effect of *eonta*. It is also possible, Democritus says, that humans, full of envy, send out *eidola* tinged with evil, who then will affect those who have become the object of envy, and "they will procure trouble and damage for both body and mind" (A 77). He was praying, Democritus said, "to meet with well-sorted [*eúloncha*] *eidola*" (B 166).

Democritus would stay at tombs for the night, we are told (A 1 = Antisthenes in Diogenes Laertius 9.38), to get knowledge through experience, to "test fantasies." This would correspond to "examples by which you could believe" about souls, besides dreams, as our Derveni text puts it.

This is "unlimited superstition," Plutarch cries out (Aemillius Paulus 1.4; not in Diels-Kranz); Plutarch was one of the last who still read Democritus. And moderns will agree: a world of ghosts right in atomism? Democritus apparently starts from traditional tales and certain experiences, which he does not dismiss as nonsense but provisionally accepts, trying to find an *aitologia*. This includes visions, even predictions and prophesies in dreams, and quasi-magical harm, e.g. by envy.

Two titles among the works of Democritus stand out in this perspective: *On Eidola or on Providence*, Περὶ εἰδώλων ἢ περὶ προνοίης (B 10a), and *On What Is in Hades*, Περὶ τῶν ἐν Ἅιδου (B 0c). This book even was famous, as it enters the tales of Democritus among the Abderites (Athenaeus 168B = VS II 130.13). We may speculate that this was transferring the "terrors of Hades" into realities of atoms that act as "souls" in our world.

It may come as a surprise, but we might seriously consider the possibility that the Derveni text is just Democritus' book Περὶ τῶν ἐν Ἅιδου. There is even a scrap of proof for the philologist: right at the end of the text preserved in col. XXVI 14, we read ἐν τῆι συγ..., and this hardly allows another supplement but ἐν τῆι συγγονῆι—we need a female noun beginning with γ κ χ—and behold, this uncommon noun is attested for Democritus: συγγονή· σύστασις. Δημόκριτος (B 137; Hesychius). The meaning σύστασις would apparently fit the context in column XXVI. Add that one sentence of the Derveni text is practically identical with a sentence of Democritus—the universe is being called "Zeus" (XIX 2 = Democritus B 30); and there is a sizable group of testimonies about Democritus and *mágoi* (Diogenes Laertius 9.34 = A 16). Is this the solution to the riddle of the Derveni text?

The answer will be a resounding "no." The world picture as developed by the Derveni author in the commentary, a world established by a ruling god who is "Intelligence," *Noûs*— "The thinking of Zeus has settled what is, what was, what will be" (col. XIX 6)—this is the very picture which Democritus is explicitly fighting; he made fun of the *Noûs* of Anaxagoras (Diogenes. Laertius 9.35). Our author is an Anaxagorean, and he declares the identity or mixture of Zeus and *Noûs* (col. XXVI 1). Democritus tried to do without *Noûs*, relying on a principle of self-organization: see the pebbles at the shore (A 128)—without an intelligent designer.

We shall go on to deal with an anonymous author, somehow between Diogenes and Democritus. The very catalogue of Democritus' writings, or of Antisthenes' writings, and the fairly contemporary collection of Hippocratic writings show what a hubbub of books was already around by that time, about and after 400 BC. Still the example of Democritus is not irrelevant. It shows the possibility of integrating traditional beliefs and practices of religion into the realities of *physis*. Our author is not a missionary of Orphism, whatever that may be, nor a priest of some sect, nor a dealer in underworld ritual, nor a practicing Iranian *mágos*. He is writing on *tà eónta*, the true face of reality, in the wake of Anaxagoras and Diogenes and somehow parallel to Democritus. He is a bit naïve, proud of his own knowledge, and far from Socratic irony, but still an interesting writer among those earlier, pre-Platonic thinkers of Greece.

Editions and Translations

[Anonymous]. 1982. "Der Orphische Papyrus von Derveni." *Zeitschrift für Papyrologie und Epigraphik* 47:1–12.

Bernabé, A. 2007. "Papyrus Derveni." In *Musaeus · Linus · Epimenides · Papyrus Derveni · Indices*, 169–269. *Poetae epici Graeci: Testimonia et fragmenta*, part II, fasc. 3. Berlin.

Betegh, G. 2004. *The Derveni Papyrus: Cosmology, Theology, and Interpretation*. Cambridge.

Burkert, W. 2006. "Orpheus und die Vorsokratiker." *Antike und Abendland* 14 (1968): 93–114 [= Burkert, *Kleine Schriften* III:62–68, Göttingen].

———. 2006. "Die altorphische Theogonie nach dem Papyrus von Derveni." In *Kleine Schriften* III:95–111.

Janko, R. 2002. "The Derveni Papyrus: An Interim Text." *Zeitschrift für Papyrologie und Epigraphik* 141:1–62.

Jourdan, F. 2003. *Le Papyrus de Derveni: Traduit et présenté*. Paris.

Kapsomenos, S. G. 1964–1965. "Ὁ Ὀρφικὸς Πάπυρος τῆς Θεσσαλονίκης." *Archaiologikon Deltion* 19:17–25.

Th. Kouremenos, G. M. Parássoglou, and K. Tsantsanoglou, eds. 2006. *The Derveni Papyrus, Edited with Introduction and Commentary*. Florence.

Readings Different from Those of Kouremenos-Parássoglou-Tsantsanoglou and Bernabé

V 4: παρίμεν, not πάριμεν (πάρεστιν/ἔθος] αὐτοῖς παρίμεν). There is no "we" in the Derveni text.

V 8: ὑπὸ τ[ῆς γαστρι]μαργίης (corresponding to "other pleasure").

The True Story of the Anonymous Edition

The first announcement of the discovery of the papyrus appeared in *Gnomon* 35 (1963): 222–223, by S. G. Kapsomenos, already bearing the subtitle "Ein Kommentar zur Orphischen Theogonie."

Then Kapsomenos published seven columns in *Deltion* 19 (1964): 23–25, which appeared *de facto* in 1965. I read it at the Center for Hellenic Studies in Washington, DC. I had just finished my book on Pythagoreans, in which the distinction between "Presocratic" and post-Platonic texts plays a major role. Martin West had already finished major parts of his book on Orphism; he had shown it to me in 1965. So we both were highly interested in the new text.

I published an analysis of the text, "Orpheus und die Vorsokratiker," in *Antike und Abendland* 14 (1968); I used it also as a test lecture in Zurich in 1968.

I got a photo of a new column from E. G. Turner in London in 1969; this resulted in a paper, "La genèse des choses et des mots," in *Les Études Philosophiques* 4 (1970).

Much more important was that Martin West went to Thessaloniki in the autumn of 1972, and he succeeded in copying, in eleven hours of intense work, what was on exhibition there in the museum. Martin communicated his texts with me. Thus we had four more columns and, in addition, ten smaller pieces. In combination with a photo in the Bulletin of the American Society of Papyrologists I could put together another column. In this form I discussed the papyrus in a seminar at UC Berkeley, in 1977. Decisive progress came in the next year, when Kapsomenos died and his successor, Kyriakos Tsantsanoglou, sent his text to E. G. Turner in London, whence it got to Martin West, and from him to me. An improved and more complete text was brought by George Parássoglou, colleague of Tsantsanoglou, to Turner in 1980. Turner did not prevent this piece from getting photocopied and hence distributed among colleagues and friends; I got my copy from Martin West once more. It was then that I found this situation impossible: Such an important discovery limited to private copying? I talked to Reinhold Merkelbach, editor of *Zeitschrift für Papyrologie und Epigraphik*, and Merkelbach decided to print the text even without authorization from Thessaloniki. Thus the main text has been available since 1982. Turner felt obliged to protest, in *Gnomon* 1982; he knew of course that the text had come from his desk. He declared that the real publication was about to appear. This process was still to last twenty-four years. I think scholarship must be grateful to Merkelbach for his courage.

There was a congress in Princeton, in 1993 (published in 1997); two commentaries appeared, by Fabienne Jourdain in French and by Gábor Betegh in English, before finally, in Florence in 2006, the real edition came out, with Theokritos Kouremenos joining Parássoglou and Tsantsanoglou. The text is now also to be found in the third volume of Bernabé's *Orphicorum fragmenta* (2007).

7

Unlocking the Orphic Doors

Interpretation of Poetry in the Derveni Papryus between Presocratics and Alexandrians[1]

Jeffrey Rusten
Cornell University

Prelude: Reader 1: The Owner of the Derveni Papyrus

The urge to attach an author's name to the Derveni Papyrus is natural for everyone who reads it, which should remind us of why *pseudepigrapha* were so popular in the ancient world. I have my own preferences, admittedly based not so much on a dispassionate consideration of the evidence as on the reason I was drawn to the papyrus myself, an interest in the forms of ancient literary scholarship. Though I have no specific proposal to make, going over the possible identities, both of its author and of its owner, and how we might argue for and against each one is in itself a useful way of evaluating the evidence we now have: it consists of the archaeological context of the find, the form of the book, the contents of the individual columns, and the quotations not only from Orpheus' theogony but also from Heraclitus and, I still believe, other authors as well.

We should really begin with the man whose ashes were found in the grave. Much has been made of the fact that any grave goods connected with Orpheus might well be thought to indicate a sort of book of the dead, and the tendency to connect this book with the complex of Orphic afterlife-doctrine attested by Pindar, Plato, the gold tablets, and other finds has proved overwhelming. The now-lost papyrus found in the right hand of a corpse in a grave at Kallatis on

[1] I am indebted to many at the conference for ideas and corrections (some acknowledged specifically below), but especially to Claude Calame, Albert Henrichs, Sarah Johnston, Franco Montanari, Glenn Most, Dirk Obbink, and Francesca Schironi. Note that in the Greek text cited below I have reproduced the brackets of KPT (for abbreviations see the appended bibliography) but not the dotted letters, which I hope is acceptable, because I do not discuss doubtful readings.

the Black Sea seems to confirm it further, as does the South Italian amphora that shows Orpheus with his lyre standing next to a seated man holding a papyrus scroll.[2] With all this background it seems almost inevitable to take the papyrus itself as a document of personal religious faith. (Note the emphasis on *pistis* in column v.) The contributions of Yannis Tzifopoulos and Dirk Obbink at the conference offered well-informed observations on this subject, and take the arguments *pro* and *con* to a much more sophisticated level.

But I am one of those who find the contents of most of the papyrus difficult to reconcile with this interpretation of its owner, and so I want to press on to other possible reasons for its inclusion in the grave goods. The collection of texts on books in burials by Wolfgang Speyer (1970), as well as studies of papyrus finds in general, reminds us that books buried with a body have multiple possible meanings. They might be the books written by the entombed—Propertius (2.10.25ff) imagines his funeral attended by no one but the books he has written for his girlfriend, whereas a malicious Horace (*Satires* 1.10.63–64) points out that Lucilius wrote far too much, so that his body could be completely burnt by his collected works without the need for any additional fuel. The sarcophagus of the Etruscan Laris Pulenas depicts him proudly holding a copy of his treatise on divination (Bonfante 2006), not really comparable with Greek burials but included here because of its religious connection and because it is more or less contemporary with the Derveni Papyrus.

Books in a grave might also be a prized possession of the owner—I know of no literary documentation of this motive, but people reading and holding scrolls was a favorite theme of Attic art, and pride in books seems likely to be behind the placement of a scroll of Timotheus near a wooden sarcophagus in third-century BC Egypt (MP3 1537, Hordern 2002 62–73), as well as luxury copies of Homer (MP3 642), Alcman (MP3 78) and perhaps Bacchylides (MP3 175) found later in burials. The body in Derveni tomb A was a military man, or, at any rate, greaves and a bridle were found among his grave goods. It may seem odd that such a man owned any books at all, but stranger things can be imagined, as in the fragment of the fourth-century comedy by Alexis, in which Linus tries to convince an unlikely pupil, Heracles, that he should develop a passion for books (Alexis, Linus *PCG* fr. 140):

ΛΙΝ. βιβλίον
ἐντεῦθεν ὅ τι βούλει προσελθὼν γὰρ λαβέ,
ἔπειτ᾽ ἀναγνώσει, πάνυ γε διασκοπῶν
ἀπὸ τῶν ἐπιγραμμάτων ἀτρέμα τε καὶ σχολῇ.
Ὀρφεὺς ἔνεστιν, Ἡσίοδος, τραγῳδίαι,

2 See Betegh 2002, and most especially Bottini 1992.

Χοιρίλος, Ὅμηρος, <ἔστ’> Ἐπίχαρμος, γράμματα
παντοδαπά. δηλώσεις γὰρ οὕτω τὴν φύσιν,
ἐπὶ τί μάλισθ’ ὥρμηκε.
ΗΡ. τουτὶ λαμβάνω.
ΛΙΝ. δεῖξον ὅ τι ἐστὶ πρῶτον.
ΗΡ. ὀψαρτυσία,
ὥς φησι τοὐπίγραμμα.
ΛΙΝ. φιλόσοφός τις εἶ,
εὔδηλον, ὃς παρεὶς τοσαῦτα γράμματα
Σίμου τέχνην ἔλαβες.

Linus: Come up and take
any book you want from here; then,
after looking quite carefully through the titles,
read quietly and at your leisure.
Orpheus is there, and Hesiod, Tragedies,
Choirilus, Homer, there’s Epicharmus, writings
of all kinds, and so you’ll reveal your nature
by what you’re eager for.
Heracles: I’ll take this.
Linus: Show me what it is first.
Heracles: *The Joy of Cooking*,
according to the title.
Linus: You’re a philosopher,
clearly: you pass by so many other writings
and seize the art of Simus.

Linus offers him Orpheus, Hesiod, tragedy, Homer, and Epicharmus—Choirilus here must be a joke—as the authors from which he can choose, and in line 7 he says “that way you will show what you’re like, your predilection.” When Heracles naturally picks up a cookbook, his flattering teacher doesn’t miss a beat, and praises his philosophical choice.

So for characterizing the owner of the book we have a range of possibilities. Even if he was not the author, but an owner-reader, he was in some sense an *addressee* of the book; why did he choose to read it? How did he read it? Was he a religious addressee, who needed to be converted and instructed? Or a philosophical addressee, hoping to find confirmation for his cosmogony in specialized interpretation? Or perhaps a reader of literature who wanted some help when reading the theogony of Orpheus? Or was the mere fact of ownership of such a finely produced book his primary aim?

Reader 2: The Author of the Derveni Papyrus and His Diverse Interests

For the author of the Derveni Papyrus, our primary evidence is of course the contents of his work, and they are not entirely homogeneous. In Figure 1 I give a conspectus of the total contents of the papyrus, with the column number, the section of the theogony discussed, and the author's interpretation and any other texts quoted.

Figure 1. Conspectus of the Contents of the Derveni Papyrus.

COL.	SECTION OF THEOGONY DISCUSSED	COMMENTATOR'S INTERPRETATION
I	?	?
II	?	"Erinyes" mentioned.
III	?	"*Daimones* ... servants of the gods" mentioned.
IV	?	Heraclitus cited (VS 22 b3, B94) on the Erinyes and the sun (εἰ γάρ τι εὔρους ἑωυτοῦ ἐκβήσεται, Ἐρινύες νιν ἐξευρήσουσι).
V		Oracles and dreams.
VI	?	Reasons for offering σπονδαί, χοαί, and πόπανα to the Eumenides.
VII	Cf. [Plato], *Alcibiades* II.147d (below)	Orpheus' poetry is αἰνιγματώδης (cites OF 13, 245.1).
VIII	Zeus succeeds Kronos (Orph. fr. 4–5)	Verses are in hyperbaton.
IX	Zeus succeeds Kronos	τὰ ὄντα were placed in disorder and prevented from recombining.
X	Oracle of Nyx (Orph. fr. 6)	φωνεῖν = λέγειν = διδάσκειν, so that πανομφεύουσαν (epithet of Nyx?) means πάντα διδάσκουσαν.
XI	Oracle of Nyx	a) ἄδυτον (of Nyx) = the depth (βάθος) of darkness; b) χρᾶν ("give prophecies") = ἀρκεῖν "(be sufficient"), with two illustrative quotations (from prose).

Col.	Section of Theogony Discussed	Commentator's Interpretation
XII	?	"Olympos" is not οὐρανός (εὐρύς), but χρόνος (μακρός).
XIII	Zeus hears θέσφατα from Kronos (Orph. fr. 7) Zeus swallows Phanes (Orph. fr. 8)	a) ? "variant reading" with ἀκούσας rejected?; b) αἰδοῖον refers to ἥλιος.
XIV	List of kings: Ouranos (Orph. fr. 10)	a) Kronos is called a child of Helios and Ge because the sun causes τὰ ὄντα to strike against each other (κρούεσθαι); b) Kronos (= Nous) "robbed Ouranos of his rule" by causing things to strike against each other.
XV	List of kings: Kronos–Zeus (Orph. fr. 10)	a) the formation of the sun (cf. XXIV); b) the present state of the *kosmos* (ἡ νῦν μετάστασις) began with rule of Kronos, who is the same as Zeus.
XVI	Creation from Protogonos (Phanes) (Orph. fr. 12–13)	What now exists was not created, but a rearrangement of previously existent matter.
XVII	"Hymn to Zeus" (Orph. fr. 14)	Aer has always existed, but received the name Zeus when the present *kosmos* took shape; he will retain this name until the previous state returns.
XVIII	"Hymn to Zeus"	The πνεῦμα in Aer was named by Orpheus Moira (= φρόνησις τοῦ θεοῦ by common usage) before Zeus received his name.
XIX	"Hymn to Zeus" (Orph. fr. 3, 31, 243, etc.)	a) Zeus (= Aer) is called "everything" because Aer can predominate in everything; b) Moira (Διὸς φρόνησις) determines past, present, and future.
XX	?	Criticism of those who seek knowledge through initiation.
XXI	Birth of Aphrodite?	a) explanation of θόρνη (?); b) μίσγεσθαι = θόρνυσθαι ("mount") = ἀφροδισιάζειν, so that Aphrodite (= Zeus, Harmonia, and Peitho) received her name when the present *kosmos* was mixed together (μιχθέντων).

COL.	SECTION OF THEOGONY DISCUSSED	COMMENTATOR'S INTERPRETATION
XXII	Rhea "becomes" Demeter (cf. Orph. fr. 1019)	Ge, Meter (= Demeter), Rhea, and Hera are the same (with an illustrative quotation from the *Hymns*).
XXIII	Creation of Okeanos (subjugation of Achelôos) (Orph. fr. 16)	Okeanos=Zeus=Aer.
XXIV	Creation of the moon (Orph. fr. 16)	a) the moon is round and ἰσομελής; b) φαίνει refers not to the brightness but to the *revelation* of the moon's seasons.
XXV		a) composition of sun, moon, and stars out of particles with varied heat and brightness; b) cross-reference back to previous account of sun's composition (cf. cols. IV, XV).
XXVI	Zeus mates with his mother (Orph. fr. 18) to produce a child	ἑᾶς = "good" (two parallels in verse); if the poet had intended "his own" he could have written ἑοῖο.

Of the twenty-six columns, the first six (on V and VI see now especially Sarah Johnston's and Fritz Graf's contributions to this volume) discuss belief in oracles and dreams, hostile *daimones*, and Erinyes.[3] But after that all except

[3] I would like to draw attention to a text that might suggest a possible poetic context for cols. III and V as well. In his dialogue *On the Face in the Moon* (ch. 26 [941F–942B], cf. *De defectu oraculorum* ch. 18 [420A]), Plutarch makes one character narrate a story he has heard from a stranger of the island of Cronus to the west, beyond Britain. The story is more or less one of a kind, but scholars have frequently pointed to its possible origin as an elaboration of an Orphic theogony-detail: after Zeus overthrows Kronos, he binds him in sleep in a cave, where he is served by *daimones* who bring him nourishment and are themselves prophetic. But the greatest oracles these *daimones* bring down to earth are the dreams of Kronos, which foresee what Zeus intends. (Speculations and earlier bibliography in Bos 1989.)

In the Orphic theogony as well as in the Derveni citations, Zeus receives prophecies not only from night, who is called *panompheuousan* in col. X, but also Kronos (note *thesphata akousas* in col. XIII). And Proclus, *In Platonis Cratylum commentaria* 27 Pasquali = Orph. fr. 239 I–V, also testifies to this double form of divination. We also see that in col. XI the *adyton* of Night and her oracular powers seem to be interpreted out of existence but to have been present in the poem. Dreams would naturally be the province of Night, as Sarah Johnston reminds me, and so perhaps Plutarch has adapted his myth from an episode in the theogony of Orpheus—many of the right elements are there, though in a different way.

Against this proposal, it must be conceded that in cols. I–VI (not to speak of col. XX) not only the *topic* but also the method of discussion seems to be different in form from the rest of the

column XX—where we seem to have a religious critique, on which see below—have a plausible reference point in Orpheus' theogony as found in the later version of the Rhapsodies. What is more, these reference points roughly concern a single complex of narrative in that poem, the succession from Kronos to Zeus and the creation that follows it, undertaken by Zeus perhaps from Protogonos on the advice of Nyx.

Column VII: The Selection of Orpheus and "Enigmatic License"

It has often been noted that the Derveni author's reinterpretations of poetry continue a well-attested tradition of tendentious interpretation of Homer by rhapsodes and Sophists (Richardson 1975). But we must not overlook one very original feature of this book: it chooses not Homer to interpret, as did almost all earlier and later allegorists, but "Orpheus." It is striking that some of the poems ascribed to Orpheus at this time seem not to have been completely distinctive in content, but compete with already-known forms and stories: the Orphic hymn to Demeter with the Homeric one, and the theogony with that of Hesiod. The difference, as Fritz Graf has pointed out in connection with the Demeter poems, is probably that the competing poems by the fictitious authors Orpheus and Musaeus "came into being within two closely related circles of theological-speculative interpretation," in other words, they appealed especially to those who sought religious significance in their poetry.[4] Thus it is not surprising that it is stated at the outset that Orpheus is "special" (col. VII):

ἔστι δὲ ξ[ένη τις ἡ] π̣όησις
κ]αὶ ἀνθρώποις[αἰνιγμ]ατώδης· [κα]ὶ ['Ορφεὺ]ς αὐτ[ὸ]ς
ἐ]ρίστ' αἰν[ίγμα]τα οὐκ ἤθελε λέγειν, [ἐν αἰ]νίγμασιν δὲ
μεγάλα ἱερ[ ]αι μὲν οὖγ καὶ ἀ[πὸ το]ῦ π̣ρώτου
ἀεὶ] μέχρι <τ>οῦ [τελε]υταίου ῥ̣ήματος. ὡ̣[ς δηλοῖ] καὶ ἐν τῶι
[εὐκ]ρινήτω̣[ι ἔπει· θ]ύ̣ρ̣ας γὰρ ἐ̣π̣ιθέ[σθαι κελ]εύσας τοῖ[ς]
ὠσὶ]ν αὐτ[οὺς οὔ]...ε̣ιμ φη[σι τοῖς] πολλο̣ῖ̣ς

---

work. Another point against any attempt to relate these early columns to the text of the poem is that col. VII introduces the foundation of the author's method of interpretation, his assumption that the poem is a riddle, and his quotation of a verse that limits the poem to a select audience.

4 Graf 1974:19. In his contribution to the conference, Graf suggested that the Derveni theogony might in fact be viewed as a cultic hymn (cf. col. V.2) that formed the *legomena* to an initiation. On *Hieroi logoi* and *Bibloi* see Henrichs 2003.

His[5] poetry is rather strange
and riddling for men; and Orpheus himself
did not wish to speak competitive riddles, but by means of riddles
(he wished to speak) great things holy[6] (?) ... therefore from the first
To the last word; he makes it clear thus also in the
Easy to understand verse: for by commanding them to "attach doors
To their ears" he does not say that he is ... ing for the many...[7]

The concept of poetry as riddle is known before this text (Struck 2004:39–50), but I find particularly interesting the variant formulation of the principle in the pseudo-Platonic dialogue *Alcibiades* II 147D. After his interlocutor has expressed frustration with interpreting a poetic text, Socrates says that in fact the text is consistent: not only this poet but almost all other poets speak in riddles, since poetry is by nature enigmatic, and is not for any chance reader to understand (ἔστιν τε γὰρ φύσει ποιητικὴ ἡ σύμπασα αἰνιγματώδης καὶ οὐ τοῦ προστυχόντος ἀνδρὸς γνωρίσαι). And in addition to its being this way by nature, when poetry is in the hands of a resentful man who doesn't wish to communicate with us but rather to conceal his wisdom as far as possible, the difficulty of understanding the thing that each poet actually means is stretched to an extreme (ἔτι τε πρὸς τῷ φύσει τοιαύτη εἶναι, ὅταν λάβηται ἀνδρὸς φθονεροῦ τε καὶ μὴ βουλομένου ἡμῖν ἐνδείκνυσθαι ἀλλ᾽ ἀποκρύπτεσθαι ὅτι μάλιστα τὴν αὑτοῦ σοφίαν, ὑπερφυῶς δὴ τὸ χρῆμα ὡς δύσγνωστον φαίνεται, ὅτι ποτὲ νοοῦσιν ἕκαστος αὐτῶν). The text that he goes on to interpret is from an improbable source, the *Margites*: he uses the tactic of word-replacement (not found in the Derveni author) to alter the meaning of the line of the *Margites* to say not that Margites knew everything badly—since to know something badly would be unacceptable to Socrates—but that it was bad for him to know all the trivial things he did know. Certainly this broad statement of principle applied to an unlikely poetic text is not meant to be taken seriously—it seems rather to be a parody of such literary interpretations, like Tiresias' linguistic reinterpretation of the birth of Dionysus in Euripides' *Bacchae* 286–296, or like the Platonic *Menexenus*, which often seems to parody the institution of the funeral oration. And yet, though Socrates is less than generous in the motives he ascribes to his allegorical poet, he claims the same enigmatic license that the Derveni author does in column VII.

5 That the author is not speaking of poetry in general but of Orpheus in particular is clarified by col. XVIII.2, 6, and the statements of method in cols. XIII.5–6, XXIII.6–7.

6 Albert Henrichs remarked that the supplement ἱερ[ολογεῖ]ται (consulted at the conference, Obbink found no trace of -εῖ-) seems somewhat bold, as it is otherwise first attested late and not in the middle or passive; but the presence of ιερ[cannot be denied. A more neutral supplement would be μεγάλα ἱερ[ὰ· ἥινικτ]αι.

7 A well-known Orphic verse = Orph. fr. 1ab, 377–378.

Identification/Equivalence as Interpretative Tool

Despite choosing a poet and a subject apt for religious interpretation and stating that he has some relation to *hiera*, the Derveni author goes on to use his license not for religious interpretation (as he had done in connection with rituals before col. VII), but to reinterpret the poem as speculative philosophy, as the "Homeric professors" like Metrodorus had done, with particular attention to cosmogony.[8]

Exactly how does he unlock his enigmatic text? When we put together a catalogue of all the licenses he takes in reading, it is somewhat surprising to discover that instead of a repertory of ingenious and sometimes outrageous misinterpretations, there is a dreary sameness and predictability to most of them. In the first instance, in contrast to Prodicus and other speakers who were interested in distinguishing the meanings of apparent synonyms,[9] the Derveni interpreter postulates word equivalencies to make his argument.

Col. V	ἀπιστίη = ἀμαθίη (μανθάνω = γινώσκω)
Col. X	λέγειν = διδάσκειν = φωνεῖν
Col. XI	χρῆσαι = ἀρκέσαι
Col. XXI	μίσγεσθαι = θόρνυσθαι ("mount") = ἀφροδισιάζειν
Col. XXI	εἴκειν = πείθειν

Identifying different verbs or concepts with each other and using this chain of synonyms to establish a new meaning is not new,[10] but is much more thoroughly practiced here than previously.

Nor is his second category of identification new: etymological interpretation of gods' names such as Kronos and Demeter is known of course from Plato's *Cratylus* and elsewhere. Heraclitus famously said that Dionysus and Hades were the same, but like many of his formulations this was surprising, complex, based partly on the sound similarity of *aidoia*, *aidôs*, and *aides*,[11] and above all expressed concisely. The Derveni interpreter runs this principle into the ground, in more than a third of the columns postulating, usually without argument, the identification of gods or abstract concepts.

Col. XII	Ὄλυμπος = χρόνος[12]
Col. XIV	Cronus = Nous

8 This paradox is noted by Laks (1997:35).

9 See most recently Sansone 2004:nn5, 56.

10 See Struck 2004:35.

11 There is another soundplay in the fragment of Heraclitus quoted in col. IV, between εὔρους and ἐξευρήσουσι.

12 On the form of argument here see Betegh 2004:250, and for its recurrence in Alexandrian Homer scholarship see Schironi 2001.

Col. XV Cronus = Zeus
Col. XVII Zeus = Aer
Col. XVIII–XIX Pneuma = Moira = *Phronesis* of Zeus
Col. XXI Aphrodite = Zeus, Harmonia, and Peitho
Col. XXII Rhea = Meter, Ge, Demeter, Hera
Col. XXIII Oceanus = Zeus = Aer

It is important to add, however, that in making such divine identifications the Derveni author had on the one hand a very congenial poetic text to work on: in column XXII he quotes from the Orphic hymns a line that identifies six different goddesses as a unity, and divine identifications are found frequently in the extant Orphic hymns;[13] on the other hand, the underlying meaning that he aimed to extract with his reinterpretations was especially well suited to divine identifications, situated as it was in the post-Parmenidean tradition that posits an ultimate unity of existence and, based on Anaxagoras and Diogenes of Apollonia, postulates basic principles like *Aer* that are the same though they appear under various names.[14]

His third method is to redefine a word, either by etymology, citation of parallel passages, or synonyms:

Col. X πανομφεύουσαν = πάντα διδάσκουσαν
Col. XI ἄδυτον = ὃ οὐ δύνει (not "cave")
Col. XI χρᾶν = "be sufficient" (not "give prophecies")
Col. XXVI ἑᾶς = "good" (not "his own")

In at least three of these cases it seems very important for him to displace the more obvious meaning, and here he inadvertently helps us in the interpretation of the poem—when he denies that a word means such and such, that, to me, is a pretty good indication of what it *did* actually mean in context.[15]

13 Morand 2001 "Les rapprochements de dieux," 156–158, 337–338. I owe this point to Claude Calame.

14 I owe this point to Glenn Most. For the physical system of the Derveni author see Laks 1997: 127–134.

15 An accompanying interpretive tactic (XXIV.7, cf. XXVI.11–12) is to hypothesize what the author *would* have written if the rejected word were his intention: this is applied already by Themistocles in interpreting the Delphic oracle on Salamis (Herodotus 7.141), Sluiter (1994) notes the same method is used for scholarly purposes in the *scholia* on *Iliad* 5.408–409, to which *P.Derv.* can also be added.

Interpreter and Text in Pre-Alexandrian Greece

Thus the value for us of the Derveni interpreter lies not so much in the originality—and certainly not the variety—of his method, but in the bulk of examples he gives us of a particular school of interpretation that was very different in intention from the Alexandrian scholarly treatment of literature in some important ways. Broadly speaking, post-Aristotelian Alexandrian scholarship is essentially canon-defending and antiquarian, motivated by the desire first to preserve, and next to study and interpret—not that there isn't considerable scope for competition, invention, and self-expression in this task,[16] but the text comes first.

The Derveni interpreter's relationship to this text is different: it is for him a vehicle of self-expression, as it probably was for others before him; the real authorities for him are not poetic texts—despite the attention he gives them—but the intellectuals and philosophers of the fifth century that he is drawing on for his physical worldview and hermeneutic tools. In the case of hermeneutics, he offers us a bounty of the sort of application of new ideas of language and meaning that was done by virtuosi before Plato; note Diogenes Laertius' description of Protagoras (9.52 = VS 80 A1):[17] "He abandoned the meaning, but discussed the word" (τὴν διάνοιαν ἀφεὶς πρὸς τοὔνομα διελέχθη). Similarly, Glenn Most's detailed study of the set piece of literary interpretation in Protagoras points to the *decontextualization* of the words of the poem as a key element of this method.[18] This is strikingly confirmed in the statement of principle in Derveni Papyrus column XIII.5–6:

> ὅτι μὲμ πᾶ[σ]αν τὴμ πόησιν περὶ τῶμ πραγμάτων
> αἰνίζεται κ̣[α]θ' ἔπος ἕκαστον ἀνάγκη λέγειν.

> Since he encodes all his poetry about materiality
> into riddles, one must speak line by line.

[16] Francesca Schironi has reminded me of Crates of Mallos especially, who is unusually innovative but still (I would maintain) working within the overall tradition of Homeric scholarship. Franco Montanari reminds me that, true as this is of Alexandrian scholarship, this period is an interpretive parenthesis: both the Presocratics before the Alexandrians and many scholars thereafter (notably the Neoplatonists) used poetry (including Orpheus) as a vehicle for their own philosophical views.

[17] Cited in the valuable survey of Sluiter (1997).

[18] Most 1994; see also his discussion of the "atomization" of Pindar's text in the hermeneutic tradition in Most 1985:36–38.

The Derveni Papyrus as Proto-Commentary

But along with being indisputably pre-Alexandrian in some respects, the book has a close affinity with Alexandrian scholarship, since—even though not all of the text seems to treat the poem of Orpheus—it clearly prefigures in many ways a commentary.[19] The book's form, surely given to it by a scribe rather than the author, is decisive for this interpretation. Scholars of ancient books have observed that the 36-character line, which accommodates the standard-length dactylic hexameter verse, is adopted as the column width of the ancient commentary so that lemmata will be independent, and the earliest example known of this phenomenon is the papyrus of Derveni.[20]

One might even speculate that the lemmatized commentary-form is an attempt to domesticate and manage the decontextualization that is inherent in the process of citation and interpretation. The most intriguing and controversial feature of this commentary-form is the use of the *paragraphos*, the symbol we associate primarily with the change of speaker in early dramatic texts. In this kind of text, that is clearly not necessary, but it appeared to me to be the scribe's aid to the readers, to orient themselves when the voice changes from the interpreter to his texts and back again. That is the way it often appears in papyrus commentaries.[21] (See the discussion in detail in the appendix.)

And it is also an important characteristic of the Derveni interpreter, at least as I read him, that, for all his cavalier treatment of texts, nevertheless just like Didymus on Demosthenes or other prolific post-Alexandrian interpreters, he would be lost without them: the poem of Orpheus is cited again and again, even in the first six columns he cites Heraclitus, and I still believe it quite possible that in column XI and column XX he cites unnamed prose texts (see the appendix). I also cling to my opinion that, although he clearly uses the technical vocabulary of citation on several occasions for effect, not all citations have to be carefully introduced or their author specified; the principle of seeking parallels and ideas from texts is sufficiently clear that one need never be surprised by a citation around the next corner, and in these cases the scribe has often given us help.

And so, although one can have reservations about the methods and the originality of this writer, nevertheless his voracious reading, intimate familiarity with his text, zest in expounding it, and use of other texts to carry his ideas further, we can agree, all deserve admiration.

19 See Dorandi 2000 and Lamedica 1992.

20 Irigoin 1984:88, Parsons at Turner and Parsons 1987:151n113, Obbink 1997:44–45n9. I owe this point to Dirk Obbink.

21 Andrieu 1954:263: "Le paragraphos est essentiallement un *signe de séparation*, et son utilisation dans le dialogue n'est qu'un aspect particulier de ses possibilités." He discusses its use in the papyri of prose authors 292–297. For Ptolemaic papyrus-commentaries using the *paragraphos* see MP3 54, 161, 466.

Appendix: Revisiting the Use of the *Paragraphos* in *P.Derv.* X.10–11, XI.8–9, XIII.5–6, XX.10 (Especially), and XXIII.7

Clearly I should have set forth this argument more thoroughly in 1985, since the interpretation of the *paragraphos* that seemed to me obvious then has met with universal resistance, and in fact there is a general tendency to deny that *paragraphoi* mark any interruptions of the authorial voice except from those texts explicitly introduced as the words of Orpheus and Heraclitus. It seems to me that *paragraphoi* have been added by the scribe to mark not only verse quotations, but shifts in the subject such as at X.10–11 (switching from the exegesis of πανομφεύουσαν to τροφόν), interruptions such as statements of method in XIII.5–6 (where μέν has no answering δέ) and XXIII.7,[22] as well as the unsourced illustrative quotation XI.8–9.[23] All these have been rejected by subsequent scholars and at least one instance has been deemed "irrational";[24] but special disfavor[25] has been reserved for my proposal that the *paragraphos* in XX.10 marks the end of a quotation (of which the beginning is lost in the previous column's end), followed by a paraphrase by the Derveni author.

I give a structural outline and a translation:[26]

ὅσοι μὲν οὖν] ἀνθρώπω[ν ἐμ] πόλεσιν ἐπιτελέσαντες [τὰ ἱε]ρὰ εἶδον,
Firstly then, those people who have observed the sacred after being publicly initiated

ἔλασσον σφᾶς θαυμάζω μὴ γ[ι]νώσκειν
these I am less surprised that they do not attain knowledge

(οὐ γὰρ οἷόν τε ἀκοῦσαι ὁμοῦ καὶ μαθεῖν τὰ λεγόμενα),
(for it is not possible to hear and learn what is being said at one and the same time);

22 Rejected by KPT, Bernabé, the latter *paragraphos* called "irrational" by Obbink (1997:44) (see below).

23 Treated as colloquial speech rather than a prose quotation by KPT, Bernabé, although elsewhere (XVIII.4, XIX.4–7, XXI.8–9, XXIII.10) the author uses φασί or λέγουσιν or λέγεται κατὰ φάτιν to introduce such colloquial expressions, and in these cases there is no scribal *paragraphos*, probably because there is no interruption of authorial voice.

24 Obbink 1997:44, on XXIII.7.

25 Already in Burkert 2006b:94n17, Lamedica 1992:328.

26 The commentary on column XX by Kouremenos in KPT 233–242 and by Bernabé (238–241) is especially full, and these, as well as my discussion in Rusten 1985:138–140, are taken for granted below.

ὅσοι δὲ παρὰ τοῦ τέχνημ ποιουμένου τὰ ἱερὰ (sc. εἶδον),
But those who (have observed the sacred) from an individual craftsman of the sacred

οὗτοι ἄξιοι
They deserve

θαυμάζεσθαι καὶ οἰκτε[ί]ρεσθαι,
both (my) surprise and pity;

θαυμάζεσθαι μὲν ὅτι
Firstly surprise: because

δοκοῦντες πρότερον ἢ ἐπιτελέσαι εἰδήσειν
although they think they will attain knowledge before they are initiated,

ἀπέρχονται
they end up

ἐπιτελέσαντες πρὶν εἰδέναι
being initiated before they attain knowledge,

οὐδ' ἐπανερόμενοι
and not asking additional questions either,

ὥσπερ ὡς εἰδότες τ̣[ι]
as if (they did not need to) because they had some knowledge

ὧν εἶδον ἢ ἤκουσαν ἢ ἔμαθον·
of what they have observed and heard and learned

[οἰ]κ̣τε<ί>ρεσθαι δὲ ὅτι
Secondly, pity: because

οὐκ ἀρκε[ῖ] σφιν τὴν δαπάνην προανηλῶσθαι
it is not enough for them to have spent their money in advance,

ἀλλὰ καὶ τῆς γνώμης[27] στερόμενοι προσαπέρχονται
But they also end up in addition being deprived of their knowledge

(*paragraphos*)

27 τῆς γνώμης στερόμενοι is a variation on μὴ γ[ι]νώσκειν in the first part, closing the ring with the opening idea. This stylistic feature explains what Kouremenos finds "a not particularly successful choice of word" (KPT 241).

> πρὶμ μὲν τὰ [ἱε]ρὰ ἐπιτελέσαι ἐλπίζοṿ[τε]ς εἰδήσειν
> Although before participating in the sacred things they hope they will attain knowledge
>
> ἐπ̣[ιτελέσ]αν[τες] δὲ στερηθέντες κα̣[ὶ τῆ]ς ἐλπί[δος] ἀπέρχονται.
> After participating they end up being deprived of their hope.

I can of course understand the impulse to vindicate the first ten lines for the author of the Derveni Papyrus: they offer a forceful expression not only of criticism[28] but of amazement and pity at certain religious practices, containing the only first-person singular verb in the entire text[29] and an abundance of highly loaded sacral and cognitive terminology, in a long, well-structured sentence with a variety of vocabulary and contrast-forms that ends in a ring with its opening words. In contrast to columns V–VI, which explain existing practices with new formulations and without criticism, column XXII gives us criticism of religious rituals without exegesis: he uses the existing traditional terminology (λεγόμενα, ἱερὰ ἰδεῖν) to make a contrast between two possible modes of initiation, the public (ἐν πόλεσιν) and the private (παρὰ τοῦ τέχνημ ποιουμένου τὰ ἱερὰ), and finds both unsatisfactory. The reader is left to wonder, is there any way to be initiated *successfully*? It is striking that, whereas in columns V–VI he was merely quoting Heraclitus, in column XX the author seems to adopt not only the vocabulary of Heraclitus (Kouremenos's commentary in KPT; see also Obbink 1997:46), but also his skeptical attitude toward ritual.

Obbink (1997:44–45) attempted to give readers good papyrological grounds to ignore the *paragraphos* here. I will quote his argument at length in three parts, with my comments interspersed. Initially, he argues that the *paragraphos* after line 10 could only indicate the *beginning* of a quotation:

> Rusten (1985) argued that the discrepancies between this column and the surrounding ones were sufficient to presume that the first 10 lines of this column are an extensive quotation from another author, the conclusion of which is marked by the *paragraphos* after line 10. Closer consideration showed otherwise. Although the author does introduce a brief prose quotation earlier (Column XI.8–9) for the illustration of an alleged meaning of a word (in addition to at least three prose lines of Heraclitus in Column IV), the scribe's consistent graphic practice when

[28] Here I differ from Graf in his contribution to the conference: he links col. XX with earlier statements to defend the view of the Derveni author as himself a religious entrepreneur (see also Burkert 2006a:202), and asserts that the author's commentary on the poem offers his answers to the questions the initiate should ask.

[29] On first-person argument in the fifth century see Thomas 1993:240–243.

> a quotation ends before the end of a line, as does line 10 of Column XX, is to fill out that line with the following text of the author's remarks. In addition, the scribe always begins the initial quotations, which serve as lemmata for the discussion (as opposed to individual words or phrases from the lemma), on a new line. The quotations are regularly marked by a paragraphos above and below the line(s) quoted. Given the fact that in Column XX line ten stops significantly short of the surrounding lines (34 letters as against 38–39 letters in the surrounding lines), and is followed by a paragraphos, lines 11ff. could well be a new (prose) quotation continuing into the lacuna at the end of Column XX, and concluding with an expression like: "so-and-so says."[30]

Obbink does not give a list of examples for his claim that a scribe always fills the line at the end of a quotation fully, but I presume he means the like of VIII.3–4, XV.5–6, 10–11 (24, 26, and 19 letter-lines respectively preceding hexameter quotations) as well as the one he cited, XI.7–8 (11 letter-line preceding an unsourced prose quotation); especially lacking, however, is evidence for the claim that a line with 34 as opposed to 38 characters is not "full." A glance at the photos in KPT shows that many lines are this short without any such external criterion, and a more important factor in line division is obviously that this scribe rarely divides syllables within words between one line and the next (XII.4–5 and XX.6–7 seem to be the only examples). In XX.10 he might have made the line slightly longer by adding πρὶν from the next sentence (as he does with short words e.g. VI.5 [new total 36 characters], XVI.8 [new total 40 characters], XVII.3 [new total 39 characters]), but at XXI.13 he *avoids* continuing a 34-character line with the available short initial words (ἦν μὲν γ[ὰρ) of a new sentence; at XX.10 there is in addition the factor of another awkward μέν without answering δέ (as at XIII.5–6), so that there are multiple reasons for beginning a new line. The "consistent graphic practice" does not operate here.

But Obbink goes on to cast doubt on the possibility of a quotation of any sort:

> Caution, however, must be exercised at this juncture. Though the scribe's graphic practice appears to be relatively consistent, the use of a paragraphos in school exercises and subliterary texts and even in some ancient critical editions is notoriously irregular, a problem that is compounded by the fact that they are overlooked or inconsistently reported

30 Obbink's initial suggestion that XX.11 is not the end but the start of a quotation would be much strengthened if it were certain that there is a *paragraphos* after XX.13, as KPT report but Bernabé does not; it is not easy to discern it on the photograph.

> by modern editors; the 19th century the *delineatores* of the Herculaneum papyri, for example, neglected to report them over 50% of the time. In the Derveni papyrus there is at least one irrationally placed paragraphos [XXIII.7], while the paragraphos at XIII.6 may mark nothing more than a strong grammatical clause, as Burkert ... notes. I have collated all *paragraphoi* recorded either in published texts or photographs of the Derveni papyrus. But I've not seen the original and am doubtless not aware of them all.

Apart from the difficulty of positing a scribe who is "consistent" at one time and "irrational" at others, the two *paragraphoi* considered anomalous (XIII.6, XXIII.7) are in fact also strikingly different from their surroundings, both being statements of interpretative method (cited above), quite possibly taken from another context (the first has μέν without answering δέ), but in any case explanatory interruptions in the process of interpretation.

Obbink concludes:

> On these grounds I conclude that lines 1–10 of Column XX are not the quoted words of another author, followed by a "feeble prose paraphrase of the last few lines" by the Derveni author. For in this case, we would expect (based on the scribe's procedure followed elsewhere) line 10 to be filled out by the author's own remarks we should also be prepared to consider that the paragraphos after line 10 may mark no more than the inception of a grammatical unit. In that case, lines 11 and 12 would represent the author's rounding out the sentence by reiterating his point in the preceding passage.

While my term "feeble prose paraphrase" was doubtless too harsh for lines 11–12, Obbink's "rounding out" and "reiterating" seem too generous for them: while lines 1–10 never use the same form twice, every word in lines 11–12 is either a word that has appeared in 1–10 or a gloss on one (πρὶμ glosses πρότερον ἢ ἐπιτελέσαι,. ἐλπίζοṿ[τε]ς + future infinitive glosses δ̣οκοῦντες + future infinitive and ἐλπίδος glosses γνώμης (i. e., the expectation of knowledge). Furthermore, these lines, although reproducing (in an anacoluthon) μὲν/ δ̣ὲ from 1–10, lack a sentence connective with what comes before.

Thus even apart from the *paragraphos*, there are good reasons for assuming a departure from the author's voice in XX.1–10: the sole first-person verb, sophisticated sentence structure at odds with the commentary form in the section (and with the author's practice even in cols. I–VI), and, between lines 10 and 11, a lack of explicit sentence-connection combined with total redundancy of contents.

Of course, it remains a matter of speculation whether the *paragraphos* here marks an actual quotation, but that does not give readers license to ignore it: the scribe is alerting the reader to some form of discontinuity in authorial voice, and we should not ignore him.[31] Interpretations of the papyrus as a whole that are founded primarily on XX.1–10 as the crucial expression of its author's views (Burkert, Laks, Janko, Graf) still seem to me to rest on less than firm ground.[32]

Bibliography and Abbreviations

Andrieu, J. 1954. *Le dialogue antique: Structure et presentation*. Paris.

Bernabé, A., ed. 2004. *Poetarum epicorum Graecorum: Testimonia et fragmenta*, pars II, fasc. 1: *Orphica*. Munich.

———. 2004–2005. *Poetarum epicorum Graecorum: Testimonia et fragmenta*, pars II, fasc. 1–2: *Orphicorum et Orphicis similium testimonia et fragmenta*. Leipzig.

———. 2007. *Poetarum epicorum Graecorum: Testimonia et fragmenta,* pars II, fasc. 3: *Musaeaus, Linus, Epimenides, Papyrus Derveni, Indices*. Leipzig.

Betegh, G. 2002. "Papyrus on the Pyre: The Derveni Papyrus and Its Archaeological Context." *Acta Antiqua Hungarica* 42:51–66.

———. 2004. *The Derveni Papyrus: Cosmology, Theology, and Interpretation*. Cambridge.

Bonfante, L. 2006. "Etruscan Inscriptions and Etruscan Religion." In *The Religion of the Etruscans* (ed. N. T. De Grummond and E. Simon) 9–26. Austin.

Bos, A. P. 1989. "A Dreaming Kronos in a Lost Work by Aristotle." *Antiquité classique* 58:88–111.

Bottini, A. 1992. *Archeologia della salvezza: L'escatologia greca nelle testimonianze archeologiche*. Milan.

Burkert, W. 2006a. "Craft versus Sect: The Problem of Orphics and Pythagoreans." In *Kleine Schriften III: Mystica, Orphica, Pythagorica,* 190–216. Ed. F. Graf. Göttingen.

———. 2006b. "Der Autor von Derveni: Stesimbrotus Περὶ Τελετῶν?" In *Kleine Schriften III: Mystica, Orphica, Pythagorica*, 89–94. Ed. F. Graf. Göttingen.

Dorandi, T. 2000. "Le commentaire dans la tradition papyrologique: Quelques cas controversés." In *Le commentaire entre tradition et innovation: Actes du*

31 The ingenious suggestion of Tsantsangolou and Kouremenos (KPT 10, 242) that XX.11–12 is an authorial variant of XX.1–10, as postulated for some passages in Aristotle, has not proved convincing. Johnson (1994) suggested (without reference to *P.Derv.*) that the *paragraphos* might serve as a reorientation point for someone reading the text aloud.

32 I suggested (Rusten 1985:140) that the "quotation" might be from the mystery criticism of Diagoras of Melos; Janko (2001), while following Obbink in rejecting it as a quotation, went on to suggest that Diagoras is the author of the entire papyrus.

Colloque international de L'institut des traditions textuelles, Paris et Villejuif, 22–25 septembre 1999 (ed. M.-O. Goulet-Cazé) 17–27. Paris.

Graf, F. 1974. *Eleusis und die orphische Dichtung Athens in vorhellenistischer Zeit.* Religionsgeschichtliche Versuche und Vorarbeiten 33. Berlin.

Henrichs, A. 2003. "'Hieroi Logoi' and 'Hierai Bibloi': The (Un)Written Margins of the Sacred in Ancient Greece." *Harvard Studies in Classical Philology* 101: 207–266.

Irigoin, J. 1984. "Livre et texte dans les manuscrits byzantins de poètes: Continuité et innovations." In *il libro e il testo: atti del convegno internazionale: Urbino, 20–23 settembre 1982* (ed. C. Questa and R. Raffaelli) 85–102. Urbino.

Janko, R. 2001. "The Derveni Papyrus (Diagoras of Melos, *Apopyrgizontes Logoi*?): A New Translation." *Classical Philology* 96:1–32.

Johnson, W. A. 1994. "The Function of the Paragraphus in Greek Literary Prose Texts." *Zeitschrift für Papyrologie und Epigraphik* 100:65–68.

KPT = Kouremenos, T., G. M. Parássoglou, and G. Tsantsanoglou, eds., *The Derveni Papyrus, Edited with a Commentary* (Studi e testi per il corpus dei pairi filosofici greci e latini 13) (Florence, 2006).

Laks, A. 1997. "Between Religion and Philosophy: The Function of Allegory in the Derveni Papyrus." *Phronesis* 42:121–142.

Lamedica, A. 1992. "Il papiro di Derveni come commentario: Problemi formali." In *Proceedings of the XIXth International Congress of Papyrology, Cairo, 2–9 September 1989* (ed. E.-M. Abd Alla Hassan) 325–333. Cairo.

Morand, A.-F. 2001. *Études sur les hymnes orphiques*. Leiden.

Most, G. W. 1985. *The Measures of Praise: Structure and Function in Pindar's Second* Pythian *and Seventh* Nemean *Odes*. Hypomnemata 83. Göttingen.

———. 1994. "Simonides' Ode to Scopas in Contexts." In *Modern Critical Theory and Classical Literature* (ed. I. J. F. de Jong and J. P. Sullivan) 127–152. *Mnemosyne* Suppl. 130. Leiden.

MP3 = *Mertens-Pack on Line*. P. Mertens and M.-H. Marganne. http://promethee.philo.ulg.ac.be/cedopal/index.htm.

Obbink, D. 1997. "Cosmology as Initiation versus the Critique of the Orphic Mysteries." In *Studies on the Derveni Papyrus* (ed. A. Laks and G. W. Most) 39–54. Oxford.

Richardson, N. 1975. "Homeric Professors in the Age of the Sophists." *Proceedings of the Cambridge Philological Society* 21:65–81.

Rusten, J. S. 1985. "Interim Notes on the Papyrus of Derveni." *Harvard Studies in Classical Philology* 89:121–140.

Sansone, D. 2004. "Heracles at the Y." *Journal of Hellenic Studies* 124:125–142.

Schironi, F. 2001. "L'Olimpo non è il cielo: Esegesi antica nel papiro di Derveni, in Aristarco e in Leagora di Siracusa." *Zeitschrift für Papyrologie und Epigraphik* 136:11–21.

Sluiter, I. 1994. "Themistocles, Labeo en de Taalkunde." *Hermeneus* 66:210–214.

———. 1997. "The Greek Tradition." In *The Emergence of Semantics in Four Linguistic Traditions: Hebrew, Sanskrit, Greek, Arabic* (ed. W. J. v. Bekkum) 149–224. Amsterdam.

Speyer, W. 1970. *Bücherfunde in der Glaubenswerbung der Antike, mit einem Ausblick auf Mittelalter und Neuzeit.* Hypomnemata 24. Göttingen.

Struck, P. T. 2004. *Birth of the Symbol: Ancient Readers at the Limits of Their Texts.* Princeton.

Thomas, R. 1993. "Performance and Written Publication in Herodotus and the Sophistic Generation." In *Vermittlung und Tradierung von Wissen in der griechischen Kultur* (ed. W. Kullmann and J. Althoff) 225–244. Scriptoralia 61. Tübingen.

Turner, E. G., and P. J. Parsons. 1987. *Greek Manuscripts of the Ancient World.* University of London Institute of Classical Studies, Bulletin Suppl. 46. London.

8

The Derveni Papyrus and the Bacchic-Orphic *Epistomia*[1]

Yannis Z. Tzifopoulos
Aristotle University of Thessaloniki

THE ENTIRE CORPUS OF THE *EPISTOMIA*[2] AND THE DERVENI PAPYRUS (*P.Derv.*) betray certain similarities—to state the most obvious ones: both are

[1] This paper first appeared in *Trends in Classics* 2 (2010): 31–63, and is printed here with minor changes.

I first heard about the Derveni Papyrus back in 1981–1982, when, as an undergraduate student, I attended at the Aristotle University of Thessaloniki a seminar by Kyriakos Tsantsanoglou and Georgios Parássoglou, who presented to a group of stunned undergraduate students their readings and interpretations of the oldest book in Europe and the problems thereof. A few years later, as a graduate student at the Ohio State University, I attended another seminar on Greek religion by Sarah Iles Johnston, who introduced to another group of stunned graduate students "unusual and out of the ordinary" texts, among them the Derveni Papyrus and the so-called Orphic texts on golden tablets. Still a few years later, this time as a lecturer at the University of Crete, I visited the Rethymno Archaeological Museum and came upon two unpublished gold *epistomia*, discovered in rescue excavations at a cemetery in Sfakaki, conducted by the 25th Ephoreia of Prehistoric and Classical Antiquities and the archaeologists Irene Gavrilaki, Stella Kalogeraki, and Niki Tsatsaki; one of the objects was incised with only two words, and the other with a longer text that demanded a re-edition and reconsideration of all the previously published *epistomia* from Crete (and elsewhere), because the new long text deviated from all previously known (for these see Tzifopoulos 2010); I am most grateful to them all, and also to Greg Nagy, Antonios Rengakos, Francesca Schironi, and Albert Henrichs for their invitation to participate in the symposium on the Derveni Papyrus held at the Center for Hellenic Studies, Washington, DC, 7–9 July 2008. For their incisive comments and criticisms I am indebted to Kyriakos Tsantsanoglou, Stavros Frangoulidis, Theokritos Kouremenos, and the audience at CHS.

[2] The word *epistomion/-a*, not in LSJ, does not appear to have been an ancient one; usually the words "tablet," "lamella," or "leaf" are employed to describe the gold incised objects discovered in graves. The word *epistomion*, however, has become a technical term among Greek archaeologists, who have no problem identifying an object by this term, when during the excavation of a grave they come upon a very small, paper-thin gold band on the mouth or near the cranium of the deceased, likely employed for covering the mouth. Not all *epistomia* are incised, and the text of those incised may be just one word, or a text of sixteen lines. Shapes of these vary, although they tend to approximate the shape and the size of the mouth. In addition to covering the mouth, sometimes the *epistomia* are placed on the chest or in the hand, and other times are folded and are placed inside the mouth, together with or instead of a burial coin (for the entire corpus of *epistomia* see Bernabé and Jiménez San Cristóbal 2008; Graf and Johnston 2007; and Tzifopoulos 2010).

associated, one way or another, with Orpheus; both are discovered in a burial context; the Derveni author comments upon ritual activities of the kind we suspect lie behind the *epistomia*; and both are rare specimens of what we may call—for lack of a better word—"religious literature," although such a genre never existed in antiquity until very late, and for which Albert Henrichs (2003a, 2003b, 2004) presented decisive definitions and distinctions. These similarities apparently, if not inevitably, invite comparison, which has led research in two directions of inquiry: on the one hand, the *epistomia* and the Derveni Papyrus are discussed as parallel examples of the same procedure and the same purpose with differences only in detail; and on the other hand, the two sets of texts are not to be associated *a priori* because evidence is lacking and at any rate the present evidence does not permit such a relation or correlation even as a working assumption.[3] The Derveni Papyrus text, an allegorical commentary of sorts of a theo-/cosmogonic poem in dactylic hexameters by Orpheus, and the small corpus of the Bacchic-Orphic gold incised *epistomia* from Italy, Crete, the northwestern Peloponnese, Thessaly, and Macedonia present analogous problems and display both similarities and differences in terms of their date, findspots, nature, content and genre (literary or otherwise), and their interrelation, if any. In what follows, first the chronological and archaeological contexts are revisited, and then the texts themselves and their contexts are examined, with emphasis on the areas where the two sets of written objects meet and where they part ways.

The chronological and archaeological issues around the Derveni Papyrus have been of primary importance because of their implications, since the time of Stylianos Kapsomenos' (1964) report at the meeting of the American Society of Papyrologists held on August 24, 1964, in Philadelphia and the discussion that followed in that meeting (that discussion is reprinted here in an appendix as a point of departure for the present line of inquiry). In their *Greek Hymns* (2001), Furley and Bremer have indicated that in dating the inscribed hymn from Palaikastro, Crete, three separate chronological issues must be distinguished: the date of the inscription itself, the date of the composition of the hymn, and the date of the cult behind the hymn.[4] These three different aspects should be distinguished for dating all of the incised *epistomia*—in fact, for dating all inscribed objects, particularly those we call "literary." In particular, the fact that the entire corpus of *epistomia* may be dated somewhere between the fourth

3 For the former see e.g. Most 1997, Betegh 2004, Bernabé and Jiménez San Cristóbal 2008, Bernabé (in this volume); for the latter: Janko 1997 and 2001, Kouremenos in KPT 2006, Burkert (in this volume), all with previous bibliography. The articles in Laks and Most 1997 are the starting point for research on *P.Derv.*; and Tsantsanoglou (this volume) outlines some areas for future study on *P.Derv.*

4 Furley and Bremer 2001:1.69–70, 2.3–4.

century BCE and the second century CE does not necessarily bespeak the date of these texts' composition, or the date of the ritual behind the texts, which undoubtedly antedates the placement of the *epistomia* inside the graves. How far back one should go in assigning a date to the text's composition, or to the ritual's appearance (whether it be the fourth, the fifth, or perhaps even the sixth century BCE), cannot be determined.

These considerations are also relevant to the date of the Derveni Papyrus. Its chronology depends primarily but not exclusively on the archaeological context, which points to the end of the fourth or the beginning of the third century BCE as the *terminus ante quem*. But this chronology is of course relative; it simply points to the date when the papyrus was placed on the pyre of the deceased individual in Derveni Tomb A. It is certainly not the date when the papyrus was written; unless someone is prepared to argue that it is an *entaphion* object, produced solely for the deceased's pyre and subsequent internment, like the famous bronze Derveni krater from Tomb B with the Dionysiac scenes. Kyriakos Tsantsanoglou (KPT, 8–9), after reviewing and comparing the script of the Derveni Papyrus and that of the earliest surviving papyri and of *dipinti*, proposes a date between 340 and 320 BCE for the writing of the text. But again, this would be the date when the Derveni Papyrus was produced somewhere (Athens? Macedonia?) by a scribe who copied another papyrus—unless again someone is prepared to argue that the surviving object is the original work (I will leave aside arguments about the professional-, amateur-, or epigraphical-like script). The third and most important date is the date of the composition of the text itself, which in turn will serve as another *terminus ante quem* for the rituals and ideas expressed and commented upon in the text of the papyrus. This date too cannot be determined, except to suppose as a *terminus ante quem* the first half of the fourth century BCE and as a *terminus post quem* the sixth century BCE.[5]

One thing, however, is certainly undeniable, as the text itself proves: the composition of the work required first that the poem by Orpheus was circulating widely (how widely is arguable); second, that a version of the Homeric *Iliad* and *Odyssey*, of Heraclitus' work and of the work of others were also public knowledge, whatever that may mean; and third, that the ritual practices commented upon in the first columns had already become something of a fashion, so as to warrant the author's corrective remarks.

The next and more complicated issue is topographical, namely the findspot of the papyrus and its provenance. Outside Egypt and the Palestine, three papyri in all have been discovered in graves, but the Derveni Papyrus is the only one

[5] According to Burkert (in this volume) the poem by Orpheus is a sixth-century text and the commentary is a work composed around 400 BCE.

that has survived its discovery, and for that we will always be indebted to Petros Themelis' discerning eye and to the extraordinary skills of Anton Fackelmann.[6] The problematics of the findspot were already heard in 1964, namely whether or not the content of the text should accommodate the findspot and vice versa—to paraphrase Bradford Welles' comment (appendix): it is one thing to ask to be buried or cremated with your valuable possession of Homer's *Iliad* and *Odyssey*, but it is another thing to ask for Aristarchus' commentary on the *Iliad* or the *Odyssey* to be placed inside the grave or on the pyre. A second and related issue that was also raised was whether this find was intrinsic to Macedonia, and at a time when, according to Welles, they "had no time for Orphism, commentated or pure," in response to which Ronald Syme pondered: "one of the things we don't know enough about is precisely the habitual culture of the landowners on the fringes of society." When Frank Walbank was asked about the history of Macedonia at this period, he posed the provocative question: "Is it possible that this scroll was merely used as inflammable material? I know Martial refers to using papyrus on funeral pyres. Would that always be blank papyrus, or might it just be some scroll that the heirs of the person were not particularly interested in preserving?" (appendix).

Not much has changed since 1964, and on present evidence both lines of argument are valid, depending on our readiness to accept their pros and cons. Richard Janko has revived Walbank's brief remark as a caveat that we should always keep in mind, although Janko himself does not dismiss completely the other extreme position, i.e. that the papyrus may have been a precious possession and like all other possessions followed the deceased to the pyre and the grave.[7] The question that begs for an answer is of course "What kind of value?"

6 The other two papyri were not carbonized, a process which, as it seems, protected and saved the *P.Derv.*: one was discovered in a fourth-century BCE grave in Callatis (modern Constanza, Romania), at the same time of the *P.Derv.* discovery, but, as soon as it came in contact with air, it disintegrated (one is reminded of the white sheet covering the remains of the deceased inside the Timpone Grande in Thourioi, Italy, which disintegrated when touched by the excavators, a grave that also contained the gold incised tablet A4); and the other papyrus was discovered a few decades later, together with writing implements, in a late fifth-century BCE grave in Daphne, a suburb of Athens (Pöhlmann and West 2012)

7 Janko 1997:62 (repeated in less detail in Janko 2001:1n1): "Let us first dismiss from our minds the fact that the papyrus was preserved by being burned on a funeral pyre. This does not necessarily prove anything about its content; its combustion could have been accidental, in that it might have been used as waste paper to help ignite the blaze, much as we use discarded newspapers. That it was burned as a roll rather than torn up might speak against this; it may after all have been a precious possession of the person with whom it was burned. Valued books could be inhumed with their owners, as perhaps in the case of the roll of Bacchylides and certainly those of Hyperides in the British Museum, the volume of Timotheus known to have been found in its owner's wooden sarcophagus at Abusir, or the roll discovered in the hand of the deceased (where it at once disintegrated) in a grave of the fourth century BC at Callatis near Constanza

It is true that "archaeological facts rarely 'speak' as clearly as do texts," as Janko (1997:62) rightly emphasized, but the corpus of the Bacchic-Orphic incised *epistomia* presents a rare case of a comparandum to the Derveni Papyrus, albeit only to complicate things even further. The *epistomia* that have been unearthed during systematic excavations have been found either on or inside the mouth, on the chest, or in the hand of the deceased, where they were placed during the inhumation process; or, if the deceased was cremated, inside an urn, where they were placed together with the deceased's remains *after* the latter were gathered from the pyre. The *epistomia* that have survived were *never* placed on the pyre to be burned with the deceased, and the reason, we all suspect, is obvious: what was written on them was intended for the deceased and his Underworld journey, and so the incised object should not have suffered any damage from the fire. It remains to be seen whether or not *epistomia* were also made of perishable material that could not have survived the intervening years. If this were true, however, it would explain, for example, the complete absence of *epistomia* from Attica, where deceased with the same ideas on afterlife certainly lived and died, otherwise Plato's castigation (on which see n29) would have been strange, to say the least.

As things stand, however, the Derveni Papyrus was not regarded in the same way the gold incised *epistomia* were. If the deceased *mystes* needed the golden texts with him/her in the grave and in the Underworld, the intention of the deceased buried in Tomb A, or at least of his family members who prepared the tomb, is quite clear: the papyrus ought to have been burned on the pyre, and ought not to have reached us. If the papyrus and its text had a function analogous to the one of the *epistomia*, as Betegh (2004:56–68 and passim) argued, trying to accommodate ritual and content,[8] then one would expect the papyrus to have been placed inside the bronze krater with the deceased's remains from the pyre, or inside the grave itself, which was full to the rim. The papyrus, however, was discovered on the slabs covering the grave (Figure 1), together with the remains of spearheads and spikes, a pair of greaves, a shield or breastplate, and all the rest with which the deceased was dressed up on the bier that was placed on the pyre. After the grave was prepared with all the *entaphia* objects (Figure 2) and

---

in Rumania; the same would presumably apply to cremations. But this book might have been valued for various reasons, speculation about which ought to follow, rather than precede, any identification of the author." At present, however, neither the sizeable number of scenes on vases where pyres are depicted nor any Greek text dated before the Roman period provides any evidence whatsoever that papyri, rolled-up or discarded, were used for kindling the funeral pyre; instead, in a number of instances we have scenes on vases of people reading and teaching from a papyrus scroll (see e.g. Figures 5 and 6).

8 See also Bernabé (in this volume); Graf (in this volume). Most (1997:117 and 134–135) and Tsantsanoglou (KPT, 2–4) suggest that the deceased may have been (a soldier) from Thessaly.

Figure 1. Derveni Tomb A, the slabs covering the tomb on which whatever remained of the pyre was strewn, among them the Derveni Papyrus (after Themelis and Touratsoglou 1997:28, fig. 5).

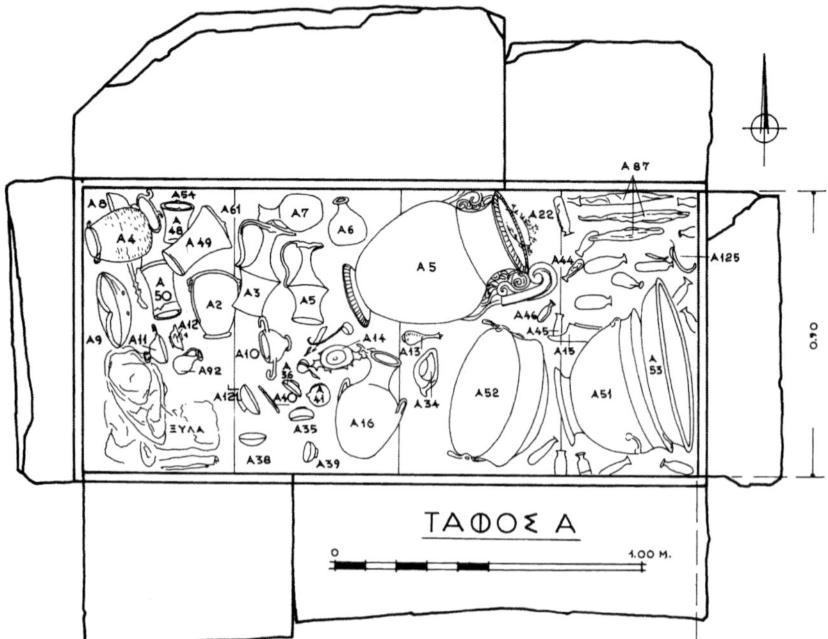

Figure 2. Derveni Tomb A, drawing of the interior of the tomb with the *entaphia* objects (after Themelis and Touratsoglou 1997:29, fig. 6).

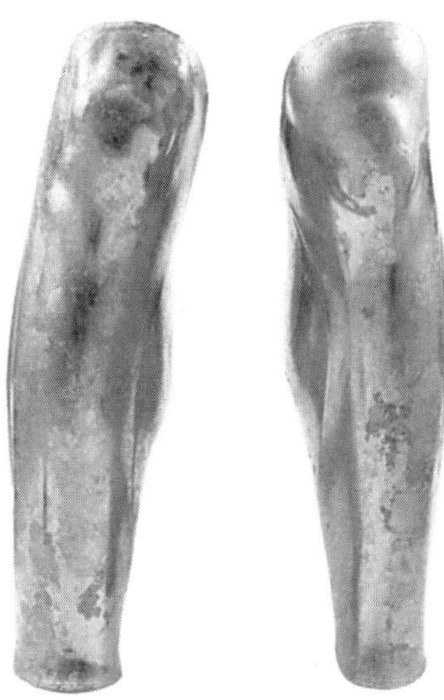

Figure 3 (*left*). Derveni Tomb A, the bronze krater inside which the remains of the deceased were laid (after Themelis and Touratsoglou 1997: pl. 1 A1).

Figure 4 (*right*). Derveni Tomb A, the second pair of bronze greaves found. inside the tomb (after Themelis and Touratsoglou 1997: pl. 7 A15).

the deceased's remains were laid inside the krater (Figure 3), the grave was shut, and whatever remained of the pyre was strewn above the grave (Figure 1).[9] Did they not see that the papyrus was not burned, or did they not care? Was the papyrus not as valuable as all these objects inside the grave, which the deceased probably needed to take with him? The deceased obviously needed a second pair of greaves (Figure 4), which was placed inside the grave, because the one he was wearing on the bier melted down on the pyre and became useless. But what was the need of the second pair? Are we to suppose that he was going to need the greaves anyway in the Underworld, but not the papyrus, or perhaps that no male in the family thought he could use the deceased's second pair of greaves? The deceased buried with the *epistomia* needed the texts with them *inside* the grave, on or inside the mouth, on the chest, or in their hands. The deceased of Tomb A did not have such a need; or rather, such a need, if there were one, is not attested in the archaeological record, because the evidence did not survive. Consequently, the scenarios pro and con for associating the text on the papyrus and the funerary ritual for the deceased are far from being conclusive.

9 Themelis and Touratsoglou 1997:28–30.

Even so, Derveni, the modern site of the ancient city Lete, is not the first place that comes to mind in relation to papyri (nor are Constanza or Daphne, for that matter). Recall Syme's wondering about "the habitual culture of the landowners on the fringes of society" (appendix). Differently formulated, this query may also extend to the deceased *mystai* carrying an *epistomion* in their grave. Because the *epistomia* originate in the "periphery or the fringes" of the Greek world—again, Italy, Crete, the northwestern Peloponnese, Thessaly, Macedonia—the deceased and the texts have been understood as a "countercultural" group with a "countercultural" or "peripheral" ideology on the afterlife, as compared to the cultural and mainstream ideology of the polis.[10] In order to discuss the "fringes" of society, however, one must also define the "center," and that center, more often than not, is Athens and its literary production, and to a lesser degree Sparta. Macedonia presents a fitting example: could the late fourth- and third-century BCE Athens still be called a center in the same way it could be in the late sixth, the fifth, and the early fourth centuries BCE? Moreover, in studying burial practices there are hardly dominant and peripheral ideologies and practices, as the decision regarding the entire funeral process rested with each individual and his/her family; patterns of similar behavior are evident, but there is always some small detail that upsets the neat and expected pattern.

At present, the evidence for the "habitual culture" in Macedonia as relates to burial practices in the fourth and third centuries BCE comprises, in addition to Derveni Tomb A, with the papyrus, the following (I have chosen only the most spectacular deviations from what would have been a consistent pattern):[11] the Derveni krater from Tomb B with its Dionysiac scenes;[12] twelve Bacchic-Orphic *epistomia*;[13] the outstanding paintings in the Judgment Tomb at Leukadia,[14] and in the Tomb of Persephone at Vergina;[15] remarkable gold foil–masks covering the faces (and sometimes the chest, arms, and legs) of male and female deceased in graves at Archontiko near Pella, Sindos, and Thessaloniki;[16] and finally, from a cist tomb at Agios Athanassios, the remarkable silver-plated cypress-*larnax* (Figure 5), inside of which the pregnant mother's bones, wrapped in purple and

10 Detienne 1975 and 2003:155–157; Edmonds 2004:41–43 and 108–109; Tzifopoulos 2011.

11 On cults and rites of passage in Macedonia see Hatzopoulos 1994, 2002, and 2006. Rizakis and Touratsoglou (2000) discuss only monuments above the grave; for altars as grave markers see also Adam-Veleni 2002:161–197 and 219–256; for the architecture of tombs in Macedonia see Miller 1982.

12 See Themelis and Touratsoglou 1997:60–92; and Barr-Sharrar 2008.

13 See Bernabé and Jiménez San Cristóbal 2008; Graf and Johnston 2007; Tzifopoulos 2010; and Edmonds 2011.

14 Petsas 1966; Miller 1992; Rhomiopoulou 1997; Brécoulaki 2006; and Kottaridou 2006.

15 Andronikos 1994, esp. 129–134 for a comparison of wall paintings in Macedonian tombs; Brécoulaki 2006; and Kottaridou 2006.

16 Chrysostomou and Chrysostomou 2001 and 2002.

Figure 5. Agios Athanassios, the interior of the tomb with the silver-plated larnax in the forefront and on the opposite wall the papyri on top of a box (after Tsimbidou-Avloniti 2000:568, fig. 2).

gold, were laid, as well as ivory fragments from the bier's decoration (a bier which, at least in one of its zones, was of a Dionysiac character). On one of the walls of this cist tomb appears a painting showing a wooden box with two scrolls of papyri on top (Figure 6). The archaeological context makes the excavator, Maria Tsimbidou-Avloniti, wonder if this may allude to the woman's musical activity.[17] Could this scene be somehow related with the Derveni Papyrus? Is this how we should also imagine the deceased in Tomb A? Could the scene represent a *cista* containing "sacred" texts? I could go on and on with scenarios, but I hope it is clear what I am getting at.

All these examples and more—the Derveni Papyrus and the *epistomia* included—point not to one common, across-the-board, pattern of burial practice and ideology on the fringes of, or peripheral to, society and polis ideology, but, as Christiane Sourvinou-Inwood (1995) has argued, to an individuation, a more personal and differentiated attitude of individuals towards death, even if only in details, which may be independent one from another or interrelated.

17 Tsimbidou-Avloniti (2000:553); I am indebted to Maria Tsimbidou-Avloniti for the photographs from this tomb and to Lillian Acheilara, in charge of the 16th Ephoreia of Prehistoric and Classical Antiquities, for permission to publish them. For another painted tomb in this area see Tsimbidou-Avloniti 2006. Katerina Tzanavari, in charge of the Derveni area and the study of the Derveni tombs, informs me that in one of them there are also intriguing scenes depicting papyri.

Figure 6. Agios Athanassios, detail of the papyri on top of a box (photo Maria Tsimbidou-Avloniti).

Finally, turning to the text of the Derveni Papyrus and how it compares with the texts on the Bacchic-Orphic gold *epistomia*, a few crucial points of contact and departure in the two sets of texts should be mentioned. Both the deceased in Derveni Tomb A and those carrying with them to the grave incised *epistomia* took the risk of their graves being looted, a very common hobby since antiquity, and the texts, if they were meant to be "secret," being publicized. The conditions of the discovery of both sets of texts indicate that they were not meant to be discovered by us, and we may safely assume that we were not the texts' intended audience: in the case of the *epistomia*, the texts contain instructions for the Underworld journey, and the intended audience is the guards of the Underworld spring or lake, the Underworld gods, and the initiate (or, at the most, during the ritual initiation and enactment, the *telestai* and the group of *mystai* present). In the case of the Derveni Papyrus,[18] it is rather far-fetched to argue that the author composed the commentary-like treatise for it to be a *hieros logos* and an *entaphion*, accompanying to the grave this individual who had similar or identical ideas. Because of the fragmentary preservation of the text, we simply do not know, except for the fact that the papyrus ought to have been burned together with his owner and his *cosmos*.

18 On some literary aspects of the *P.Derv.* ὑπόμνημα/commentary see Hunter (in this volume), Calame (in this volume), and Sistakou (in this volume).

In referring to the poetry by Orpheus he is quoting—and about which he has set about to write an interpretive commentary—the Derveni author defines it in column VII as "enigmatic" (*ainigmata*): Orpheus composes his poetry in allegories, because this is the only way he can speak covertly about a *hieros logos* (in lines 7 and perhaps also 2) and present it to the public, i.e. in performance; this secret(?) *logos* is not to be spoken or heard of openly, but then the author proceeds to uncover and explain it in this treatise. This is not the expected, narrow definition of *hierologein* (Henrichs 2003a:233 with n86),[19] and in the Derveni author's mind other texts are also closely related to Orpheus' poem, to which he refers in order to strengthen his interpretation: the *Iliad*, the *Odyssey*, Heraclitus, oracles, and other "epic" poetry (col. IV lines 5–7, col. XXII line 12, and col. XXVI lines 4 and 6–7). That Orpheus was a kind of "theologian," as was the Cretan Epimenides, as well as a number of other notables of the Archaic period,[20] is not new; the fact that Homer, Heraclitus, and who knows who else, as the papyrus is fragmentary, were also considered to be such is something new for so early a period.[21] It implies an additional level of understanding not of all poetry, but specifically of the poetry touching upon matters divine. This understanding is achieved not while the poetry and presumably the rituals are performed in public, but in *exegesis*, i.e., according to Harvey Yunis,[22] poetic interpretation through critical reading, similar to the one advocated by the rhapsode Ion in Plato, an *exegesis* which may or may not have been publicly performed.

Of the poem in question by Orpheus, approximately twenty-four lines in dactylic hexameters survive; the poem's formulaic language, as it compares to that of Homer and Hesiod, remains a desideratum. Apart from verbal echoes

19 During the discussion at the CHS Conference, Albert Henrichs raised doubts about the supplement ἱερ[ολογεῖ]ται in *P.Derv.* column VII line 7 (and possibly in column VII line 2), and Dirk Obbink upon consultation found no trace of -ει- in the photograph of column VII. Rusten (in this volume) proposes a more neutral supplement: μεγάλα ἱερ[ά· ἤινικτ]αι; see also Janko 2008:39; and KPT, 74–75, 171–173, pl. 7 I59 (Tsantsanoglou informs me that the epsilon after the lacuna is almost certain and the space between it and the next tau cannot but admit an iota; hence ιερ[....] ε̣ι̣ται).

20 Tsantsanoglou 1997:121–122; Most 1997; Betegh 2004:362–364; KPT, 75, 172–173; Bierl (in this volume). Albeit a late source, the *Suda* characterizes a number of Epimenides' works as "riddling," for which see Tzifopoulos 2010, with previous bibliography.

21 On the surprising accommodation of theology to philosophy and vice versa see Laks 1997. For the reference to Heraclitus' poetry by the Derveni author and the interaction between the philosopher and "Orphism" see Sider 1997 and in this volume; for Heraclitus and the mysteries see also Schefer 2000 and Drozdek 2001. Granger (2000) convincingly argues that the foolish and ignorant are portrayed by Heraclitus as living a life like the Homeric dead souls. On the complex issue of Orphism and the Presocratics see Burkert 1968 and 1997; Finkelberg 1986; the essays in Laks and Most 1997; and Bernabé 2002.

22 Yunis 2003:195–198; and also Edwards 1991; Henry 1986.

between the texts on the *epistomia* and the Derveni Papyrus—which in and of themselves may or may not be significant—there is one line which presents a striking parallel (col. XIII line 4): αἰδοῖον κατέπινεν, ὃς αἰθέρα ἔκθορε πρῶτος. The verb ἔκθορε in the Orphic poem does not present an *enigma* for the author in this place. Later, however, in column XXI, forms of the verb θόρνυμι occur, which may, arguably but not certainly, be related to the verb θρῴσκω. Interestingly, the infinitive of this verb θόρνυσθαι follows ἀφροδισιάζειν in XXI lines 5–6 (Ἀφροδίτη Οὐρανία καὶ Ζεὺς καὶ ἀφροδισιάζειν καὶ θόρνυσθαι), upon which follows the commentary on ἀφροδισιάζειν, and after that we may suppose followed the commentary on θόρνυσθαι; for in the next column, XXII, the author comments on the many names of the female procreator.

Be that as it may, the choice of the verb θρῴσκω is remarkable, all the more so because in Hesiod's *Theogony*, where procreation is bursting profusely, this verb occurs only once (281): from Medusa's head ἐξέθορε Χρυσάωρ τε μέγας καὶ Πήγασος ἵππος. Elsewhere in Archaic poetry, the verb is employed for only two divine births: in the *Homeric Hymn to Apollo* 119: Apollo ἐκ δ' ἔθορε πρὸ φόως; and in the *Homeric Hymn to Hermes* 20: Hermes μητρὸς ἀπ' ἀθανάτων θόρε γυίων.[23] In the remaining attestations a certain kind of movement is described: in the *Homeric Hymn to Demeter* 430, Persephone narrates Hades' rush towards her from the opening of the earth: τῇ δ' ἔκθορ' ἄναξ κρατερὸς πολυδέγμων, Hades who, albeit not a newborn, sees the light of day of the earth and moves suddenly and overwhelmingly to accomplish the abduction. In the numerous Homeric attestations (far more in the *Iliad* than in the *Odyssey*), the verb again describes the movement of the heroes or gods in battle or in action, and more specifically, the way in which they jump from the chariot or rush towards and overwhelm the enemy.[24]

The same verb is also attested in the texts of three *epistomia*, one from Pelinna, Thessaly (side A lines 7–10, side B lines 9–11): ταῦρος εἰς γάλα ἔθορες,

[23] On this line and its interpretative problems see Calame 1997:66–72; Jourdan 2003, *ad loc.*; Janko 2002, *ad loc.*; Burkert 2004:89–93; Betegh 2004:113; *PEG* 2004, 8 F; KPT, *ad loc.*; Bernabé 2007:79–85.

[24] Greeks on Trojans or vice versa: *Iliad* 8.252, 11.70, 12.462, 14.441, 15.380, 15.573, 15.582, 15.623, 16.770, 20.381, 21.233, 21.539 (Apollo), *Odyssey* 17.233 (Odysseus); jumping from chariot: *Iliad* 8.320, 10.528, 16.427, 23.509; lot jumping out: *Iliad* 7.182, 23.353, *Odyssey* 10.207; Athena's landing *Iliad* 4.79; Iris' sea-landing 24.79; *Odyssey* 23.32, Penelope from bed, at the moment when she identifies the beggar with Odysseus (23.25–31), and not earlier when Eurykleia announces to her Odysseus' return (23.4–9) (for which see Winkler 1990:156–157). These movements are sometimes likened in similes to those of animals (the lion, the dog, the eagle) attacking their prey, or to the movement of the sea: *Iliad* 5.161 (lion on cattle), 15.577 (dog on young deer), 16.773 (flying arrows), 21.18 (Achilles like a *daimon*); *Odyssey* 22.303 (eagles on birds; compare *Iliad* 16.427–430). One instance in which both verbs are employed (as in the text from Pelinna) is Hector's overwhelming attack, likened to that of a wave crushing a swift ship (*Iliad* 15.623–625): αὐτὰρ ὃ λαμπόμενος πυρὶ πάντοθεν ἔνθορ' ὁμίλῳ, | ἐν δ' ἔπεσ' ὡς ὅτε κῦμα θοῇ ἐν νηΐ πέσῃσι | λάβρον ὑπαὶ νεφέων ἀνεμοτρεφές.

αἶψα εἰς γάλα ἔθορες, κριὸς εἰς γάλα ἔπεσες; and in two texts from Thourioi (A1 lines 15–16 and A4 lines 5–6): ἔριφος ἐς γάλα ἔπετες.[25] In the text from Pelinna, at least, the expression does not seem to refer exclusively to birth, but also to movement, because in the beginning of the text the expected verb γίγνομαι is employed (νῦν ἔθανες καὶ νῦν ἐγένου, τρισόλβιε, ἄματι τῶιδε κτλ.), as in the Thourioi A4 text (ἐγένου). Finally, in a controversial text, a hymn *kletikos* discovered in the temple of Dictaean Zeus in Palaikastro near Itanos, Crete, the expression, in strong anaphora, θόρ' ἐς (θρῴσκω εἰς) is employed in two strophes as an appeal to the god to come and reappear (reborn?), and jump/rush onto cattle, sheep, trees, the *oikoi*, the poleis, the ships, the young citizens, *themis*, in order to effect fertility.[26]

These instances strongly suggest that epic, hymnic, and ritual poetry seems aware of the verb's semantics. Apparently, in certain texts the verb θρῴσκω is almost a technical term for describing the birth and the first movements of a god or a hero,[27] and the semantics of the phrase in these lexical contexts implies a fusion of two motifs: the way a particular child is born and the newborn's erratic jumping movements when out of the womb, as well as the overwhelming charge of an animal or human when attacking—both motifs with special emphasis on new beginnings of a particular kind, be it birth, rebirth, or movement.

25 On these expressions see Tsantsanoglou and Parássoglou 1987:13; and Tzifopoulos 2010; Iakov (2010) advances a challenging interpretation of the expression in the Pelinna text, i.e. that "milk" denotes the Milky Way, to which the epithet "starry" and the name Asterios in the B-texts are also related; in this way, the animals mentioned in the expression as falling headlong into the milk are probably the stars and constellations on the sky (which may indicate a number of reincarnations of the soul as well); there the soul of the *mystes* stays in transit, until it becomes itself a star, or returns to its star, reaching its final destination.

26 Guarducci in *IC* III.ii [Dictaeum Fanum].2, line 24ff, commentary (pp. 16–17): ἀ[μῶν δὲ θόρ' ἐς ποί]μνια, καὶ θόρ' εὔποκ' ἐς [μῆλα], [κὲς λάϊ]α καρπῶν θόρε κὲς τελεσ[φόρος οἴκος]. [θόρε κὲς] πόληας ἁμῶν, θόρε κὲς ποντο<π>όρος νᾶας, θόρε κὲς ν[έος πο]λείτας, θόρε κὲς θέμιν κλ[ειτάν]; West 1965:157–158; and Furley and Bremer 2001:2.16–17. Perlman (1995:162 with n11) has noted a discrepancy between the *Hymn*, where fertility is important and receives emphasis, and the Pelinna text, where the "ritual matrix ... does not stress fertility." For the verb θρῴσκω in the texts of the lamellae and the Palaikastro hymn, Alonge 2005. Depew (2000:61–65 and 69–77) and Furley and Bremer (2001:1.1–62) discuss the problematic distinctions between the genres of hymn and prayer. Calame (2009:177–228) in his semiotic analysis of the dialogue in the texts on the lamellae and *epistomia*, and in hymns and prayers, concludes that in both sets of texts there is an interesting interplay in the roles: poet–addressee (man/woman)–god.

27 In the hymnic invocation of Dionysus by the women of Elis, preserved in Plutarch's *Moralia* (299a–b), "the hero Dionysus, worthy bull, is to come ... to the temple storming on bovine foot" (Furley and Bremer 2001:1.369: ἐλθεῖν, ἥρω Διόνυσε, | Ἀλίων ἐς ναὸν | ἁγνὸν σὺν Χαρίτεσσιν | ἐς ναὸν τῷ βοέῳ | ποδὶ θύων. | ἄξιε ταῦρε (they translate ἥρω as "Lord" on the basis of Mycenaean Greek ἥρα/ἥρως being equivalent to "Lady/Lord"; 2.374–375); for extensive commentary and the previous bibliography see Furley and Bremer 2001:1.369–372; 2.373–377; Scullion 2001; and Tzifopoulos 2010.

This striking instance may also indicate that the Derveni author, in addition to being well versed in poetry and rituals of all kinds, was also aware of the semantics of the verb in different lexical contexts, and so also perhaps of the texts on the *epistomia*, or at least of the *legomena* and *dromena* in the rituals to which he refers in columns I–VII and XX. The texts on the *epistomia* (and perhaps other texts as well, among them the Derveni poem by Orpheus) formed part of the *legomena* and the *dromena* in an initiatory ritual that promised a blessed afterlife. These texts need not be the ritual's *hieros logos*, unless the meaning of the term is broadened, as is done by the Derveni author, with the exception of the *symbola* or *synthemata*—these enigmatic, as the Derveni author would have called them, passwords for identification and entrance into a special place in the Underworld.

However one understands the Derveni author—as a *mantis*, a *prophetes*, a *chresmologos*, an *(orpheo)telestes*, an *agyrtes*, a *magos*, a *góes* or *goês*, an *Orphikos*, a *physikos*, a philosopher-poet (and that is the easy part, even though he may have been comfortable with one term and uncomfortable with the other)[28]—what needs to be emphasized is that his methodology and commentary presuppose that the works ascribed to Orpheus and circulating in written form and through performances since at least the sixth century BCE, *and* the related literature (Homer, Heraclitus, and others), *and* the rituals (Dionysiac, Eleusinian, and other) in fashion during the Derveni author's time, were also thought of as texts, actions, beliefs, and ideas in need of interpretation by an intermediary.

His being an "intermediary" between the human and the divine/*cosmos* and its true understanding accentuates the difficulty of our perception of him, because these intermediaries were more or less trusted by people, who had specific needs. In his harsh criticism of these charismatics in the famous *Republic* passage (364b–365a), Plato distinguishes two kinds of needs that peoples and cities have, and then addresses the way in which false religious practitioners accommodate their preaching to suit those needs. The first need involves an

[28] For discussion of these columns and the problematic identity of their author see Obbink 1997; Kahn 1997; West 1997; Tsantsanoglou 1997 and 2008; Most 1997:118; Janko 2001:18–24; Burkert 2004:99–124; Betegh 2004:74–91; and KPT, 45–59, 70–75, 82–83, 86–87, 161–174, 186–189, 193–197. Graf and Johnston (2007:90–96, 158–164, 178–184) propose that the authors of the texts on the lamellae and *epistomia* may have been local or itinerant *orpheotelestai* (also called *bricoleurs*), a term which combines all (or almost all) the religious activities mentioned by Plato (n29); also Edmonds 2004:4. Torjussen (2005) argues that Dionysus was most probably absent from the commentary, whose author used Orpheus as an authority. According to Andrei Lebedev's (1996) hypothesis, Pharnabazos, the diviner of Hermes, and Aristoteles were two such individuals, both magicians and *orpheotelestai*, at work in Olbia, and, because of competition, they were writing curse-tablets against one another. In a parallel case, Emmanuel Voutiras (1998) has proposed that Timarete from Corinth most probably was an itinerant female magician active in fourth-century BCE Pella.

interest in this life: people want assurances and blessings during their lifetime. The second need of people involves what happens to them after death.[29] This appears also to be the case in column V of the Derveni Papyrus, although the text is fragmentary, where reference is made to oracles, but also to dreams, both of which are not misunderstood in what they say about Hades' *deina*.[30]

Even though Plato's and the Derveni author's views cannot be taken as representative or mainstream, they both attempt to distinguish between true and false attitudes, true and false knowledge: a misunderstanding and ignorance of what the rituals and their accompanying texts are really referring to when they touch upon matters divine and *cosmic*. Although perceptions are difficult to grasp, a bad poet does not make poetry bad, just as a bad *mantis*, *prophetes*, *chresmologos*, *orpheotelestes*, *agyrtes*, *magos*, philosopher-poet does not make these arts bad by definition.[31]

29 Plato *Republic* 364b–365a (translation Shorey 1937, modified): "But the strangest of all these speeches are the things they say about the gods and virtue, how so it is that the gods themselves assign to many good men misfortunes and an evil life, but to their opposites a contrary lot; and *agyrtai* and *manteis* go to rich men's doors and make them believe that they, by means of sacrifices [θυσίαις] and incantations [ἐπῳδαῖς], have accumulated a treasure of power from the gods that can expiate and cure with pleasurable festivals any misdeed of a man or his ancestors, and that if a man wishes to harm an enemy, at slight cost [μετὰ σμικρῶν δαπανῶν] he will be enabled to injure just and unjust alike, since they are masters of spells and enchantments [ἐπαγωγαῖς τισιν καὶ καταδέσμοις] that constrain the gods to serve their end. And for all these sayings they cite the poets as witnesses [μάρτυρας ποιητάς], with regard to the ease and plentifulness of vice ... And others cite Homer as a witness to the beguiling of gods by men ... And they produce a bushel of books of Musaeus and Orpheus [βίβλων δὲ ὅμαδον παρέχονται Μουσαίου καὶ Ὀρφέως], the offspring of the Moon and of the Muses, as they affirm, and these books they use in their ritual [καθ' ἃς θυηπολοῦσιν], and make not only ordinary men but states believe that there really are remissions [λύσεις] of sins and purifications [καθαρμοί] for deeds of injustice, by means of sacrifice and pleasant sport [διὰ θυσιῶν καὶ παιδιᾶς ἡδονῶν] for the living, and that there are also special rites for the defunct, which they call *teletai*, that deliver us from evils in that other world [αἳ τῶν ἐκεῖ κακῶν ἀπολύουσιν ἡμᾶς], while terrible things await those who have neglected to sacrifice [μὴ θύσαντας δὲ δεινὰ περιμένει]." Betegh (2004:80) understands Plato's attitude as negative and that of the Derveni author as positive; for a discussion of this passage and the one in *Laws* 909a–b see also Voutiras 1998:123–127; and KPT, 45–59. Cf. Theophrastus *Characters* 16.11; and Plutarch *Sayings of Spartans* 224e.

30 KPT, 70–71 and 161–166; Ferrari 2007:207–208; Janko 2008:50–51. On oracles and divination, see Johnston in this volume.

31 As in everything else, so in all these activities there were both true and false intermediaries, interpreters, and practitioners who catered to people's needs, and among them there were also fakes, who tried to earn a living by playing on people's superstitions and fears, and some may indeed have been local or Panhellenic jokes (Burkert 1987:30–53). The usual but not always convincing distinctions we draw among these intermediaries and practitioners (religious or not) are abolished by Plato and the Derveni author, so as to emphasize their message, but neither Plato nor the Derveni author believe that the art itself is to blame; blame and reprobation must fall on the ignorant, self-proclaimed intermediaries, who misunderstand and misapply the art with ridiculous results (see n28, the example of the two magicians' dog-fight in Olbia). Betegh (2004:364–370), correctly in my view, understands the interpretative method followed by the

The Derveni Papyrus and the gold incised *epistomia* reveal points of contact and departure both in terms of their chronological and archaeological contexts, and in terms of their texts. Neither of these, however, is strong enough and conclusive in either direction. Even so, both are unique representatives of discourses on the nature of the divine and the *cosmos*, and on the afterlife and its ritual poetics that must have proliferated from at least the sixth century BCE onwards, if not earlier, vying for an attentive audience. More research will no doubt enhance further our understanding of them both, particularly the nature of the relation, if any, between the texts on the *epistomia* and the poem by Orpheus commented upon by the Derveni author, both of which present analogous problems in need of interpretation by an intermediary.

But until then, and in spite of Plato's and the Derveni author's warnings against ignorance, and in spite of their discourses on the true nature of things, Greeks continued business as usual: they attended initiation rituals, procured a gold incised *epistomion*, and, when time came, they were buried with it. At least for these deceased we know this much: they were buried content and assured that special treatment awaited them in the Underworld in the belief that they had "earned" what we would call, for all intents and purposes, "paradise." For the deceased individual in Derveni Tomb A, who took with him on the pyre the allegorical commentary on a theo-cosmogonic poem by Orpheus, alas, we do not know even this much.

Derveni author as similar to that of interpreting oracles, but this need not be different from allegorical interpretations; see also Johnston (in this volume). For Plato's pronouncements in the *Republic* as prophetic see Virvidakis 1996; for the Orphic and anti-Orphic Plato see Kingsley 1995:112–132; Cosi 2000:146–150; and for the terminology of the mysteries employed by the philosopher, Riedweg 1987.

Appendix

The following discussion among Eric Turner, Georges Daux, Bernhard van Groningen, Claire Préaux, Charles Bradford Welles, Herbert Youtie, Kurt von Fritz, Hugh Lloyd-Jones, Frank Walbank, Sir Ronald Syme, and Herbert Musurillo followed Kapsomenos' (1964) presentation at the Annual Meeting of the American Society of Papyrologists in Philadelphia, August 24, 1964 (*Bulletin of the American Society of Papyrologists* 2 [1964]:15–23). It is offered here not for the sake of the history of classical scholarship, but in order to show that, in spite of the fact that at the time knowledge about the text was very limited, nonetheless the questions and issues raised were and still remain fundamental for understanding the Derveni Papyrus.

Professor Eric G. Turner, University College, London

I must say how much I, personally, have enjoyed this exposition. It was so clear. I also enjoyed the opportunity to see so many pictures. The point that has occurred to me in regard to these pictures is the relative size of the writing, and also its purpose. Is it a good book hand? Was the papyrus of Derveni the work of a practiced scribe? I am sure that we must admit that it is so, but I suspect that it is a very small handwriting, whereas the *Timotheus* was a large one. This was obscure, I think, in our pictures.

The immediate thing that comes to mind when I think of papyri like the one of Derveni is in fact the *Crito* of Plato, which is, of course, early third century. It is a very small handwriting, and the letters are tiny. Now the individual forms of the letters are not very much like those of the Derveni hand, but the impression of the hand and the style as a whole is, and this does warn one, I think, to be a little careful where we have such a small amount of comparative material, because this is very definitely a book and a book hand. The *Timotheus* is a very poorly written book in my opinion—a very gross hand—and the contract of 311 is after all a business document written by a scribe of quite different character. Again, it is very difficult to compare inscriptions because there you are working with a chisel and not with a pen.

These are the sorts of cautions which enter my mind. At the same time, I have not seen anything quite like the letter forms or the layout so clearly set out, and this is what makes me think that it ought to go into the fourth century. Whether it is earlier or, perhaps, a little bit later, I do not know, but I believe that it is the earliest Greek papyrus. I would be ready to support that. Of course we are apt to compare material from different places, from different environments, and from different media. This is still a caution which must be maintained. It is not merely a question of Egyptian and Greek inscriptions; it is even Macedonia. But no more shall I say.

Professor Georges Daux, L'École Française d'Archéologie

I think that there is not much to await from the inscriptions. I do not think that the examples which we have so far would prove anything. I think that the most important thing is the writing from the papyrological point of view, and in light of the evidence it is quite certain that it belongs to the fourth century on the whole. There is also an inscription which was not mentioned; certainly the inscription on the vase belongs clearly to the fourth century. So I think that the contribution of archaeology and of epigraphy and of the form of the inscription on the vase are very important factors for the dating of the manuscript of the papyrus.

Professor Bernhard A. van Groningen, University of Leiden

There is just one thing I would like to mention, because I think it is rather too often forgotten. Now my age is seventy, and I write practically in the same way as when I was twenty. If after two thousand years there is a scrap of manuscript which was written by me, it could not possibly be said whether it was written in 1964 or in 1904, and I say that we must always be careful and not be too precise in our datings, because you always have the difference of half a century in one man's life.

Professor Claire Préaux, University of Brussels

I should say that the papyrus shows us that the cursive style of writing was not formed in the fourth century BC. I was struck by the fact that the marriage contract of Elephantine was written exactly in a book style. We see the cursive writing being formed under our eyes in the beginning of the first half of the third century BC, and when you look at the writing of even a man like Zenon, the famous manager of Apollonius' estate, it is not exactly cursive. This man must have learned writing in Caria, not in Egypt. He brings with him the type of writing for documents as well as for books which was in use in the Greek world at the end of the fourth century or at the beginning of the third.

So this papyrus then confirms us in what we could deduce from the papyri of Egypt—that there probably was no cursive writing in Greece in the fourth century BC. We must imagine that Plato, Aristotle, or Demosthenes wrote this way, which is just the unique way of writing Greek, whether it is on stone or papyrus, either quick-writing or not quick-writing. This adds a social meaning, because it means that probably writing was not so much known, after all—less known among people than we would perhaps expect.

Professor Charles B. Welles, Yale University

Mlle. Préaux and others have introduced the term "cursive." I don't know what it means, of course, and probably no one else does either, but it is conveniently used to indicate a style of writing in which the pen is lifted as little as possible from the papyrus. It has seemed to me sometimes in practice to study almost as if it were Japanese—the sequence of strokes with which a writer makes letters, if indeed there is a sequence of strokes and not all one stroke.

One letter struck me particularly in this papyrus of Professor Kapsomenos, and seemed to be extremely interesting. I had the impression that the sigma was actually made in one stroke without lifting the pen from the paper. It seemed to me also that at least in some cases the omega was made in the same fashion, that is, starting at the left with a little loop, then going up looping again, and off. Would Professor Kapsomenos like to comment on that point? (Professor Kapsomenos agreed that the sigma was made in a single stroke.)

Professor Herbert C. Youtie, University of Michigan

The word "cursive" has, of course, always bothered us. It always needs definition. Actually, it is a word which could conveniently be abandoned. Mlle. Préaux, I think, almost instinctively gave us the better approach. I, myself, am trying to remember this too. She said, "quick or not so quick." This is the secret, of course. The quicker it gets, the more cursive it gets. I need not go through what the elementary books say to explain it. So actually I am now trying to say "fast writing," and I don't use "slow writing" usually, since ordinarily I am dealing with documents. They are all relatively fast, and therefore, they are all more or less cursive. The faster they are, the more cursive they will get because the scribe will make more loops.

I would say that we could very well abandon the word "cursive." It has traditional value so that one hates to let the word go, but it is much vaguer than "quick or fast writing." Even that is a relative term, of course, but perhaps in current English "fast" is a more intelligible word than "cursive." That is about as much as one can say.

About the date of this papyrus, I agree with everyone that this is a fourth-century hand. I feel strongly that it is a fourth-century hand, but I agree with Professor van Groningen in the point of his remarks. I feel that the attempt to date undated literary manuscripts in anything under a century is not today going to succeed. We don't know that much. It is one thing to have an inscription which tells you it was written in 346 BC, but if the papyrus doesn't tell you when it was written, if it is not a fast hand, you are really in trouble. And everyone is in trouble every time he tries to date a literary hand. He feels in trouble, and that is his best indication. I always feel in difficulty with an undated papyrus, and often even when it is a document, I must pull my forces together, and look and compare and depend upon all my predecessors for a judgment. It is so comforting to open Schubart or something similar, and find an adjusted list of cursive documents. Much of this is secure, but not so secure that we can hope to date within twenty-five or even fifty years. I can't do it! Grenfell and Hunt were perhaps the only ones who had the feeling that they could date within decades. They were under an illusion. We know today that unless they were really much, much more imbued with ancient handwriting than anyone living today, that they could not do it. My own feeling is that I can't do it and I have not met anyone who can.

Professor Welles

Would you, before you leave the microphone, explain whether you regard this particular papyrus as fast written or slow written, or something in between?

Professor Youtie

Within the limits of visual judgment that we use, I think that most of us would put this among the slow moving. But you must compare it with Mlle. Préaux's ostraka, if you want really fast writing. And of course, it is all relative. Mlle. Préaux wrote—if you don't mind my referring to your beautiful article on the ostrakon palaeography—a magnificent thing. It is a masterpiece, and anyone who wants to know about fast writing would do well to read Mlle. Préaux's article in the *Journal of Egyptian Archaeology*, volume 40. Now, that is fast writing, and then it slows down to what we call a literary hand. If you call a papyrus a literary hand, then you mean that it is slow. If you call it a document, then you usually mean that it is fast.

Professor Welles

I think that since we are friends here, and only our voices are being recorded, I might say that I do not entirely agree with my colleague from Michigan that it is impossible to make a fairly accurate dating of a literary hand, but I respect his judgment, and it is second to none.

Professor Kurt von Fritz, University of Munich

Professor Kapsomenos has told us how this carbonized papyrus was unrolled by Mr. Fackelmann from Vienna. Now this seems to open further possibilities. As everyone knows, there are a great many carbonized papyrus rolls which may contain most interesting material. The question then arises whether the time might now have come to try to unroll them and to make an attempt to read them. Of course, this is a very difficult question in various ways. In the first place, one might say that it would be better to wait until still more improved methods have been developed because at present, there is of course always some kind of destruction. So far, it has not been possible to unroll the rolls in such a way that every bit is preserved.

On the other hand, when I was in Vienna last April I was told that after Mr. Fackelmann had done some work for Professor Kapsomenos and his Greek colleagues, he had improved his method by experimenting with papyrus rolls which he himself had carbonized. In other words, there is a possibility of very great improvement in the near or distant future.

In the second place, the rolls are in the hands of our Italian colleagues, and they of course are very anxious to preserve these rolls and not have them experimented with, unless there is a very good prospect of them being harmed as little as possible. But at the same time, I thought it might be interesting to all of you at least to mention the problem, and perhaps we could ask some of our Italian colleagues who may be here whether they have talked to their colleagues at Naples about it, or whether they might be able to discuss it with them, and if in the future such an enterprise were entered into, whether some money might be found to do something about it.

Perhaps we might start in this way, that we would not at first start by trying to unroll these papyrus rolls, but rather get some money for further experimentation for the next few years so that then, if an entirely satisfactory method should be developed, we could proceed with great safety to the papyri.

Professor Hugh Lloyd-Jones, Oxford University

I have heard a most careful, excellent exposition, and then comments by some of the greatest experts in the world on papyri, and the consensus of their impressions that the date is fourth century is most impressive. Well, if they are right, this is a most sensational fact from the point of view of content. Who ever knew that the Greeks were writing commentaries on poetry, and on Orphic poetry at that, as early as the fourth century? Professor Kapsomenos in his learned commentary regarding possibilities, possible authors, at the end of his paper mentioned Metrodorus of Lampsacus and Epigenes, but unfortunately these are shadowy figures. We know very little about them. In the case of Epigenes, the whole question of date is a very open one.

It may well be that the manuscript is not as early as most speakers today have thought. We clearly have so little material for the history of Greek writing in the period in question that even though most of the experts who discussed the paper have the impression that the find must be as early as the fourth century, I think we should be rash if we regarded that as an absolute certainty. How strong the archaeological evidence is for the dating is not yet clear. But if the text really is so early, its importance for the history of scholarship and of Greek religion is very great. As impressive as the consensus in favor of the early date has been, we have so little of Greek writing of this period that it would be exceedingly dangerous if the hypothesis of an early date were to be generally accepted without careful consideration of all the difficulties involved.

Professor Daux

Now I must say that I quite agree that it is impossible to date a papyrus within about fifty years, but for epigraphy it is not exactly so for the fourth century. As I said, there is an inscription on this beautiful vase which was found, published since and it will be published more—and there is no doubt that the inscription and the dialect are from the fourth century. There is no doubt that the archaeological finds are from the fourth century. There is no doubt about it.

I am very skeptical about dates in general, but in the fourth century, in this period of Greek art, you can be certain of the dates of certain magnificent works. You could not date this vase from the third century. It is quite impossible. You can discuss it between 350 and 330—perhaps about 320—but you cannot put it in the third century. I think this is one of the cases where the archaeological and epigraphical evidence brings some security to papyrology. I insist on that and I believe it.

Professor van Groningen

I am sorry, ladies and gentlemen, to detain you just one moment more, but I would like to say something. If I remember well, Plato commented on a poem of Simonides in the *Protagoras*, and if Plato did that, I think we can presume that such interpretations and spoken commentaries were rather usual. If such things were done verbally, I hardly doubt that they should have been written down from time to time. So I do not think that this commentary is such a big surprise. Of course, I could be mistaken, but I just give my impression.

Professor Welles

What does surprise me in a certain sense is not so much that a man might have wished to have buried with him some Orphic hymns or might choose to have manuscripts of Orphic hymns consumed in his funeral pyre, which I suppose would remain with him just as effectively, but that he should have done this with a commentary seems to me a little remarkable. And it also interests me that this should have occurred in Macedonia, in a rather exciting period of Macedonian history, when someone might think that the Macedonians had no time for Orphism, commentated or pure.

Professor van Groningen

No, no, no, no, no!

Professor Welles

No?

Professor van Groningen

Well, of course, as you might know, I wasn't there either. However, I would like to say this. My country was occupied during the war for five years, and the situation was very, very, difficult, but nevertheless very good work, even on classical epigraphy, was done in that time, so why not in Macedonia?

Professor Welles

I was working around rather to another matter, but since we have here someone who knows very much about Macedonia at least in the later period, and certainly in the earlier period too, I wonder if we might hear from Professor Walbank.

Professor Frank W. Walbank, University of Liverpool

I have nothing to say, except to pose a question. Is it possible that this scroll was merely used as inflammable material? I know Martial refers to using papyrus on funeral pyres. Would that always be blank papyrus, or might it just be some scroll that the heirs of the person were not particularly interested in preserving?

Sir Ronald Syme, Oxford University

I would say that the presence of a commentary on poetry or any literary work at so early a period does seem to me to be remarkable. But one of the things we don't know enough about is precisely the habitual culture of the landowners on the fringes of society. We might find parallels in the South of France for this sort of thing, might we not?

Professor Herbert Musurillo, Fordham University

I would like to agree with Dr. Lloyd-Jones on the question of the sensationalism of this commentary in one respect, that as far as I know this would be the first excellent commentary using the allegorical method for Homer. You remember that Horace in Epistles I and II, *Trojani belli scriptorem*, speaks of the allegorical interpretation of the *Iliad* and the *Odyssey*, and we don't have any commentaries of this sort. This would be, so far as I know, the first sizeable piece.

In this connection, Philo of Alexandria regularly used the allegorical method, and we are not quite sure where he derived it from. It not only came undoubtedly from the Midrashi method of interpreting the Pentateuch, but in this case we will have a sort of background for saying that Philo was adapting some of the methods of the Greek commentators and grammarians. So, from this point of view I agree with the sensational method of the commentary on this papyrus, and I would like to see some more work done on this aspect of it.

Professor Kapsomenos

It is not a commentary on Homer, because Homer is just quoted to explain some words in the poem.

Professor Musurillo

I did not mean Homer specifically, but the use of the allegorical method in general.

Professor Welles

We shall conclude this first report of our meeting by congratulating Professor Kapsomenos on his work and the extraordinary nature of his discovery and assuring him that we all shall wait with bated breath for the full evidence to appear in print.

Abbreviations

IC = *Inscriptiones Creticae*, ed. Margarita Guarducci, opera et consilio Friderici Halbherr collectae, vols. I–V (Rome, 1935–1950).

KPT = Theokritos Kouremenos, Giorgos M. Parássoglou, and Kyriakos Tsantsanoglou, eds., *The Derveni Papyrus. Edited with Introduction and Commentary* (Studi e Testi per il Corpus dei Papiri Filosofici Greci e Latini 13) (Florence, 2006).

PEG 2004, 2005, 2007 = *Poetae epici graeci testimonia et fragmenta*, pars II: *Orphicorum et orphicis similium testimonia et fragmenta*, fasc. 1–3, ed. Adalberto Bernabé. Munich and Leipzig.

Bibliography

Adam-Veleni, Polyxeni. 2002. *Μακεδονικοί βωμοί: Τιμητικοί και ταφικοί βωμοί αυτοκρατορικών χρόνων στη Θεσσαλονίκη, πρωτεύουσα της επαρχίας Μακεδονίας, και στη Βέροια, πρωτεύουσα του Κοινού των Μακεδόνων*. Δημοσιεύματα Αρχαιολογικού Δελτίου 84. Athens.

Alonge, Mark. 2005. "The Palaikastro Hymn and the Modern Myth of the Cretan Zeus." *Princeton/Stanford Working Papers in Classics*, Dec. 2005. http://www.princeton.edu/~pswpc/papers/papers.html.

Andronikos, Manolis. 1994. *Βεργίνα II: Ο τάφος της Περσεφόνης*. Βιβλιοθήκη τῆς ἐν Ἀθήναις Ἀρχαιολογικῆς Ἑταιρείας 138. Athens.

Barr-Sharrar, Beryl. 2008. *The Derveni Krater: Masterpiece of Classical Greek Metalwork*. Ancient Art and Architecture in Context 1. Princeton.

Bernabé, Adalberto. 2002. "Orphisme et Présocratiques: Bilan et perspectives d'un dialogue complexe." In *Qu'est-ce que la philosophie présocratique?* (ed. André Laks and Claire Louguet) 205–247. Cahiers de Philologie 20. Villeneuve-d'Ascq.

———. 2007. "Autour de l'interprétation des colonnes XIII–XVI du Papyrus de Derveni." *Rhizai: A Journal for Ancient Philosophy and Science* 1:77–103.

Bernabé, Adalberto, and Ana Isabel Jiménez San Cristóbal. 2008. *Instructions for the Netherworld: The Orphic Gold Tablets*, trans. Michael Chase (Religions in the Graeco-Roman World 162), Leiden (=*Instrucciones para el más allá. Las laminillas órficas de oro*, apéndice iconográfico de Ricardo Olmos, Ilustraciones de Sara Olmos, Madrid 2001).

Betegh, Gábor. 2004. *The Derveni Papyrus: Cosmology, Theology, and Interpretation*. Cambridge.

Brécoulaki, Hariclia. 2006. *La peinture funéraire de Macédoine: Emplois et fonctions de la couleur, IVe–IIe s. av. J.-C.* (Meletemata 48), Athens [= a summary version in “La peinture funéraire de Macédoine,” in *Rois, cités, nécropoles: Institutions, rites et monuments en Macédoine. Actes des Colloques de Nanterre (Décembre 2002) et d'Athènes (Janvier 2004)* (ed. Anne Marie Guimier-Sorbets, Miltiade B. Hatzopoulos, and Yvette Morizot) 47–61 (Meletemata 45) (Athens, 2006)].

Burkert, Walter. 1968. “Orpheus und die Vorsokratiker: Bemerkungen zum Derveni Papyrus und zur pythagoreischen Zahlenlehre.” *Antike und Abendland* 14:93–114 [= Fritz Graf, ed., *Walter Burkert Kleine Schriften III: Mystica, Orphica, Pythagorica*, 62–88 (Hypomnemata Suppl. 2.3) (Göttingen, 2006)].

———. 1987. *Ancient Mystery Cults*. Cambridge, MA.

———. 1997. “Star Wars or One Stable World? A Problem of Presocratic Cosmogony (*PDerv*. Col. XXV).” In Laks and Most 1997:167–174.

———. 2004. *Babylon, Memphis, Persepolis: Eastern Contexts of Greek Culture*. Cambridge, MA.

Calame, Claude. 1997. “Figures of Sexuality and Initiatory Transition in the Derveni Theogony and Commentary.” In Laks and Most 1997:65–80.

———. 2009. *Poetic and Performative Memory in Ancient Greece: Heroic Reference and Ritual Gestures in Time and Space*. Hellenic Studies 18. Washington, DC.

Chryssostomou, Anastassia, and Pavlos Chryssostomou. 2001. “Ανασκαφή στη δυτική νεκρόπολη του Αρχοντικού της Πέλλας κατά το 2001.” *Το Αρχαιολογικό Έργο στη Μακεδονία και Θράκη* 15:477–488.

———. 2002. “Ανασκαφή στη δυτική νεκρόπολη του Αρχοντικού της Πέλλας κατά το 2002.” *Το Αρχαιολογικό Έργο στη Μακεδονία και Θράκη* 16:465–478.

Cosi, Dario M. 2000. “Orfeo e l'Orfismo: Tra continuità e innovazione.” In *Tra Orfeo e Pitagora: Origini e incontri di culture nell'antichità: Atti dei Seminari Napoletani 1996–1998* (ed. Marisa Tortorelli Ghidini et al.) 139–159. Naples.

Depew, Mary. 2000. “Enacted and Represented Dedications: Genre and Greek Hymn.” In *Matrices of Genre: Authors, Canons, and Society* (ed. Mary Depew and Dirk Obbink) 59–79, 254–263. Cambridge, MA.

Detienne, Marcel. 1975. “Les chemins de la déviance: Orphisme, dionysisme et pythagorisme.” In *Orfismo in Magna Grecia: Atti del quattordicesimo convegno di studi sulla Magna Grecia, Taranto, 6–10 Ottobre 1974*, 49–79. Naples.

———. 2003. *The Writing of Orpheus: Greek Myth in Cultural Contact*. Trans. Janet Lloyd. Baltimore, MD.

Drozdek, Adam. 2001. “Heraclitus' Theology.” *Classica et Mediaevalia* 52:37–56.

Edmonds, Radcliffe G., III. 2004. *Myths of the Underworld Journey: Plato, Aristophanes, and the “Orphic” Gold Tablets*. Cambridge.

———, ed. 2011. *The "Orphic" Gold Tablets and Greek Religion: Further Along the Path*. Cambridge.

Edwards, Mark J. 1991. "Notes on the Derveni Commentator." *Zeitschrift für Papyrologie und Epigraphik* 86:203–211.

Ferrari, Franco. 2007. "Note al testo delle colonne II–VII del papiro di Derveni." *Zeitschrift für Papyrologie und Epigraphik* 162:203–211.

Finkelberg, Aryeh. 1986. "On the Unity of Orphic and Milesian Thought." *Harvard Theological Review* 79:321–335.

Furley, William D., and Jan M. Bremer. 2001. *Greek Hymns: Selected Cult Songs from the Archaic to the Hellenistic Period*, vol. 1: *The Texts in Translation*, vol. 2: *Greek Texts and Commentary*. Studien und Texte zu Antike und Christentum 9–10. Tübingen.

Graf, Fritz, and Sarah Iles Johnston. 2007. *Ritual Texts for the Afterlife: Orpheus and the Bacchic Gold Tablets*. London.

Granger, Herbert. 2000. "Death's Other Kingdom: Heraclitus on the Life of the Foolish and the Wise." *Classical Philology* 95:260–281.

Hatzopoulos, Miltiade B. 1994. *Cultes et rites de passage en Macédoine*. Meletemata 19. Athens.

———. 2002. "Λατρεῖες τῆς Μακεδονίας· τελετὲς μεταβάσεως καὶ μυήσεις." In *Λατρείες στην 'Περιφέρεια' του Αρχαίου Ελληνικού Κόσμου* (ed. Aphrodite Avagianou) 11–29. Athens.

———. 2006. "De la vie à trépas: Rites de passage, lamelles dionysiaques et tombes macédoniennes." In *Rois, cités, nécropoles: Institutions, rites et monuments en Macédoine. Actes des Colloques de Nanterre (Décembre 2002) et d'Athènes (Janvier 2004)* (ed. Anne Marie Guimier-Sorbets, Miltiade B. Hatzopoulos, and Yvette Morizot) 131–141. Meletemata 45. Athens.

Henrichs, Albert. 2003a. "*Hieroi Logoi* and *Hierai Bibloi*: The (Un)written Margins of the Sacred in Ancient Greece." *Harvard Studies in Classical Philology* 88: 205–240.

———. 2003b. "Writing Religion: Inscribed Texts, Ritual Authority, and the Religious Discourse of the Polis." In *Written Texts and the Rise of Literate Culture in Ancient Greece* (ed. Harvey Yunis) 38–58. Cambridge.

———. 2004. "Sacred Texts and Canonicity: Greece." In *Religions of the Ancient World: A Guide* (ed. Sarah Iles Johnston) 633–635. Cambridge, MA.

Henry, Madeleine. 1986. "The Derveni Commentator as Literary Critic." *Transactions of the American Philological Association* 116:149–164.

Iakov, Daniel. 2010. "Milk in the Gold Tablets from Pelinna." *Trends in Classics* 2:64–76.

Janko, Richard. 1997. "The Physicist as Hierophant: Aristophanes, Socrates, and the Authorship of the Derveni Papyrus." *Zeitschrift für Papyrologie und Epigraphik* 118:61–94.

———. 2001. "The Derveni Papyrus (Diagoras of Melos, *Apopyrgizontes Logoi*?): A New Translation." *Classical Philology* 96:1–32.

———. 2002. "The Derveni Papyrus: An Interim Text." *Zeitschrift für Papyrologie und Epigraphik* 141:1–62.

———. 2008. "Reconstructing (Again) the Opening of the Derveni Papyrus." *Zeitschrift für Papyrologie und Epigraphik* 166:37–51.

Jourdan, Fabienne. 2003. *Le Papyrus de Derveni: Texte présenté, traduit et annoté*. Vérité des mythes 23. Paris.

Kahn, Charles H. 1997. "Was Euthyphro the Author of the Derveni Papyrus?" In Laks and Most 1997:55–63.

Kapsomenos, Stylianos. 1964. "The Orphic Papyrus Roll of Thessalonica." *Bulletin of the American Society of Papyrologists* 2:2–14 [= Ἀρχαιολογικὸν Δελτίον 19 (1964): 17–25].

Kingsley, Peter. 1995. *Ancient Philosophy, Mystery, and Magic: Empedocles and Pythagorean Tradition*. Oxford.

Kottaridou, Angéliki. 2006. "Couleur et sens: L'emploi de la couleur dans la tombe de la reine Eurydice." In *Rois, cités, nécropoles: Institutions, rites et monuments en Macédoine. Actes des Colloques de Nanterre (Décembre 2002) et d'Athènes (Janvier 2004)* (ed. Anne Marie Guimier-Sorbets, Miltiade B. Hatzopoulos, and Yvette Morizot) 55–168. Meletemata 45. Athens.

Laks, André. 1997. "Between Religion and Philosophy: The Function of Allegory in the Derveni Papyrus." *Phronesis* 42:121–142.

Laks, André, and Glen W. Most, eds. 1997. *Studies on the Derveni Papyrus*. Oxford.

Lebedev, Andrei. 1996. "Pharnabazos, the Diviner of Hermes: Two Ostraca with Curse Letters from Olbia." *Zeitschrift für Papyrologie und Epigraphik* 112: 268–278.

Miller, Stella G. 1982. "Macedonian Tombs: Their Architecture and Architectural Decoration." In *Macedonia and Greece in Late Classical and Hellenistic Times* (ed. Beryl Barr-Sharrar and Eugene N. Borza) 152–171. Studies in the History of Art 10. Washington, DC.

———. 1992. *The Tomb of Lyson and Kallikes: A Painted Macedonian Tomb*. Mainz.

Most, Glen W. 1997. "The Fire Next Time: Cosmology, Allegoresis, and Salvation in the Derveni Papyrus." *Journal of Hellenic Studies* 117:117–135.

Obbink, Dirk. 1997. "Cosmology as Initiation vs. the Critique of Orphic Mysteries." In Laks and Most 1997:39–54.

Petsas, Photios M. 1966. *Ὁ τάφος τῶν Λευκαδίων*. Βιβλιοθήκη τῆς ἐν Ἀθήναις Ἀρχαιολογικῆς Ἑταιρείας 57. Athens.

Pöhlmann, Egert, and Martin L. West. 2012. "The Oldest Greek Papyrus and Writing Tablets: Fifth-Century Documents from the 'Tomb of the Musician' in Attica." *Zeitschrift für Papyrologie und Epigraphik* 180:1–16.

Rhomiopoulou, Katerina. 1997. *Lefkadia, Ancient Mieza*. Athens.

Riedweg, Christoph. 1987. *Mysterienterminologie bei Platon, Philon und Klemens von Alexandrien*. Untersuchungen zur antiken Literatur und Geschichte 26. Berlin.

Rizakis, Athanassios, and Ioannis P. Touratsoglou. 2000. "*Mors Macedonica*: Ὁ θάνατος στὰ ἐπιτάφια μνημεῖα τῆς Ἄνω Μακεδονίας." *Ἀρχαιολογικὴ Ἐφημερίς* 139:237–281.

Schefer, Christina. 2000. "'Nur für Eingeweihte!' Heraklit und die Mysterien (Zu Fragment B1)." *Antike und Abendland* 46:46–75.

Scullion, Scott. 2001. "Dionysos at Elis." *Philologus* 145:203–218.

Shorey, Paul. 1937. *Plato*, vol. 5: *The Republic, Books 1–5*, rev. ed. Loeb Classical Library. Cambridge, MA.

Sider, David. 1997. "Heraclitus in the Derveni Papyrus." In Laks and Most 1997: 129–148.

Sourvinou-Inwood, Christiane. 1995. *Reading Greek Death to the End of the Classical Period*. Oxford.

Themelis, Petros G., and Ioannis P. Touratsoglou. 1997. *Οι τάφοι του Δερβενίου*. Δημοσιεύματα του Αρχαιολογικού Δελτίου 59. Athens.

Torjussen, Stian. 2005. "Phanes and Dionysos in the Derveni Theogony." *Symbolae Osloenses* 80:7–22.

Tsantsanoglou, Kyriakos. 1997. "The First Columns of the Derveni Papyrus and their Religious Significance." In Laks and Most 1997:93–128.

———. 2008. "Magi in Athens in the Fifth Century BC?" In *Ancient Greece and Ancient Iran: Cross-Cultural Encounters. 1st International Conference (Athens, 11–13 November 2006)* (ed. Seyed Mohammad Reza Darbandi and Antigoni Zournatzi) 31–39. Athens.

Tsantsanoglou, Kyriakos, and Giorgos M. Parássoglou. 1987. "Two Gold Lamellae from Thessaly." *Hellenika* 38:3–16.

Tsimbidou-Avloniti, Maria. 2000. "'... λάρνακ' ἐς ἀργυρέην ...' (*Ιλ.* Σ, 413)." In *Μύρτος. Μνήμη Ιουλίας Βοκοτοπούλου* (ed. Polyxeni Adam-Beleni) 543–575. Thessalonike.

———. 2006. "La tombe macédonienne d'Hagios Athanasios près de Thessalonique." In *Rois, cités, nécropoles: Institutions, rites et monuments en Macédoine. Actes des Colloques de Nanterre (Décembre 2002) et d'Athènes (Janvier 2004)* (ed. Anne Marie Guimier-Sorbets, Miltiade B. Hatzopoulos, and Yvette Morizot) 321–331. Meletemata 45. Athens.

Tzifopoulos, Yannis Z. 2010. *"Paradise Earned": The Bacchic-Orphic Gold Lamellae of Crete.* Hellenic Studies 23. Washington, DC.

———. 2011. "Centre, Periphery, or Peripheral Centre: A Cretan Connection for the Gold Lamellae of Crete." In *The "Orphic" Gold Tablets and Greek Religion: Further Along the Path* (ed. Radcliffe Edmonds III) 165–199. Cambridge.

Virvidakis, Stelios. 1996. "Η προφητεία του φιλοσόφου: Πολιτικές εξαγγελίες στην πλατωνική Πολιτεία." In *Ιεροί λόγοι: Προφητείες και μαντείες στην ιουδαϊκή, την ελληνική και τη ρωμαϊκή αρχαιότητα* (ed. Dimitris I. Kyrtatas) 115–132. Athens.

Voutiras, Emmanuel. 1998. *ΔΙΟΝΥΣΟΦΩΝΤΟΣ ΓΑΜΟΙ: Marital Life and Magic in Fourth-Century Pella.* Amsterdam.

West, Martin L. 1965. "The Dictaean Hymn to the Kouros." *Journal of Hellenic Studies* 85:149–159.

———. 1997. "Hocus-pocus in East and West: Theogony, Ritual, and the Tradition of Esoteric Commentary." In Laks and Most 1997:81–90.

Winkler, John J. 1990. *The Constraints of Desire: The Anthropology of Sex and Gender in Ancient Greece.* New York.

Yunis, Harvey. 2003. "Writing for Reading: Thucydides, Plato, and the Emergence of the Critical Reader." In *Written Texts and the Rise of Literate Culture in Ancient Greece* (ed. Harvey Yunis) 189–212. Cambridge.

9

The Derveni Papyrus between the Power of Spoken Language and Written Practice

Pragmatics of Initiation in an Orpheus Poem and Its Commentary[1]

Claude Calame
École des Hautes Études en Sciences Sociales, Paris

Translated by Nicholas Snead

FOR US, EVER SINCE THE SECOND QUARTER OF THE SIXTH CENTURY BCE, Orpheus sings. Indeed, in its depiction of the Argonauts' voyage, the famous frieze on the Siphnian Treasury at Delphi calls attention to Orpheus' role as a bard. Standing in the bow of the ship that carries the Greek heroes and holding what is probably a lyre in his hand, Orpheus seems to be guiding the vessel with his song.[2] The voice of the singer of Thrace is active as well in the long epic narrative poem recounting the legend of the Argonauts by the Hellenistic poet Apollonius of Rhodes. During their passage near the flowering island, the Greek heroes, like Odysseus, run the risk of being seduced by the soft, enchanting, and destructive songs (*molpaí*) of the Sirens, daughters of the Muse Terpsikhore. But the melody (*mélos*) of Orpheus' rhythmic chant (*aoidé*) as he plays the phorminx

1 Focused on the Derveni Papyrus, the present article originated as a much shorter piece published in Italian (Guidorizzi and Melotti 2005:28–45). A longer version, translated into Spanish, was published in Bernabé and Casadesús 2009:841–866. The present version benefited not only from exchanges at a July 2009 conference at the Center for Hellenic Studies but also from being presented during my 2009–2010 seminar on the anthropology of Greek poetics at the École des Hautes Études en Sciences Sociales. Special thanks to Ioanna Papadopoulou for her active role during that seminar. An abridged version of the second part of this article was included in "The Authority of Orpheus, Poet and Bard: Between Oral Tradition and Written Practice," in Ph. Mitsis and Ch. Tsagalis, eds., *Allusion, Authority, and Truth: Critical Perspectives on Greek Poetic and Rhetorical Praxis* (Berlin, 2010) 13–35.

2 *LIMC*, s.v. "Orpheus," 6 (see also "*Argonautai*," II 1, 593n2); a black-figure vase in Heidelberg, dated to around 580, could be a representation of Orpheus between two Sirens: see Riedweg 1996:1275.

responds to the "lily-like" voices of these young women with bird bodies. And the melody of the Thracian singer ultimately triumphs over the deceptive voices of the young women.[3]

1. Incantatory Practices between Orality and Writing

In poetic tradition as in classical iconography, Orpheus is famous as much for the melodious qualities of his instrumental music as he is for the enchanting and spellbinding powers of his voice as *aoidos*.

In classical poetry, for example, Pindar does not hesitate in *Pythian* 4 to insert the "renowned" poet Orpheus in the catalogue of Greek heroes who participate in the long account of the Argonauts' voyage. Son of Apollo or at least inspired by the god, the cithara-playing hero Orpheus, conductor of the Muses, is presented as the father and therefore the inventor of song (*aoidaí*); from the Homeric poems onward, this term generally denotes the song in epic diction.[4] In this manner, Orpheus assumes the role of creator and player of the phorminx (*phormigktés*); this role is the one Apollo himself takes on, for example, in Aristophanes, who for his part presents Orpheus as the creator of *teletaí*, or initiatory rites:[5] Orpheus is singer, bard, and master of initiation.

In contemporary iconography, the power of Orpheus' voice is incarnated by the singing hero's head, separated from the body that carried it. The singer of Thrace is in this way reduced to his pure vocality through a probable allusion to the legend in which he falls victim to the *sparagmos* of the maenads, who were spurred on by a Dionysus jealous of the exclusive honors Orpheus paid to Apollo. Aeschylus made this legend the tragic subject of the *Bassarids*.[6] Yet

3 Apollonius of Rhodes 4.891–911; other instances of the effects of Orpheus' music have been collected and discussed by Riedweg (1996:1273–1279); see also Bernabé 2001:63–76; on the hero's participation in the voyage of the Argonauts, see Graf 1987:95–99.

4 Pindar *Pythians* 4.176–177 = *Orphica* 899 I T/1006 T Bernabé, cf. sch. *ad loc.* (II, p. 139 Drachmann) = *Orphica* 899 II and III T Bernabé, as well as the accounts gathered as *Orphica* 985 T and 896 T Bernabé. On the genealogy of Orpheus, cf. Pseudo-Apollodorus *The Library* 1.3.2 = *Orphica* 901 II T Bernabé. On Orpheus as the son of Calliope and Oeagrus or Apollo see also Ovid *Metamorphoses* 10.187 and 11.8 = *Orphica* 897 T and 1035 II T Bernabé: Orpheus divine son of Apollo (*vatis Apollineus*).

5 Aristophanes Frogs 231, and 1035–1036 = *Orphica* 547 I T Bernabé. On the broader meaning of *teleté* as a general ritualistic practice of initiation, see Burkert 1987:9–11; for the more specific meaning as a rite of initiation into the Orphic mysteries, see Morand 2001:140–146.

6 Aeschylus *Bassarids: TrGF* pp. 138–139 Radt = Eratosthenes *Catasterismi* 24 = *Orphica* 536 T and 1033 T Bernabé. For modern readers, the episode where Orpheus' head arrives at Lesbos and becomes an oracle appears most notably in Philostratus *Heroicus* 28.7–11 = *Orphica* 1056 T Bernabé; other texts in Graf 1987:85–86 point out additionally that the scene of the Orphic *sparagmos* at the hands of the Thracian women appears as early as 480: cf. *LIMC*, "Orpheus," 32–51. On the legend of the complex relationship linking Orpheus, Apollo, and Dionysus, see Detienne 1989:124–132.

along with other similar artifacts, the frieze of a red-figure vase at Cambridge stages for us the confrontation between a seated young man and a man standing with his right hand stretched out in front of him (this image appears opposite a musical scene depicting two young women). Because of the laurel branch that he is holding in his left hand, it makes sense to identify the second young man as the god Apollo or as one of the priests who serve as his mortal representatives. In the center of this musical scene, the head of Orpheus is resting on the ground: while the head is singing, the seated ephebe's role seems to be to transcribe the words coming from the mouth of the immortalized poet onto a two-leaved tablet coated in wax. As for the god or his priest, he is guiding with his right hand the movements of the young man transcribing to the diptych. The presence of Apollo or of his representative confers an oracular quality to the voice of Orpheus, which is perhaps part of a practice of necromancy.[7] Is this an "oral dictated text," according to the hypothesis formed by Albert Lord to describe the written transcription of poems transmitted orally under the name "Homer"? Whatever the case, the oral and even melodious expression of Orpheus, under the authority of the god of the lyre and of the oracles, leads to a practice of writing.

Plato was very much aware of this paradox in a frequently analyzed passage of the *Republic* where he denounces the charlatans and roaming diviners (*agúrtai kaì mánteis*) who attempt to profit from the divine powers conferred upon them by sacrificial practices and incantatory formulas. The latter are designated as charms with magical powers (*epagogaîs kaì katadésmois*). These charlatans are quick to bring forth piles of papyrus scrolls (*bíblon hómadon*) whose authority they attribute to Musaeus and Orpheus, "descendants of the Moon and of the Muses." They pull sacrificial formulas from these scrolls that they address both to individuals and to civic communities while claiming to liberate and purify them (*lúseis kaì katharmoí*) from injustice through what they call initiations (*teletaí*).[8] Officiants at rites of initiation, the roaming priests who invoke the authority of Orpheus readily entrust to writing and record in books the memory of the vocal and ritual powers of the incantatory formulas!

This is the great paradox that the Derveni Papyrus presents: it offers citations of a cosmo-theogonic poem in epic and rhapsodic diction proffered by the spoken voice of Orpheus while at the same time inaugurating for us the long

7 Red-figure vase (*ARV*^{2} 1401.1) = *LIMC*, "Orpheus," 70 = "Apollon," 872; other representations of Orpheus' singing head are listed in Schmidt 1972. In regards to two cuneiform Mesopotamian documents and to magical Greek texts invoking Apollo through a head or a skull, Faraone presents the hypothesis of scenes of necromancy (2005:71–83).

8 Cf. Plato *Republic* 364b–365a = 573 I–II F Bernabé; for a well-done discussion of the incantatory formulas and practices of initiation attributed to Orpheus, see Jiménez San Cristóbal 2008a.

tradition of the *hypómnema*, a written practice if ever there was one. This means that the hybrid text presented in the Derveni Papyrus provides an example of a practice of written orality. The meanings at stake in this practice will be examined below.

2. The Derveni Papyrus as a Document

As a rapid introduction to the Derveni Papyrus, it is important to recall that the scroll was discovered in the tomb of a realitively well-off citizen-soldier in Macedonia. Placed on the slabs covering the tomb instead of next to the remains of the departed with the other objects meant to accompany him in the afterlife, the papyrus roll was without a doubt supposed to have been burned with the cadaver on the funeral pyre. Half-consumed, it presents passages taken from an Orphic poem in the form of lemma and fragments of a commentary written around 330.[9] The verses commented upon come themselves from a cosmo-theogonic poem that is repeatedly attributed to Orpheus and can be dated with certainty to the mid-fourth century BCE.

In his *Laws*, Plato in fact alludes to an ancient discourse (*palaiòs lógos*) in which the "god" (in this case Zeus) is presented as "the beginning, the end, and the center of everything that exists"; this discourse is characterized as Orphic by the scholiast who explicates the passage. Yet it turns out that Plato is in fact paraphrasing a well-known verse found with one variation in a fragment of a poem in hexameter that is cited in the treatise *De mundo*. This treatise is attributed to Aristotle and is often incorrectly identified as part of an Orphic hymn to Zeus. This extract is found with several variations in a longer passage cited by the early Church father Eusebius of Caesarea. This passage is certainly a later version of the Orphic narration referred to as the *Hieroì lógoi* and comprising twenty-four rhapsodies. Dating from the second century CE, this version, which is also celebrated in the commentary of Damascius, probably represents a development of the later version passed on by the Peripatetic philosopher Eudemus of Rhodes.[10] All this shows that the cosmo-theogonic poem widely cited by

9 Bibliographic information on the archeological circumstances of the discovery and on the dating of the document are available in Bernabé 2002:91–93; Betegh 2004:56–68; and Kouremenos, Parássoglou, and Tsantsanoglou 2006:1–9.

10 Plato *Laws* 715e = *Orphica* 31 III F Bernabé and schol. Plato *Laws* 715e (p. 317 Greene) = *Orphica* 31 IV F Bernabé, through probable reference to the version later cited by Pseudo-Aristotle *De mundo* 401a25–31 = *Orphica* 31 I F Bernabé, then by Eusebius *Praeparatio evangelica* 3.8.2 (= Porphyry fr. 354 Smith) = *Orphica* 243 F Bernabé; cf. West 1983:218–220 and 239–241. For the three versions of the orphic cosmo-theogony cf. Damascius *De principiis* 123–124 (III, pp. 159–162 Westerink) = *Orphica* 20 I F, 75 F and 90 T Bernabé; in reference to the three versions, see Brisson 1995:2875–2915.

Neo-Platonic philosophers in its rhapsodic version descends, through numerous variations and reconfigurations, from an Orphic poem in epic diction that was already in circulation during the period the Derveni Papyrus was composed.

Yet in an unexpected manner, to say the least, the Derveni commentator not only offers an interpretation of this verse but also cites it in the form in which it appears in the "Eudemus version" and in the *Sacred Discourses in 24 Rhapsodies*: "Zeus the head, Zeus the middle, from Zeus everything is made." In addition, the Derveni author responds a little later in the exegesis to another verse that is integrated in this same rhapsodic extract: "Zeus the king, Zeus the foundation of all things, with his exploding thunder."[11]

3. The Explicated Poem: Rhapsodic and Orphic Diction

Corresponding at least partially with the version known as the "Eudemus" version and with the much later rhapsodic version, the verses cited in the Derveni commentary are taken from a cosmo-theogonic poem in epic diction; this poem narrates in a nonlinear chronology the different phases of the creation of the cosmos and its re-creation by Zeus. From an analytic perspective, the now-classic narrative distinction between *Erzählzeit* and *erzählte Zeit* is essential: this double temporality is combined with the temporality of the uttered enunciation. I have tried to demonstrate this elsewhere in relation to the way Hesiod unfolds the story of the five generations of mortal men in *Works and Days* in order to insert it into the enunciation and into the pragmatic workings of his didactic poem.[12]

Despite the mutilations of the half-consumed papyrus, we can see the following cosmo-theogonic moments in the temporal succession of the five generations: Zeus succeeds Kronos; Zeus receives oracles from Nyx and his father Kronos concerning his future reign on Olympus; Zeus consumes the phallus (*aidoîon*), probably the virile member of Uranus transformed into the Sun. This primordial phallus, as we will see, was gushing in the Ether, and as the "firstborn" sovereign, Zeus swallows it. From him, the gods and goddesses are (re)born, with the rivers and springs, but also the earth, the sky, the river Okeanos, and the moon—in other words, all that comes into being. Recasting

11 Derveni Papyrus, col. XVII 12 and XIX 10 = *Orphica* 14, 2 and 4 F Bernabé (who was able to use the Derveni commentary to reconstruct four verses of this passage of the Orphic poem dedicated to the pervasive unity of Zeus); concerning the *Orphic Hymn* 15 addressed to Zeus, see Ricciardelli 2000:298–300.

12 See Calame 2009:5–24 and 59–94, attempting to place this narrative in its poetic and enunciative context, in contrast to the numerous structural analyses of the Hesiodic, wrongly called, "mythe des races."

the original act of cosmic creation in an apparently inverted order, this second demiurgic act prompts the citation and the commentary on the verses in poetic praise of Zeus mentioned above: Zeus is at the same time the artisan and the foundation of all things. The master of creation is therefore himself assimilated with Moira, if not with the celestial Aphrodite. He can unite with his mother Rhea, who is likely assimilated in the poem itself with Gaia and also Meter and Hera! The burning of the papyrus has unfortunately denied us these last steps—if they existed—of the creation of the world through the intermediary of the genealogy of the gods. Thus there is no primordial Kronos as in the rhapsodic version, nor any mention of the Titans, nor any allusion to Dionysus or to the anthropogony, at least not in the current state of the text.[13]

Neither the Homeric diction used nor the qualifications and functions of Zeus partially visible in the shredded fragments of the lines cited and explicated present any aspect that departs from the grand discursive tradition of Greek traditional cosmo-genealogical poetry; the dactylic rhythm implies a recitation analogous to those chanted in the Rhapsodies. Without a doubt focused on the story of Zeus, these verses could not be part of a hymn, as some of their modern readers have proposed.[14] Rather, the specificity of what is left of the explicated poem lies in its content. Particularly distinctive is Zeus' swallowing of the phallus, with a play on words perhaps already present in the poem itself. This *aidoîon* is in fact probably assimilated with the member of Sky and with Sun. The primordial *pudendum* certainly plays the same role as Eros-Phanes, the luminous golden-winged deity, firstborn and sprung from the primordial egg in other versions of the orphic cosmo-theogony.[15] If it is perhaps Kronos who severs the member of Uranus, it is not at any rate he who swallows it! The progression of the Orphic narrative does not follow the logic of Hesiod's *Theogony*, where it is Uranus himself who ingests his own sons, preventing development of the theogonic process.

Transferred from Kronos to Zeus, the act of ingestion leads to two narrative and theological moments that are specific to Orphic cosmological thought: the

13 These different phases of the poetic cosmo-theogony explicated in the papyrus have been reconstituted recently by Bernabé (2002:102–123); see also Betegh 2004:92–137 as well as an overly normalized version in Jourdan 2003:XVIII–XXIV. In their commentary, Kouremenos, Parássoglou, and Tsantsanoglou remain much more cautious regarding reconstructions that rely too heavily on the model provided by the first phases of Hesiod's cosmic creation in the *Theogony*. On the absence of Kronos, see Betegh 2004:157–158.

14 See West 1983:74–75 and 96–104; Betegh (2004:136–138) develops an argument against the hypothesized hymn despite the term *hú]mnon* that can be established in col. VII 2 (cf. II 8 as well); Kouremenos, Parássoglou, and Tsantsanoglou 2006:171.

15 On the figure of Phanes-Protogonos-Eros, see Calame 1991:231–237; concerning the functioning of the double meaning of *aidoîon* in the poem itself, see Calame 1997:66–72, Bernabé 2002:104–107, Brisson 2003, and Betegh 2004:111–122 and 171–172.

second creation of the universe and the erasing of generations in the blurring of genealogical relationships. Through temporal flattening and vicarious incest, these two narrative processes allow the differentiations of the demiurgic and genealogical process to merge in the unity of an all-powerful divine figure, the beginning and end of all things.[16] We find in the few verses cited and explicated by the *sophós* of Derveni—echoing to some extent these cosmological and theogonic processes—enunciative phrasings that characterize the Orphic re-elaboration of Homeric diction. These include the paratactic asyndeton for the naming and qualifications of the divinity, the phonetic play of assonance in the descriptions and invocation, the repetition of the divinity's name in key positions of clauses in the dactylic hexameter, etc. I have analyzed these stylistic elements in another study, to be published soon. These different forms of phonetic and semantic wordplay on the names of the major entities and divinities at work in the creation and the re-creation of the cosmos stress the incantatory nature of epic diction in a rhapsodic recitation that takes on accents made familiar by the *Orphic Hymns*.[17] The Homeric diction of the rhapsodies developed then into a truly Orphic diction, which likely had ritual significance.

4. Interpretative Procedures

To the eyes and ears of the reader-listener in the fourth century, the poetic utterances of a cosmogony and genealogical narrative believed to be the poetic work of Orpheus are thought of as pertaining to the *aínigma*; these hexameters in Homeric and Orphic diction are considered by the Derveni author to be "enigmatic" (*ainigmatódeis*). It is therefore appropriate to examine the interpretive procedures and the modes of enunciation of a hermeneutic voice that is itself enigmatic. It is worth noting that while the written voice of the commentary attributes spoken verses to Orpheus, that written voice itself remains entirely anonymous.

The anonymous commentator expresses himself in general in an entirely assertorial manner. According to him, when the poet says something like "[Zeus] took in his hands [the strength of his father]," he is speaking in implied meaning (*ainízetai*). Often brought up in Greek texts, this manner of speaking in enigmatic terms is, in particular, that of the man who, according to a dream

16 The process of re-creating a cosmos in unity has been discussed in Calame 1997:66–74 and Bernabé 2002:114–118.

17 On the structure, lexicon, and formulaic language of the *Orphic Hymns*, see the two studies by Rudhardt (1991:267–274 and 2008:177–250) as well as the strong analysis of Hopman-Govers (2001). See also Morand 2001:58–76 on wordplay and 101–137 for the titles that generally refer to smoke offerings.

recounted by Herodotus, addresses Hipparchus in dactylic hexameter on the eve of his fatal participation in the Panathenaea: "Bear, you lion, unbearable pains with a patient heart; there is no one, among men who commit injustice, who shall not pay for it." The error in understanding these two prophetically phrased hexameters would prove fatal for the young tyrant despite the warnings given by the dream interpreters (*oneirópoloi*) that we find working already in the *Iliad*.[18]

In the same way, the Derveni commentator presents as "enigmatic" the hexameter that makes Zeus into the head, the center, and therefore the cause of all things created. This Orphic verse, let us not forget, figures in the *hieròs lógos* from Plato's *Laws* cited above as part of a dialogue that is itself more or less contemporary with the Derveni text. According to the anonymous interpreter, who focuses his attention on the term *kephalé* (the head), Orpheus is not only speaking in hidden meanings in this verse (*épos*), he is also making revelations (*semaínei*). We recall that Heraclitus, in a famous passage, attributes this mode of revealing to the oracle of Delphi: the role of the Pythic voice is to "signify." Herodotus assigns this same semiotic mode to his own historiographical undertaking when, in its opening, he attributes a quasi-judiciary role to his *lógos* in regards to elucidating the causes of the Greco-Persian wars. According to the Derveni author, the poet Orpheus "indicates" (*semaínei*: that present things are the product of existing things) when he tells of how the gods as well as the elements were born from "the first-sovereign, the venerable," the unique principal. To support his assertion, the interpreter cites no fewer than four hexameters taken from the Orphic poem he is explicating: the voice of the poet speaking on the cosmogonic role taken on by Protogonos is designated as a simple "statement" (*légei*), while the lines cited are presented as hexameters ("in these lines": *en toîs épesi to[îsde]*).[19]

Furthermore, when a cosmo-theogonic term can take on two meanings, the simple "say" or "tell" (*légein*) of the poem in epic diction becomes "explain." This is the case for instance with the now-famous adjective *aidoîos* describing the object that first gushed in the ether and was in the end consumed by Zeus: "venerable," which also denotes the *pudendum* of Uranus incorporated into the Sun. To introduce the double interpretation of this term that is indeed polysemic and to justify the word-for-word interpretation of the poetic expression, the

[18] Derveni Papyrus col. IX 10; cf. Herodotus 5.56.1–2 and Homer *Iliad* I.63. In the following passage of the text, which is greatly fragmented, the commentator seems to strongly affirm that he has made visible that which is not readily apparent.

[19] Derveni Papyrus col. XVII 11–13 and col. XVI 1–7 (for the use of the form *semaínei*, see also col. XXV 13, in relation to *gignóskein*); cf. Heraclitus fr. 22 B 93 DK and Herodotus 1.5.3. On the Orphic verses explicated in this passage, see n11 above.

commentator readily declares that "[Orpheus] proceeds in enigmas regarding reality through the entire poem"; moreover, from this perspective the poet Orpheus "reveals" (*deloî*) at the same time he "speaks."[20] The quasi-oracular process attributed to the poem implicitly conforms to the legendary tradition of the prophetic qualities attributed to the voice of the immortal Orpheus. In addition, this process without a doubt corresponds to the oracular role attributed to Nyx in regards to Zeus in the very narration of the process re-creating the universe.

The oracular nature of the voice assumed by the Orphic poem is clearly summarized in the beginning of the commentary. There the interpreter in fact declares, as a sort of introduction to his exegesis, that the whole of the poem is *ainigmatódes* and that Orpheus (?) "did not want to tell of contestable enigmas but of great things through enigma." The conclusion here: the author of the poem is presenting a sacred discourse (*hier[log]eîtai*). The key to a poetic composition that appears from the outset as a *hieròs lógos* is thus given. The Derveni commentator ends up effectively paraphrasing the famous orphic verse that recommends the profane close their ears: "I'm going to sing [*aeíso*] for those who comprehend [*xunétoisi*]; close the doors, you the profane [*bébeloi*]"; or, in a formulaic variation that allows for retaining the divisions of the rhythmic structure of the hexameter: "I'm going to speak [*phthégxomai*] to whom it is permitted; close the doors, you the profane."

Presented by the Derveni commentator as a "truly distinct" or "truly recognizable" verse (*en tôi [euk]rinéto[i épei*), this poetic injunction could be read as the first line of the cosmo-theogonic hexameter attributed to Orpheus; it could mark the beginning of the poem proper like a sort of seal or password. It is at any rate construed this way by modern editors of the *Orphica* who place this enunciation, with its double formulation, at the head of their collection of Orphic fragments.[21] The anonymous poetic voice that speaks in what is likely the opening of the classical cosmo-theogonic poem has thus become, for the sage of Derveni, the voice of Orpheus.

The specific Orphic character of the mechanics of the poem explicated by the author of Derveni resides more in the fact that it is certainly considered

[20] Derveni Papyrus col. XIII 1–5; bibliography on the question of the use of the term *aidoîon* available above in n15.

[21] Derveni Papyrus col. VII 3–11, in the new text presented and annotated by Tsantsanoglou (1997: 95 and 117–128), with the commentary of Kouremenos, Parássoglou, and Tsantsanoglou (2006: 171–174); the verse paraphrased by the Derveni author is reconstructed and published as *Orphica* 3 F Bernabé (cf. 2 T as well as 101 F Bernabé) in reference to the double enunciation 1a and 1b F Bernabé cited above; on this formulaic introductory verse, see the remarks by West (1983:82–84) and Burkert (2005:49–51). On Orphic discourse as *hieroì lógoi*, see Baumgarten 1998:89–97 and Henrichs 2003:237–244.

a "sacred discourse" than in its "enigmatic" features. From this perspective, we might very well recall Socrates' remark in Plato's *Alcibiades* upon hearing the citation of gnomic Homeric verse when the poet is thought to be speaking in enigmas. In response to the citation, Socrates points out that poetry as a whole is ultimately by its nature *ainigmatódes*; as a result, not everyone will be able to understand it.[22] We also know that, at least as far back as Theagenes of Rhegium around the end of the sixth century, Homeric (and consequently rhapsodic) poetry could be understood in terms of "insinuation" (*hypónoia*), to quote the expression used by Perikles, according to Thucydides. It is in this manner that the Athenian statesman refers to the mode of meaning typical to Homeric poetry.

Enigmatic expression is then a fundamental feature of all epic poetry, and the thematic implications of this enunciative mode are explored within the poems. For example, in *Works and Days,* when Hesiod turns to the unjust "kings," he presents the story of the nightingale captured by the hawk as *aînos.* The former represents the bard reduced to the cries of the owl having fallen into the hands of the latter, all this while the master lays claim, through the authority of his sovereign speech, to a discretionary power. In a manner of speaking, the animal allegory is decoded through etymological definition.[23]

It makes sense then that the Derveni commentator reiterates in several places that a poem written in an enigmatic manner, like the one he repeatedly attributes to Orpheus, cannot be addressed to the ignorant (usually described as *ou gignóskontes*), and that it is reserved for those "in the know" (*gignóskontes*). This term must certainly refer to the "initiate" (*xunetoîsi*) addressed in the famous verse already cited, which—in a strong and performative affirmation of the poet, speaking in the first person—functions perhaps as the opening of the cosmo-theogonic poem: *aeíso xunétoisi.* But "Orpheus" is not alone in reserving his poetry for an initiate audience. In the fifth century, both Pindar and Bacchylides say that their own poetic language is intended solely for this same "intelligent" audience! We find in this parallel to exclusive poetry further proof that the group of Orpheus' followers, while made up of the initiate, cannot be considered a "sect." This classification is nothing more than a supplementary projection of a Christian-inspired concept onto the Orphic following, a projection in line with

22 Plato *Alcibiades* II 142ac; see also Aristotle *Poetics* 22.1458a, which condemns enigma as an over-use of metaphorical expression, and *Rhetoric to Alexander* 35.18, where "enigmatic expression" (*ainigmatodôs hermeneúein*) is understood as a way of saying one thing by employing terms that denote something else.

23 Thucydides 2.41.3–4; Hesiod *Works and Days* 202–212; for the relationship between the procedure of *aînos* and the first "allegorical" readings of Homeric poetry, see Nagy 1990:147–150 and 425–430, as well as Ford 2002:62–75, along with the numerous bibliographic references I gave on the subject in 1997:65n2.

one of the major traditions of the modern history of religions. But the Orphic groups can be compared to the privileged in each city who possessed the knowledge necessary to access the word of the poets who served as *sophoí*.[24]

Addressing himself in this way to those in the know, the scholarly Derveni commentator recuperates to some extent in his use of the form *he* the enunciative mechanism produced by the strong voice of the poet-*I*, who happens to be an Orphic rhapsode. We see here the Orphic oxymoron divided between the oral and the written, and this is particularly the case in column VII of the papyrus, positioned at the juncture between the ritualistic instructions and the commentary on the poem itself.

5. Erudite Practices

Given the double meaning attributed to poetic enunciation of the explicated poem, both the graphic procedures of citation and the discursive and interpretive modes of the anonymous author in the papyrus also align closely with those of the Alexandrian scholar. Indeed, the work of editing the classic texts collected in the library created by Ptolemy calls for a commentary. While performing this work of edition (*ékdosis*), the scholar would write down notes, or *hypomnémata*: actual commentary to the poems from the Archaic and Classical periods, with meanings that began to escape readers because of historic shifts in the cultural and social paradigm of the Hellenistic period. These poems were later archived in libraries where they were read and no longer the object of a musical, oral "performance."[25]

Following the model that would become Alexandrian philological practice, the verses explicated in the Derveni Papyrus are presented as actual lemmata, marked by an obelus or a *paragraphos*. These citations are often followed by a formulation using *hóti* ("because") that explains why the poetic expression should be understood (or not understood) to have a certain meaning. This is the case, for example, with the hexameter stating Zeus' royalty: the god is called king because he corresponds to a unique principle that has power over multiple things in existence. Further along in the explicated poem, the mention of the river Okeanos, in a verse that is now lost, provokes the following commentary: "this verse [*épos*] was composed in a deceptive manner; this is not obvious

[24] Derveni Papyrus IX 2, XII 5, XVIII 5, XX 2–3 and 8, XXIII 2 and 5, XXVI 8; cf. *Orphica* 1a F Bernabé, Pindar *Olympian* 6.83–85, and Bacchylides 3.85 (*garúo* as well). Recently Bremmer (2010:22–29) criticized using the notion of a "sect" to describe the groups of Orphic followers.

[25] On the original meaning of *hypómnema* as a "written note," see Plato *Phaedrus* 249c and *Politicus* 295c. On the subject of commentary as a scholarly genre in the Hellenistic period, see Pfeiffer 1968:212–227.

though for most [*toîs póllois*], but clear [*eúdelon*] for those with the proper knowledge [*toîs orthôs ginóskousin*] because Okeanos is the air and the air is Zeus." We learn here that those who do not know (*ou gignóskontes*) remain content with the appearance maintained by the words of common language that Orpheus uses to "signify" (*semaínei*) his own opinion; because of this qualification the uninitiated continue to believe that Okeanos is a river, satisfied with the surface meaning.

Only then those with proper knowledge have access to the second meaning that the commentary itself reveals. Reserved for the initiate—that is, for the beneficiaries of the *teletaí* that Orpheus himself is thought to have founded—the meaning explicated by the Derveni commentator generally stems from the physical conception of the world developed by thinkers and sages commonly referred to as "pre-Socratic."[26] The essential feature of the Derveni Papyrus is not so much the explicit reference to Heraclitus—apparently considered to be a *mythológos* or *astrológos* and cited by the commentator in the context of an aphorism demonstrating the role played by the Erinyes in the control and respect for the order of the cosmos, particularly in relation to Helios[27]—but rather the likely eclecticism of the Derveni author. In his explanation of the Orphic version of the cosmo-theogonic creation, he brings up different processes taken from physical, and more specifically atomistic, understandings of the world. In this context and because the interpretation itself presents no precise authorial indications, it is not useful to stubbornly apply the modern conception of an individual author to the Derveni commentator; the numerous attempts to attach the name of a known "philosopher" to the document are therefore futile.[28]

6. Questions of Authorship

While Anaxagoras, Diogenes of Apollonia, Euthyphro, and Leucippus have all been mentioned in turn by modern scholars not as authors of the commentary but simply as possible sources of inspiration for the Derveni commentator, the

[26] Derveni Papyrus XIX 10–15 and XXIII 1–10; for a reconstruction of the verses concentrating on Okeanos, see most recently Bernabé 2002:119–120 and Kouremenos, Parássoglou, and Tsantsanoglou 2006:256–260; for explanations of speculations about classical physical thinkers, see in particular the references given by West (1983:80–81) and by Laks (1997:127–134); see also Brisson's recent attempt to link the Derveni author's materialist interpretation to Stoic thought and allegorical practice, 2009:33–39.

[27] Derveni Papyrus IV, 5–9 citing Heraclitus frr. 22 B 3 and 94 DK; cf. Sider 1997:129–144 (who reads *hiero]lógoi*; bibliography on this passage 130n5), and Tsantsanoglou 1997:96–109 (who adds *mytho]lógoi*), as well as Kouremenos, Parássoglou, and Tsantsanoglou 2006:153–157.

[28] The unfruitful efforts of modern scholars at authorial attribution are listed by Betegh (2004:64–65 and 373–380), and discussed by Kouremenos, Parássoglou, and Tsantsanoglou (2006:58–59).

discourse seems to be most essentially characterized by a nebulous atomism that is supported by references to a cosmological outlook close to that of Empedocles. The processes of creation and re-creation of the cosmos are thus more or less regularly compared to processes of separation and combination of physical particles. But these cosmogonic processes are put into motion by forces of the divine order, such as Harmonia, Peitho, Aphrodite, and of course Zeus. It's worth noting that in Hippocratic thought in particular we see this same blend of physically, empirically based explanations with references to the forces at work in polytheist theology.[29]

This is the case, for example, with the gushing or spurting movement that animates the cosmos, according to the Orphic creation. In mentioning this movement, "Orpheus" refers to the process of reciprocal attraction of the elements and basic physical properties such as the cold. He demonstrates (*deloî*) that particles moving in the air couple together through the affinities they have for each other:

> ... nor cold with cold. And "through a gushing movement" is the formula he [i.e. Orpheus] uses to demonstrate [*deloî*] that after having been divided into smaller pieces, the elements moved through the air and gushed, and in gushing, they came together with each other to form anew. Yet they continued gushing until that moment when each went towards its partner. "Celestial Aphrodite," "Zeus," "enjoy the pleasures of Aphrodite," "gush," "Persuasion," and "Harmonia," these words all are used to refer to the same god. ... Indeed, when existing realities [*tà eónta*] were mixing with each other, Zeus received the name "Aphrodite" and that of "Persuasion," because the elements yielded to each other.

We notice the etymological wordplay with the term *thórnei*, which can refer to the noun ("a gushing movement" or "ejaculation") or to a form of the verb ("he gushed" or "he mated with"). The original "gushing" is in this way first associated with the physical movement of the fundamental elements divided into particles of an atomist nature; but this "gushing" is in turn linked, through an assimilation of the verb *thórnusthai* and the verb *aphrodisiázein*, to the action of Celestial Aphrodite and Zeus. These two gods themselves are soon after assimilated with the "lesser divinities" Peitho and Harmonia, who serve the goddess of love. Persuasion becomes the force that makes beings give in to one another, while Harmonia is the power that arranges their coming together.[30]

29 See for instance Holmes 2010:121–191 and Lloyd 2003:40–61.

30 Derveni Papyrus XXI 1–12; on this cosmic movement, see Calame 1997:70–74 (with n7) as well as Laks and Most 1997:21n53 on the form and meaning of *thórnei* and Bernabé 2002:118–119, along

From an enunciative perspective, the explanation is introduced as a general assertion by a *hóti* that recalls the explicative procedure described above. The explicative *hóti* aligns this general *we*-truth with revelation by the voice of Orpheus that "says" (*lég[on] deloî hóti*): "through a gushing movement." Through the intermediary of Aphrodite's involvement, this gushing movement of the particles in the air from the past is aligned with the present state of "things that exist" and their mixing in a generalized sexual union. The whole of this argument is captured in a circular structure found in other explications. In pragmatic fashion, this succession establishes a rhapsodic rhythm in the commentary that doubtless echoed the rhythm of the poem being explicated.[31] From a visual perspective, the *parágraphoi* that indicate the citations from the poem attributed to Orpheus add a graphic cadence to a text that was probably meant to be read aloud; didactic in nature, this reading surely took place within a circle of Orphic initiates.

The interpretive relationship between the theological cosmogony of the rhapsodic poem attributed to Orpheus and its commentary in terms of "pre-Socratic" physics is established then by a subtle dialectic movement. This interpretive movement combines purely material processes and interventions of divine forces. In the hermeneutic tradition, already detectible in the Homeric poems, that Plato firmly established with his *Cratylus*, etymological practices naturally provide a royal path towards an exegesis based on the meanings that the very forms of words inspire.[32]

The defining feature of the interpretive mode adopted by the Derveni commentator resides then in his return to explanations of divine powers that are based on physical principles. "Ocean is the air, and the air is Zeus," he claims in an explicative statement, discussed above, about those who have the knowledge necessary to comprehend the implied meanings of the cosmo-theogonic poem: reciprocity between the physical and the divine is established! Similarly, Zeus' swallowing of the "venerable" sovereign firstborn and the cosmic unity resulting from this act are interpreted as the definitive establishment of the reign of Noûs through the intermediary of a likely etymological pun on the poetic form *moûnos*, "only."[33] Again the hermeneutic discourse leads to the confirma-

---

with the comparative remarks by Burkert (2005:55–60), and recently the extended commentary of Kouremenos, Parássoglou, and Tsantsanoglou (2006:243–252).

31 The prose narratives in Plato's *Timaeus* and *Critias* can adopt the rhapsodic rhythm of the Homeric poems recited at the Great Panathenaea: Nagy 2002:52–69.

32 The analogies between the etymological procedures of the Derveni commentator and those accumulated in Plato's *Cratylus* are pointed out in particular by Kahn 1997:60–63. For the combinations of physical explanations and references to divine figures, see Laks 1997:130–137.

33 Derveni Papyrus XXIII 1–3 (see n26 above) and XVI 3–14 (n19 above and Kouremenos, Parássoglou, and Tsantsanoglou 2006:214–217).

tion of a principle that is more theological than physical. For both the rhapsodic poet "Orpheus" and his anonymous commentator, the definitive establishment of the reign of Zeus as a unique demiurgic and divine principle takes precedent. By this measure, the authority of an interpretation, which is both physical and theological, can only be that of an initiate in the rites of Orpheus; it is the interpretation of an *orpheoteléstes*, actually an initiator.[34]

7. Itineraries of Initiatory Writing

Everything occurs as if the commentator were struggling to recast in physical terms a theological outlook that he is trying to reinforce by means of a mixed exegesis. In this context of discursive practice of interpretation adopted by an Orphic initiate or by a master of Orphic initiation, the allusion to the rites of initiation following the affirmation of Zeus' power acquires its full significance. Through a likely comparison to those who are incapable of understanding the cosmo-theogonic poem because of their ignorance, and through the intermediary of a rather strong enunciative intervention, those who perform civic rites and hear the spoken words of the poem without understanding them are condemned. It is impossible to see, hear, or learn while performing the ritual without a certain prerequisite knowledge, a knowledge somewhat similar to vision (*hos eidótes, eidésein*, etc.):[35]

> [Concerning] those men who saw the sacred rites, having performed them in the cities, I'm not all that surprised that they do not understand —it is not possible, in fact, for them to hear and to learn at the same time the words pronounced. But those [who performed these rites] in the presence of a man who has chosen the sacred rites as his art, they are the ones who warrant shock and pity. ... While before performing the sacred rites they hope they will know, once they have performed them they find they are deprived even of their hope.

Consequently, it becomes somewhat clearer why the anonymous commentary of this *póesis ainigmatódes*, of which the diction and composition are attributed to Orpheus, is introduced in the papyrus by a series of prefatory remarks on the performance of ritual gestures. Even if these remarks are disputed in modern readings because of the fragmented condition of the papyrus, it is clear

34 Kouremenos, Parássoglou, and Tsantsanoglou (2006:45–58) conclude in their review of the different theses advanced on this subject that "the Derveni author is not Orphic or even anti-Orphic" (52) and not "a religious professional" (53). Contrary to their conclusion, we refer to the proposition of Fritz Graf (in this volume), who sees the Derveni author as an *orpheotelestés*.

35 Derveni Papyrus XX 1–12; for references on this passage, see Calame 1997:77–78.

that the ritual acts that they allude to in the preface of the poetic commentary are performed by the adept seeking to win the favor of the Erinyes, who themselves are assimilated with the souls.[36] Whether or not there are allusions in these severely mutilated lines to those adept in the Eleusinian mysteries, to oracular practices, or to specifically Orphic ritual gestures, there is a straightforward reference to those who succeed neither in learning nor knowing and who therefore mistrust the rites.

On the enunciative level, the voice in the commentary seems in this passage to be incorporating the authorial *I* into a collective *we*. While the form *párimen* should be understood in this way, the enunciative *we* stands in opposition to all the uses of *they* that refer to the individuals who lack the knowledge necessary to understand the ritual gestures they perform or the oracular responses they solicit. This means that from a metadiscursive perspective, the anonymous author of the commentary is presenting himself as a member of the same group of initiates; corresponding to the "knowing" to whom the anonymous interpretation is addressed, these Orphic initiates would possess the knowledge necessary to decipher efficiently the ritual practices and cosmo-theogonic verse placed under the authority of Orpheus.[37] We discover in this manner the power of the voice of Orpheus associated with a didactic procedure and the practices of initiation.

By this measure, the passage introducing the exegesis of the rhapsodic poem originating in the mouth of Orpheus takes on, to some extent, the role of the initial formulaic line that we encountered in its two versions above. In the variations presented, this line, functioning as both an authorial and an initiatory seal, seems to mark the beginning of the different versions of the Orphic cosmo-theogony.[38] "I'm going to sing" (*aeíso*) or "I'm going to proclaim" (*phthégxomai*)—this verbal and poetic act responds to the same didactic and initiatory requirements of knowledge as the discursive practice represented in the commentary of the cosmo-theogonic poem attributed to Orpheus. As I have argued elsewhere,[39] the

36 These remarks cover cols. II–VI of the Derveni Papyrus, particularly col. V 5–13. See Tsantsanoglou 1997:96–117 and Kouremenos, Parássoglou, and Tsantsanoglou 2006:144–171 as well as the new reading proposed by Ferrari (2011b:74–82) that develops a parallel with practices of Persian *magi* (see also 2011a:51–54).

37 Derveni Papyrus V 3. According to Most (1997:120 and 130), this enunciative *we* refers to a group of professionals opposed to both the priests of civic cults and individuals who claim to be experts on the sacred rites (on the latter, see also Betegh 2004:78–83); this reading runs counter to Kouremenos, Parássoglou, and Tsantsanoglou (2006:53–54 and 161–162), who interpret the form *párimen* as an infinitive and the equivalent of *pariénai* (see Burkert, in this volume, p. 113).

38 *Orphica* 1a and b F as well as 3 F and 101 F Bernabé; cf. Derveni Papyrus VII 9–10 and n21 above.

39 Calame 1997:77–80; see also Obbink 1997:40–47 and Laks 1997:138140. The parallel sometimes established with initiatory itineraries presented in gold lamellae, funerary texts incorrectly associated with Orphism, is not relevant here: see Calame 2011a; as a result, Most (1997:125–134)

Derveni commentary can be considered a sort of intellectual itinerary of initiation because of its dual erudite and theological qualities. Spoken in a primarily assertive mode by an anonymous author, it is offered to an Orphic initiate of the future. As a discursive practice, it is likely that the commentary was read to prepare or to accompany certain ritual gestures of initiation described in the text itself.

Following the circular progression of Zeus' demiurgic actions narrated in the poem as it develops, the discourse in the exegesis accomplishes a return to the cosmogonic unity proposed to adepts claiming to be under the authority of the poet and original singer Orpheus. In doing so, the Derveni commentator uses the same rhapsodic rhythm, but he uses it to transition from a traditionally oral poem to the practice of reading and writing. For this reason, it is possible to see the figure of Orpheus presented by the Orphic Derveni interpreter as not only the representative of a melodious voice with oracular qualities but also the generic emblem of Orphic cosmo-theogonic poetry in its various rhapsodic forms. Similarly, this is often the case with the figure of "Homer," cited by classical authors less for being the author of the *Iliad* or the *Odyssey* and more as the representative of the epic genre embodied in the rhapsodic tradition.[40] In addition, this "enigmatic" poetry, with the didactic decoding it requires, makes Orpheus the master of initiation, as he is for Aeschylus in Aristophanes' *Frogs*.

Through the discursive procedures specific to erudite commentary, the text of the Derveni Papyrus is presented paradoxically as an articulated discourse on practices of worship. It is without a doubt strengthened in this function by the ritual utility conferred through the corresponding intellectual itinerary, both cosmogonic and initiatory, that it seems to offer to the Orphic initiates invited to read it. Resulting from a practice of writing and probably meant less for an oral recitation than for an individual reading ("ritual reading?"), the exegetic Derveni text, with its rhapsodic organization, nevertheless appears as a discourse carrying the marks of poetic utility and meant for initiatory purposes. Its ritual function is apparently double: this discourse serves without a doubt in education, in initiation, and to integrate the new initiate into the group of Orphic officiants before it accompanies him as a text in a second rite of passage, his burial, where the mortal body is destroyed by flames on the funeral pyre. Meant to reveal the hidden meanings of the poem's Orphic cosmo-theogony transmitted by an inspired voice of poetic authority, the erudite commentary is itself put to use in this didactic and initiatory double function of epistemological as well as ritual nature.

---

certainly goes too far in his claims that the Derveni commentary is an "eschatological theology" in the form of "soteriological physics."

40 See my analysis of the significance of the name and figure of Homer (2004:26–31).

8. The Oxymoron of Oral Writing

This paradox of using written scholarly methods to enhance the enchanting powers of a particularly effective poetic voice of initiation is already present in the earliest existing accounts of classical Orphism. While in Euripides' *Hypsipyle* the melody of Orpheus' Thracian cithara accompanies the chant of the Asiatic elegy that provides the cadence for the beating of the Argonauts' oars, in a famous passage from *Hippolytus* Theseus accuses his son, guilty of exclusive devotion to Artemis, of belonging to the Orphic following: "Proclaim now your glory; for all nourishment show off your vegetarian diet; with Orpheus as your master join the Bacchants and honor the smoke of numerous writings."[41] Since the end of the Classical period then, the poetic and initiatory authority of Orpheus had been attached to written texts; and there was immediate distrust and scorn expressed about these texts, as in Plato half a century later.

Alcestis, also by Euripides, provides another contrasting example. On one hand, Admetus, attempting to retrieve his wife from Hades, relates his hope of using the melodious voice (*glôssa kaì mélos*) of Orpheus to charm Persephone, daughter of Demeter, through song (*húmnoisi*). On the other hand, the chorus later contrasts the sovereign power of Ananke, or Necessity, with the uselessness "of the tablets of Thrace where the voice [*gêrus*] of Orpheus was inscribed [*katégrapsen*]."[42] Whether its effect is positive, as Admetus envisions it, or negative, as in the case of the chorus, who form an analogy with the ineffective drugs that Apollo offered to the followers of Asclepius, the melodious and enchanting word of Orpheus possesses the unique power to inscribe itself onto wooden tablets; the tablets' origin in Thrace evokes the poet and singer's native land. By definition the melodious voice of Orpheus is written.

Indeed, the paradox of writing down oral discourses offering narrative and didactic forms of poetry that borrow from the tradition of Homeric diction is captured in a way in the image appearing on a famous Apulian amphora attributed to the Ganymede Painter (Figure 1). Dating from the last quarter of the fourth century, this image is contemporary to the Derveni Papyrus. In a shrine representing a tomb, a young Orpheus with his lyre, wearing a Phrygian headdress, is playing, singing, and dancing in front of an old man, who is holding a papyrus scroll in his hand.[43] Regardless of the purpose for the old man of the discourse

41 Cf. Euripides *Hippolytus* 948–954 (= *Orphica* 627 T Bernabé) as well as Euripides *Hypsipyle* fr. 752g, 8–14 Kannicht (= *Orphica* 1007 Bernabé); see also fr. 759a, 1614–1623 Kannicht (= *Orphica* 1009 T Bernabé).

42 Euripides *Alcestis* 357–362 (= *Orphica* 980 T Bernabé) and 962–971 (= *Orphica* 812 T Bernabé); see also Calame 2002:397–400.

43 Apulian amphora by the Ganymede Painter, Antikenmuseum Basel inv. S 40 (= *LIMC*, "Orpheus," 20); see the detailed commentary in my recent study, Calame 2011b.

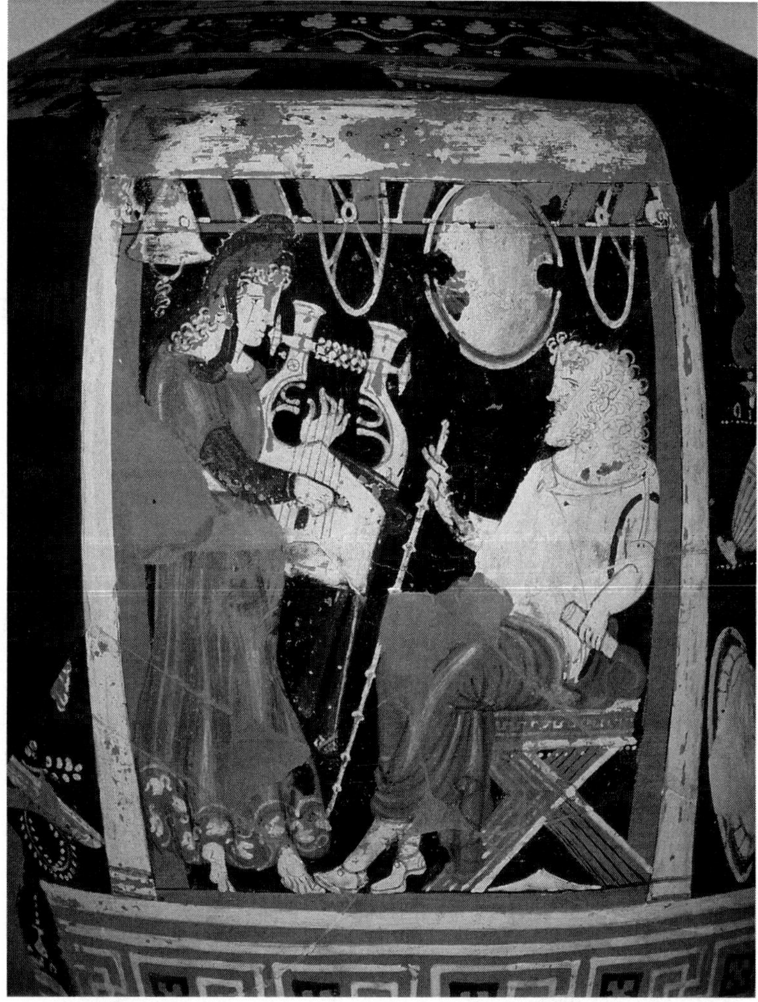

Figure 1. Apulian amphora by the Ganymede Painter. Antikensammlung Basel S 40. Photo, Antikenmuseum Basel und Sammlung Ludwig / Andreas F. Voegelin.

captured in writing, this strange funeral scene evokes the enchanting voice of Orpheus. But this poetic and musical voice is eternalized in a text meant for the deceased, which evokes the figure of the citizen whose remains, consumed by fire, were laid to rest at Derveni. This striking iconographic representation of the oral–written oxymoron related to Orpheus' authoritative voice suggests all at once the nature, the function, and the circumstances of the first initiatory Orphic text discovered by modern scholars.

Bibliography

Baumgarten, R. 1988. *Heiliges Wort and heilige Schrift bei den Griechen: Hieroi Logoi und verwandte Erscheinungen*. Tübingen.

Bernabé, A. 2001. "Orfeo: De personaje del mito a autor literario." *Quaderns Catalans de Cultura Clàsica* 18:61–78.

———. 2002. "La théogonie orphique du papyrus de Derveni." *Kernos* 15:91–129.

Bernabé, A., and F. Casadesús, eds. 2008. *Orfeo y la tradición órfica: Un reencuentro*. 2 vols. Madrid.

Betegh, G. 2004. *The Derveni Papyrus: Theology, Cosmology, and Interpretation*. Cambridge.

Borgeaud, Ph., ed. 1991. *Orphisme et Orphée. En l'honneur de Jean Rudhardt*. Geneva.

Bremmer, J. 2010. "Manteis, Magic, Mysteries, and Mythography: Messy Margins of the Polis Religion?" *Kernos* 23:13–35.

Brisson, L. 1995. *Orphée et l'Orphisme dans l'antiquité gréco-romaine*. Aldershot.

———. 2003. "Sky, Sex, and Sun: The Meanings of *aidoîos/aidoîon* in the Derveni Papyrus." *Zeitschrift für Papyrologie und Epigraphik* 144:19–29.

———. 2009. "Zeus Did Not Commit Incest with His Mother: An Interpretation of Column XXVI of the Derveni Papyrus." *Zeitschrift für Papyrologie und Epigraphik* 168:27–39.

Burkert, W. 1987. *Ancient Mystery Cults*. Cambridge, MA.

———. 2005. "La teogonia originale di Orfeo secondo il papiro di Derveni." In Guidorizzi and Melotti 2005:46–64.

Calame, C. 1991. "Éros initiatique et la cosmogonie orphique." In Borgeaud 1991:227–247.

———. 1997. "Figures of Sexuality and Initiatory Transition in the Derveni Theogony and Its Commentary." In Laks and Most 1997:65–80.

———. 2002. "Qu'est-ce qui est orphique dans les Orphica? Une mise au point introductive." *Revue de l'histoire des religions* 219:385–400.

———. 2004. "Identités d'auteur à l'exemple de la Grèce classique." In Calame and Chartier 2004:11–39.

———. 2005. *Masques d'autorité: Fiction et pragmatique dans la poétique grecque antique*. Paris. [Translated into English 2005, as *Masks of Authority: Fiction and Pragmatics in Ancient Greek Poetics*, Ithaca, NY.]

———. 2009. *Poetic and Performative Memory in Ancient Greece: Heroic Reference and Ritual Gestures in Time and Space*. Hellenic Studies 18. Washington, DC.

———. 2011a. "Funerary Gold Lamellae and Orphic Papyrus Commentary: Same Use, Different Purpose." In *The "Orphic" Gold Tablets and Greek Religion: Further along the Path* (ed. R. G. Edmonds III) 203–218. Cambridge.

———. 2011b. "L'écriture de la voix enchanteresse d'Orphée (OF 1)." *Tracing Orpheus: Studies in Orphic Fragments* (ed. M. Herrero de Jáuregui et al.) 7–12. Berlin.

Calame, C., and R. Chartier, eds. 2004. *Identités d'auteur dans l'antiquité et la tradition européenne*. Grenoble.

Detienne, M. 1989. *L'écriture d'Orphée*. Paris.

Faraone, Ch. A. 2005. "L'ultima esibizione di Orfeo: Necromanzia e una testa cantante a Lesbo." In Guidorizzi and Melotti 2005:65–85.

Ferrari, F. 2011a. "Frustoli erranti: Per una ricostruzione di P. Derveni coll. I–III." *Studi e testi per il corpus dei papiri filosofici greci e latini* 16:39–54.

———. 2011b. "Rites without Frontiers: *Magi* and *Mystae* in the Derveni Papyrus." *Zeitschrift für Papyrologie und Epigraphik* 179:71–83.

Ford, A. 2002. *The Origins of Criticism: Literary Culture and Poetic Theory in Classical Greece*. Princeton.

Graf, F. 1987. "Orpheus: A Poet among Men." *Interpretations of Greek Mythology* (ed. J. Bremmer) 80–106. London.

Guidorizzi, G., and M. Melotti, eds. 2005. *Orfeo e le sue metamorfosi: Mito, arte, poesia*. Rome.

Henrichs, A. 2003. "*Hieroi logoi* and *Hieroi bibloi*: The (Un)Written Margins of the Sacred in Ancient Greece." *Harvard Studies in Classical Philology* 101:207–266.

Holmes, B. 2010. *The Symptom and the Subject: The Emergence of the Physical Body in Ancient Greece*. Princeton.

Hopman-Govers, M. 2001. "Le jeu des épithètes dans les *Hymnes orphiques*." *Kernos* 14:35–49.

Jiménez San Cristóbal, A. I. 2008a. "El ritual y los ritos órficos." In Bernabé and Casadesús 2008:731–770.

———. 2008b. "Los orfeotelestas y la vida órfica." In Bernabé and Casadesús 2008: 771–799.

Jourdan, F. 2003. *Le Papyrus de Derveni*. Paris.

Kahn, Ch. H. 1997. "Was Euthyphro the Author of the Derveni Papyrus?" In Laks and Most 1997:55–63.

Kouremenos, T., G. M. Parássoglou, and K. Tsantsanoglou. 2006. *The Derveni Papyrus, Edited with Introduction and Commentary*. Florence.

Laks, A. 1997. "Between Religion and Philosophy: The Function of Allegory in the Derveni Papyrus." *Phronesis* 42:121–142.

Laks, A., and G. W. Most, eds. 1997. *Studies on the Derveni Papyrus*. Oxford.

Lloyd, G. E. R. 2003. *In the Grip of Disease: Studies in Greek Imagination*. Oxford.

Morand, A.-F. 2001. *Études sur les* Hymnes orphiques. Leiden.

Most, G. W. 1997. "The Fire Next Time: Cosmology, Allegoresis, and Salvation in the Derveni Papyrus." *Journal of Hellenic Studies* 117:117–135.

Nagy, G. 1990. *Pindar's Homer: The Lyric Possession of an Epic Past*. Baltimore.

———. 2002. *Plato's Rhapsody and Homer's Music: The Poetics of the Panathenaic Festival in Classical Athens*. Cambridge, MA.

Obbink, D. 1997. "Cosmology as Initiation vs. the Critique of Orphic Mysteries." In Laks and Most 1997:39–54.

Pfeiffer, R. 1968. *History of Classical Scholarship: From the Beginnings to the End of the Hellenistic Age*. Oxford.

Ricciardelli, G. 2000. *Inni orfici*. Milan.

Riedweg, Ch. 1996. "Orfeo." *I Greci: Storia cultura arte società* II.1 (ed. S. Settis) 1251–1280. Turin.

Rudhardt, J. 1991. "Quelques réflexions sur les Hymnes orphiques." In Borgeaud 1991:263–288.

———. 2008. *Opera inedita. Essai sur la religion grecque. Recherches sur les Hymnes orphiques*. Kernos, Suppl. 19. Liège.

Schmidt, M. 1972. "Ein neues Zeugnis zum Mythos vom Orpheushaupt." *Antike Kunst* 15:128–137.

Sider, D. 1997. "Heraclitus in the Derveni Papyrus." In Laks and Most 1997:129–148.

Tsantsanoglou, K. 1997. "The First Columns of the Derveni Papyrus and Their Religious Significance." In Laks and Most 1997:93–128.

West, M. L. 1983. *The Orphic Poems*. Oxford.

10

"Riddles over Riddles"

"Mysterious" and "Symbolic" (Inter)textual Strategies

The Problem of Language in the Derveni Papyrus

Anton Bierl
University of Basel

1. Introduction

THE OFFICIAL AND AUTHORITATIVE *EDITIO PRINCEPS* of the Derveni Papyrus by Kyriakos Tsantsanoglou and George M. Parássoglou, with translation, papyrological apparatus, and photographs, and the first full commentary in English by Theokritos Kouremenos, has given our knowledge a secure textual foundation.[1] Finally, with this new footing, we can go into the deeper hermeneutical problems of a text that is still so full of riddles for us. Important progress has also been made by Alberto Bernabé's edition, with its *apparatus criticus* that is a thesaurus of supplementary knowledge and alternative readings.[2] And Gábor Betegh's first monograph on the papyrus, an admirably full-fledged interpretation finished shortly before KPT,[3] is a great achievement to which my modest thoughts owe a great deal. However, even now there are still numerous open points.

My contribution will focus on several important questions that are essential for understanding the Derveni Papyrus as a whole: (1) What are the exegetical methods of the Derveni author? (2) What is the importance of the riddling and how is it linked to the allegorical method? (3) What is the point of view of the Derveni author—is he an anti-Orphic who applies a radical, natural scientific allegoresis to a canonical Orphic text, or is he himself part of the Orphic

1 Kouremenos, Parássoglou, and Tsantsanoglou 2006 (= KPT). See also the useful commentary by Jourdan (2003). In this article I quote the KPT *editio princeps*.

2 Bernabé 2007a:169–269. See also the interim text with a good apparatus by Janko (2002).

3 Betegh 2004.

movement? If the latter, in what way? (4) Further, does Presocratic thinking about nature have anything to do with Orphic thinking? (5) Does the text provide proof for the view of Wilhelm Nestle and many others who plead for a clear-cut progression from μῦθος to λόγος,[4] or does it give any evidence that such an evolutionary process has to be modified to accommodate interpenetration between these discourses?[5] Glenn Most's work is essential for me in this regard.[6] I am also indebted to a recent article by Spyridon Rangos and the work of others who have explored the hermeneutical strategies of the Derveni author.[7] Until recently, following the revision of the evolutionist view of the progression from μῦθος to λόγος, it had become almost the *opinio communis* that the Derveni author was somehow linked to Orphism and at least influenced by religious thoughts and practices.[8] The volume edited by André Laks and Glenn Most had a big impact on this view,[9] and Betegh encapsulates it in his first book-length study on the Derveni Papyrus. However, there have always been voices against such an opinion: some scholars have argued that the Derveni author was an anti-Orphic and natural scientist radically opposed to such obscure mystic thinking.[10] With his line-by-line commentary in the authoritative edition of KPT Kouremenos now strongly sides with the latter group and seems to tip the scales. My contribution is meant to counterbalance such an argument and to give a nuanced pro-Orphic interpretation.

The entire debate is also connected to the problem of how to link columns 1–6 to the allegorical reading of a theogony of Orpheus in the rest of the text.[11] Formerly the text was called a Presocratic allegorical commentary on an Orphic poem, written from a strong perspective of natural science.[12] However, it seems that this cannot be the whole story. Michael Frede has recently pointed out that the author is not really interested in an overall scientific interpretation.[13] The entire apparatus of Presocratic science elaborated in an eclectic way is rather underdeveloped. What might then be the intention of the author and the context of the primary recipient? Like many critics I am convinced that it must

4 Nestle 1940. For the *P.Derv.*, see e.g. Burkert 1968.

5 Most 1997 and in general Most 1999.

6 Most 1997 and Most 1999. See also Laks and Most 1997.

7 Rangos (2007) has worked along similar lines, though I began to think about this independently before. See also Henry 1986 and Sistakou and Calame in this volume.

8 E.g. West 1983:68–115; West 1997; and the work of Burkert, in particular Burkert 1999:59–86, esp. 78–86; Burkert 2006; Bernabé 2007b.

9 Laks and Most 1997.

10 E.g. Henrichs 1984, esp. 255; Rusten 1985:140; Casadio 1987:386; Janko 1997; Janko 2001:6: "sophist" (but also "at once a sophistical Orphic and an Orphic sophist" [5]); KPT 52.

11 See Johnston, Graf, Bernabé in this volume.

12 E.g. Burkert 1968; Janko 2001:1–6.

13 Frede 2007, esp. 9–12.

somehow have to do with the ritual columns. I strongly believe that the Derveni author is a reform Orphic, as Most has put it.[14] The *we*-form of the first-person plural πάριμεν in col. 5.4 speaks in favor of this opinion.[15] But does the appropriation of the Orphic text only function as a statement against the fear of the "Fire next time," in a ritual soteriological and burial context, the primary *Sitz im Leben*?[16] Betegh seems to be on the right path in associating the ritual passages with the δρώμενα, and the exegetical passage then with the λεγόμενα in the sense of a ἱερὸς λόγος.[17] And Rangos makes a very good point in underlining the obfuscating quality of the text in order to make evident the latent nuances.[18]

2. The Derveni Author, a Riddling *Orpheotelestes*?

It goes without saying that riddling is a major feature of our text (e.g. cols. 7, 9, and 13).[19] The hermeneutical tools of allegory and allegoresis imply that readers presume the author of the canonical text to intend something other than what the literal sense indicates. What is striking in the allegoresis of the Derveni Papyrus is the fact that the target discourse, natural science, remains rather vague, a strange, eclectic blend of Presocratic natural theory. Does this render our author an incompetent who fails to reach his intellectual goal?[20] I do not think so; he most likely aims at something other than pure allegoresis. Like his source, the supposedly riddling Orpheus, the Derveni author himself riddles. Thus we have two-tier riddling, or "riddles over riddles," which makes it so difficult to grasp the authorial register. The author does not intend to give a nuanced logocentric view in the vein of science. Rather, nature is part of the mystical and eschatological discourse upon which Presocratics like Heraclitus, Parmenides, and Empedocles are based. That these early philosophers are not completely embedded in λόγος, but deeply rely on myth and ritual discourse, has recently been made more and more evident.[21]

Initiation and soteriology do not necessarily possess only metaphoric value for abstract philosophy. Insight into nature and the cosmos is still intrinsically

14 Most 1997:122–124.

15 πάριμεν̣ [εἰς τὸ μα]ν̣τεῖον ἐπερ̣[ω]τ̣ή̣σ̣[οντες] ("we enter the oracle in order to ask," 5.4).

16 Most 1997, with "we" at 120. However, see Burkert in this volume, suggesting that πάριμεν is an infinitive.

17 Betegh 2004, esp. 349–359; the Derveni author designates the poem as *hymnos* (7.2). For hymn as unmarked term for an epic poem in its performance, see Nagy 1990:353n77. Often there is a cyclical logic. For *hieroi logoi*, see Henrichs 2003; he is skeptical about applying this term to the *P.Derv.*: see pp. 213–214, 232–233.

18 Rangos 2007. See also Betegh 2004:364–370.

19 See 7.5–6, 9.10, 10.11, 13.6, 17.13.

20 Rusten 1985:122; West 1983:79.

21 See the literature cited in Bierl 2007:45n254; Gemelli Marciano 2008.

associated with wisdom in general and with eschatology, a realm of knowledge concerned with the afterlife of the soul.[22] Heraclitus himself, whom our author cites (DK 22 B 3 and 94, in col. 4), uses a dark, aphoristic prose that reflects the grounding of his thought in death.[23] Language and play with linguistic elements are part of his philosophical thinking, which aims at triggering a lightning-like intuition.[24] Other authors and forms display language play as well: the αἶνος, a story with a deeper meaning behind the surface,[25] achieves its effect through the use of defamiliarized, strange, and riddling language (αἰνίγματα); Anaximander produces a rather poetic prose full of metaphors;[26] Parmenides seems to be based on mystical insights.[27] Peter Kingsley has aptly demonstrated the ways in which both Parmenides and Empedocles are deeply involved in the religious discourse of mystery cults in Magna Graecia.[28] Empedocles poses as a god, μάντις, prophet, and healer who teaches with an oracular language that involves nature and the future of the soul.[29] Thus his style is strange, poetic, and dark. Like Heraclitus, he uses paretymologies; furthermore, he applies polyptota, metaphors, metonymies, and kennings—he breaks loose the bond between signifier and signified and employs new, defamiliarized forms and vocabulary. Empedocles' poetical and "studied ambiguity" produces an alienating style that makes the recipient "stop thinking at the right moment" in order to reach the sudden, mystical insight.[30] Parmenides embeds his view on φύσις and cosmogony in poetry and in a mystical journey through the elements. Empedocles seems, as Andreas Willi, among others, points out, to resort to a divine language, which is typical of Indo-European culture.[31] For him, the problem of communication and knowledge seems to lie in naming as a means of human designation. Human beings notoriously err in their use of language, but by reverting to another, higher language, closer to the putative origin, the recipient can reach higher knowledge. This is part of the initiation into mystery cults like Orphism, where the initiands are directed by ἱεροὶ and riddling λόγοι, by συνθήματα and σύμβολα to higher cognition. Whereas the thoughts of men are led astray by faulty naming, gods and divine authorities like Orpheus possess

22 See Seaford 1986.

23 Thurner 2001.

24 See e.g. Schefer 2000; Bremer 1990. On Heraclitus and *P.Derv.*, see Seaford 1986 and Sider 1997.

25 Nagy 1979:235–241, esp. 240; Nagy 1990:31.

26 Simplicius *De physica* 24.20–21: ποιητικωτέροις οὕτως ὀνόμασιν αὐτὰ λέγων (DK 12 A 9; after the famous fragment of Anaximander, DK 12 B 1).

27 Gemelli Marciano 2008.

28 Kingsley 1995; Kingsley 1999.

29 Bierl (forthcoming). For these designations regarding the Derveni author, see Tzifopoulos in this volume.

30 Willi 2008:193–229. For the citation, see Millerd 1908:21, referred to at Willi 2008:221.

31 Willi 2008:230–263, esp. 243–254.

the true language, which is located in the realm of θέμις, divine order. In other words, the denotations of men are only θέσις or νόμος, while the true content is pure φύσις.[32]

3. The Method of the Derveni Author: Inclusion and Exclusion as Principles of Understanding in Initiatory Contexts

First I would like to look at column 7:

...(.)]οcε̣[
..ὕ]μνον̣ [ὑγ]ι̣ῆ καὶ θεμ[ι]τ̣ὰ λέγο[ντα· ἱερουργεῖ]τ̣ο γὰρ
[τῆ]ι ποήσει. [κ]αὶ εἰπεῖν οὐχ οἷόν τ[ε τὴν τῶν ὀ]νομάτων
[λύ]σιν καίτ[οι] ῥηθέντα. ἔστι δὲ ξ[ένη τις ἡ] πόησις
[κ]α̣ὶ ἀνθρώ[ποις] αἰνι̣[γμ]ατώδης, [κε]ὶ ['Ορφεὺ]ς̣ αὐτ[ὸ]ς̣
[ἐ]ρίστ' αἰν[ίγμα]τα οὐκ ἤ̣θελε λέγειν, [ἐν αἰν]ίγμασ̣[ι]ν δὲ
[μεγ]άλα̣. ἱερ[ολογ]ε̣ῖ̣ται μὲν οὖν καὶ ἀ̣[πὸ το]ῦ πρώτου
[ἀεὶ] μέχρι οὗ̣ [τελε]υ̣τ̣α̣ίου ῥήματος. ὡ̣[ς δηλοῖ] καὶ ἐν τῶι
[εὐκ]ρινήτω̣[ι ἔπει· "θ]ύ̣ρας" γὰρ "ἐπιθέ[σθαι" κελ]εύσας τοῖ̣[ς]
["ὠσὶ]ν" αὐτ[οὺς οὔτι νομο]θ̣ε̣τ̣εῖν φη[σιν τοῖς] πολλοῖς
τὴ]ν ἀκοὴν [ἁγνεύο]ντας κατ̣[ὰ]
]ς̣ειτ̣[..].
]ωι τ[..]εγ.[...]..[
ἐν δ]ὲ τῶι ἐχομ[έ]ν̣ωι πα[
].τ̣..ε̣ι̣γ.[.]κ̣ατ̣[

... a hymn saying sound and lawful words. For [a sacred rite was being performed] through the poem. And one cannot state the solution of the [enigmatic] words though they are spoken [*i.e. not secret*]. This poem is strange and riddling to people, though [Orpheus] intended to tell not contentious riddles but rather great things in riddles. In fact he is speaking mystically, and from the very first word all the way to the last. As he also makes clear in the well-recognized verse: for, having ordered them to "put doors to their ears," he says that he is not legislating for the many [but addressing himself to those] who are pure in hearing ... and in the following verse ...[33]

[32] For Empedocles and the *P.Derv.* author, see Betegh 2004:370–372.

[33] All translations of the *P.Derv.* are from KTP, from Betegh 2004, or from a combination of them with slight modifications.

Orpheus probably sings a hymn in the form of a ἱερὸς λόγος, uttering things that are sound or even healthy and that are in accord with divine θέμις. He is the healer and divine authority who composes according to divine language—at least he thinks so. Words can have a salubrious effect. They have to do with health because, through the recitation of poetry, a sacred rite is being performed. The words of poetry have a special and sacred aural effect as λεγόμενα in accompaniment with δρώμενα. Since the poem is a holy text, and in accordance with mystery rites, it is forbidden to overtly solve its riddles. This means that there is a choice: one must either allegorize—rendering the discourse no longer holy—or simply utter the obscure words. It cannot be approached in both ways at the same time. However, our author tries to establish a *modus* that cuts between both options, a typically Orphic paradoxical mode that concentrates on the mystic workings of nature.[34]

The poem of Orpheus is strange because it defamiliarizes, deestablishes, fixed meanings; it loosens the link between signified and the signifier and occupies a zonal territory in between. To an average audience, therefore, it seems to be a riddling, enigmatic work. Yet Orpheus does not intend to use this technique for contentious purposes, or to show off in a rhetoric ἀγών. No, according to the Derveni author Orpheus wants to say great things in riddles, that is, he wants to help the initiated, the μύσται, to grasp the circumstances of nature and the cosmos, the quintessential message of Orphic and/or mystery cult in general. The Derveni author can prove this with Orpheus' standard entrance verse, which is characteristic of mysteries:

> ἀείσω ξυνετοῖσι· θύρας δ' ἐπίθεσθε, βέβηλοι
> φθέγξομαι οἷς θέμις ἐστί· θύρας δ' ἐπίθεσθε, βέβηλοι
>
> *OF* 1 and 3

Orpheus, as well as the Derveni author, has the key. The entrance formula reflects the standard notion of mystic exclusion and inclusion. The initiated and "pure in hearing" are included—they, as μύσται, are able to hear and learn what is divine law, θέμις. To "put doors to the ears" means to exclude the others, the profane or βέβηλοι. The door stands for the barrier between inside and outside, and the image associates hearing with special access. Thus the sacred space of the sanctuary is metonymically shifted to the private space of the auditory canal of the τελεστής or μύστης. The formula mirrors the central verb μύω, which designates the act of listening to an authoritative voice of θέμις as well as the signal to keep the mouth and ears shut.[35] The initiated should open their

[34] Cf. Rangos 2007, esp. 70: "He wants it both ways." Cf. also Most 1997.

[35] Nagy 1990:31–32 (with the link to *mythos*).

ears and eyes so that they can experience the sacred message; the masses must be kept outside. The imperative suggests the drawing of a boundary around a zonal space where the truth of φύσις becomes evident, but in latent and enigmatic terms. The word βέβηλοι comes from βαίνω; the uninitiated masses have to *go*, to keep away from the closed doors that shut up the inner space of their ears. By employing the formula the author says that Orpheus is not "legislating" (νομο]θ̣ε̣τεῖν, 7.10) for the many—i.e. using the style of νόμοι and θέσις to express what is merely conventional signification—but addressing his poem to the "pure in hearing," who have access to the special and marked space and who are allowed to hear what is divine and, thus, the essence of φύσις.

With new riddles the Derveni author then tries to tease out deeper meaning: the authoritative meaning of αἶνος is hidden and has to be made manifest. However, the author does not convey this meaning in an evident sense, but adds a second enigmatic layer. The reason Orpheus riddles, according to the Derveni author, is to comply with the taste of the recipients, ordinary men who like to give names. Compare the following expressions: Ὀρφεὺς γὰ`ρ´ / τὴν φρόνησ[ι]ν Μοῖραν ἐκάλ̣εσεν· ἐφαίνετο γὰρ αὐτῶι / τοῦτο προσφερέστατον ε[ἶ]ν̣αι ἐ̣ξ̣ ὧν ἅπαντες ἄνθρωποι / ὠνόμασαν· ("For Orpheus called thought Moira. This seemed to him to be the most suitable of the names that all people had given," 18.6–9); πάν̣[τ' οὖ]ν ὁμοίω[ς ὠ]νόμασεν ὡς κ̣άλλιστα ἠ[δύ]ν̣ατο / γινώσκ̣ων τῶν ἀνθρώπων τὴν φύσιν ("So he named all things in the same way as finely as he could, knowing the nature of men ...," 22.1–2); and ὁ δὲ σημαίνει τὴν αὐτοῦ γνώμην / ἐν τοῖς λεγομέν[ο]ις καὶ νομιζομένοις ῥήμασι ("But he indicates his own opinion in current and customary expressions," 23.7–8). Even an initiated audience, according to Orpheus, thinks in customary ways. People are used to mythical figures in theogonic poems. Thus, the Derveni author argues, Orpheus clothes his ideas in such traditional figures with a putatively different intention.

If, as Parmenides and Empedocles say, naming is the great problem of mankind—with ὀνόματα people might reach false conclusions—a poet needs poetic metaphors to meet the taste of his audience. In *Rhetoric* 1407a32–1407b6 Aristotle criticizes Empedocles (Emp. test. 31 A 25) for his ambiguities—ἀμφίβολα is a feature of oracular language—and in *Meteorologica* 357a24–28 he assails him for his metaphorical style, which is apt for poets, but not suitable πρὸς δὲ τὸ γνῶναι τὴν φύσιν. Therefore, according to Aristotle, Empedocles lacks the principle of clarity that should accompany a philosopher, something which might also be said of Orpheus. But a goetic and mystical wonder-worker and μάντις-poet resorts to metaphors in order to provoke thinking. Intentional ambiguity is used to reach intuitive insights. The Derveni author is part of the Orphic system, too—he wants to radicalize and enforce such riddling strategies.

4. The Cognitive and Didactic Purpose and the Derveni Author as a Figure between Philosopher and Orphic Wisdom Practitioner

It is my contention that the Derveni text is hardly concerned with burial ritual;[36] rather, it has its *Sitz im Leben* in a didactic context.[37] The Derveni author—as oracular priest, healer, and prophet—appropriates the canonical text of the great guru Orpheus to convey initiatory and cognitive messages. But for him Orpheus' theogony as αἴνιγμα is not radical enough, even though Orpheus is known as the founder of bizarre myths and wisdom. Still, the paradoxical blurring of opposites that is typical for myth and ritual triggers unifying cognition for the μύσται.

Orphic ideology is a bricolage comprising the canonical Hesiodic theogony and many other variants that blend traditional Greek views with new Oriental and other external influences.[38] As διφυής *par excellence* Orpheus is the marked and fictionalized sign for such knowledge based on moralistic and biotic rules. Compared to the ordinary Olympian theology, the main principle of his lore seems to be a grounding of life in death and a spiritual foregrounding of Night and other chthonic elements.[39] The Derveni author himself behaves like a priest and Orphic μάγος and γόης.[40] Through magic and special rituals, he attempts to secure the passage of souls to death and Night (cf. cols. 1–6). And symbolic analogy is his primary method.

The Orphic group and rival "extra-ordinary" practitioners honor the Erinyes with χοαί and something birdlike, since souls are compared to birds (col. 6)—like goes to like—and all is fitted to music and musical performance, poetry (col. 2). The chthonic Erinyes, as avengers, are assistants of the Olympic gods and guarantors of the current cosmos and Zeus' system of δίκη (col. 3). Binary oppositions can be subverted; what harms can also help to maintain order. The author cites Heraclitus fragments 3 and 94, on the sun and its tendency to overstep boundaries and on the role of the Erinyes, Δίκης ἐπίκουροι, who hunt down transgressors (col. 4). The word ὑπερβατόν (4.10) is the verbal adjective for violating the limits of the cosmic order as well as the *terminus technicus* for suspending the syntactical standard order and sense (cf. 8.6).[41]

[36] See Most 1997:131–135.

[37] See Calame 1997:77–80; Betegh 2004:360–370; and also Calame and Graf in this volume.

[38] For bricolage, see Edmonds 2004:4.

[39] See e.g. Bremmer 1991; Burkert 1999:59–86.

[40] Edmonds (2008:34–35) rightly stresses that our author has to deal with rivals and so believes him to be a *mystes*, not a *magos*. However, I believe that it is in principle possible for him to be a *magos*, too (see also Edmonds 2008:35n83; Betegh 2004:81–82); much depends on how one interprets the *magoi* in column 6. The first-person plural in 5.3 might be an indication that he includes himself. On *magos*, see also Bernabé, Graf, and Johnston in this volume.

[41] See Rusten 1985:125n10 (with reference to *scholia* (A) *Iliad* 14.1); Jourdan 2003:47n7.

Column 5 deals with the terrors of Hades, and with the disbelievers: "For them we go into oracular shrines to inquire for oracular answers" (αὐτοῖς πάριμεν [εἰς τὸ μα]ντεῖον ἐπερ[ω]τήσ[οντες], / τῶν μαντευομένων [ἕν]εκεν, 5.4–5). The uninitiated are afraid of the horrors of the underworld because they do not have access to the truth. Dream interpretation, however, yields a deeper knowledge in the same way that oracular language does. Both are ambiguous and seem to be lacking in logic, both move on metonymies and metaphors, and both provide signs, σήματα or παραδείγματα (5.8), in a loose and ambivalent structure. In this respect one can compare Heraclitus, who says of the Delphic oracle: Ὁ ἄναξ, οὗ τὸ μαντεῖόν ἐστι τὸ ἐν Δελφοῖς, οὔτε λέγει οὔτε κρύπτει ἀλλὰ σημαίνει (fr. 93 DK).

The use of cryptic and enigmatic language in the way of an exegesis of dreams and oracles is precisely the strategy adopted by our anonymous "extraordinary" practitioner to produce deeper insight. But our author is aware of the fact that, because of "fault" (ἁμαρτίη) or "pleasure" (ἡδονή) (5.8–10), some do not apprehend dreams or care about latent signs. These undesirable behaviors result in "disbelief" (ἀπιστίη) and "lack of understanding" (ἀμαθίη) (5.10). Moreover, moral aberration is analogous to the deviation from initiatory wisdom. Ritual acts and enchanting songs allow μάγοι like him to remove the impeding δαίμονες: "As if they pay a penalty" (ὡσπερεὶ ποινὴν ἀποδιδόντες, 6.5), they offer a sacrifice (see column 6). Μάγοι, in the same way as μύσται, communicate with the Erinyes through fluids and knobbed cakes. The performance of ritual and speech acts can accomplish diametrical change: in such a way, Erinyes, who harm, become Eumenides, who are emblematically benevolent (see col. 6), and disbelievers can be turned into believers. Analogy and symbolic similarity are the principal ideas behind such thinking and doing, and they are the features of exegetical speech as well.

The Derveni author clarifies his standpoint in a sort of parenthesis in column 20: for him the performance of rites is important, but it has to be complemented by knowledge. People performing the mystery rites in the cities have only seen the holy things. But he wonders whether they have knowledge (γινώσκειν): "For it is not possible to hear and at the same time to understand what is being said" (οὐ γὰρ οἷόν τε / ἀκοῦσαι ὁμοῦ καὶ μαθεῖν τὰ λεγόμενα·, 20.2–3). Mere listening does not automatically lead to understanding, which is why he tries to deepen the discourse with new riddling that leads to learning and sudden insight. Seeing the holy things is one thing, and true knowledge of such signs another. Therefore, the Derveni author is against other rival priests and ritual wonder-workers as well, and he pities those who follow them. Only he has access to the necessary wisdom, and only he can teach it.

5. Learning about *Physis* through Fragmentation and Playing with the Orphic Text

In answer to the question "How does the Derveni author approach his goal?," I contend that he applies linguistic and exegetical strategies based on his religious intentions and desire to enlighten. Thus he invents new σύμβολα and συνθήματα that are similar to the many strange συνθήματα dispersed in the gold tablet Thurii 2 (Graf 4, *OF* 492), which has already been connected with our text by Betegh.[42] He achieves this by unfastening (λύσις) and splitting the great canonical theogony of Orpheus into many symbolic, mysterious, and oracular parts. In other words, he fragments the continuous epic hexameters of Orphic narration. Furthermore, he loosens its syntagmatic and syntactic structure, and, not least, its sense.

By defamiliarizing habitual meaning, by splitting and rendering the signifier ambiguous, the Derveni author tries to activate thought in order to establish a new harmonized sense. This activation is accomplished through a performative speech act, such as teaching or the reading aloud of a new text by a priest or recipient. In other words, a textual σπαραγμός is applied to Orpheus, the emblematically διφυής poet. And when Orpheus, symbol of free invention by bricolage, meets new bricolage, the enchantment and strange diction that produce a dissolution of sense can yield new intuitive understanding. Therefore, our text is not a commentary, a logocentric exegesis of a poem whose meaning, having become questionable, must be legitimized. Instead, the author's method creates unity in plurality, reinforcing an Orphic principle. All in all, the Derveni text is not just an accommodationist's transformation to a new sense.[43] Nor is it poetry explained by science, since the Presocratic system of targeting is imprecise and unclear. Rather, source and target meet and overlap in a syncretistic association, and both maintain a bricolage of common physical ideas based on nature and the cosmos. Cosmogony, cosmology, and the knowledge of φύσις and its evolution form this common ground, which means that both texts are intrinsically Orphic.

According to the Derveni author, Orpheus' poem reflects the taste of the masses: they demand the existence of mythological figures who stand for traditionally associated knowledge. By splitting, defamiliarizing, and reassembling the text in unusual lemma-like catchwords the author can produce new meaning from these associations. The source is a holy text to which he applies the poetical and hermeneutical tools of paretymology and allegoresis. His

[42] Betegh 2004:333–337. See also Rangos 2007:65 on "new syntheses of telestic Orphic myths with cosmogonical and cosmological processes" and 65–67 for σύμβολα.

[43] Most 1997:124.

intention is to break up, disrupt, and shift the meaning. Therefore, the Derveni author must be seen as an Orphic making use of new linguistic techniques. He draws on philosophers who base their writings in myth and religious concepts, in order to convey the same message as theirs by using Orpheus: everything is nature, and understanding nature—the cosmos, sun, moon, and stars—provides the μύστης with eschatological knowledge. The putative ὑπερβατά (4.10, 8.6) and false syntactical connections are wrong and unjust, i.e. unsound readings: since Sun tends to transgress, the Erinyes come to set it back on the right path; moral behavior and cosmic behavior are assimilated and interrelated. In the same way, as one tries to appease the Erinyes and make them benevolent (see cols. 1–6), he helps to create cosmos—order—in language.[44] The fragments the Derveni author singles out are put together to form new, concise, and symbolic συνθήματα, material that fosters thought.[45]

6. The Presocratic and Orphic System of *Physis*

The author's physical and eclectic system of Presocratic science is fairly easy to comprehend:[46] instead of a single force, we have two: Sun, the fomenting and striking energy of fire responsible for mixing and making the particles of Being float, and Night, which joins things in certain configurations: "Sun dissolves by heating, night unites by cooling those things which the sun heated" (ὁ ἥλι̣[ος θερμαίνων δι]α̣λ̣ύει ταῦ̣τα ἡ νὺξ ψύ[χουσα] / συ[νίστησι.........] ἅσσα ὁ ἥλιος ἐ̣θ̣ε̣ρ[μ, 10.12–13). Furthermore, in Sun and Night we have the four qualities of early ancient medicine: warm and dry versus cold and humid. Fire, the pure energy, has to be removed to a certain distance so that everything does not melt and commingle. Thus things stand apart and coagulate into a certain formation: our world (ἡ νῦν μετάστασις, 15.9). Separating, dissolving in order to make stand in distance (διαλύειν, διιστάναι), and assembling, putting together (συνιστάναι), are the two actions responsible for the configurations of the eternal beings. These actions mirror the Empedoclean forces of Philia/Philotes and Neikos.

On the level of textual montage, as we have seen, the Derveni author acts on separation and reassembly, fragmenting and connecting as well. Column 10, where the author assimilates saying, uttering, and teaching, is important for

44 And maybe even music; see 2.8: καὶ] ἐ̣π̣έθηκε[ν ὕμνους ἁρμ]οστο[ὺ]ς τῆ̣ι̣ μ̣ουσ̣ι̣κῆι; the subject could be Orpheus himself or a rival Orphic priest.

45 I need only recall sentences like αἰδοῖον κατ̣έπινεν, ὃς αἰθέρα ἔκθορ̣ε πρῶτος (13.4) or Οὐρανὸς Εὐφρονίδης, ὃς πρώτιστο̣ς βασίλευσεν (14.6). Compare also the riddling: Ζεὺς κεφα̣[λή, Ζεὺς μέσ]σ̣α̣, Δ̣ιὸς δ' ἐ̣κ [π]άντα τέτ̣[υκται (17.12) or Ζεὺς βασιλεύς, Ζεὺς δ' ἀρχὸς ἁπάντ̣ω̣ν ἀργικέραυνος (19.10).

46 See Burkert 1968; Betegh 2004:278–348; KTP 28–45. Jourdan (2003:xvii–xviii) provides a useful summary of the system.

assembly in a didactic context. In the same way that Orpheus' Night utters, says, and teaches her understanding of the world, so too does our anonymous Orphic. By disjoining the sense and defamiliarizing the syntax and context, the Derveni author provides συνθήματα as sayings; in uttering them with his voice (φωνή) he produces poetic enchantment. The dual-natured Orphic system, the paradoxical harmony of binary opposites, is reinforced by teaching through fragmented citations. The symbolic catchwords then trigger the desired sudden, enlightening insight.

The arcane, chthonic, and mysterious are here as important as the evident. Life is grounded in death and Night, who serves as "nurse" (τροφός, 10.11). Night has knowledge and proclaims her oracle from the innermost shrine (ἐξ ἀδύτοιο), where she is "never setting" (ἄδυτον, col. 11). Night does not set as φῶς, but rather remains in the same place after being struck by a beaming light. Parmenides discusses the same dual system of light and night:

μορφὰς γὰρ κατέθεντο δύο γνώμας ὀνομάζειν·
τῶν μίαν οὐ χρεών ἐστιν—ἐν ὧι πεπλανημένοι εἰσίν—
τἀντία δ' ἐκρίναντο δέμας καὶ σήματ' ἔθεντο
χωρὶς ἀπ' ἀλλήλων, τῆι μὲν φλογὸς αἰθέριον πῦρ,
ἤπιον ὄν, μέγ' [ἀραιὸν] ἐλαφρόν, ἑωυτῶι πάντοσε τωὐτόν,
τῶι δ' ἑτέρωι μὴ τωὐτόν· ἀτὰρ κἀκεῖνο κατ' αὐτό
τἀντία νύκτ' ἀδαῆ, πυκινὸν δέμας ἐμβριθές τε.
τόν σοι ἐγὼ διάκοσμον ἐοικότα πάντα φατίζω,
ὡς οὐ μή ποτέ τίς σε βροτῶν γνώμη παρελάσσηι.

Mortals have settled in their minds to speak of two forms, one of which to name alone is not right,[47] and that is where they go astray from the truth. They have assigned an opposite substance to each, and marks distinct from one another. To the one they allot the fire of heaven, light, thin, in every direction the same as itself, but not the same as the other. The other is opposite to it, dark night, a compact and heavy body. Of these I tell you the whole arrangement as it seems to men, in order that no mortal may surpass you in knowledge.

fr. 8, 52–61

And Parmenides continues:

αὐτὰρ ἐπειδὴ πάντα φάος καὶ νὺξ ὀνόμασται
καὶ τὰ κατὰ σφετέρας δυνάμεις ἐπὶ τοῖσί τε καὶ τοῖς

[47] Here I follow Hölscher 1969:27, 104. The translation is after John Burnet, with small changes.

πᾶν πλέον ἐστὶν ὁμοῦ φάεος καὶ νυκτὸς ἀφάντου
ἴσων ἀμφοτέρων, ἐπεὶ οὐδετέρωι μέτα μηδέν.

Now that all things have been named light and night; and the things which belong to the power of each have been assigned to these things and to those, everything is full at once of light and dark night, both equal, since neither has aught to do with the other.

fr. 9

Night has the identical σήματα of Being as light, since neither can be said to be Nothing. To name one alone, as if it were only the negative opposite, is fallacious.[48] Night is unconscious—as the lightweight and mild light she is self-identical—and possesses material substance. The decisive knowledge stems from the subconscious, oracular and dreamlike (see col. 5). Night resides in a sacred shrine because she has an oracular status and because, as paretymologically explained, she does not set. For this etymological play one might compare Heraclitus fr. 16 DK: τὸ μὴ δῦνόν ποτε πῶς ἄν τις λάθοι; ("How could anyone not realize that which never sets?"). Thus human beings, at least the initiated ones, have to deal with and refer to Night, Hades, and Death. In this formulation, Night becomes the basis of life. The Orphic bone tablets of Olbia testify: ΒΙΟΣ ΘΑΝΑΤΟΣ ΒΙΟΣ ("Life-Death-Life," *OF* 463). People, or at least mantic priests, γόητες and μάγοι, must initiate ritual contact with Night to appease her horror and bring forth benevolence, wealth, blessings, and knowledge.

Our author also follows another Parmenidean principle: there is no becoming/coming into being or destruction/perishing; things—τὰ ἔοντα—are and have always been.[49] In the course of time we come into contact with different κόσμοι and configurations of particles through separation and mixture. There is development toward the order of Zeus, but Zeus is already there from the beginning and he operates as a mastermind (*Nous*) in the world. The temporal process from Night, through Ouranos and Kronos, to Zeus is subsumed under a universal divine plan, and the paradox of temporal succession and self-identity is made clear by συνθήματα.[50]

In such a riddling exegesis the bond between cause and effect is often dissolved; in our text it happens quite often that cause and effect are established and produced in retrospect. Human beings have difficulty understanding the

48 Hölscher 1969:103–105. The mistake lies in the duality—in reality both sides belong together in a complementary way.

49 For Parmenides and the Derveni Papyrus, see KPT 32.

50 For the central role of Zeus, see Bernabé 2007b:125–126 ("Thus, he is a kind of harmonization of contradictions [a characterization reminiscent of Heraclitus' formulation of the divine]" [125]).

mystery of life—a difficulty stemming from denomination (ὀνομάζειν). When they conceptualize generation, development, and process, they think in terms of sexual intercourse (see cols. 13 and 21). Common theogonies and cosmogonies account for these notions: *phallos*, sexual encounters, and other scandalous stories are signs, screens, or symbols; by reading them one can reach their implicit truth. Moreover, many mystery cults work with such sexual rites and tokens as well—Orpheus and Orphic initiations are notorious for doing so.[51]

7. Going through the Theogony

The textual and hermeneutical strategies regarding columns 8ff. that explain how Zeus was installed are most riddling, but they lead to insight in φύσις: Orpheus' theogony is pure poetry and ὀνόματα. By means of an *in medias res* order and the use of ring composition, the importance of Zeus, the guarantor of this κόσμος, is mirrored on the level of compositional and poetic structure.[52] The decisive paradox of Orphic cyclicity is conveyed by systematically playing down the violence in the succession of mighty divine rulers. Regime change happens only insofar as the configuration of succession develops toward the now-existing natural order of Zeus. However, Zeus is the real ἀρχή from the very beginning, as he dominates the world. Therefore, he is paradoxically identical to all former personifications of this evolution.

Let us have a look at how the Derveni author delineates this development, picking out fragmented verses—the fragmentary use does not imply, as West and other critics have argued, that according to the logic of a stemma we can reconstruct an abridged Derveni theogony as a lineage of an Orphic Protogonos theogony:[53]

> "Ζεὺς μὲν ἐπεὶ δὴ π̣α̣[τρὸς ἑο]ῦ πάρα θέ[σ]φατον ἀρχὴν
> [ἀ]λκήν τ' ἐν χείρεσσι ἔ[λ]αβ[εν κ]α̣[ὶ] δαίμον[α] κυδρόν."
>
> "And when Zeus took from his father the prophesied rule
> And the strength in his hands and the glorious *daimon*."
>
> 8.4–5

Truth is again brought about by linguistic means, by loosening the syntax, the grammatical order. The Derveni author claims: "It has escaped notice that

51 Burkert 1987:67, 74, 80, 95–96, 104–108, 134n12, 156n44. For the allegoresis on the isotopy of sexuality, see Calame 1997:66–75.

52 For the "flashback device," see Bernabé 2007b:113–114.

53 West 1983:82–115, esp. 87, 95n44. Bernabé (2007b:126) thinks as well that it was "a brief poem that took for granted the knowledge of other poems."

these words are transposed" ([τ]α̣ῦτα τὰ ἔπη ὑπερβατὰ ἐό[ν]ṭα λανθάν̣[ει·], 8.6). ὑπερβατά—the putative transgression—lies in the use of language. This syntactical transposition has to be restored to the correct order, just as the sun must be returned to normal δίκη by the Erinyes when it oversteps its boundaries (see col. 4). The decisive words are πατρὸς ἑοῦ and πάρα; if πάρα is not in anastrophe, it does not go with the genitive "from his father" but with the accusative "contrary to divine decrees"—πα̣ρὰ̣ θέσφατα (8.11). Our author points at a morally dangerous poetic and syntactical ambivalence. Thus he purifies it by reinstalling a clear reference, and he reads: "Zeus, when he took the strength from his father and the glorious *daimon*" (Ζεὺς μὲν ἐπεὶ τὴ̣[ν ἀλ]κ̣ὴν / [πα]ρὰ πατρὸς ἑοῦ ἔλαβεν καὶ δαίμονα [κυδρ]όν, 8.7–8).

The Orphic exegete does not want to draw on variants of the saga in which Zeus listens to his father. For him the fact that Zeus took the *strength* is decisive. He understands "strength" in the sense of "a natural force": strength automatically joins with the strongest, as in the phrase "equal with equal" (ὅμοιον ὁμοίῳ). The author tries to play down the revolutionary, violent act of succession as much as possible; in his own reading he leaves out ἀρχὴν in its sense of "reign, regime." Those who do not understand the meaning of the word associate it with a real deposition of sovereigns. In reality it means removing the fire, the partitioning of the sun at a safe distance so that it does not hinder things from coagulating and coming together (see col. 9). Zeus is installed "so that he may rule on the lovely abode of snow-capped Olympus" (ὡς ἂν̣ ἔ̣[χοι κά]τα καλὸν ἕδ̣ος νιφόεντος Ὀλύμπου, 12.2). Surprisingly, he associates Olympus with time, not with heaven, because time is long. Zeus rules for eternity, over the long span of temporal extension. Time is snow-capped because it has the quality of Night, who is white, cool, gray, and bright (12.11–13).

The author returns to the succession of Zeus in column 13: the variant πατρὸς ἑοῦ πάρα̣ [θ]έ̣σφατ' ἀκούσα[ς] (13.1) gives the Orphic rhetorician and equivocator evidence that succession is not necessarily due to listening to Zeus' father or to Night, who might have given orders to seize power. The sense of the verb lies in listening to the oracular voice of Night, which possesses the deepness of *Nous*. Zeus deposes Ouranos by swallowing his αἰδοῖον, the male member, which first ejaculated αἰθήρ (or which first sprang into αἰθήρ).[54] Much ink has been spilled in attempts to explain 13.4 (αἰδοῖον κατ̣έπινεν, ὃς αἰθέρα ἔκθορε πρῶτος):[55] I side with Burkert's interpretation, based on a Hittite mythic parallel, the *Song of Kumarbi*, recently confirmed by Berna-

54 Burkert 1999:82; Burkert 2006:102–103. For "ejaculate," see also Jourdan 2003:63.

55 For θόρε resp. θρῴσκω and θόρνυμι in the Orphic-Bacchic gold-leaves, see Tzifopoulos in this volume.

bé,[56] and against West, whose domesticated reading has also gained its adherents. West, followed by many other critics,[57] combines 8.5 ([ἀ]λκήν τ' ἐν χείρεσσι ἔ[λ]αβ[εν κ]α̣[ὶ] δαίμον[α] κυδρόν) with 13.4 and reconstructs for the Orphic poem ...καὶ δαίμονα κυδρὸν / αἰδοῖον κατέπινεν, in which case αἰδοῖον acts as an adjective modifying *daimon*, i.e. "reverend" Protogonos-Phanes, and not as the word for the scandalous phallus.

But the Derveni author goes on: "Since he is speaking through the entire poem allegorically [αἰνίζεται κ̣[α]θ' ἔπος ἕκαστον] about real things, it is necessary to speak about each word in turn. Seeing that people consider all birth to depend on the genitals [ἐν τοῖς α[ἰδοίο]ις ὁρῶν τὴν γένεσιν τοὺς ἀνθρώπου[ς]] and that without the genitals there can be no birth, he used this [word] and likened the sun to a genital organ [αἰδοίωι εἰκάσας τὸν ἥλιο[ν]]" (13.6–9). The scandalous action of an ejaculation of *aither* is expressed as a metaphor, an image of the sun and its effect on the formation of natural life. Thus *phallos* must have stood here; otherwise, the author would be making a double replacement, from the august *daimon* Protogonos, to *phallos*, to Sun. West, on the contrary, believes that he must restore a "faulty" text that has come into the hands of our author.[58] But there is a higher probability that the Orphic wisdom practitioner breaks the canonical text of the master into enigmatic pieces, which seem to be incorrect, for his own didactic purposes. While these συνθήματα might include different readings in close narrative context, it is a mistake to reconstruct the right text in terms of textual criticism, as if we had variants in a textual transmission.

The sentence "[He made] to leap, the brightest and hottest having been separated from himself" ([ἐ]κθό̣ρηι τὸν λαμ̣πρότατόν τε [καὶ θε]ρμ̣ό[τ]ατον / χωρισθὲν ἀφ' ἑωυτοῦ, 14.1–2) might again depict the mythical ejaculation, focusing on the energy of semen. Moreover, the dissociation of the hottest, i.e. *phallos*/sun, from himself is an allusion to the famous castration in prospect, since Ouranos is deprived of his *phallos*: "So he says that this Kronos was born from the sun to the earth because he became the cause through the sun that they were struck against each other" (τοῦτον οὖν τὸν Κρόνον / γενέσθαι φησὶν ἐκ τοῦ ἡλίου τῆι Γ̣ῆι, ὅτι αἰτίαν ἔσχε / διὰ τὸν ἥλιον κρούεσθαι πρὸς ἄλλ̣ηλα, 14.2–4). "The great deed" (ὃς μ̣έγ' ἔρεξεν, 14.5) is the castration. Kronos is born from the union of Sun/Ouranos' *phallos* with Ge—through the sun he becomes the cause (αἰτίαν ἔσχε, 14.3) setting all things in motion. Kronos is etymologized to κρούειν/κρούεσθαι

[56] Burkert 1999:82; Burkert 2006:101–111; Bernabé 2002:105–112; Bernabé 2007b:107–110; and cf. Betegh 2004:109–122, esp. 113–122.

[57] West 1983:85 (cf. 114); KTP 21–28. Brisson 2003 and Jourdan 2003:60–63 are against Burkert's suggestion and argue for an ambiguous polysemy between the adjective and noun. See Sider in this volume.

[58] West 1983:85.

'strike'. After Ouranos is dethroned by castration, Kronos is established as the natural force, albeit retrospectively, by his great deed. He is the "Striker," but the energy stems from the cutting off of his father's *phallos*—the removal, as a means of distancing, is the act of concentrating fire's loose energy in the ball of Helios: this is how the sun comes to give the energy that all things draw from in order to grow and move. Encircling the striking energy allows things to condense and prevents them from standing apart from one another (cf. κρọύε<i>ν αὐτὰ πρọ̀[ς ἄλ]λ̣ηλα κα̣[ὶ] ποήσηι τὸ [πρῶτ]ον / χωρ̣ισθέντα διαστ̣ῆναι δίχ' ἀλλήλων τὰ ἐ̣ọ́ντα·, 15.1–2). "For when the sun is separated and encircled/distanced, he coagulated in the middle and held fast both the things that are above and those which are below the sun" (χωρ̣[ι]ζομένου γὰρ τοῦ ἡλίου καὶ ἀπολαμβανομένου / ἐν μ̣έσωι πήξας ἴσχει καὶ τἄνωθε τοῦ ἡλίου / καὶ τὰ κάτωθεν, 15.3–5). *Nous*—that is, Zeus, the highest principle—fixed the sun in the middle, removing its dangerous potential to a safe distance so that fire would not prevent things from joining (cf. col. 9).

By uttering Orpheus' riddling poetry the Derveni author metaphorically produces and performatively reenacts the natural process of distancing energy, concentrating and encircling it in one huge ball of fire, the sun. Ouranos ejaculates the sky; by castrating his father, Kronos separates the *phallos*: the fire is distanced and fixed in the sky. The absorption (καταπίνειν) of the *phallos* iconically reenacts the encirclement of the sun in rings (as shown in Anaximander and Parmenides).[59] The stomach of Zeus is then, poetically speaking, the cosmos enclosing the *phallos* of Ouranos, from which the sun qua *aither* and the first state of mixed energy comes. In *aither* fire is merged with air in an undifferentiated blend. In the next step fire has to be separated, concentrated, and spaced. Zeus swallows the *phallos*, thus notionally and poetically enacting the image of the sun encapsulated. Zeus/*Nous* then fixes the sun in the middle (15.4), and we meet again the interplay of a διιστάναι and συνιστάναι, a breaking apart and putting together.[60] Only with the separation of the sun through Kronos, as "striking" energy, can he be performatively produced and become Κρούων. The effect is the cause, so to speak. And as Zeus swallows the *phallos* of Ouranos, he encircles and encapsulates the sun: only by doing so does he become the principle of our *kosmos* (ζῆν; cf. τὸν Ζῆνα, 18.15, and τὸν Ζᾶνα, 23.4).

Even in the first generation Ouranos/Sky is only retrospectively produced by the action of ejaculating *aither* into the sky. In column 16 the citation says:

59 Parmenides DK 28 A 37 and B 12.1. In the middle is the *daimon* who rules everything (B 12.2), comparable to *Nous*/Zeus.

60 διιστάναι (15.2, 15.9) vs. συνιστάναι (9.6, 10.13, 17.2, 17.8, 17.15, 21.3, 25.9). See also Calame 1997: 72–73.

Πρωτογόνου βασιλέως αἰδοίου· τῶι δ' ἄρα πάντες
ἀθάνατ̣οι προσέφυν μάκαρες θεοὶ ἠδ̣ὲ θέαιναι
καὶ ποταμοὶ καὶ κρῆναι ἐπήρατοι ἄλ̣λα τε πάντα,
ἅ̣σσα τότ' ἦν γεγαῶτ', αὐτὸς δ' ἄρα μοῦνος ἔγεντο.

with the phallus of the first-born king [i.e. Ouranos, not Phanes-
Protogonos], upon which all
the immortals grew, blessed gods and goddesses
and rivers and lovely springs and everything else
that had been born then; and he himself became solitary.

16.3–6

When Mind (*Nous*/Zeus) swallows the *phallos*, which is solitary and separated, Sun and Mind become separated and are then alone. But from this cosmos everything grows; by means of this solitary Mind, Zeus plans/contrives (ἐμήσατο, 23.4) the entirety of life (τὸν Ζᾶνα, 23.4). In the naming lies the problem,[61] because all is in existence before it is named.[62] Men believe in birth and temporal succession by attaching different names (see col. 17), but in reality all that has ever been and all gods are constituted in Zeus. Air is Zeus; Ouranos and Kronos are Zeus, who is therefore head (i.e. beginning), middle, and end. From Zeus all things have their being (col. 17); therefore, the text culminates in the brief "hymn to Zeus": "Zeus the head, Zeus the middle, and from Zeus all things are fashioned" (Ζεὺς κεφα[λή, Ζεὺς μέσ]σ̣α̣, Διὸς δ' ἐκ̣ [π]άντα τέτ̣[υκται], 17.12).[63]

All things are present in the air/breath (πνεῦμα) (18.2); Orpheus calls it *Moira*, which is the φρόνησις or *Nous* (col. 18), hence Zeus, who is equated with a king dominating everything, as the ἀρχή (col. 19). "Zeus, the ruler of all with the bright bolt" (Ζεὺ̣ς βασιλεύς, Ζεὺς δ' ἀρχὸς ἁπάντ̣ω̣ν ἀργικέραυνος, 19.10), rules like the Heraclitean fire, principle of thought and energy.[64]

By "mating" Orpheus putatively means the congress of the particles of being: similar goes to similar—ὅμοιον ὁμοίῳ̣. Aphrodite, Peitho, and Harmonia are the κατὰ φάτιν (21.8–9) designations of mixing, gathering, and joining (col. 21). The many names for *Ge* are names of convention as well, which make sense etymologically (col. 22). Through greed, moral deviations, and lack of understanding (22.6), people use this plethora of different names—but in reality they all mean the same thing.

[61] For ὄνομα, see 7.3, 17.7, 19.9, 21.7, 22.10, 23.12. For ὀνομάζω, see 12.7, 14.7, 14.9, 17.1, 17.5, 17.7, 18.3, 18.9, 18.12, 21.10, 21.13, 22.1, 22.10. On the naming, see Burkert 1970.

[62] π[ρ]ό̣τερον ἦν πρ[ὶν ὀν]ο̣μ̣α̣σ̣θῆνα̣ι̣, ἔ̣π̣[ει]τα ὠ̣νομάσθ̣η· (17.1).

[63] For the "hymn to Zeus" (*OF* 14), see Bernabé 2007b:116–118; for Zeus as center of the poem and highest being, ibid., 125–126.

[64] Cf. Heraclitus DK 22 B 64: τὰ δὲ πάντα οἰακίζει Κεραυνός.

In column 23 the Derveni author presents a riddling equation featuring Okeanos, air, and Zeus. Okeanos and Achelous are not water: the expression "he placed in the sinews" implies a human or divine figure. Choerilus metaphorically calls the network of all rivers γῆς φλέβες (*TrGF* I 2 F 3). How can water be air? Here, I again suggest paretymological play.[65] The Orphic verse ἶνας δ' ἐγκ̣α̣τ̣[έλε]ξ' Ἀχελωΐου ἀργυ̣[ρ]οδίν̣ε̣[ω (23.11) he explains with τὰ[ς] δ' ἶνα[ς ἐγκ̣αταλ]έξαι ἐστ[ὶ ...] δ̣ε ἐ̣γκ̣α̣τῶ̣[σ]α̣ι̣[66] (23.13). The utterance τὰ[ς] δ' ἶνα[ς can be understood as τὰ[ς] δίνα[ς—the vortices of air, already present in the epithet ἀργυ̣[ρ]ο-δίν̣ε̣[ω] 'silver-eddying'. Water is both Air and Zeus, who is the energy of the vortex, because it is the whirl of the air that strikes and moves, contriving everything.[67]

Then the author speaks about the moon (cols. 24–25). It is circular, equally measured, and of equal limbs. Orpheus calls the moon the one "who shines for many articulate-speaking humans on the boundless earth" (ἣ πολλοῖς φαίνει μερόπεσσι ἐπ' ἀπείρονα γαῖαν, 24.3). One could disagree with this, since the moon might shine more at her zenith (ὑπερβάλλειν, 24.4–6). However, this is not Orpheus' meaning. According to the author, the phrase alludes to the moon's role in time-keeping. He comes back to the two important principles of the sun and night (col. 25): the moon is bright, but cold; the stars are invisible and latent, but during the night they are visible and manifest themselves. They float at a certain distance, but this is out of a cosmic necessity, i.e. *Nous* or Zeus. Without the distance, another sun would coagulate. But there is only *one* sun.

At this point the author inserts an additional methodological statement: "And the words that follow he puts before [as a screen], not wishing all men to understand" (τὰ δ̣' ἐ̣πὶ τούτοις ἐπίπροσθε π[ο]ιεῖται / [οὐ β]ου[λό]μενο̣[ς] πάντας γιν[ώ]σκε̣[ι]ν̣, 25.12–13). Orpheus uses poetic expressions to conceal the meaning, and the author tries to reveal it. At the same time, by using new terms, he covers the truth with new screens.

In the last column (26) the author deconstructs the story of the incest between Zeus and Rhea/Demeter, from which Dionysus, the last ruler, is born.[68] If Zeus encompasses all gods, we must assume that he also has his mother inside of him. Therefore, a sexual generation is impossible. Mother is just another metaphor for Mind. Again he makes his argument at the micro-linguistic level,

65 Discussed by Obbink at the CHS conference. For another explanation—a borrowing from Akkadian *înân*—see D'Alessio 2004, esp. 23–29.

66 Or Betegh: ἐστ[ὶν τ]ὸ̣ ἐγγε̣[νέσθ]αι.

67 For δῖνος, see Anaxagoras DK 59 A 57; for δίνη, see Empedokles DK 31 B 35.4; B 115.11. At the same time τὰ[ς] δ' ἶνα[ς could be read as accusative plural of ἴς 'strength'. See KPT 259–260.

68 See Bernabé 2007b:121–122.

playing with sound-ambiguities.[69] By overlapping the genitive of the feminine adjective ἐύς with the feminine possessive pronoun ἑός the inventive author claims that Zeus' new creation does not come from "his own" (ἑᾶς) mother, but from his "good" (ἐᾶς instead of ἐῆος) mother. The adjective ἐύς is, of course, not identical with the possessive pronoun ἑός. However, the erroneous confusion was quite frequent among grammarians.[70] The Mother is good, since Zeus mingles in love not with his mother, but with Mind—it is identical with the good Mind, the mother of all.

As a textual example he cites Hermes, the giver of goods, δῶτορ ἐάων in *Odyssey* 8.335[71] and the two urns in the famous passage from *Iliad* 24: "for two urns are placed down on Zeus' floor—of gifts such as they give: of evils, and the other one of goods [ἐάων]" (δοιοὶ γάρ τε πίθοι κατακήαται ἐν Διὸς οὔδει / δώρων, οἷα διδοῦσι, κακῶν, ἕτερος δέ τ' ἐάων, 527–528).[72] Besides the linguistic sophistry the reference to Hermes might not be by chance. As ψυχοπομπός, he is linked to Hades and the passage into the underworld, where all goods are waiting for those who behave properly in both a ritual and intellectual sense. What is harmful has to be changed into good. The idea of jars (πίθοι) filled with different qualities on Zeus' floor shows that Zeus epitomizes and encompasses everything—that is, all the binary opposites, even good and evil. Further, this fits in with chthonic Hades, since moral behavior decides if the δεινά of Hades can turn out good.

8. Conclusion

By bizarrely riddling over an Orphic text, which is itself putatively riddling but quite traditional, the Derveni author introduces a radical *Umwertung* of values and meanings. The μεθιστάναι (6.3) happens both through ritual and through speech-acts; that which is latent is highlighted by obscurely spoken words. Through both fragmented and decontextualized sentences the sense is distorted, twisted, and changed.

What our author intends to convey with such enigmatic utterances often remains uncertain: it is not a clear-cut and lucid commentary in terms of

69 For parallels to the practice of early Alexandrian philology and its *hypomnema* exegesis, see Rusten in this volume.

70 LSJ s.v. ἐύς; ἑός = ἀγαθός; see Apollonios Dyskolos *Syntax* 213.7–8 Uhlig on *Iliad* 24.292 and KPT 271 *ad loc.* and Jourdan 2003:104–105. The play on semantic ambiguity is easier to grasp if we print in 26.2 ἑᾶς (as Jourdan 2003:26 and Betegh 2004:54–55) instead of ἐᾶς (as KPT 113; Janko 2002:52).

71 Only here, in *Odyssey* 8.325, and in the passage of the *Iliad* 24.528 do we have the variant with *spiritus asper* δῶτορ ἑάων. See Hainsworth 1988:369 *ad Odyssey* 8.325.

72 See also Brügger 2009:189 *ad loc.*

Presocratic natural science. But by means of abstruse remarks, some light can be shed on the basic mechanisms of φύσις 'nature'. *Physis* as eternal cosmic being is a miracle. People tend to err because of incorrect names (ὀνόματα), since the language of φύσις or the gods is basically lost. However, φύσις and κόσμος speak for themselves. Human language, on the contrary, is not φύσει, but νόμῳ, by convention, or θέσει. Yet some great poets and guru-prophets might still have access to pure φύσις and physical language, though they may make concessions to the audience and their tastes. Furthermore, the cosmos, sun, moon, and stars are also part of the soteriological reflections. By understanding φύσις people can reach deep insights about life, including its basis in night and death.

Our Derveni author seems to be an Orphic with philosophical knowledge. He is neither inept and clumsy nor unintelligent. He is certainly not a modern scientist, but he wants to trigger reflection and deep thoughts on the paradoxical workings of nature. Insight is activated by short and bizarre distortions of sense. Therefore, the Orphic poem is treated as an oracular message from the dark. Deeper meaning is teased out by further riddling, by fragmentation, by a loosening of syntactic and semantic order, by highlighting poetic ambiguity, by opening up the nuances. The canonical text is decontextualized, cut to pieces, and fragmented into defamiliarized morsels of words. Just as συνθήματα unite opposites to a paradoxical utterance, nature encompasses two principles: separation and reassembly. The aphoristic, obscure oracular mode à la Heraclitus paves the path to sudden insight. The συμβάλλειν of fragmented words, the dark re-transpositions of παραγωγά, ὑπερβατά, the distortions of sense and structure, and the poetic and magic logic of analogy initiate understanding. Through these games of language the mystic sense of φύσις can flare up like a sudden bolt.

All in all, the context of the Derveni papyrus is clearly didactic, and the text does seem to be situated in Orphic circles and its teachings. However, according to the enlightening ideas of its author, it is not enough to perform Orphic rites, to listen to ἱεροὶ λόγοι, or to see σύμβολα 'sacred things'. While the λεγόμενα and ὁρώμενα should provoke thought, insight, and understanding, the message that the text offers to μύσται can be grasped not by means of logocentric discourse, but only through its hints at the mysteries of φύσις. These are the mysteries I refer to as "riddles over riddles."

Bibliography

Bernabé, A. 2002. "La théogonie orphique du papyrus de Derveni." *Kernos* 15:91–129.

———. 2004–2005. *Orphicorum et Orphicis similium testimonia et fragmenta. Poetae epici Graeci: Testimonia et fragmenta*, part II, fasc. 1–2. Munich. [Cited as *OF*, with fragment number.]

———, ed. 2007a. *Musaeus · Linus · Epimenides · Papyrus Derveni · Indices. Poetae epici Graeci: Testimonia et fragmenta*, part II, fasc. 3. Berlin.

———. 2007b. "The Derveni Theogony: Many Questions and Some Answers." *Harvard Studies in Classical Philology* 103:99–133.

Betegh, G. 2004. *The Derveni Papyrus: Cosmology, Theology, and Interpretation*. Cambridge.

Bierl, A. 2007. "Literatur und Religion als Rito- und Mythopoetik: Überblicksartikel zu einem neuen Ansatz in der Klassischen Philologie." *Literatur und Religion*, 1: *Wege zu einer mythisch-rituellen Poetik bei den Griechen* (ed. A. Bierl, R. Lämmle, and K. Wesselmann) 1–76. Berlin.

———. Forthcoming. "Empedokles: Philosoph, Arzt, Dichter und religiöser Prophet. Vom Mythos zum Logos?" Inauguration Lecture, Basel, 13 May 2003.

Bremer, D. 1990. "Logos, Sprache und Spiel bei Heraklit." *Synthesis Philosophica* 10:379–391.

Bremmer, J. 1991. "Orpheus: From Guru to Gay." *Orphism et Orphée en l'honneur de Jean Rudhardt* (ed. P. Borgeaud) 13–30. Geneva.

Brisson, L. 2003. "Sky, Sex, and Sun: The Meanings of αἰδοῖος/αἰδοῖον in the Derveni Papyrus." *Zeitschrift für Papyrologie und Epigraphik* 144:19–29.

Brügger, C. 2009. *Homers Ilias. Gesamtkommentar* VIII: *Vierundzwanzigster Gesang* (ed. A. Bierl and J. Latacz). Berlin.

Burkert, W. 1968. "Orpheus und die Vorsokratiker: Bemerkungen zum Derveni-Papyrus und zur pythagoreischen Zahlenlehre." *Antike und Abendland* 14:93–114 (= *Walter Burkert, Kleine Schriften*, III: *Mystica, Orphica, Pythagorica* [ed. F. Graf] 62–88. Göttingen).

———. 1970. "La genèse des choses et des mots: Le papyrus de Derveni entre Anaxagore et Cratyle." *Les Études Philosophiques* 25:443–455.

———. 1987. *Ancient Mystery Cults*. Cambridge, MA .

———. 1999. *Da Omero ai Magi: La tradizione orientale nella cultura greca*. Venice.

———. 2006. "Die altorphische Theogonie nach dem Papyrus von Derveni." *Walter Burkert, Kleine Schriften* III: *Mystica, Orphica, Pythagorica* (ed. F. Graf) 95–111. Göttingen.

Calame, C. 1997. "Figures of Sexuality and Initiatory Transition in the Derveni Theogony and Its Commentary." In Laks and Most 1997:65–80.

Casadio, G. 1987. "Adversaria Orphica: A proposito di un libro recente sull'Orfismo." *Orpheus* 8:381–395.

D'Alessio, G. B. 2004. "Textual Fluctuations and Cosmic Streams: Ocean and Acheloios." *Journal of Hellenic Studies* 124:16–37.

Edmonds, R. G., III. 2004. *Myths of the Underworld Journey: Plato, Aristophanes, and the "Orphic" Gold Tablets*. Cambridge.

———. 2008. "Extra-ordinary People: *Mystai* and *Magoi*, Magicians and Orphics in the Derveni Papyrus." *Classical Philology* 103:16–39.

Frede, M. 2007. "On the Unity and the Aim of the Derveni Text." *Rhizai* 4.1:9–33.

Gemelli Marciano, M. L. 2008. "Images and Experience: At the Roots of Parmenides' *Aletheia*." *Ancient Philosophy* 28:21–48.

Hainsworth, J. B. 1988. "Book VIII." *A Commentary on Homer's Odyssey, vol. 1: Introduction and Books i-viii* (ed. A. Heubeck, S. West, and J. B. Hainsworth) 341–385. Oxford.

Henrichs, A. 1984. "The Eumenides and Wineless Libations in the Derveni Papyrus." In *Atti del XVII Congresso Internazionale di Papirologia*, II, 255–268. Naples.

———. 2003. "*Hieroi Logoi* and *Hierai Bibloi*: The (Un)written Margins of the Sacred in Ancient Greece." *Harvard Studies in Classical Philology* 101:207–266.

Henry, M. 1986. "The Derveni Commentator as Literary Critic." *Transactions of the American Philological Association* 116:149–164.

Hölscher, U. 1969. *Parmenides, Vom Wesen des Seienden: Die Fragmente, griechisch und deutsch*. Frankfurt.

Janko, R. 1997. "The Physicist as Hierophant: Aristophanes, Socrates, and the Authorship of the Derveni Papyrus." *Zeitschrift für Papyrologie und Epigraphik* 118:61–94.

———. 2001. "The Derveni Papyrus (Diagoras of Melos, *Apopyrgizontes Logoi*?): A New Translation." *Classical Philology* 96:1–32.

———. 2002. "The Derveni Papyrus: An Interim Text." *Zeitschrift für Papyrologie und Epigraphik* 141:1–62.

Jourdan, F. 2003. *Le Papyrus de Derveni: Texte présenté, traduit et annoté*. Paris.

Kingsley, P. 1995. *Ancient Philosophy, Mystery, and Magic: Empedocles and Pythagorean Tradition*. Oxford.

———. 1999. *In the Dark Places of Wisdom*. Inverness, CA.

Kouremenos, T., G. M. Parássoglou, and K. Tsantsanoglou, eds. 2006. *The Derveni Papyrus, Edited with Introduction and Commentary*. Florence. [Cited as KPT.]

Laks, A., and G. W. Most, eds. 1997. *Studies on the Derveni Papyrus*. Oxford.

Millerd, C. 1908. *On the Interpretation of Empedocles*. Chicago.

Most, G. W. 1997. "The Fire Next Time: Cosmology, Allegoresis, and Salvation in the Derveni Papyrus." *Journal of Hellenic Studies* 117:117–135.

———. 1999. "From Logos to Mythos." *From Myth to Reason? Studies in the Development of Greek Thought* (ed. R. Buxton) 25–47. Oxford.

Nagy, G. 1979. *The Best of the Achaeans: Concepts of the Hero in Archaic Greek Poetry*. Baltimore. Rev. ed. 1999.

———. 1990. *Pindar's Homer: The Lyric Possession of an Epic Past*. Baltimore.

Nestle, W. 1940. *Vom Mythos zum Logos: Die Selbstentfaltung des griechischen Denkens von Homer bis auf die Sophistik und Sokrates*. 2nd ed. 1975. Stuttgart.

Rangos, S. 2007. "Latent Meaning and Manifest Content in the Derveni Papyrus." *Rhizai* 4.1:35–75.

Rusten, J. S. 1985. "Interim Notes on the Papyrus from Derveni." *Harvard Studies in Classical Philology* 89:121–140.

Schefer, C. 2000. "'Nur für Eingeweihte!' Heraklit und die Mysterien." *Antike und Abendland* 46:46–75.

Seaford, R. 1986. "Immortality, Salvation, and the Elements." *Harvard Studies in Classical Philology* 90:1–26.

Sider, D. 1997. "Heraclitus in the Derveni Papyrus." In Laks and Most 1997:129–148.

Thurner, M. 2001. *Der Ursprung des Denkens bei Heraklit*. Stuttgart.

West, M. L. 1983. *The Orphic Poems*. Oxford.

———. 1997. "Hocus-pocus in East and West: Theogony, Ritual, and the Tradition of Esoteric Commentary." In Laks and Most 1997:81–90.

Willi, A. 2008. *Sikelismos: Sprache, Literatur und Gesellschaft im griechischen Sizilien (8.–5. Jh. v. Chr.)*. Basel.

11

Reading the Authorial Strategies in the Derveni Papyrus[1]

Evina Sistakou
Aristotle University of Thessaloniki

IF THE COMMENTARY INCLUDED IN THE DERVENI PAPYRUS were a literary text, one could legitimately read it from a formalistic viewpoint. As this is not the case, scholars have justly focused on the religious-initiatory and the exegetical-allegorical aspects of this peculiar commentary on the Orphic theogony. On the basis of the distinction between literary and nonliterary, the form and content of the Derveni Papyrus have been interpreted within a ritual and/or philosophical context—some occasional remarks or even deliberate attempts to theorize about it being the exception that proves the rule.[2]

Whatever the generic identity of the Derveni document, it appears to be a far cry from the concept of *literariness*: it can no more be regarded as "literature" than the Homeric scholia or Aristotle's treatises, at least in the narrow sense of the word. Yet, as the voice resonating throughout the commentary strikes us with its exceptional clarity and vigor, the fact that the profile of the Derveni author has attracted considerable attention by each and every scholar studying the papyrus should not come as a surprise. In my view, all readings of the author's voice in the Derveni Papyrus entail, albeit implicitly, the acknowledgment that what we have here is far more than a set of religious/philosophical technicalities on how to understand the Orphic theogony. Design and intention, arrangement and style point towards a conscious, imaginative speaker (or writer) who is well aware of his ability to manipulate his audience by methodically creating his own authorial persona. It is the question of which devices are employed for this purpose that I will be addressing in the present study.

1 I am grateful to Gregory Nagy for inviting me to present a first draft of this paper at the Derveni Conference (held at the Center for Hellenic Studies, 7–9 July 2008) and for granting me permission to publish it in *Trends in Classics* 2 (2010): 18–30. I am also indebted to Antonios Rengakos, Franco Montanari, and Yannis Tzifopoulos for their insightful comments.

2 See e.g. Calame 1997 and Obbink 1997.

Approaching the Derveni document as a unified *text* rather than as a heterogeneous collection of two different texts—i.e. a poetic theogony and an exegetical commentary—provides a useful starting point for my discussion. The same principle underlies Madeleine Henry's rendering of the Derveni commentator as a literary critic, when she notes that "our present and nearly universal habit of characterizing the Derveni document as a poem and commentary thereon may be harmfully inaccurate, for such a perceptual stance diverts us from viewing the entire document as an autonomous object of study"; subsequently, she describes all the objects of the author's scrutiny—i.e. the Orphic poem, the dreams, the oracles and the rites, and the interpretation itself—as "text."[3] If the Derveni document is viewed from this unifying perspective, it is natural to suppose that its creator assumes the role of the "author" in that he develops an overall strategy for controlling his "text," in much the same way as any writer of literature does. Therefore, I suggest that the Derveni "text" lends itself to an analysis based on the same criteria—stylistic, rhetorical, narratological—that underlie the study of literature.[4]

1. A Staged Theology?

A peculiar feature of the Derveni commentary, as contrasted to other technical texts, is that it explicitly refers to a setting. To define this setting in terms of (narrative?) space would amount to its analysis by means of various parameters, such as the existence of an environment, the description of the objects included in it, the implication of a temporal dimension, and the demonstration of the ways in which this environment interacts with human experience.[5]

The preserved text begins with a description of Orphic ritual practices, which are probably not enacted in real time to the accompaniment of the commentator's words (cols. I–VII).[6] What strikes us most is the detailed depiction of how these rituals are performed, as the below-mentioned citations clearly demonstrate (italics are mine):

> ... *libations are poured down in drops* for [Zeus] *in every temple*. Further, one must *offer exceptional honors to [the Eumenides]* and *burn a bird to each [of*

3 Henry 1986:151–152.

4 In my citation of the Derveni Papyrus I follow the Kouremenos, Parássoglou, and Tsantsanoglou 2006 edition (henceforth referred to as KPT); I have also adopted their translation of the Greek original.

5 See *RENT* s.v. "Space in narrative."

6 E.g. Bernabé 2007a:124: "It can be a ἱερὸς λόγος related as λεγόμενα to a ritual, but it is impossible to determine which ritual it would be and whether it had something to do with the ones alluded to by the commentator himself." On a thorough overview of the discussions of these columns, primarily from the viewpoint of Greek religion, see Betegh 2004:74–91.

> *the daimones]*. And he added *[hymns] adapted (or: poems well adapted) to the music.*
>
> Col. II.5–8

> ... *consult an oracle* ... *they consult an oracle* ... for them we *enter the oracle* in order *to ask*, with regard to those seeking a divination, whether it is proper ...
>
> Col. V.2–5

> This is why the *magi perform the sacrifice*, just as if they are paying a retribution. *And on the offerings they pour water and milk, from which they also make the libations to the dead. Innumerable and many-knobbed are the cakes they sacrifice*, because the souls too are innumerable.
>
> Col. VI.4–8

> On their account anyone who is going to sacrifice to the gods *must first [sacrifice] a bird*...
>
> Col. VI.10–11

> *For [a sacred rite was being performed]* through the poem.
>
> Col. VII.2–3

The text is fraught with difficulties as regards the type and number of rituals described, the subjects of these rituals (Greek and/or Persian *magi*, initiates), and their connection to Orphic or other mystical cults. However, my focus is on the means by which the commentator livens up his theological account. There is at least one space referred to explicitly, namely the oracle (col. V.4: [εἰς τὸ μα]ντεῖον).[7] But the theological background prompts the speculation that the space towering above the others might be a tomb, the place where the *choai* were traditionally performed.[8]

The spatialization of the mysteries provides the basis for action to unfold, for ritual to be symbolically enacted. As in any ceremony, the action is not connected with a fixed point in time, but instead its repeatedness and duration

7 If we follow the KPT edition, a temple may be mentioned at col. II.5 κατὰ π]άντα να[όν. But, since the reference to a temple is unlikely within an Orphic context, we may adopt another reconstruction, e.g. κατὰ π]άντα να[σμόν (suggested by Ferrari [2007:205]).

8 Cf. Betegh 2004:76: "*Choai* were most often made to the deceased at the grave. This would certainly fit well with the archaeological context of the roll, and raises the possibility that the text refers to such funerary rituals as were conducted also at the tomb at Derveni."

are stressed. Thus, the numerous verbs describing the ritual are set in the present ([χ]έονται, χρησ[τ]ηριάζον[ται, πάριμεν, μ[ειλ]ίσσουσι, π[οιοῦσι[ν], ἐπισπένδουσιν, θύουσιν, προθύουσι). Corresponding to the activities in which the *magi* and the initiates are regularly engaged, these verbs stress the dramatic present. Dramatization is further reinforced as the commentator provides a detailed record of how these rituals are performed: the libations, the burning of birds, the hymning and the playing of music, the sacrifice, and the offering of water, milk, and cakes set the scene for an almost theatrically enacted ceremony.

Three key concepts appear within this theological staging—the Erinyes, the Eumenides, and the *daimones*—in connection to the souls of the deceased. Several suggestions have been made as to the identification of each category with the other two, and as to their philosophical/religious significance.[9] However, more important to my reading are the dynamics of their presence within the space implied, the eschatological interface they create between the (real or fictional) setting and the enactment of the ritual. Regardless of whether the ritual context implied here is that of an initiation or a funeral,[10] the Erinyes, the Eumenids, and the *daimones* are shown to inhabit its spatial environment. It is their epiphany that lends a strong feeling of death, an eschatological atmosphere, to this staged theology.

2. The Author's Voices

A distinguishing characteristic of the Derveni commentary, separating it from other texts within the same generic category, is its polyphonic quality. By the term *polyphony* narratologists describe either (a) the plurality of voices that can be heard within a text and are not subordinate to a single authorial hierarchy or (b) the fact that the main narrator's utterance is in itself many-voiced.[11] Although point (a) is also applicable to the Derveni text, as will be shown in the next sections, it is point (b), the variety of the authorial voices, that I will be dealing with presently.

Since the identity of the Derveni author is highly controversial and chiefly reconstructed by his mirror image in the text,[12] we are only able to give an account of the implied author and his narrative persona as reflected within the commentary. Thus, rather than searching for the Derveni author as a historical

9 E.g. Henrichs 1984 and Tsantsanoglou 1997.

10 Betegh 2004:88–89.

11 See *RENT* s.v. "Polyphony."

12 Fundamental is the discussion about the problem of the authorship of the Derveni Papyrus by Janko (1997). On the profile of the Derveni author, as sketched out in the text, see Betegh 2004: 349–372.

entity, we should instead focus on the ways in which he manifests himself in the textual world through the employment of three different voices: the omniscient, the exegetical, and the didactic, respectively.

The underlying premise of this textual world is that it represents the theological and philosophical truth of the Orphic theogony; but, since the revelation of this truth is a question of interpretation, the author, qua interpreter, adopts an overall omniscient voice:

> And *one cannot state the solution of the [enigmatic] words* though they are spoken [i.e. not secret]. *This poem is strange and riddling to people* though [Orpheus] himself did not intend to say contentious riddles but rather great things in riddles. In fact *he is speaking mystically*, and from the very first word all the way to the last.
>
> Col. VII.3–8

> With regard to the phrase "he took in his hands," *he was allegorizing* just as in everything else *which formerly seemed uncertain but has been most certainly understood.*
>
> Col. IX.10–12

The author's persona highlights the strange (col. VII.4 ξ[ένη τις ἡ] πόησις), enigmatic (col. VII.5 ἀνθρώ[ποις] αἰνι[γμ]ατώδης), mystical (col. VII.7 ἱερολογεῖται), and allegorical (col. IX.10 ἠινίζετο) nature of the Orphic poem. The above-mentioned expressions capture Orpheus' intention—or, to be more accurate, what the author has us believe to be Orpheus' intention—of creating a sacred speech, a *hierologia*; his aim was to communicate theological truth to believers in a nonexplicit way,[13] thus rendering his speech incomprehensible to the many (cf. the repeated use of αἰνιζόμενος ἔφη / αἰνίζεται "allegorizing/speaking in an enigmatic way"). This deliberate obscurity calls for the superhuman intervention of an interpreter who is able to "translate" the divine discourse of Orpheus and, more importantly, to reveal the (hypothetical) intentionality behind his theogony. Textual markers such as σκέψασθαι δὲ χρή "one has to consider..." followed by ἐδήλωσεν "he made clear that...," κ[α]θ' ἔπος ἕκαστον ἀνάγκη λέγειν "it is neccessary to speak about each word in turn," διὰ τοῦτο λέγει "for this reason he says...," δῆλον "it is clear...," σημαίν]ει δὲ [τ]όδε "and this indicates this...," and the like suffice to illustrate the point. Occasionally, the author exceeds his role as a go-between between the Orphic text and the community, and grows into a

13 Orpheus' intention to deliver a mystical speech is more effectively expressed if we take Orpheus to be the subject of the verbs, see KPT 171–172.

prophet himself, not only by assessing Orpheus' theology (col. XXII.1–3 "so he named everything in the same way as best he could knowing the nature of men, that not all have the same (nature) nor all want the same things"), but also by judging divine providence (col. XXV.9–10: "if the god did not wish the present ἐόντα to exist, he would not have made the sun").

Undoubtedly, the Derveni text resonates chiefly with its author's exegetical voice.[14] Despite the religious/philosophical subject of the commentary, the most striking feature of the commenting voice is its emphasis upon textual and linguistic analysis. In effect, the Derveni author focuses so intensely on the exploration of the potentialities and limitations of language that his exegesis of the Orphic religion has plausibly been likened to the type of literary criticism undertaken by Plato and Aristotle.[15] Going one step further, we may argue that the Derveni author views Orphic religion through a literary prism in interpreting its textual rendition in terms of poetic language: this is why he highlights the ambiguity of language, the use of metaphor, and the paramount importance of context as vital parameters for the correct understanding of the Orphic text.[16]

Here is an instance of pure textual criticism:

> It has escaped notice that *these words are transposed; in fact they are as follows:* "Zeus, when he took the power from his father and the glorious *daimon.' [In this] word order the prevailing meaning is not that Zeus hears his father but that he takes power for him. [In the other] word order the impression would be given that he took the power contrary to the prophecies.*
>
> Col. VIII.6–12

Elsewhere semantic analysis for the terms deployed by Orpheus is provided, as for example in the interpretation of πανομφεύουσαν:

> Therefore, "teaching" was not considered different from "saying" and "saying" from "uttering," but "uttering," "saying," and "teaching" mean the same. *Thus nothing prevents "all-voicing" and "teaching all things" from being the same thing.*
>
> Col. X.6–10

14 Edmonds (2008:33 and n78) stresses the fact that the Derveni author displays his expert knowledge through the explication of a difficult poetic text, i.e. the Orphic theogony; moreover, he draws a very interesting parallel between the Derveni interpretation of Orpheus and the exegesis of the Simonides poem in Plato *Protagoras* 339a–347a.

15 See Henry 1986:150–151.

16 These features are brilliantly discussed by Henry (1986:151–163).

In column XXII the author identifies various deities, namely Ge, Gaia, Demeter, Meter, Rhea, and Hera, with each other by suggesting the etymological affinity between their names; even if the idea forms part of the Orphic religion,[17] the emphasis on tautology should be credited to the commentator himself. The etymologizing of other divine names, such as Aphrodite from ἀφροδισιάζω, Peitho from εἴκω-πείθω, and Harmonia from ἁρμόζω in column XXI, displays the curious mixture of philological and philosophical discourse used by the Derveni author.[18]

As has been said, the Derveni text is polyphonic in more ways than one: its author, via his exegetical voice, engages repeatedly in an (intertextual?) dialogue with previous interpreters.[19] To reconstruct their identity is an almost impossible task, as their figures remain nameless and shadowy; their voice is subsumed into the author's discourse; their presence is only vaguely sensed, as for example in the following passage:

> *Those who think that Olympus and heaven are the same are mistaken*, because *they do not realize* that heaven cannot be long rather than wide ...
>
> Col. XII.3–6

Scholars have made reasonable assumptions about the origin of the beliefs criticized here, linking them primarily with views expressed in the Homeric epics as interpreted by pre-Hellenistic commentators.[20] However, in contrast with explicit references to other thinkers, such as Heraclitus in column IV.5 (κατὰ [ταὐτ]ὰ Ἡράκλειτος μα[ρτυρόμενος] τὰ κοινά "in the same manner Heraclitus invoking common truths..."), the Derveni author opts to roughly outline the profile of "those who misunderstand" the theological truths. In addition, the opinions of the ordinary people are objected to:

> *So when they say that* "Moira spun," *they are saying that ...*
>
> Col. XIX.4–5

Or:

17 Betegh 2004:189–190.

18 For a thorough discussion of the commentator's technique of applying the numerous divine names used by Orpheus to very few divinities, see Betegh 2004:185–205.

19 On the agonistic aspect of such criticism, see Edmonds 2008:33n79.

20 For a thorough analysis of this reference within the context of ancient scholarship, see Schironi 2001. Cf. Kouremenos in KPT 189–191, esp. the concluding remark on p. 191: "It is unclear whether in rejecting the identification of Olympus with the sky the Derveni author objects to the absence of a clear distinction between Olympus and the sky in Homer, to a pre-Zenodotean interpretation of the Homeric Olympus as the sky, or to the use of the noun 'Olympus' as a name for the outermost heavens in the natural philosophy of his day."

> But *those who do not understand the words spoken think that* Zeus takes the power and the *daimon* from his own father.
>
> Col. IX.2–4

There is an undertone of contempt for the anonymous misinterpreters throughout the Derveni text; this undertone marks the transition from the exegetical to the didactic voice. By assuming the role of the initiator and the instructor at the same time, the Derveni author constructs a textual world modeled on the conventions of didactic literature, the most crucial of which is the opposition of an addresser and an addressee.[21] To this opposition I will now turn my attention.

3. Devising the Addressees

Were the textual world of the Derveni Papyrus to be inhabited only by the implied author, our reading experience would have been definitely less exciting, less dramatic, and less personalized than it is now. It is exciting because otherwise the text would have been monophonic; it is dramatic because the author animates his protagonists; it is personalized because the addressees function as (anti)models for the reader himself.

Nevertheless, it should be stressed that the Derveni author differentiates his commentary from traditional initiatory texts: no direct apostrophes to the addressees are included, nor do the initiates produce their own utterances. Claude Calame, in comparing initiatory texts known from the gold leaves and the Derveni Papyrus, remarks that

> from the enunciatory point of view, these texts either constitute direct addresses to the initiand, praising the initiatory process he is in the process of performing, or are placed in the mouth of the initiand himself, who thereby expresses his hope for salvation. With the performative value they receive by being spoken in the second or first person, these texts diverge greatly from the Derveni commentary, which is characterized by the distance of the interpretations stated in the third person.[22]

In the Derveni Papyrus teaching is normally voiced by this distanced rhetoric; however, the author's didactic activity does not take place in a vacuum.[23]

21 On the didactic function, see Calame 1997:77–80.

22 Calame 1997:79, n23.

23 Even more so, if he had been a practitioner, probably a *mantis*, as Tsantsanoglou (1997:98) thinks: "But it is noticeable that this is not the didactic tendency of a theological thinker, but the desire of a religious practitioner to disseminate his professional secrets to the faithful."

The paradox of the Derveni text, then, is the lack of a *direct* dramatization of the intended initiatory act, whereas, on the other hand, the experience of an *actual* ritual is hinted at by reference to a staging, an instructor, and a community of worshipers. The Derveni author is not alone in his textual world. Having already stressed the theatricality of the ritual space and the different personae adopted by him, I will now focus on the vivid account of his addressees.

As noted above, there is no trace of a direct address to a hearer (or reader) in the Derveni text; its author opts for a third-person form of address, as "when the point is to emphasize unequal status between speaker and addressee, for instance, to show respect or scorn."[24] The latter is the case here, since the author constantly juxtaposes the addressees with his own ability to comprehend and reveal the religious truth to people. The author's strategy is to introduce only the ill-informed and the profane into his textual world, thus excluding those who understand—a trace of the latter is to be found in the following passage:

> This verse is composed so as to be misleading; it is unclear to the many, *but quite clear to those who have correct understanding,* that "Oceanus" is the air and that air is Zeus.
>
> Col. XXIII.1–3

To gain in effectiveness, the author represents his instruction as a process of enlightenment; we may record the different stages of this process by observing the various portrayals of the addressees. At first, they seem to disbelieve on the basis of their ignorance:

> *Why do they disbelieve* in the horrors of Hades? *Without knowing* (the meaning of) dreams or any of the other things, *by what kind of evidence would they believe? For overcome both by error and pleasure as well, they neither learn nor believe.*
>
> Col. V.6–10

Disbelievers are those who cannot decipher the signs sent by the gods in the form of dreams—signs clearly hinting at the horrors of Hades. Crucial to their misinterpretation is the fact that they have given themselves over to pleasure.[25] Are they to be identified with the many who have no hope of understanding?

24 *RENT* s.v. "Address."

25 On the association of disbelief and pleasure within an eschatological context in Plato, see Kouremenos in KPT 164–166.

> ...having ordered them to "put doors to their ears," he says *that he is not legislating for the many [but addressing himself to those] who are pure in hearing...*
>
> Col. VII.9–11

The implied audience has been selected according to the main criterion applying to Orphic mysticism, namely the exclusion of the unholy.[26] A few, uninitiated but with a prospect of understanding, are eventually accepted as recipients of the Orphic teaching and its interpretation.[27] Now, their lack of knowledge (οἱ δ' οὐ γινώσκον[τες) is due to the misinterpretation of the Orphic theogony (δοκοῦσιν / οἱ δὲ δοκοῦντες), which in turn may be attributed to the ambiguity of the poetic language deployed;[28] the point is best illustrated in the following example:

> But *those who do not understand the word think that it means "of his own" [i.e. ἑᾶς] mother.* But if he wanted to show the god "desiring to mingle in love with his own mother," he could have said, *altering (a few) letters,* "ἑοῖο mother."
>
> Col. XXVI.8–12

Shifting from eschatology to mysticism and from philosophical exegesis to literary interpretation, the Derveni author manipulates his implied audience into accepting his view of Orphism; given that this view is subjective and refracted through the authorial strategies deployed, I will finally review the Derveni commentary as a complex, multilayered text, mainly by examining its relation to the Orphic original.

4. The Quoter and the Quotee

To address the question of the nature and the generic quality of the Derveni text is not an easy task. Should we classify it as secondary literature or as an autonomous essay on Orphism? Does its importance stem from its religious function as an initiation text, or is it merely a philological source for the reconstruction

26 On this *topos* of Orphic and related literature, see the *testimonia* collected by Bernabé (2007b, *ad loc.*).

27 Bernabé (2007a:100–102), on the contrary, argues that the listeners are already initiated and therefore the poem is not *sensu stricto* an initiation poem.

28 We may even find a counterexample implied in col. XIII.7–9: "*Seeing that people consider all birth to depend on the genitals* and that without the genitals there can be no birth, *he used this (word)* and likened the sun to a genital organ." See e.g. Kouremenos (KPT 196), who remarks that the Derveni author in explaining the word αἰδοῖον appeals to common beliefs in order to justify the explanation that Orpheus employs in his own poem.

of the lost Orphic poem?[29] The fact that it has been variously labeled—as commentary, *hypomnema*, theogony, *hieros logos*, allegorical exegesis, *syngramma*, and so on—reflects the difficulty of identifying the Derveni text with a well-defined subliterary generic category.[30] The following remark by Henry provides a useful starting point for reconsidering the issue:

> The Derveni author interprets the Orphic poem on behalf of an untrained audience. By rereading and rewriting the text for that audience, the commentator implies that all criticism is a species of rewriting as well as of rereading. It is self-justifying because in thus guiding the audience to what he believes are important questions, the Derveni author creates his own "model readers."[31]

The key to understanding this device may be found in the author's notion of the quotation. In effect, the Derveni author (the *quoter*) is rereading and rewriting a theogonic poem attributed to Orpheus (the *quotee*) by embedding brief excerpts from it (the *quotational inset*) into his own initiatory/exegetical discourse (the *discoursal frame*).[32] The way in which these four parameters interact with each other creates a series of consequences. First, the author, acting as an intermediary reader, controls both the Orphic pretext and his audience; thus, his reliability is put to the test, as the reader has to rely on the author for the selection, arrangement, and accurate citation of the pretext.[33] Second, by juxtaposing his own voice with the Orphic, the Derveni author renders his text polyphonic but, more importantly, transgeneric, in that he combines the Orphic (hymnic or epic) theogonic poem with philosophical, theological, and exegetical discourse. Moreover, not only does the quoter enhance his prestige by invoking the authority of Orpheus, but also the quotee, via his cited theogony, may challenge the validity of the author's explanation.[34]

All this amounts to a new "genre" which encompasses the Orphic original as adapted to the intra- and extra-textual standards applied by the author—the

29 The various possibilities of classifying subject matter and genre of the Derveni text are listed by Betegh (2004:349–350).

30 For an overview of this debate, see Funghi 1997.

31 Henry 1986:163–164.

32 On the terminology, see *RENT* s.v. "Quotation theory."

33 For a reconstruction of the Orphic theogony on the basis of (a) the literally quoted fragments and (b) "the content of the text the commentator read but did not quote," see Bernabé 2007a; cf. Betegh 2004:92–131.

34 There is a dissonance between the Orphic theogony and the author's cosmogonic views; see e.g. Betegh 2004:275, noting that "there is hardly anything connecting the two. This is why it is customarily held that the author—as indeed all who engage in the business of allegoresis—loses sight of and violates the apparent meaning of the text."

authorial strategies, rhetoric, and style belong to the first, and the ritual, religious, and philosophical requirements of the author's cultural environment to the latter.[35] Our inability to securely define, or even name, this genre stems from its multidimensional character. Dirk Obbink, in arguing that the Derveni author combines cosmology with initiation, concludes that this mixed genre is

> an alternative to the view of the Derveni papyrus as a composition of a single dimension: a philological commentary, philosophical treatise, or literary *paignion* ... Certainly some of the exegetical techniques invoked by the commentator derive from a shared early stage of critical activity dating to the late fifth century. But the mobilization of those techniques in the linking of myth and idea at the expense of clarity in reasoning has ritual and social motivation.[36]

To conclude: The Derveni author imposes his highly personalized, subjective view upon the Orphic material; he devises his readers and communicates his own perspective of Orphism to them; this results in a text where citation, commentary, instruction, and apologetic converge. In my opinion, there are some interesting parallels with late antique and Byzantine texts, all of which can be regarded as "commentaries" on great works of the past—in the broadest sense of the term. These may include such diverse genres as philological criticism (especially Eustathius' and Tzetzes' personalized commentaries on Greek poetry), Christian apologetic, and Neoplatonic treatises, as well as works such as Basil's *Hexaemeron* or Philon's *Quaestiones*. We would benefit considerably by reading the Derveni text in the light of these works—but this is a subject for another study.

Bibliography

Bernabé, A. 2007a. "The Derveni Theogony: Many Questions and Some Answers." *Harvard Studies in Classical Philology* 103:99–133.

———. 2007b. *Poetae epici Graeci: Testimonia et fragmenta*, pars II, fasc. 3. Berlin.

Betegh, G. 2004. *The Derveni Papyrus: Cosmology, Theology, and Interpretation*. Cambridge.

35 On the philosophical affiliations of the Derveni author, see Janko 1997:61–66. Cf. the suggestion of Janko (2002–2003) that the Derveni author was probably regarded by his contemporaries as an "atheist" for the fact that he applied allegory and etymology to the interpretation of the holy texts of Orphism.

36 Obbink 1997:54.

Calame, C. 1997. "Figures of Sexuality and Initiatory Transition in the Derveni Theogony and Its Commentary." In Laks and Most 1997:65–80.

Edmonds, R. G. 2008. "Extra-Ordinary People: *Mystai* and *Magoi*, Magicians and Orphics in the Derveni Papyrus." *Classical Philology* 103:16–39.

Ferrari, F. 2007. "Note al testo delle colonne II–VII del papiro di Derveni." *Zeitschrift für Papyrologie und Epigraphik* 162:203–211.

Funghi, M. S. 1997. "The Derveni Papyrus." In Laks and Most 1997:25–37.

Henrichs, A. 1984. "The Eumenides and the Wineless Libation in the Derveni Papyrus." In *Atti del XVII Congresso Internazionale di Papirologia (Napoli 1983)* II:255–268. Naples.

Henry, M. 1986. "The Derveni Commentator as Literary Critic." *Transactions and Proceedings of the American Philological Association* 116:149–164.

Janko, R. 1997. "The Physicist as Hierophant: Aristophanes, Socrates, and the Authorship of the Derveni Papyrus." *Zeitschrift für Papyrologie und Epigraphik* 118:61–94.

———. 2002–2003. "God, Science, and Socrates." *Bulletin of the Institute of Classical Studies* 46:1–17.

KPT = Th. Kouremenos, G.-M. Parássoglou, and K. Tsantsanoglou, *The Derveni Papyrus, Edited with Introduction and Commentary* (Florence, 2006).

Laks, A., and G. W. Most, eds. 1997. *Studies in the Derveni Papyrus*. Oxford.

Obbink, D. 1997. "Cosmology as Initiation vs. the Critique of Orphic Mysteries." In Laks and Most 1997:39–54.

RENT = D. Herman, M. Jahn, and M.-L. Ryan, eds., *The Routledge Encyclopedia of Narrative Theory* (London, 2005).

Schironi, F. 2001. "L'Olimpo non é il cielo: Esegesi antica nel papiro di Derveni, in Aristarco e in Leagora di Siracusa." *Zeitschrift für Papyrologie und Epigraphik* 136:11–21.

Tsantsanoglou, K. 1997. "The First Columns of the Derveni Papyrus and Their Religious Significance." In Laks and Most 1997:93–128.

12

The Orphic Poem of the Derveni Papyrus

David Sider
New York University

ALTHOUGH THERE ARE SOME FEW PLACES where I argue for something new, the chief aim of this essay is to present a text and provisional commentary on the Orphic poem (OP) contained within the Derveni Papyrus.[1] I draw my knowledge of the readings of the papyrus solely from the text of Parássoglou and Tsantsanoglou, as well as the photographs in KPT (see below, pp. 252–253, for abbreviations used herein); the conjectures and many of the parallel texts and alternate readings come from Bernabé's Teubner edition. If nothing else, this chapter will allow for one-stop shopping, as it combines the distinct non-overlapping sets of data from these two sources, as well as taking other scholars' observations into account.[2] Much of the work on the poem over the past years has been to evaluate its religious and philosophical content, as well as the use made of it by the Derveni author (herein simply the Author), and to this I add nothing; but there still seems to be a place for a study that concentrates on Orpheus' words as poetry. Note that I follow the editorial practice found in collections of poetry such as Page's *Poetae Melici Graeci* (*PMG*); that is, phonology has been regularized (thus, e.g., αἰδοῖον κατ- for αἰδοῖογ κατ-) and

[1] Several of the textual notes suggested here were first presented at the conference on the Derveni Papyrus held at the Center for Hellenic Studies, July 2008. In addition to my audience in Washington for their comments at the time, I am grateful to Francesca Angió, Alberto Bernabé, Gábor Betegh, Marco Fantuzzi, and Richard McKirahan for their helpful remarks on an earlier draft of this paper, as well as to Andrew Ford for a spirited discussion that followed a briefer version of this chapter presented at the APA meeting in San Antonio, Texas, Jan. 6, 2011. This is a slightly revised version of the online publication; note in particular that references have been added to Santamaría, who in turn refers to the earlier online version of this chapter.

The Orphic verses of the Derveni Papyrus are gathered in Bernabé 1.14–32 (= 3–18 F), Betegh 96–97, KPT 21, West 1983:114–115 ("an *exempli gratia* reconstruction"). Bernabé (2007a) offers a running commentary on the Orphic poem, but his interest is not primarily literary.

[2] The lack of a critical apparatus in KTP has been noted in the reviews; see R. Janko, *BMCR* 2006.10.29; A. Laks, *Rhizai* 4 (2007): 156.

elision is printed where the papyrus has *scriptio plena*, although half-brackets and dotted letters are printed. (The use of half-brackets here will be discussed below.)

To cover familiar ground briefly: The Derveni Papyrus contains (more familiarly, "is") a prose work (to choose the broadest possible term) that frequently quotes from Heraclitus,[3] Homer,[4] an anonymous hymn,[5] and, most extensively, a dactylic poem attributed to Orpheus, who is identified as the author of the "hymn" in column 6.[6] That scholars cannot agree on the point of view of the Author—is he atheist, literary critic, natural philosopher, or committed Orphic?—is not of concern here. When he wrote is also unknown, but composition is usually placed between the end of the fifth century and the middle of the fourth, which would also give us a *terminus ante quem* for the date of the Orphic poem, which has been placed as early as ca. 500 BC.[7] The story that Onomacritus inserted (ἐμποιέων) his own verses into a text of Musaeus—a mythical figure of a status similar to Orpheus—serves as a vivid reminder that even as early as the late sixth century, texts allegedly written by a poet of great (if not mythical) ancestry were altered if not outright forged.[8] And in fact, according to Diogenes Laertius 8.8, Ἴων δὲ ὁ Χῖος ἐν τοῖς Τριαγμοῖς φησιν ἔνια ποιήσαντα

3 In addition to the passage in col. 4 explicitly credited to Heraclitus, Janko (2001:23n119) thinks that a prose passage set off by *paragraphoi* in col. 11.8–9 is also by Heraclitus: χρᾶν τόνδε τὸν θεὸν νομίζοντ[ες ἔρ]χονται πευσόμενοι ἅσσα ποῶσι. Even if the quotation is not meant merely—so Ts. (1997:14n12)—to echo common sentiment, I find nothing particularly Heraclitean in the style of these words, however much they may represent his general beliefs.

4 Despite the fact that the Author introduces them with δηλοῖ, which elsewhere assumes Orpheus as subject, it seems to me highly unlikely that two passages quoted one after the other on col. 26 solely to demonstrate that ἐάων means "good things," a meaning the Author would foist on OP**24** ἑᾶς, should also just happen to be (*Iliad* 24.527–528) or closely resemble (*Odyssey* 8.335) two passages from Homer, *pace* Obbink (Laks and Most 1997:41), Janko 2001:31n186; cf. Betegh 100. Bernabé regards these two passages as coming from a separate Orphic hymn; see his comments to F 686–687.

5 Col. 22.12 Δημήτηρ [Ῥ]έα Γῆ Μήτηρ Ἑστία Δηιώι, which the Author's language cites as ἐν τοῖς Ὕμνοις εἰρ[η]μένον, phraseology that seems to imply Orphic authorship, but also to preclude it from coming from the main poem under discussion. It is not included as part of the Orphic Derveni poem by either Bernabé or KTP. For the scansion of this entirely spondaic line, see Kouremenos *ad loc.*

6 The Derveni Papyrus aside, the first author explicitly to attribute hymns to Orpheus is Plato (*Laws* 829e). For the ways in which this poem is and is not typically hymnic, see Calame 2010:20–21.

7 See West 1983:82–94, 108–113. He considers the poem quoted in the papyrus to be an abridgement of the *Protogonos* theogony, but, even if this is true, it may be the Author who is doing his own abridging in that he may not cite every line of the poem he has in front of him.

8 Herodotus 7.6 = Onomacritus T 1 D'Agostino: ἐξηλάσθη γὰρ ὑπὸ Ἱππάρχου τοῦ Πεισιστράτου ὁ Ὀνομάκριτος ἐξ Ἀθηνέων, ἐπ' αὐτοφώρῳ ἁλοὺς ὑπὸ Λάσου τοῦ Ἑρμιονέος ἐμποιέων ἐς τὰ Μουσαίου χρησμὸν ὡς αἱ ἐπὶ Λήμνῳ ἐπικείμεναι νῆσοι ἀφανιοίατο κατὰ τῆς θαλάσσης. Cf. E. D'Agostino, *Onomacritus: Testimonia et fragmenta* (Pisa, 2007) 33 ff.

(*sc.* Πυθαγόραν) ἀνενεγκεῖν εἰς Ὀρφέα (*sim.* Clement of Alexandria *Stromateis* 1.131.4).[9]

The extant columns of the Derveni Papyrus contain only the upper third to half of their original height. Since the Author writes in part in a form that soon became (and still is) standard—citation of a brief passage followed by a commentary that frequently repeats words from the citation before or the one to follow—we can often detect a poetic word in the prose commentary that echoes in part the now-lost lemma/citation. These provide one-word fragments such as those which we are all too familiar from the fragments of other poets, where the word is fairly secure even if we cannot be sure that, now accommodated to the citator's own sentence, the precise morphological case, person, etc., has been reproduced. When the embedded poetic word picks up a lemma only partially legible, it may help in its constitution. In these cases, it seems proper, however unusual, to make use of half-brackets, which are normally found when a completely separate author with his own manuscript tradition (e.g. Athenaeus or Plutarch) cites a passage that is also found on a papyrus. The Author's practice of repeating words from the lemma in his commentary satisfies the essential idea behind the use of half-brackets. Although I do not present a complete survey (let alone a commentary) of these isolated fragments, as does Betegh (103–105), I refer to many of them in the commentary.

It is not clear whether the Author quotes from one poem, which he calls a hymn of Orpheus (col. 6.2, 5), in the order in which the lines occur in the poem, as Betegh persuasively argues,[10] or whether he hops about in an attempt to make some point of his own, quoting from various places in the poem as he sees relevant. In either case, we can in our ignorance do no better than follow the Author's own order. As Betegh says (*per litt.*), "even if the commentary is not necessarily line-by-line, the order of the verses as they appear in the papyrus makes good sense."

Orpheus' reputation as supreme singer begins early (unlike, say, his homosexuality, which is a Hellenistic innovation).[11] General praise is found in Ibycus

[9] Turnabout is fair play: Suidas s.v. Ὀρφεύς says that it was Orpheus who wrote the *Triagmoi*. On the other hand, the sophist Hippias boasted that he incorporated into his own work verses of Orpheus, among others (Clement of Alexandria *Stromateis* 6.15 = Hippias B 6 D-K).

[10] Betegh 105–108.

[11] Cf. Phanocles fr. 1.9–10 *CA* πρῶτος ἔδειξεν ἐνὶ Θρῄκεσσιν ἔρωτας | ἄρρενας. Plato *Republic* 620a does refer to Orpheus' hatred of the tribe of women, but this is because it was women who killed him! References to "Orpheus musicus" are collected by Bernabé 428–443, whose T numbers are given. Note also *P.Oxy*. 3698 ed. Haslam = F 1005a, Ο]ἰ̣άγρο̣υ φ[ί]λ̣ος υἱ̣[ὸς | πλήκ̣τ̣ρω̣ι̣ ἐπ̣ε̣[ιρήτιζε, which A. Debiasi, *Zeitschrift für Papyrologie und Epigraphik* 143 (2003): 1–5 attributes to Eumelus' *Corinthiaca*. What follows is but a mere sketch of Orpheus the poet; for a far richer account, see Calame 2010.

306 *PMG* = 864 T ὀνομάκλυτον Ὀρφήν; Pindar *Nemean* 4.177 = 972 T ἐξ Ἀπόλλωνος δὲ φορμιγκτὰς ἀοιδᾶν πατήρ | ἔμολεν, εὐαίνητος Ὀρφεύς; and Timotheus *Persians* 221–223 = 902 T πρῶτος ποικιλόμουσος Ὀρφεὺς <τέχν>αν ἐτέκνωσεν υἱὸς Καλλιόπα<ς> Πιερίαθεν. More specific praise, namely that his playing has the power to move birds, plants, fish, and rocks, still solidly fifth century, occurs in Simonides 567 *PMG* = 943 T τοῦ [*sc.* Ὀρφέως, acc. to Tzetzes] καὶ ἀπειρέσιοι | πωτῶντ' ὄρνιθες ὑπὲρ κεφαλᾶς | ἀνὰ δ' ἰχθύες ὀρθοὶ | κυανέου 'ξ ὕδατος ἅλλοντο καλᾷ σὺν ἀοιδᾷ; Aeschylus *Agamemnon* 1630 = 946 T ὁ μὲν γὰρ ἦγε πάντα που φθογγῆς χαρᾷ ("He leads all things with the power of his tongue in delight"); Euripides *Bacchae* 561–564 = 947 T ... θαλάμαις, ἔνθα ποτ' Ὀρφεὺς κιθαρίζων | σύναγεν δένδρεα μούσαις, | σύναγεν θῆρας ἀγρώτας; Euripides *Iphigenia at Aulis* 1211–1215 = 948 T (Ἰφ.) εἰ μὲν τὸν Ὀρφέως εἶχον ... λόγον, | πείθειν ἐπᾴδουσ' ὥσθ' ὁμαρτεῖν μοι πέτρας | κηλεῖν τε τοῖς λόγοισιν οὓς ἐβουλόμην, | ἐνταῦθ' ἂν ἦλθον· νῦν δέ, τἀπ' ἐμοῦ σοφά, δάρκρυα παρέξω; *Tragica Adespota TGrF* 129.6–8. Later, water is added: Phanocles fr. 1.20; Apollonius of Rhodes 1.27. And of course he charms people as well: Euripides *Hypsipyle* fr. 752g.10–12, = 1007 T Θρῇσσ' ἐβόα κίθαρις [Ὀρφέως] ... ἐρέτᾳσι κελεύσματα μελπομένα, Euripides *Alcestis* 357–362, 962–972; Euripides *Medea* 542–543; to say nothing of his charming Hades and Persephone (first in Euripides *Alcestis* 357–359).[12]

The most likely source of this reputation is the early epic tale of the voyage of the Argo,[13] where tales of rocks and trees "sequacious of the lyre" (Dryden) were part of the narrative and Orpheus' own words, whether actually quoted or not, were characterized as extraordinarily beautiful.[14] On the other hand, the verses quoted in the Derveni Papyrus or those few other Orphic lines that can be dated

[12] To all of which we can add a joking statement that Orpheus' music could animate torches; Euripides *Cyclops* 646–648.

[13] Cf. the *Hypsipyle* fragment, above, where Orpheus sings to encourage the rowers of the Argo. There is, however, no explicit testimony that such an early epic existed; the closest we have is *Odyssey* 12.70 Ἀργὼ πᾶσι μέλουσα, which is usually, and reasonably, understood to refer to an early epic *Argonautica*. (That it narrates the adventures of the generation before that of the Trojan warriors does not entail that the poem too antedates Homer.) See P. Dräger, *Argo Pasimelousa* (Stuttgart, 1993) 12–18, for a review of Homer's references to this tale, which could have existed only in the form of an oral epic; and M. L. West, "*Odyssey* and *Argonautica*," *Classical Quarterly* 55 (2005): 39–64; reprinted in id. *Hellenica* I: *Epic* (Oxford, 2011) 277–312.

[14] To retroject from Apollonius 4.891–911 and the *Orphic Argonautica* 1268–1285, Orpheus would have engaged in and won a singing contest with the Sirens, which would have provided an excellent excuse for the early epic poet to lavish praise on Orpheus' divine singing and to narrate a magical episode in which rocks, etc., were animated. According to the fifth/fourth-century historian Herodorus, the ἀσθενής Orpheus was brought on board only to contest with the Sirens, not to take his turn at the oars; Herodorus *Argonautica* fr. 39 FHG = 1010 II T. Orpheus has also been identified as a figure between two Sirens on a vase dated to ca. 580 BC (*LIMC* Orpheus 6); see further Calame 2010:14.

to the classical period,[15] although not unattractive, are far from the dazzling performance of the mythical Orpheus, an inconcinity that seems to have bothered almost nobody in the ancient world. But note that Orpheus' poetry—that is, the poetry that was published under his name, such as that in the Derveni Papyrus—was compared unfavorably to Hesiod's by Menander Rhetor *Διαίρεσις τῶν ἐπιδεικτικῶν* 3.340 Spengel [= Hesiod T 126 Most] παρέσχετο δὲ τὴν μὲν ἐν ποιήσει ἀρετὴν Ἡσίοδος, καὶ γνοίη τις ἂν μᾶλλον, εἰ τοῖς Ὀρφέως παραθείη.

It is possible that in this early *Argonautica*, Orpheus indeed sang beautifully (of what we cannot know, tempting as it is to guess that at least once it was of a cosmogonical and cosmological nature), but the poem as a whole seems not to have survived long enough to be cited in the fifth century,[16] by which time the figure of Orpheus took on a separate and distinct existence as the author of τελεταί τε καὶ χρησμῳδίαι (Plato *Protagoras* 316d) and ἐπῳδαί (Euripides *Cyclops* 614) exclusively; cf. Aristophanes *Frogs* 1032. We shall thus never know whether his singing in this lost epic was reported directly (and was in fact stunningly beautiful) or merely said to be so by the *Argonautica* poet. It is almost as if there were two distinct Orpheis, which is in fact exactly what the historian Herodorus said.[17] Who was Orpheus when he was not sailing? A bard like Homer, as suggested by Plato *Ion* 536b? This would be consistent with Pindar *Pythian* 4.176, where he is called φορμιγκτὰς ἀοιδᾶν πατήρ; cf. Timotheus 221–224 = 883 T. Unlike Homer, however, Orpheus is often associated with the wilds of mountains, where those sequacious animals, trees, and rocks are to be found.[18] Later, this led him to be thought of as a pastoral poet, but this is probably due more to his origins as a shamanistic figure somewhat like Dionysus, who too is associated with sites outside the city.[19]

15 Fourth-century citations of Orphic verses are Plato *Cratylus* 402bc = 22 F λέγει δέ που καὶ Ὀρφεὺς ὅτι «Ὠκεανὸς πρῶτος καλλίρροος ἦρξε γάμοιο, | ὅς ῥα κασιγνήτην ὁμομήτορα Τηθὺν ὄπυιεν»; Plato *Philebus* 66c = 25 F «Ἕκτῃ δ' ἐν γενεᾷ,» φησὶν Ὀρφεύς, «καταπαύσατε κόσμον ἀοιδῆς»; [Aristotle] *De mundo* 401a25 = 31 F (some of whose nine verses will be quoted below). This is not to deny that later citations, such as those in Damascius, who cites Eudemus, may be of equally early origin—some of them in fact are the same as is found in *P.Derv.*—but in a text as subject to accretions as this one, the earlier the citation, the better.

16 At any rate, it is never cited, even by as little as its title, in any extant text; hence its complete absence from Kinkel's, Bernabé's, Davies's, and West's collections of epic fragments.

17 Scholion in Apollonius of Rhodes 1.23 = 967 T, clearly truncated in transmission, Ἡρόδωρος δύο εἶναι Ὀρφεῖς φησιν, ὧν τὸν ἕτερον συμπεπλευκέναι τοῖς Ἀργοναύταις. The other one, presumably, is the religious seer and author of cosmological/theogonic poetry, in which latter role he was included by some among the Seven Wise Men; cf. Diogenes Laertius 1.42 = 887 T.

18 Cf. Euripides *Bacchae* 560–564: ἐν ταῖς πολυδένδροισιν Ὀλύμπου | θαλάμαις, ἔνθα ποτ' Ὀρφεὺς κιθαρίζων | σύναγεν δένδρεα μούσαις, | σύναγεν θῆρας ἀγρώστας.

19 See e.g. M. Detienne, "Un polythéisme récrit: Entre Dionysos et Apollon: Mort et vie d'Orphée," *Archives de sciences sociales des religions* 59 (1985): 65–75; West 1983:4–7.

Fragments of the Orphic Poem

With the prefix OP attached, the fragments are numbered as they are by Kouremenos in KPT 21, except for the first one, which comes from Bernabé. In parentheses are their locations within the Derveni Papyrus. Concordances with Betegh and Bernabé are made difficult because each editor makes different joins between lines quoted separately in the papyrus.

OP**3 F** (*P.Derv.* col. 7)

[φθέγξομαι οἷς θέμις ἐστι· θ]⌊ύρας δ' ἐπίθε⌋[σθε βέβηλοι]

I shall proclaim to those for whom it is proper; close the doors, o profane ones

v. comm.

OP**1** (*P.Derv.* col. 8.2)

[ο]ῒ Διὸς ἐξεγ̣ένοντο [μεγασθεν]έος βασιλῆ̣ος

... who were born from great-minded king Zeus

[ο]ῒ *ZPE** [μεγασθεν]έος Sider [ὑπερμεν]έος *ZPE** [περιφραδ]έος Santamaría (*iam tent.* Sider) [περισθεν]έος Janko (2002)

OP**2** (*P.Derv.* col. 8.4–5)

Ζεὺς μὲν ἐπεὶ δὴ̣ π̣α̣[τρὸς ἑο]ῦ πάρα θέ[σ]φατον ἀρχὴν
⌊ἀ⌋λκήν τ' ἐν χείρεσσι ⌊λ⌋ά̣β[εν, κ]α⌊ὶ⌋ δαίμον̣⌊α⌋ κυδρόν ...

Zeus, when from his father he took into his hands his divine rule and valor, (he) — the glorious daimon ...

1 θέ[σ]φατον (*ZPE**) ἀρχὴν Π θέσφατ' ἀκούσας Calame 1997 (i.e. = OP7) **2** [ἀ]λκήν *ZPE** χείρεσσι ⌊λ⌋ά̣β[εν Sider χείρεσσι ε[Π χείρεσσι ⌊λ⌋ά̣β[εν Rusten 126 χείρεσσ' ἔ⌊λ⌋α̣βεν Janko (2002) χείρεσσ' ἔλαβεν West 84 cf. col. 8.8–10

OP**4**–OP**5** (*P.Derv.* col. 11.1, 11.10)

ἐξ ἀ̣δύτοιο (.?.)
⌊Νὺξ⌋ ἔχρησεν ἅπαντα τά οἱ θέ[μις ἐκτελέεσ]θ̣αι

From the innermost sanctuary Night proclaimed all that it was right for him [i.e. Zeus] to accomplish.

⌊Νὺξ⌋ Sider [ἣ δέ] *ZPE** [Νὺξ] Santamaría [ἥ οἱ] West 114 [ἣ δέ] Bernabé θέ[μις] *ZPE** [ἐκτελέεσ]θ̣αι Sider [ἦν τελέεσ]θ̣αι Santamaría (*iam tent.* Sider) [ἦν ἀνύσασ]θ̣αι Ts. *ap.* Bern. For ἦν ἀ., Ts. also considers [ἐξανύσασ]θ̣αι and [(ἐξ- or ἦν)ανύεσ]θ̣αι. [ἦεν ἀνύσσ]αι West [ἦεν ἀκοῦ]σ̣αι Janko (2002) [αὖθι τελέσσ]αι Burkert

OP**6** (*P.Derv.* col. 12.2)

ὡς ἂν̣ ἔ̣[χοι κά]τα καλὸν ἕδ̣ος νιφόεντος Ὀλύμπου

So that he might hold sway over the noble seat of snow-clad Olympus.

ἂν ἔ̣[χοι κά]τα Ts. *ap.* Brisson 1997:152n10 ἄ[ρξαι κα]τά West ἄρ̣ξ[ηι κα]τά Janko (2002) ἄ[ρξηι Burkert ἄ[.... κα]τά *ZPE**

OP**7** (*P.Derv.* col. 13.1)

Ζεὺς μὲν ἐπεὶ δὴ̣ π̣ατρὸς ἑοῦ πάρα̣ [θ]ἐ̣σφατ' ἀκούσα[ς,]

Zeus, upon hearing the prophecies from his father....

ἔπει[τ' ἄφραστα θεᾶς] West 114 [θ]ἐ̣σφατ' ἀκούσα[ς Ts., *iam* [θέ]σφατ' ἀκούσα[ς *ZPE**

OP**8** (*P.Derv.* col. 13.4)

αἰδοῖον κατ̣έπινεν, ὃς αἰθέρα ἔκθορ̣ε πρῶτος

He gulped down the revered one, who was first to spring from the aither

αἰθέρα Π αἰθέρος Lamberton

OP**9** (*P.Derv.* col. 14.5)

ὃς μ̣έγ' ἔρεξεν

...who wrought a great thing.

OP**10** (*P.Derv.* col. 14.6)

Οὐρανὸς Εὐφρονίδης, ὃς πρώτιστ̣ος βασίλευσεν

Ouranos the son of Night, who was first to become king.

Οὐρανὸς Εὐφρονίδης Π -ον -ην Kouremenos (*iam* –ον̣ -ην̣ West), *qui iunxit haec verba cum* fr. 9

OP**11** (*P.Derv.* col. 15.6)

ἐκ τοῦ δὴ Κρόνος α̣ὖτις, ἔπειτα δὲ μητίετα Ζεύς
From whom was Kronos in turn, and then Zeus the planner

α̣ὖτις Bernabé [α]ὖτις *ZPE**

OP**12** (*P.Derv.* col. 15.13–15)

μῆτιν κα.[*ca.* 14]ε̣ν βασιληίδα τιμ̣[ήν]
εc.[ ].α̣ι ἶνα̣ς ἀ̣π.[
ει̣[

1 μῆτιν (Bernabé) *vel* Μῆτιν (*ZPE**)]ε̣ν *possis*]ω̣ν Ts. κάπ̣[πινων] Burkert κάπ̣[πινεν καὶ ἔχ]ε̣ν Santamaría καὶ̣ [μακάρων κατέχ]ων West (*sed iota non legendum*; P-Ts.) εἶχ]εν *vel* κάτεχ]εν Janko (2002) τιμ̣[ήν] *ZPE** **2** ἀ̣πά̣[σας Janko (2002)

OP**13**–OP**14**

OP**13** (*P.Derv.* col. 16.3–6)

πρωτογόνου βασιλέως αἰδοίου, τῷ̣ δ' ἄρα πάντες
ἀθάνατ̣οι προσέφυν μάκαρες θεοὶ ἠδ̣ὲ θέαιναι
καὶ ποταμοὶ καὶ κρῆναι ἐπήρατοι ἄλ̣λα τε πάντα,
ἅ̣σσα τότ' ἦν γεγαῶτ', αὐτὸς δ' ἄρα μοῦ̣νος ἔγεντο.

...of the revered first-generating king; to him were joined all the immortal blessed gods and goddesses, as well as rivers, delightful springs and all else that had then been born; but he himself came to be all by himself.

***ante* 1** <κατέπινεν μένος> Brisson 2003 (*melius*: μένος κατέπινεν|) **1** τῷ̣ Ts. Betegh τοῦ̣ *ZPE** **4** ἅ̣σσα Ts. *ap*. Bernabé [ὅ]σσα *ZPE**

OP**14** (*P.Derv.* col. 16.14)

[νῦν δ' ἐστὶ]ν βασιλεὺς̣ πάντ̣[ων καί τ' ἔσσετ' ἔπ]ειτα
Now he is king of all and will be hereafter

omnia suppl. West *excepto* βασιλεὺς πάντ̣[ων *ZPE**

OP**15** (*P.Derv.* col. 18.12–13)

Ζεὺς πρῶ̣τος [γέν]ε̣το, ⌞Ζεὺς⌟ ⌞ὕστατος⌟ [ἀργικέραυνος]
Zeus was first, Zeus of the bright lightning bolt is last

v. comm.

OP**16** (*P.Derv.* col. 17.12)

Ζεὺς κεφα̣⌞λή⌟, [Ζεὺς μέσ]σ̣α̣, Δ̣ιὸς δ’ ἐκ̣ [π]άντα τέτ̣[υκται]
Zeus is the head/first, Zeus is the middle, from Zeus are all things fashioned

*suppl. ZPE**

OP**17** (*P.Derv.* col. 18)

[Ζεὺς πνοίη πάντων, Ζεὺς πάντων ἔπλετο] ⌞μοῖρα⌟
Zeus is the breath of all; of all is Zeus the share/fate

h.v. composuit Merkelbach *e verbis Auctoris; v. comm.*

OP**18** (*P.Derv.* col. 19.10)

Ζεὺ̣ς βασιλεύς, Ζεὺς δ’ ἀρχὸς ἁπάν̣τ̣ων ἀργικέραυνος.
Zeus is king, Zeus of the shining lightning is the ruler of all

OP**19** (*P.Derv.* col. 21.5–7)

(Πειθώ θ’ Ἁρμονίην τε καὶ Οὐρανίην Ἀφροδίτην)
Persuasion, Harmony, and Aphrodite Ourania

h.v. composuit Kouremenos *e verbis Auctoris; v. comm.* θόρνῃ δ’ Ἀφροδίτη | Οὐρανίη καὶ Πειθώ θ’ Ἁρμονίη τε *e.g.* Merkelbach

OP**20** (*P.Derv.* col. 23)

μήσατο <δ’> Ὠκεανοῖο μέγα σθένος εὐρὺ ῥέοντος
— contrived the great might of widely flowing Okeanos

h.v. West *composuit e verbis Auctoris*: "Ὠκεανός," "ἐμήσατο," "σθένος μέγα," " εὐρὺ ῥέοντα" μήσατο δ’ Ὠκεανὸν βαθυδίνην εὐρὺ ῥέοντα *e.g.* Burkert

OP**21** (*P.Derv.* col. 23.11)

ἶνας δ' ἐγκ̣α̣τ̣[έλε]ξ̣' Ἀχελωΐου ἀργυ̣[ρ]οδίν̣ε̣⸤ω⸥
And within he placed the sinews of Acheloios with its silvern eddies

cf. *P.Oxy.* 221 col. 9.1–2 .]νας [δ' ἐ]γκατέλεξ(α) | Ἀχελωίου ἀργυροδίνεω

OP**22** (*P.Derv.* col. 24.3)

ἣ πολλοῖς φαίνει μερόπεσσ' ἐπ' ἀπείρονα γαῖαν
She [*sc.* the Moon] shines on many mortals over the boundless earth

μερόπεσσι ἐπ' Π

OP**23** (*P.Derv.* col. 25.14)

[αὐτ]ὰ̣ρ̣ [ἐ]π̣εὶ δ[ὴ πάν]τ̣α Διὸ[ς νοῦς μή]σατ̣[ο ἔ]ρ̣γ̣α̣
but when the mind of Zeus contrived all deeds.

omnia rest. Ts. (*monente* West), *excepto* νοῦς (Sider); φρήν Ts.

OP**24** (*P.Derv.* col. 26)

μητρὸς ἑᾶς ἔθελεν μιχθήμεναι ἐν φιλότητι
He wished to lie in love with his own mother

h.v. composuit Ts. *e verbis Auctoris*: "μητρός," "ἑᾶς," "θέλοντα μιχθῆναι," "ἐν φιλότητι" ἤθελε μητρὸς ἑᾶς μιχθήμεναι ἐν φιλότητι *e.g.* Ts. ὁ δ' ἤθελεν ἐν φιλότητι μητρὸς ἑῆς ⏑⏑— μιχθήμεναι *e.g.* Merkelbach

Commentary

In a lost transition between the end of column 6 (on sacrifices, prayers, and souls) and the beginning of column 7, the Author turns to extensive quotation and commentary on a "sound and orthodox" hymn of Orpheus—ὕ]μνο̣ν [ὑγ]ι̣ῆ καὶ θεμ[ι]τ̣ὰ λέγοντα (*sc.* Ὀρφέα)—which he characterizes as wholly holy: [Ὀρφεὺ]ς̣ ... [μεγ]άλα̣ ἱερ[ολογ]ε̣ῖ̣ται μὲν οὖν καὶ ἀ̣[πὸ το]ῦ πρώτου [καὶ] μέχρι <τ>ο̣ῦ [τελε]υτ̣α̣ί̣ου ῥήματος (7.5–8). (The nature and quality of the Author's interpretations need not concern us.)

OP**3 F** [φθέγξομαι οἷς θέμις ἐστι· θ]⌊ύρας δ' ἐπίθε⌋[σθε βέβηλοι]

The Author continues his introduction (see above) to the discussion and exegesis of Orpheus by saying [θ]ụ́ρας γὰρ ἐπιθέσ[θ]ε ὁ [κελ]εύσας τοῖ̣[ς | ὠσὶ]ν αὐτ[ούς]—see Janko 2008:39 for the text—which Burkert recognized as the formulaic line end at the beginning of several religious poems. Cf. e.g. Plato *Symposium* 218b (Alcibiades): οἱ δὲ οἰκέται, καὶ εἴ τις ἄλλος ἐστὶν βέβηλός τε καὶ ἄγροικος, πύλας πάνυ μεγάλας τοῖς ὠσὶν ἐπίθεσθε. That covering one's ears hinders hearing hardly needs a classical parallel, but it may be that Odysseus' description of the wax put in his crew's ears so that they would not hear the Sirens alludes to something similar in the episode in the early *Argonautica*, where, as we saw above, Orpheus helped the crew sail past the Sirens; cf. *Odyssey* 12.177 ἑτάροισιν ἐπ' οὔατα πᾶσιν ἄλειψα [*sc.* κηρόν], 199–200 αἶψ' ἀπὸ κηρὸν ἕλοντο ἐμοὶ ἐρίηρες ἑταῖροι, | ὅν σφιν ἐπ' ὠσὶν ἄλειψ', ἐμέ τ' ἐκ δεσμῶν ἀνέλυσαν. Either word for "ear" could well have appeared in the line following 3 F, but in both Clement of Alexandria *Protrepticus* 7.74.4 and Ps.-Justinus Martyr, *Cohortatio ad gentes* p. 15 C Morel (both of whom attribute the verses to Orpheus) we find φθέγξομαι οἷς θέμις ἐστί· θύρας δ' ἐπίθεσθε βέβηλοι | πάντες ὁμῶς.

There are, however, two possible first halves to this line, (i) the one printed above and ἀείσω ξυνετοῖσι (attributed to Orpheus by Cyril of Alexandria *Contra Julianum* 1.35, but to Pythagoras by others), both of which are in accord with what the Author says after the above: οὔτι νομο[θετεῖν φη[σιν τοῖς] πολλοῖς [... *ca.* 14... τὴ]ν ἀκοὴν [ἁγνεύο]ντας .... See further Santamaría 2012:55–56.

OP**1** [ο]ἳ Διὸς ἐξεγẹ́νοντο [μεγασθεν]έος βασιλῆ̣ος

[ο]ἳ Διὸς ἐξεγẹ́νοντο: = *Iliad* 5.637 (of mortals); cf. *Homeric Hymn to the Dioscuri* 17.2 οἳ Ζηνὸς Ὀλυμπίου ἐξεγένοντο; and often in early epic in this sense, most notably in Hesiod's genealogical poems; cf. *Theogony* 106 οἳ Γῆς ἐξεγένοντο καὶ Οὐρανοῦ ἀστερόεντος; Bernabé (2007a:102–103) notes the emphasis laid on Zeus at this early point in the poem. Xenophanes B 33 begins the process of using the verb to indicate coming into being, while still maintaining its earlier biological sense:

> πάντες γὰρ γαίης τε καὶ ὕδατος ἐκγενόμεσθα,

—a process which Empedocles B 59 continues to develop:

> αὐτὰρ ἐπεὶ κατὰ μεῖζον ἐμίσγετο δαίμονι δαίμων,
> ταῦτά τε συμπίπτεσκον, ὅπῃ συνέκυρσεν ἕκαστα,
> ἄλλα τε πρὸς τοῖς πολλὰ διηνεκῆ ἐξεγένοντο.

It remained for Parmenides B 10.1–3 to apply it solely to inanimate substances:

> εἴσῃ δ' αἰθερίαν τε φύσιν τά τ' ἐν αἰθέρι πάντα
> ... ὁππόθεν ἐξεγένοντο.

If, as has been suggested, the Author quotes the lines in the order of the poem, this early reference to Zeus demonstrates his importance here.

[μεγασθευ]έος: *ZPE**'s [ὑπερμεν]έος, adopted by all but Janko and Santamaría, is acceptable but can be improved upon. It calls for hiatus after ἐξεγένοντο, which can only barely be justified; Homer has a number of examples of hiatus before ὑπὲρ(-)[20]—eleven (some examples below) vs. fifty times in the *Iliad* where there is elision or correption, but only one where, as here, the preceding syllable is short (23.820 Τυδεΐδης δ' ἄρ' ἔπειτα ὑπὲρ σάκεος μεγάλοιο). Moreover, there is never hiatus before ὑπερμεν- in Homer. On the other hand, hiatus after a short syllable, when it does occur, is found at the midline trochaic caesura, as here (and at the bucolic diaeresis); and of these occurrences over 25 percent are after -ο(ν)το; cf. Munro, *Homeric Grammar,* ¶382, citing O. V. Knös *De digammo homerico* (Uppsala, 1872–1879) 42–45. And ὑπερμεν- is an epithet (of the right shape) of Zeus in Homer. Janko's conjecture evokes Zeus' strength more explicitly, but it is rather rare and applied only to mortals—even serving as a proper name—or objects.

[μεγασθεν]έος, which is regularly applied to gods, is preferable; cf. Bacchylides 3.67–68 μεγασθενὴ[ς] Ζεύς, Aeschylus *Eumenides* 61 [Apollo], Aristophanes *Clouds* 566 and Pindar *Olympian* 1.25 [Poseidon], Quintus of Smyrna 2.140 Ζηνὶ μεγασθενέι. It also occurs five times in the Orphic hymns. Another possibility is [περιφραδ]έος (Apollo, *Homeric Hymn to Hermes* 464). [ἐρισθεν]έος, also suggested by Janko, is, with seven letters restored, said by Kouremenos to be too short, which suggests that a restoration of eight letters is possible. At 13.4 αἰθέρα ἔκθορ̣ε is an example of hiatus at the bucolic diaeresis after a short vowel; in the verse of a good poet, this might be thought of as vivid writing; more on this later.

βασιλῆ̣ος: Zeus is never called by this title in Homer, but he is in Hesiod and the hymns—a well-known fact, which also serves to remind us that, although Homer offers guidance whenever the text of Orpheus is in doubt, allowance should always be made for changes in metrics, vocabulary, and myth.

Between OP**1** and OP**2**, the Author writes ὅπως δ' ἄρχεται ἐν τῶ[ιδε δη]λοῖ, leaving the subject of the verb unclear. Tsantsanoglou and Parássoglou take it to

[20] That is, where a long final syllable or diphthong does not experience epic correption: *Iliad* 3.299 ὁππότεροι πρότερο̲ι̲ ὑ̲πὲρ ὅρκια πημήνειαν ~ 4.67 = 4.72 ~ 4.136 ~ 4.271, 6.458, 11.297, 14.413, 17.24, 23.73, 23.820.

be τὰ νῦν ἐόντα, while Bernabé prefers Ζεύς, which is indeed strongly suggested by 2.1 Ζεὺς ... ἀρχήν, although the phrase "how Zeus rules" is odd; an inceptive aorist would convey the thought better. "How Zeus begins" (Betegh) should allude to his birth, not, *simpliciter*, to the beginning of his rule. If the Author, in the manner of a textual commentor, worked his way through the Orphic poem in order, and OP**2** followed directly on OP**1**, as has been argued by, among others, Betegh (105–108), it would seem that in this particular telling of the story the emphasis is on Zeus, but this cannot be determined.

OP**2** Ζεὺς μὲν ἐπεὶ δ̣ὴ̣ π̣α̣[τρὸς ἑο]ῦ πάρα θέ[σ]φατον ἀρχήν
⸤ἀ⸥λκήν τ' ἐν χείρεσσι ⸤λ⸥ά̣β[εν, κ]α̣⸤ὶ⸥ δαίμον⸤α⸥ κυδρόν ...

For the words restored in half-brackets, see column 8.8–10. These lines may have come immediately after OP**1**; cf. West 1983:114, Betegh 109. This line and OP**7** Ζεὺς μὲν ἐπεὶ δὴ̣ π̣ατρὸς ἑοῦ πάρα̣ [θ]έ̣σφατ' ἀκούσα[ς] are, ignoring the different morphology of the penultimate words, the same except for the last words. There are some examples of this in Homer and other early epic; cf. B. Hainsworth, *The Iliad: A Commentary* III (Cambridge, 1993) 19–21; R. Janko, *Homer, Hesiod, and the Hymns* (Cambridge, 1982) 129–130. This near repetition, however, is especially reminiscent of Empedocles, who also plays with the idea of oral formulas, reworking his own lines so closely that editors frequently merge what I believe to be two (or more) distinct quotations into one fragment (as I hope to show in detail elsewhere). Cf. B 121.4, as quoted by most sources, Ἄτης ἂν λειμῶνα κατὰ σκότος ἠλάσκουσιν, and the same line as quoted by Proclus, Ἄτης ἐν λειμῶνι κατὰ σκότος ἱλάσκονται, where the appropriateness of ἄν(α) ... ἠλάσκουσιν and ἐν ... ἱλάσκονται argue against scribal error. For a more sophisticated example, compare also B 115.1, as quoted by Plutarch *On Exile* 607c, ἔστι τ(ι) ἀνάγκης χρῆμα, θεῶν ψήφισμα παλαιόν, with ἔστιν Ἀνάγκη, χρῆμα θεῶν, σφρήγισμα παλαιόν, as quoted by Simplicius *On Aristotle's Physics* 1184.9–10 = Empedocles fr. 110 Bollack. This literary play with one's own words/formulae was adopted by Lucretius; cf. e.g. 2.82 *avius a vera longe ratione vagaris* ~ 2.229 *avius a vera longe ratione recedit*; see further J. D. Minyard, *Mode and Value in the* De Rerum Natura: *A Study in Lucretius' Metrical Language* (Wiesbaden, 1978) 44–45. It would be interesting to know whether Empedocles is at all indebted in his own near self-quotation to this Orphic poem. This discussion shows that Calame (1997:67n3) is on weak ground when he argues that OP**2**.1 should be altered to the reading of OP**7**.

μέν: "Emphaticum," Bernabé 3.207 (citing Denniston, *Greek Particles*, 359–361), but this cannot be sure and it remains quite possible that this clause was followed by one with δέ; see below.

χείρεσσι ˪λ˩ạ́βεν: What I print is a simple combination of Rusten's and Janko's readings. The latter, followed by Bernabé, is surely right to regard the Author's requoting this verse six lines later in a different word order as the equivalent of a separate quotation that calls for half-, not full, brackets; see the introductory paragraph, above. Π has *scriptio plena* elsewhere, if [ἡ δὲ] ἔχρησεν is correctly restored at col. 11.10, where there is space for three letters; note also 16.9 δὲ ἄρα (prose) and 24.3 μερόπεσσ(ι) ἐπ'. At 13.4 there is hiatus which for metrical reasons cannot be mitigated by elision: αἰθέρα ἔκθορε. The reason for choosing Rusten's avoidance of elision is that λαβ- is most common in Homer among past indicatives (thirty-nine times), but the choice of this, ἐλαβ- (six times), or ἔλλαβ- (nineteen times) is determined in all places but one by metrical convenience, the exception, also at the midline caesura, being *Iliad* 8.116 ἐν χείρεσσι λάβ', where no manuscript offers the variant χείρεσσ' ἔλαβ'. The same words occur at 15.229, but here the verb is imperative; i.e. no temporal augment is possible. For elision of this word at the midline caesura, cf. *Odyssey* 19.356 δεξαμένη χείρεσσ' | ὅτε κτλ., West, *Greek Metre,* 36.

δαίμον̣˪α˩ κυδρόν: Gods can be glorious; cf. Hesiod *Theogony* 442 κυδρὴ θεὸς, *Works and Days* 257 (Dike), *Odyssey* 11.580, etc. (Hera), *Homeric Hymn to Demeter* 179 (Demeter), *Homeric Hymn to Hermes* 461 (Apollo), etc. In Orphic poetry, Eros receives this epithet, *Orphic Argonautica* 14. The problem is the syntax. As quoted, this phrase would seem to be the direct object of ἔλαβεν, which presents an odd picture, or perhaps a striking syllepsis, especially with the phrase "in his hands." It is easy, though, to imagine that the Author, quoting whole lines, has truncated the grammar, so that (as my commas and translation indicate) ἔλαβεν takes only "rule and valor." It is true that in "correcting" the word order, the Author again presents a text that on the surface allows δαίμονα to be another object, but once more he may be simply finishing the line but not the syntax. This was the view of Rusten and West, both of whom attempted to find from the Author himself the line containing the verb governing δαίμονα.

OP**4**–OP**5** ἐξ ἀδύτοιο (.?.)
˪Νὺξ˩ ἔχρησεν ἅπαντα τά οἱ θέ[μις ἐκτελέεσ]θ̣αι

The Author quotes OP**5** as a single line, but has anticipated it on line 1 of this column, which begins with ... [τ]ῆς Νυκτός· «ἐξ ἀ[δύτοι]ο» δ' αὐτὴν [λέγει] χρῆ̣σ̣αι .... It is thus quite likely that the words ἐξ ἀδύτοιο immediately preceded OP**5** (same phrase and same sedes at *Iliad* 5.512, *Orphic Argonautica* 956; cf. Aristophanes *The Knights* 1015–1016 Ἀπόλλων ἴαχεν ἐξ ἀδύτοιο). Bernabé joins the two fragments, along with *ZPE**'s ἡ δὲ.

⌞**Νύξ**⌟: Night, as is clear from col. 11.1; see last lemma. Three letters are needed; hence, ἡ δέ in *scriptio plena* (= ἡ δ' in meter) was restored by *ZPE**, which is better than reading the repeated οἱ in West's ἥ οἱ. The choice between ἡ δέ and Νύξ depends in large part on how one understands the line introducing OP**5:** τάδ' [ἐν ἐχομέν]ωι (Janko or [ἐπὶ τούτ]ωι Ts.) λέγει·. If the Author is proceeding to a new point, an anaphoric ἡ δέ (or better, ἥδε) is appropriate; but if he, as often, cites a passage to illustrate a point made earlier (cf. his quoting Heraclitus in col. 4, or the way col. 8.1 and 8.3 lead respectively to the quoting of 8.2 and 8.4–5), then Νύξ seems more likely. Since, as reconstructed here, Νύξ is not the first word of the sentence, there is no need for a connecting particle in any case, since, as Calame (2010:20) notes, there is frequent asyndeton in this poem.

⌞**Νὺξ**⌟ **ἔχρησεν**: A violation of Meyer's first law. West's conjecture is metrically less likely, but cf. 8 ἔκθορε̆ πρῶτος.

οἱ: Almost certainly Zeus, although Rusten (1981:131f.) is hesitant; see next lemma.

θέ[μις]: θέμις normally derives from the gods and rarely applies to gods themselves; cf. Hesiod *Theogony* 396 τὸν δ' ἔφαθ', ὅστις ἄτιμος ὑπὸ Κρόνου ἠδ' ἀγέραστος, | τιμῆς καὶ γεράων ἐπιβησέμεν, ἣ θέμις ἐστίν, but here it is generalized, unlike the Derveni restoration. See further H. Lloyd-Jones, *The Justice of Zeus* (Berkeley, 1971) 166n23, with bibliography. Athena can tell Ares what not to do («Ἆρες, ἔπισχε μένος κρατερὸν καὶ χεῖρας ἀάπτους· | οὐ γάρ τοι θέμις ἐστὶν ἀπὸ κλυτὰ τεύχεα δῦσαι | Ἡρακλέα κτείναντα,» [Hesiod] *Shield of Heracles* 446–448). Θέμις can come from Zeus or another god: υἷες Ἀχαιῶν ..., οἵ τε θέμιστας πρὸς Διὸς εἰρύαται (*Iliad* 1.237–239); cf. [Hesiod] *Shield of Heracles* 22 ὅ οἱ Διόθεν θέμις ἦεν. But what is the supposed sense of the restoration here? That it is "right" for Zeus to accomplish these things; or that he "should" do so? The former is possible (Night to Zeus would be like Athena to Ares); the latter may seem too strong, but is probably correct: Zeus here is subject to the demands of fate, just as any mortal is. And a god's "prophecy" may command rather than merely predict; cf. Thucydides 1.134.4 ὁ δὲ θεὸς ὁ ἐν Δελφοῖς τόν τε τάφον ὕστερον ἔχρησε τοῖς Λακεδαιμονίοις μετενεγκεῖν οὗπερ ἀπέθανε.

[ἐκτελέεσ]θ̣αι: The word to be supplied seems to have been paraphrased in the Author's preceding sentence as ποῶσι, the best Homeric word for which is (ἐκ)τελέεσθαι: *Iliad* 7.353, 12.217; cf. [Hesiod] *Shield of Heracles* 21–22 = fr. 195. ἐκτελέσαι μέγα ἔργον, ὅ οἱ Διόθεν θέμις ἦεν—whereas neither ἀνύσασθαι nor ἀνύεσθαι occurs in early epic, and indeed the middle occurs only once, at *Odyssey* 16.373 (as either ἀνύσσεσθαι or ἀνῦσεσθαι), and then not again until Pindar *Pythian* 2.49; cf. V. Magnien *Le futur grec* (Paris, 1912) 1.111; and the middle is generally rare. See Santamaría (2012:59–60), who prefers my second suggestion, ἦν τελεέσθαι.

OP**6** ὡς ἂν ἔ[χοι κά]τα καλὸν ἕδος νιφόεντος Ὀλύμπου

ἂν ἔ[χοι κά]τα: According to the papyrological description of Tsantsanoglou and Parássoglou, the restorations of West, Burkert, and Janko are inconsistent with the horizontal trace before the lacuna that could be the top only of Γ, Ε, Ζ, Ξ, Σ, or Τ. For tmesis with anastrophe when the preposition follows its verb, see H. W. Chandler, *Greek Accentuation*[2] (Oxford, 1881) ¶¶922–923. Kouremenos compares *Iliad* 2.699 τότε δ' ἤδη ἔχεν κάτα γαῖα μέλαινα, and *Odyssey* 9.6 ἢ ὅτ' ἐϋφροσύνη μὲν ἔχῃ κάτα δῆμον ἅπαντα. ὡς ἄν + optative (or subjunctive) is normal in Homer and epic in general, often at the beginning of the line and always so in Orphic literature; cf. *Orphic Hymn* 87.12 ὡς ἂν ἔοι, 62.11, 63.13.

The usual sense of this verb in early poetry (and prose) is, in order of increasing metaphorical sense, (i) "hold down, cover," (ii) "pervade," (iii) "suppress/control," (iv) "rule" (which is a political overlap and extension of [iii]). E.g. (i) *Odyssey* 11.302 τοὺς ἄμφω ζωοὺς κατέχει φυσίζοος αἶα; cf. *Iliad* 3.243. (ii) *Odyssey* 13.269 νὺξ δὲ μάλα δνοφερὴ κάτεχ' οὐρανόν. (iii) Bacchylides *Dithyramb* 3.28–29 [σ]ὺ δὲ βαρεῖαν κάτεχε μῆτιν; Theognis 602–603 τοιάδε καὶ Μάγνητας ἀπώλεσεν ἔργα καὶ ὕβρις, οἷα τὰ νῦν ἱερὴν τήνδε πόλιν κατέχει. (iv) Sophocles *Antigone* 609–610 (Ζεῦ,) δυνάστας | κατέχεις Ὀλύμπου | μαρμαρόεσσαν αἴγλαν; Euripides *Hecuba* 79–81 ὦ χθόνιοι θεοί, σώσατε παῖδ' ἐμόν, | ὃς μόνος οἴκων ἄγκυρ' ἔτ' ἐμῶν | τὴν χιονώδη Θρήικην κατέχει; *Orphic Hymn* 2.6 κατέχεις οἴκους πάντων; cf. ibid. 18.4, 27.5. Kouremenos considers the use of the verb in the *Antigone* passage equivalent to that in the Derveni Papyrus. Note, however, that the statement quoted is in direct answer to the chorus' own rhetorical question, τεάν, Ζεῦ, δύνασιν τίς ἀνδρῶν ὑπερβασία κατάσχοι; (604–605). That is, Sophocles' sentence entails the political sense of κατέχω, which perhaps cannot be dated before the second half of the fifth century, thus perhaps too late for a poem that quickly (how quickly depends on when one dates the Author) came to be taken as a work of Orpheus. Sense (iii) is probably best here.

ἕδος νιφόεντος Ὀλύμπου: Cf., with Bernabé, *Homeric Hymn to Heracles* 15.7–8 (Zeus) κατὰ καλὸν ἕδος νιφόεντος Ὀλύμπου | ναίει; Apollonius of Rhodes 1.503–504 (Orpheus) ἤειδεν δ' ὡς πρῶτον Ὀφίων Εὐρυνόμη τε | Ὠκεανὶς νιφόεντος ἔχον κράτος Οὐλύμποιο; *Orphic Hymn* 15.7 ἕδος νιφόεντος Ὀλύμπου; *Iliad* 24.144 ἕδος Οὐλύμποιο, 18.615 Ὀλύμπου νιφόεντος; Hesiod *Theogony* 42 νιφόεντος Ὀλύμπου. I omit the parallels adduced where Olympus is the ἕδος of the gods. Note also Hesiod *Theogony* 117–118 Γαῖ' εὐρύστερνος, πάντων ἕδος ἀσφαλὲς αἰεὶ | ἀθανάτων οἳ ἔχουσι κάρη νιφόεντος Ὀλύμπου (118 = 794 = *Orphic Hymn* 25.7 = 59.2).

OP**7** Ζεὺς μὲν ἐπεὶ δὴ π̣α̣τρ̣ὸς ἑοῦ πάρ̣α̣ [θ]ἐ̣σφατ' ἀκούσα[ς

See above, on OP**2**.

OP**8** αἰδοῖον κατ̣έπινεν, ὃς αἰθέρα ἔκθορ̣ε πρῶτος

Bernabé adds this line to OP**4**–OP**5**, which would indeed fit nicely, but the word ἀφα[ιρεῖ]ν in the sentence preceding the citation of CP**6** suggests that another line or two was quoted in the lines lost after OP**5**. Furthermore, the two lines can be consecutive only if αἰδοῖον is neuter, arguments against which I lay out below.

αἰδοῖον: Since Orphic verses tell of Zeus' swallowing of Protogonos, who is called αἰδοῖος at OP**13**.1 by Zeus, it is likely that αἰδοῖον is masculine singular; so West 1983:85–86 and Brisson 2003. Many, however, take the Author's allegoresis as fact, maintaining that αἰδοῖον is neuter, meaning "penis,"[21] but this sense of this word in the singular first appears only toward the end of the fifth century (three times in Herodotus, but he uses it far more often in the plural; Philolaos[?] B 13). The Author (of the late fifth, as I think, or early fourth century) himself uses the singular αἰδοῖον = genital organ only when specifically interpreting the αἰδοῖον of the poem in this way (col. 13.9 αἰδοίῳ εἰκάσας τὸν ἥλιον, 16.1 [αἰδοῖ]ον τὸν ἥλιον ἔφ[η]σεν εἶναι); elsewhere he reverts to the more normal plural; cf. col. 13.7–9 ἐν τοῖς α[ἰδοίο]ι̣ς ὁρῶν τὴν γένεσιν τοὺς ἀνθρώπου[ς] νομίζον̣[τας εἶ]ν̣αι τούτῳ ἐχρήσατο, ἄνευ δὲ τῶν̣ αἰδοίων̣ [οὐ γίν]ε̣σθαι, αἰδοίῳ εἰκάσας τὸν ἥλιο[ν]. In any case, it seems quite unlikely that an epic poet of the fifth century would use the singular in this sense. It is true that, as Burkert ibid. shows, there are Near Eastern stories with parallels for the swallowing of a god's penis, but it may well be that stories such as these led the Author to his interpretation.

Wild allegoresis is one thing; willful misreading something else. The Author, as Betegh (*per litt.*), emphasizes, must have understood the poem in this way. How could the Author, who presumably saw a complete poem, have gone so wrong? West (1983:85) thinks that his text was faulty. Perhaps the preceding line named Protogonos, which he took as an ordinary compound adjective, πρωτόγονος (as accented by editors) or, more likely, πρωτογόνος; cf. e.g. Orphic fr. 140 (cited several times by Damascius *De principiis*):

πρῶτον δαίμονα σεμνόν
Μῆτιν σπέρμα φέροντα θεῶν κλυτόν, ὅν τε Φάνητα
πρωτογόνον μάκαρες κάλεον.

21 E.g. Betegh 163; Janko (2001:24); Burkert, *Babylon, Memphis, Persepolis* (Cambridge, MA, 2004) 90–91; Bernabé (2007b:70–84).

"...the first august *daimon* to carry the seed of the gods, famed Metis, whom the blessed ones called Phanes *protogonos*" (where the epithet is clearly active). Cf. Orphic fr. 243.9 [*sc.* Ζεύς ἐστι] Μῆτις πρῶτος γενέτωρ. Damascius paraphrases as follows: Εἰ δὲ ὁ παρ' Ὀρφεῖ πρωτογόνος [again, I print paroxytone] θεὸς ὁ πάντων σπέρμα φέρων τῶν θεῶν ἀπὸ τοῦ ᾠοῦ πρῶτος ἐξέθορε. See further on OP**13**.1. It wouldn't take a great leap of allegoretic skill to apply the meaning "that which is the primary progenitor" to *aidoion* understood as a noun = "penis." For the paroxytone accentuation and the active meaning, see John Philoponus *De vocabulis*, recensio a π 20 πρωτογόνος· ἡ πρώτως τεκοῦσα παροξύνεται.

ὅς reads more easily in this one line with a masculine αἰδοῖον, but of course its antecedent could easily have been a genitive in the preceding line; Bernabé 1.19 suggests βασιλῆος or Οὐρανοῦ.

κατ̣έπινεν: Regularly used of the gulping down of solids, most notably and pertinently in Hesiod's *Theogony*, of Cronus' swallowing his children: 459 τοὺς μὲν κατέπινε μέγας Κρόνος, 467, 473.

αἰθέρα ἔκθορ̣ε: As in Hesiod, Aither, Chaos, and Chronos are early gods in Orphic cosmogonies. The *aither* from which the Orphic Phanes (who is nowhere named in the Derveni poem) derives is called "clouds" in later prose paraphrases; cf. Damascius *De principiis* 124 [I 317, 2–4 Ruelle] εἰς δὲ τὴν δευτέραν τελεῖν ἤτοι τὸ κυούμενον καὶ τὸ κύον ᾠὸν τὸν θεόν, ἢ τὸν ἀργῆτα χιτῶνα, ἢ τὴν νεφέλην, ὅτι ἐκ τούτων ἐκθρώσκει ὁ Φάνης. Attempts to read αἰθέρα as a terminal accusative are thus misguided, as the parallels in Orphic texts show. Furthermore, ... [ἐ]κ̣θό̣ρηι τὸν λαμπρότατόν τε [καὶ θε]ρ̣μ̣ό[τ]ατον (col. 14.1) shows that the Author copied his exemplar correctly; i.e. αἰθέρα ἔκθορ̣ε cannot be considered an error on his part. Even if he read the accusative as direct object, there is no reason for us to follow him; cf. Bernabé 2007b:86–87.

Why not the more usual genitive, as in Homer (*Iliad* 10.94–95 κραδίη δέ μοι ἔξω | στηθέων ἐκθρῴσκει) and everywhere else? αἰθέρος ἔκθορε would also avoid hiatus. The only parallel (adduced by Kouremenos) is from an anonymous late epigram, *Greek Anthology* 9.371.1 δίκτυον ἐκθρῴσκοντα πολύπλοκον ἄρτι λαγωόν, where Scaliger may have been right to conjecture δικτύου ... πολυπλόκου. It is possible that the hiatus was intentional, to make the leap vivid. And if we are willing to credit this Orphic bard with this bit of vivid writing, let us also note both that αἰθέρα and ἔκθορ̣ε each filling a dactylic foot gives the line what it is easy to call a jumpy aural effect, and that, although there is a midline break after ὅς, the line is in accord with Bulloch's law, for which see A. W. Bulloch, "A Callimachean Refinement to the Greek Hexameter," *Classical Quarterly* 20 (1970): 258–268. On this still vexed question, see Santamaría 2012:61–64 and Maria Scermino, "P. Derveni coll. XIII–XVI: Un mito, due frammenti, un rompicapo," in *Papiri filosofici: Miscellanea di Studi* VI. *Studi e testi per il corpus dei papiri filosofici greci e latini* (Florence, 2011) 55–90.

OP**9**–OP**10** ὃς μ̣έγ' ἔρεξεν
Οὐρανὸς Εὐφρονίδης, ὃς πρώτιστο̣ς βασίλευσεν

Between quoting these two lines, the Author says only τὸ δ' ἐπὶ τούτῳ·, which lacks the ἐχόμενον he uses elsewhere that would make it explicit that OP**10** followed immediately upon OP**9**, as West and Kouremenos believe, reading (see the *apparatus criticus*) Οὐρανὸν Εὐφρονίδην. The sense would now be Κρόνος μέγ' ἔρεξεν Οὐρανόν, i.e. "Cronos greatly harmed Ouranos." For ἔρεξεν as a euphemism (here for castration), see Burkert, *Homo Necans* (Berkeley, 1983) 3, who notes how this verb often substitutes for the act of killing in a sacrificial ritual; cf. Epicasta, ἣ μέγα ἔργον ἔρεξεν ἀϊδρείῃσι νόοιο | γημαμένη ᾧ υἷϊ (*Odyssey* 11.272–273), which conveys a similar sense of religious awe. For the double accusative construction that would be produced, cf. *Iliad* 3.354 ξεινοδόκον κακὰ ῥέξαι. Reading accusatives would furthermore account for what now looks like asyndeton in OP**10**, although, as Betegh (123n87) observes, this is not a major obstacle to retaining the nominatives; one can imagine that Οὐρανὸς Εὐφρονίδης is enjambed with a preceding nominative word or phrase. It would also be inept of Orpheus to link one ὅς-clause to another after only four words. On the whole, then, it seems best, or at any rate more cautious, to follow Π and retain the two nominatives.

Εὐφρονίδης: Cf. T. Corsten, *Die Inschriften von Kios* (Bonn, 1985) 21.6 (Late Hellenistic to early Imperial date) = *Epigrammatum Anthologia*, Appendix, ed. Cougny 4.49 Οὐρανὸς Εὐφρονίδης. Matronymics are unusual in Greek; cf. Apollo/Artemis Letoïdes, Cheiron Philyrides, Perseus Danaides, Ares Enyalios (< Enyo). Herakles is often called "the son of Alcmene," although no single matronymic is used, except for Bacchylides 5.71 Ἀλκμή<ν>ιος θαυμαστὸς ἥρως. Musaeus is the son of Μήνη (Hermesianax fr. 7.15). And the Molionĕ (dual) are called after their mother Molionē, according to Eustathius *Commentarii ad Homeri Iliadem* 3.319.4–11 van der Valk. Cf. further Herodian *Orthography* 3.2.435 Τὰ εἰς δης μητρωνυμικὰ διὰ τοῦ ι γράφεται οἷον Λητωΐδης ὁ υἱὸς τῆς Λητοῦς, Δαναΐδης ὁ υἱὸς τῆς Δανάης, Φιλυρίδης ὁ υἱὸς Φιλύρας. ὅθεν Νιοβίδης ὁ τῆς Νιόβης. ὅθεν τὸ Φιλομηλείδης τὸ παρ' Ὁμήρῳ οὐ λέγομεν εἶναι πατρωνυμικὸν οὐδὲ λέγομεν τὸν υἱὸν τῆς Φιλομήλας. ὄνομα κύριόν ἐστιν. εἰ γὰρ ἦν μητρωνυμικόν, διὰ τοῦ ι ὤφειλεν εἶναι· καὶ ὁ Διονύσιος λέγει ὅτι ἀπὸ μητέρων οὐ σχηματίζει πατρωνυμικὸν ὁ Ὅμηρος. W. R. Paton and E. L. Hicks, *Inscriptions of Cos* (Oxford, 1891) nos. 10 and 367 list citizens by both patronymic and matronymic. (Other cultures assign matronymics more freely, such as Russians and Ashkenazi Jews; see B. O. Unbegaun, *Russian Surnames* [Oxford, 1972] 21–22, 105–108, 124–125, 342–344.) For Ouranos as son of Night in Orphic theology, cf. Alexander of Aphrodisias *On Aristotle's Metaphysics* 821.11–12 κατ' Ὀρφέα τὸ Χάος γέγονεν, εἶθ' ὁ Ὠκεανός, τρίτον Νύξ, τέταρτον ὁ Οὐρανός, quoting the verse Οὐρανός, | ὃς πρῶτος βασίλευσε θεῶν μετὰ μητέρα Νύκτα.

Night might be given prominence by this matronymic because of her role as nurse in Orphic theology; cf. col. 10.11 **τροφ[ὸν** δὲ λέγων αὐ]τ̣ὴ̣ν̣ α̣ἰ̣ν̣ί̣[ζε]τ̣αι, which Kouremenos 184 reasonably combines with col. 10.9 **πανομφεύουσαν** (a hapax, obviously repeated from a lost lemma) and with Proclus *On Plato's Cratylus* 404b = 112 F θεῶν γὰρ τροφὸς ἀμβροσίη Νὺξ λέγεται (although not identified as an Orphic view by Proclus) to suggest that the missing line was —⏑ πανομφεύουσα θεῶν τροφὸς ἀμβροσίη Νύξ (6 F). Santamaría suggests [Ζηνὶ] πανομφεύουσα ⌊θεῶν⌋ τρόφος ἐξ ἀ̣[δύτοι]ο. There is also the question, as Betegh (*per litt.*) points out, "whether Ouranos had a father at all."

Night is euphemistically called *euphrone* as early as Hesiod *Works and Days* 560. Note also Heraclitus B 26, 57, 99, and, most interesting, 67, a fragment of Orphic-like polarities quoted by Hippolytus *Refutation of All Heresies* 9.10.8 ὁ θεὸς ἡμέρη εὐφρόνη, χειμὼν θέρος, πόλεμος εἰρήνη, κόρος λιμός. The word is then common in all three major tragedians, but to judge from its frequent occurrence in Hippocrates and Herodotus, *euphrone* became the usual word for "night" in Ionic (which includes Heraclitus).

βασίλευσεν: The aorist of this and similar verbs is often inceptive and must certainly be so in a genealogical narrative. With **πρῶτος**, the sense is that there was no king before Ouranos; that is, there was no hierarchy among the gods.

OP**11** ἐκ τοῦ δὴ Κρόνος α̣ὖτις, ἔπειτα δὲ μητίετα Ζεύς

α̣ὖτις[5½]: A frequent *sedes* for this word in early epic, but the sense "in turn, next," although frequent in Hesiod (especially, as here, in genealogies) and the Hymns, is not found in Homer; cf. *LfgrE* s.v. 3 b β. The alpha is dotted "because the foot of a right-hand oblique can be seen in the photograph and there is no other possibility of reading it" (Bernabé, *per litt.*).

μητίετα: The Author adduces the transparent meaning of this common early epic epithet of Zeus (thirty-five times) to argue that Orpheus equates Zeus with Nous, i.e. μῆτις.

OP**12** μῆτιν κα.[*ca.* 14]ẹν βασιληίδα τιṃ[ήν]
εσ.[ ].ạι ἶνạς ἀπ.[
εị[

1 μῆτιν: Since these lines are cited in order to show that Zeus is Nous (see above), lower-case *metis* is probably preferable (so Bernabé and Betegh 162–163) to seeing a reference to the distinct deity Metis (as in *ZPE**), who in Orphic texts is masculine and equated to Phanes and Zeus. And if this is indeed what the Author is doing, it is also likely that here at least he is adducing this passage from elsewhere in the poem.

βασιληίδα τιṃ[ήν]: The kingly honor in question is the very one of being king; cf. Proclus *On Plato's Cratylus* 105 μόνος ὁ Κρόνος, τὴν τετάρτην βασιλικὴν τάξιν κληρωσάμενος, παρὰ πάντας τοὺς ἄλλους ὑβριστικῶς δοκεῖ κατὰ τὸ μυθικὸν πρόσχημα προσδέχεσθαι καὶ ἐκ τοῦ Οὐρανοῦ τὸ σκῆπτρον καὶ μεταδιδόναι τῷ Διΐ· καὶ γὰρ ἡ Νὺξ παρ' ἑκόντος αὐτὸ λαμβάνει τοῦ Φάνητος·

σκῆπτρον δ' ἀριδείκετον εἷο χέρεσσιν
θῆκε θεᾶς Νυκτός, <ἵν' ἔχῃ> βασιληΐδα τιμήν. (168 F)

For this line end, always preceded by a form of ἔχειν (the simplex only), cf. Hesiod *Theogony* 462 ἐν ἀθανάτοις ἔχοι βασιληίδα τιμήν, Isyllus 64, and two oracles of Apollo (71.3, perhaps of the early fifth century, and 431.1 P-W), as well as in some later writers. It is therefore unlikely that a form of κατέχω (West, Janko) is to be read here.

2–3: Because no *paragraphos* is present in the left-hand margin and the poetic word ἶνας appears (as in OP**21**), it is likely that these two lines continue the poetic quotation, as noted by Ts.

OP**13** πρωτογόνου βασιλέως αἰδοίου, τῷ δ' ἄρα πάντες
ἀθάναṭοι προσέφυν μάκαρες θεοὶ ἠδ̣ὲ θέαιναι
καὶ ποταμοὶ καὶ κρῆναι ἐπήρατοι ἄλ̣λα τε πάντα,
ἅ̣σσα τότ' ἦν γεγαῶτ', αὐτὸς δ' ἄρα μοῦ̣νος ἔγεντο.

This, the longest fragment in the papyrus, presenting no textual problems (two alternate readings in *ZPE** can no longer be entertained), lays out the notion of a cosmic Zeus, who contains within himself all that was and all that is to be, as close parallels from other Orphic verses make clear, especially 243 and 245 F, which will be cited below. On the join between OP**13** and OP**14**, see below.

1 πρωτογόνου: See above, where I argue that the sense is not the passive "protogenous" (an archaic English word), but the active "first progenitor." Note 243.5 F Ζεὺς αὐτὸς ἁπάντων ἀρχιγένεθλος (where the immediate context strongly suggests an active meaning).

βασιλέως: On the vexed question of who this is (which would take us beyond our immediate concern with the poetic text), see Betegh 118–119, who argues for Ouranos.

1–4 πάντες ... ἄ̣λ̣λα τε πάντα: A similar listing of Zeus-contained gods also appears in the parallel texts; see e.g. 241.5–9 F:

αἰθέρος εὐρείης ἠδ' οὐρανοῦ ἀγλαὸν ὕψος,
πόντου τ' ἀτρυγέτου γαίης τ' ἐρικυδέος ἕδρη,
Ὠκεανός τε μέγας καὶ νείατα τάρταρα γαίης
καὶ ποταμοὶ καὶ πόντος ἀπείριτος ἄλλα τε πάντα
πάντες τ' ἀθάνατοι μάκαρες θεοὶ ἠδὲ θέαιναι.

2 προσέφυν: For this third-person-plural form, see *Odyssey* 5.481 ἀλλήλοισιν ἔφυν; Pindar *Pythian* 1.42 περίγλωσσοι τ' ἔφυν. This verb usually indicates close/tight attachment of something that still retains its distinct nature; see *Odyssey* 12.433 (Odysseus holding on to the rock between Scylla and Charybdis) τῷ προσφὺς ἐχόμην. Aristotle uses it frequently of eggs and embryos attached to the womb, which seems an apt parallel; cf. *Historia animalium* 538a10 ἐν τῇ ὑστέρᾳ [*sc.* τὰ ᾠά] ἔχει καὶ προσπεφυκότα.

As noted above, similar Orphic verses spell out the meaning here, so that we can rule out "be born in addition"; cf. Hesychius π 3751 Hansen προσέφυ· προσεγένετο (for which in this sense, see LSJ s.v. 2). Orphism equates many gods and contains many stories of gods being swallowed by others, only to be reborn; that is, to regain their separate existence later. This fragment describes the time(s) when Zeus *protogonos* contains the others gods within himself. Cf. 243.7–10 F [Ζεύς] ἐν ᾧ τάδε πάντα κυκλεῖται ... πάντα γὰρ ἐν μεγάλου Ζηνὸς τάδε σώματι κεῖται (~ 245.5 F πάντα γὰρ ἐν Ζηνὸς μεγάλῳ τάδε σώματι κεῖται), 241.2 F τῶν πάντων δέμας εἶχεν ἐνὶ γαστέρι κοίλῃ.

θεοὶ ἠ̣δ̣ὲ θέαιναι: A variation of the epic formula (πάντες τε) θεοὶ πᾶσαί τε θέαιναι (*Iliad* 8.5, 20, 19.101, *Odyssey* 8.341, *Homeric Hymn to Apollo* 311).

4 ἅ̣σσα τότ' ἦν γεγαῶτ': The list given at 241.5–9 F (see above) is likewise followed by ὅσσα τ' ἔην γεγαῶτα. The Orphic author may have been influenced by Ibycus, who alludes to the birth of the Moliones from a silver egg: τούς τε λευκίππους κόρους | τέκνα Μολιόνας κτάνον, | ἅλικας ἰσοκεφάλους ἑνιγυίους | ἀμφοτέρους γεγαῶτας ἐν ὠέῳ | ἀργυρέῳ (fr. 285 *PMG*).

OP**14** [νῦν δ' ἐστὶ]ν βασιλεὺς πάντ̣[ων καί τ' ἔσσετ' ἔπ]ειτα

The Author may introduce this line with the words [ἔτι δὲ ἐν τῶι ἐχ]ο̣μένωι, "and then in the following line," which, if correctly restored, would indeed make for a nice fit with OP**13**.

βασιλεὺς πάντ̣[ων: Cf. Hesiod fr. 308.1 M-W αὐτὸς γὰρ πάντων βασιλεὺς; Corinna fr. 654.iii.13 *PMG* Δεὺς πατεὶ[ρ πάντω]ν βασιλεύς; and, most famously, Pindar fr. 169.1 Νόμος ὁ πάντων βασιλεὺς θνατῶν τε καὶ ἀθανάτων.

OP**15** Ζεὺς πρῷτος [γέν]ẹτο, ⌊Ζεὺς⌋ ⌊ὕστατος⌋ [ἀργικέραυνος]

The first three words are (re)quoted ([λέ]γẹι) at col. 18.12–13. Since OP**16** (on which see below) appears twice elsewhere in Orphic poetry preceded by this line, the Author's statement (col. 17.6) that ὕστατον ἔφησεν ἔσεσθαι τοῦτον (hence the "will be" in the translation) strongly suggests that it did so here as well.

[ἀργικέραυνος]: Zeus' epithet below, OP**18**, as well as three times in Homer (in the vocative), Pindar *Olympian* 8.3, Bacchylides 5.58 (by sure conjecture), and Cleanthes 1.32.

OP**16** Ζεὺς κεφạ⌊λή⌋, [Ζεὺς μέσ]σ̣α̣, Δ̣ιὸς δ' ἐκ̣ [π]άντα τέτ̣[υκται]

= 31.2 = 243.2 F.

OP**17** [Ζεὺς πνοίη πάντων, Ζεὺς πάντων ἔπλετο] ⌊μοῖρα⌋

Col. 18 begins '[τὴν δὲ Μοῖρα]ν φάμενος [δηλοῖ]' τήνδ[ε γῆν] καὶ τἆλλα πάν[τ]α̣ εἶναι | ἐν τῶι ἀέρι̣ [πνε]ῦμα ἐόν. τοῦτ' οὖν τὸ πνεῦμα Ὀρφεὺς | ὠνόμασεν Μοῖρα̣ν, which, as Merkelbach (*ZPE* 1 [1967]: 24) saw, looks like a prose paraphrase of 31.5 F Ζεὺς πνοίη πάντων, comparing col. 19.1–4. Further supporting this is that Orpheus in the papyrus is cited for some of the same lines as are found in 31 F, as well as in the similar 243 F; see comm. on OP**16** and OP**18**. Merkelbach (ibid.) completed the line with a conjecture that accounts for Μοῖρα, replicating the frequent asyndeton found in 31 and 243 F, but since Moira does not figure much in other Orphic verses, the second half cannot be as persuasive as the first. On the whole, though, Merkelbach's line is more convincing than West's [Ζεὺς πάντων τέλος αὐτὸς ἔχει, Ζεὺς] Μοῖρα [κραταιή].

OP**18** Ζεὺς βασιλεύς, Ζεὺς δ' ἀρχὸς ἁπάν̣τ̣ων ἀργικέραυνος.

= 31.7 F. Cf. also 243.4–5 F Ζεὺς βασιλεύς, Ζεὺς αὐτὸς ἁπάντων ἀρχιγένεθλος. | ἓν κράτος, εἷς δαίμων, γενέτης μέγας, ἀρχὸς ἁπάντων.

ἀρχός: In Homer, exclusively of mortals; in *Homeric Hymn to Hermes* 292, Hermes is the ἀρχός of thieves; next again used of a god (Helios) by Pindar *Olympian* 7.71. Perhaps there is meant to be an echo here of 2 ἀρχήν, as suggested by Bernabé (2007a:104).

OP**19** (Πειθώ θ' Ἁρμονίην τε καὶ Οὐρανίην Ἀφροδίτην)

Orpheus has clearly been joining several gods under the same name—Ἀφροδίτη Οὐρανία | καὶ Ζεὺς καὶ ἀφροδισιάζειν κ̣αὶ θόρνυσθαι καὶ Πειθὼ | καὶ Ἁρμονία τῶι αὐτῶι θεῶι ὄνομα κεῖται (col. 21.5–7)—but his syntax cannot be recovered and Kouremenos' reconstructed line is best accepted only *exempli gratia*. This fragment number would be better served with the one word **θόρνῃ** (cf. col. 21.1 θόρ{ν}ηι δὲ λέγ[ων]), a *hapax* which the context clearly associates with other words (such as ἀφροδισιάζειν, col. 21.8) for sexual intercourse, a metaphorical sense of "jump" found elsewhere; cf. Nicander *Theriaca* 99 with *schol. ad loc.* θορνύντα· ὀχεύοντα. (Ts. [1997:19n53] tentatively suggested that θόρηι should be retained.)

OP**20** μήσατο <δ'> Ὠκεανοῖο μέγα σθένος εὐρὺ ῥέοντος

As noted in the *apparatus criticus*, West, quite convincingly, puts together a verse from the poetic words embedded in the Author's text. The subject is almost certainly Zeus, but in a context where one god goes under many names, I've left a blank in the translation.

εὐρὺ ῥέοντος: Ending the line likewise four times in Homer: *Iliad* 2.849, 16.288, 21.157, 186.

OP**21** ἶνας δ' ἐγκ̣α̣τ̣[έλε]ξ' Ἀχελωΐου ἀργυ̣[ρ]οδίν̣ε̣⌞ω⌟

ἶνας ... ἀργυ[ρ]οδίν̣ε̣⌞ω⌟: The Author not only sees veins within Acheloius literally (by means of allegoresis; see next lemma), he also seems to detect it in Orpheus' words; that is, ἶνας ἀργυροδίνεω. This is shown by the Author's unusual use of the demonstrative adjective, so that aurally τάσδ' ἶνας ~ τὰς δίνας (col. 23.13)—unusual for him, that is; he uses the demonstrative pronoun often enough, but not the demonstrative adjective. Since the usual phrase is in the singular—cf. *Iliad* 21.356 ἲς ποταμοῖο, Pindar fr. 70 + *249b ἲς Ἀχελωΐου—something like this may have been in the mind of the poet as well as of the Author; cf. Kouremenos KPT 259. The adjective is used exclusively of rivers and quite often of Acheloius: Hesiod *Theogony* 340; Panyassis fr. 28.1 Matthews = 31.1 Bernabé; Callimachus *Hymn to Demeter* 13; Dionysius Periegetes 433, 1140.

Ἀχελωΐου: There are several fifth-century passages where "Acheloius" is used for water in general: Euripides *Andromache* 167, *Bacchae* 625, *Hypsipyle* fr. 753, fr. 365; Sophocles *Athamas* fr. 5; Achaeus *Aithon* 20 F 9 *TrGF*; Aristophanes *Lysistrata* 381 (water in a bucket, an inappropriate and hence intentionally pompous example); cf. Bond on *Hypsipyle* fr. 753 (p. 86). These can be regarded as simple metonymy, but as the adjective ἀργυροδίνεω shows (see below), Orpheus is referring to Acheloius not only in his original role as river, but more specifically as the river that once seems to have had something of the same status as Oceanus. Cf. Servius on Vergil *Georgics* 1.8 = Orpheus F 154 Bernabé *nam, sicut Orpheus docet et Aristophanes comicus et Ephorus historicus tradunt, Acheloon generaliter propter antiquitatem fluminis omnem aquam veteres vocabant*; Ephorus *ap.* Macrobius *Saturnalia* 5.18.7 = *FGrHist* 70 F 20a τοῖς μὲν οὖν ἄλλοις ποταμοῖς οἱ πλησιόχωροι μόνοι θύουσιν, τὸν δὲ Ἀχελῷον μόνον πάντας ἀνθρώπους συμβέβηκεν τιμᾶν, οὐ τοῖς κοινοῖς ὀνόμασιν ἀντὶ τῶν ἰδίων <ὀνομάζοντες τοὺς ἄλλους ποταμούς, ἀλλὰ> τοῦ Ἀχελῴου τὴν ἰδίαν ἐπωνυμίαν ἐπὶ τὸ κοινὸν μεταφέροντας. τὸ μὲν γὰρ ὕδωρ ὅλως, ὅπερ ἐστὶν κοινὸν ὄνομα, ἀπὸ τῆς ἰδίας ἐκείνου προσηγορίας Ἀχελῷον καλοῦμεν, τῶν δὲ ἄλλων ὀνομάτων τὰ κοινὰ πολλάκις ἀντὶ τῶν ἰδίων ὀνομάζομεν τοὺς μὲν Ἀθηναίους Ἴωνας, τοὺς δὲ Λακεδαιμονίους Πελοποννησίους ἀποκαλοῦντες. τούτου δὲ τοῦ ἀπορήματος οὐδὲν ἔχομεν αἰτιώτατον εἰπεῖν ἢ τοὺς ἐκ Δωδώνης χρησμούς· σχεδὸν γὰρ ἐν ἅπασιν αὐτοῖς προστάττειν ὁ θεὸς εἴωθεν Ἀχελῴῳ θύειν, ὥστε πολλοὶ νομίζοντες οὐ τὸν ποταμὸν τὸν διὰ τῆς Ἀκαρνανίας ῥέοντα, ἀλλὰ τὸ σύνολον ὕδωρ Ἀχελῷον ὑπὸ τοῦ χρησμοῦ καλεῖσθαι, μιμοῦνται τὰς τοῦ θεοῦ προσηγορίας. σημεῖον δὲ ὅτι πρὸς τὸ θεῖον ἀναφέροντες οὕτω λέγειν εἰώθαμεν· μάλιστα γὰρ τὸ ὕδωρ Ἀχελῷον προσαγορεύομεν ἐν τοῖς ὅρκοις καὶ ἐν ταῖς εὐχαῖς καὶ ἐν ταῖς θυσίαις, ἅπερ πάντα περὶ τοὺς θεούς. Note also *schol. ad Iliad* 21.195 (*P.Oxy.* 221 col. 9.21) Ἔφορος δ' ἐν β΄ [φησὶ] τὸ ἐν Δωδώνῃ μαντεῖον σχεδὸν ἐν ἅπασι τοῖς χρησμοῖς προστάττειν Ἀχελῴῳ θύειν, ὅθεν τοὺς Ἕλληνας πάν[τ]ạ[ς] πọτạμ̣ὸν νομίζειν Ἀχελῷον; *schol. ad Iliad* 24.616b Erbse καὶ πᾶν ὕδωρ Ἀχελῷόν φασιν. See further Betegh 215–217. Note, however, *Iliad* 21.194–195, where Acheloius and Oceanus are distinguished (οὐδὲ ... Ἀχελώϊος ... οὐδὲ ... Ὠκεανός).

ἐγκ̣ạτ̣[έλε]ξ̣': Although the Author glosses this word (in the infinitive) as ἐ̣γ̣κ̣ạτῶ̣[σ]ạι (23.13), a *hapax* presumably meaning something like "push down in(to)," an unknown sense of ἐγκαταλέγω, it may be that Orpheus' meaning is rather "assigned/allotted," as in Hesychius ε 210 ἐγκεκλάρωται· ἐγκαταλέγει. The first word is found elsewhere only at Aelian *Varia historia* 8.1 (*v.l.* συγκεκ-), applied to Socrates' daimonic voice. Moreover, the sense "assigned" for ἐγκαταλέγειν is found nowhere else. Nonetheless, for all the tenuousness of these links, the meaning of this line may be something like "Zeus assigned the veins of Acheloius"; that is, with Acheloius = water in general—as the Author says and as D'Alessio has shown to be an early belief—"Zeus allotted each of the veins of water," which now means that Zeus ordered the disposition of the earth's various bodies of water (πάντες ποταμοὶ καὶ πᾶσα θάλασσα | καὶ πᾶσαι κρῆναι καὶ φρέατα μακρά, *Iliad* 21.196–197, introduced by ἐξ οὗ, whose reference D'Alessio shows is Acheloius, not Oceanus).

Thus the primary sense of ἶνας is indeed "sinews" or "veins," not "strength," although, as D'Alessio argues, the latter is not totally to be precluded from the semantic range of this word in poetic texts, especially given μέγα σθένος Ὠκεανοῖο (*Iliad* 18.607 = 21.195). Veins, though, are to be understood metaphorically as the various flowing bodies of water, all of which derive from Oceanus/Acheloius—in other words "the veins of Acheloius" is a kenning, as West saw, comparing Choerilus 2 *TrGF* γῆς φλέβας [*sc.* τοὺς ποταμούς]; cf. I. Wærn, *ΓΗΣ ΟΣΤΕΑ: The Kenning in Pre-Christian Greek Poetry* (Uppsala, 1951) 95–96. The image is spelled out in [Hippocrates] *De Hebdomadibus* c.6 1.22ff. Roscher *aqua ... fluminum imitatio est venae et qui in venis est sanguinis*, a text dated ca. 60–30 BC by J. Mansfeld, *The Pseudo-Hippocratic Tract Περὶ Ἑβδομάδων Ch. 1-11 and Greek Philosophy* (Assen, 1970) 229–230. That is, the Author has taken the Homeric ἲς ποταμοῖο (*Iliad* 21.356), where the sense is "the river's strength," made it plural, and returned the metaphor to its original meaning. Note too that the Choerilus phrase is parallel only with φλέβες = ἶνες; the genitives are different. γῆς is possessive; Ἀχελῴου is the same to a certain extent (they are indeed his veins), but also and more so genitive of material; i.e. veins (consisting) of water.

This sense seems preferable to that of LSJ s.v. 1 "build in," for which they adduce Thucydides 1.93.2 πολλαί τε στῆλαι ἀπὸ σημάτων καὶ λίθοι εἰργασμένοι ἐγκατελέγησαν and (in the Suppl.) Callimachus *Aetia* fr. 64.7 Pf. (*The Tomb of Simonides*) πύργῳ δ' ἐγκατέλεξεν ἐμὴν λίθον, where the reference (the embedding of carved stelae into other structures) is so close to Thucydides' that one wonders whether there is an allusion here to Simonidean inscribed epigrams being used to build Themistocles' Long Walls. See also Suda ε 77 Ἐγκατελέγησαν λίθοι: ἀντὶ τοῦ ἐγκατῳκοδομήθησαν.

OP**22** ἣ πολλοῖς φαίνει μερόπεσσ' ἐπ' ἀπείρονα γαῖαν

Since immediately before adducing this line, the Author says the following of the moon: ὅσα δ[ὲ μ]ὴ κυκλοειδέα οὐχ οἷόν τε **ἰσομελῆ** εἶναι, it seems almost certain that he found the hexametrical *hapax* ἰσομελῆ (though not necessarily in the accusative) in a nearby verse, which, context suggests, must apply to the moon. Merkelbach tentatively conjectured ἰσομελὴς δ' ἄρ' ὑπέρβαλεν ἄστρα σελήνη. For a moon with limbs, cf. Empedocles B 31, which refers to the γυῖα of the Sphere; see further Kouremenos (in KPT) *ad loc.*, against Betegh 247–248, who prefers to take the "limbs" literally and have them refer to the horns of the moon. These do in fact figure in many lunar descriptions, but this epithet is largely meaningless, since the horns must needs always be equal. All that can differ is whether the line drawn through the points of the horn are upright or tilted; cf. Theophrastus *De signis* 27.

This verse is introduced with the words δηλοῖ δὲ τόδε, which elsewhere in the papyrus assumes a poet as subject, most likely Orpheus, although in these cases the verb is fleshed out with ἐν τούτῳ/τούτοις. Kouremenos would thus seem to be justified in assuming τὸ ἔπος as subject here from the words of the Author immediately following: τοῦτο τὸ ἔπος δόξειεν ἄν τις ἄλλως ε<ἰ>ρῆσθαι.

ἥ: Selene, as the Author's context makes clear. Elsewhere in Orphic literature, Zeus is either simply equated with Selene (Ζεὺς Ἥλιος ἠδὲ Σελήνη 31.6 F), or, in a descriptive passage on Zeus' body reminiscent of the Metaphysical poets, the sun and the moon are his eyes, ὄμματα δ' ἠέλιός τε καὶ ἀντιόωσα σελήνη (243.16 F). In another fragment, Selene is listed with fire, water, earth, heaven, Phanes, and night as the ἀθανάτων γεννήτορας (619 F). There is nothing so overtly theological or allegorical in this isolated line, but it could readily serve as a descriptive expansion in such a context. Cf. Hesiod *Theogony* 372 ἣ πάντεσσι ἐπιχθονίοισιν φαείνει.

ἐπ' ἀπείρονα γαῖαν: = *Iliad* 7.446; *Odyssey* 25.79, 17.386; Hesiod *Theogony* 187, *Works and Days* 487, fr. 43a.83 (same *sedes*); *Iliad* 24.342; *Odyssey* 1.98.

OP**23** [αὐτ]ὰ̣ρ̣ [ἐ]π̣εὶ δ[ὴ πάν]τ̣α Διὸ[ς νοῦς μή]σατ̣[ο ἔ]ρ̣γ̣α̣

[αὐτ]ὰ̣ρ̣ [ἐ]π̣εὶ δ[ή]: Twenty-eight times in Homer, and often in the *Homeric Hymns*.

νοῦς: The φρήν can be "turned" (of Zeus; *Iliad* 10.45), and can remember, learn, and experience various feelings, but, although there is no reason why the *phren* should not actively plan and execute, nowhere in early Greek literature does it actually do so. It is significant that the only time the nominative singular occurs in Homer (see above), it is the subject of a passive verb. The plural nominative is common in Homer, but whether steadfast or not, they do not serve in any executive role; note e.g. *Iliad* 1.103–104 = *Odyssey* 4.661 μένεος δὲ μέγα φρένες ἀμφιμέλαιναι πίμπλαντ', 10.10 τρομέοντο δέ οἱ φρένες ἐντός. Elsewhere mental activity occurs *in* or *in accord with* one's *phren*; cf. S. D. Sullivan, *Psychological Activity in Homer* (Ottawa, 1988) 188, "nowhere [*sc.* in Homer] will it be said that it is *phrenes* that make a choice." The closest one finds in later literature are several passages where one's own *phren* "makes" or "puts" a person in one or another state of mind; cf. Aeschylus *Persians* 769 φρένες γὰρ αὐτοῦ θυμὸν ᾠακοστρόφουν, Aristophanes *Lysistrata* 708–709. Note, though, Aeschylus *Suppliants* 598–599 ἔπος σπεῦσαί τι τῶν βούλιος φέρει φρήν; Euripides *Iphigenia Among the Taurians* 655 ἔτι γὰρ ἀμφίλογα δίδυμα μέμονε φρήν.

Nous, on the other hand, unlike *phren*, figures often in the Author's text, sometimes suggesting that it was in an Orphic verse, most notably soon after quoting OP**23**: col. 26.1 μήτηρ ὁ Ν̣ο̣ῦ̣ς ἐστιν τῶν ἄλλων̣. *Nous*, furthermore, plays an active role in the formation of the universe in Anaxagoras' cosmology; cf. B 12 καὶ γνώμην γε περὶ παντὸς πᾶσαν ἴσχει καὶ ἰσχύει μέγιστον [*sc.* νοῦς]· καὶ ὅσα γε ψυχὴν ἔχει καὶ τὰ μείζω καὶ τὰ ἐλάσσω, πάντων νοῦς κρατεῖ. καὶ τῆς περιχωρήσιος τῆς συμπάσης νοῦς ἐκράτησεν, ὥστε περιχωρῆσαι τὴν ἀρχήν....καὶ τὰ συμμισγόμενά τε καὶ ἀποκρινόμενα καὶ διακρινόμενα πάντα ἔγνω νοῦς. καὶ ὁποῖα ἔμελλεν ἔσεσθαι καὶ ὁποῖα ἦν, ἅσσα νῦν μὴ ἔστι, καὶ ὅσα νῦν ἐστι καὶ ὁποῖα ἔσται, πάντα διεκόσμησε νοῦς, καὶ τὴν περιχώρησιν ταύτην, ἣν νῦν περὶ χωρέει τά τε ἄστρα καὶ ὁ ἥλιος καὶ ἡ σελήνη καὶ ὁ ἀὴρ καὶ ὁ αἰθὴρ οἱ ἀποκρινόμενοι; see also B 13. Note too Euripides *Trojan Women* 886 Ζεὺς εἴτ' ἀνάγκη φύσεος εἴτε νοῦς βροτῶν. This would provide yet another link between the Derveni Papyrus and Anaxagoras, and perhaps Diogenes of Apollonia as well; cf. W. Burkert, "Orpheus und die Vorsokratiker," *Antike und Abendland* 14 (1968): 93–114; Janko 2002:3–4; A. Laks, *Diogène d'Apollonie*[2] (Sankt Augustin, 2008) 269–274 ("À propos du papyrus de Derveni").

Normally one should not restore in violation of Naeke's (or anybody's) law, but this is acceptable here (whether with νοῦς with or φρήν) because in our small sample of Orphic verses in the papyrus we find 13.1 αἰδοίου|[8], 16 Δ̣ιὸς δ' ἐκ |[8] (where ἐκ looks backward not forward), and 18 ἁπάντων|[8].

μή]σατ̣[ο ἔ]ρ̣γα̣: As in *Iliad* 10.289; *Odyssey* 3.261, 24.199, 24.444; Hesiod *Theogony* 166, 172.

OP**24** μητρὸς ἑᾶς ἔθελεν μιχθήμεναι ἐν φιλότητι

As the *apparatus criticus* shows, this verse can be regarded only as a re-creation *exempli gratia*, however reasonable and attractive, and as such does not warrant much comment.

μιχθήμεναι ἐν φιλότητι: The preposition is not necessary, but cf. *Iliad* 2.232 μίσγεαι ἐν φιλότητι, 14.237 παραλέξομαι ἐν φιλότητι; *Homeric Hymn to the Dioscuri* 33.5 init. μιχθεῖσ' ἐν φιλότητι.

Bibliography and Abbreviations

Bernabé [*simpliciter*] = Alberto Bernabé, *Poetae epici Graeci: Testimonia et fragmenta*, pars 2, fasc. 1–3 (Berlin, 2004–2007).

Bernabé, Alberto. 2007a. "The Derveni Theogony: Many Questions and Some Answers." *Harvard Studies in Classical Philology* 103:99–133.

———. 2007b. "Autour de l'interprétation des colonnes xiii–xvi du Papyrus de Derveni." *Rhizai* 4:77–103.

Betegh = Gábor Betegh, *The Derveni Papyrus: Cosmology, Theology, and Interpretation* (Cambridge, 2004).

Brisson, Luc. 1997. "Chronos in Col. XII of the Derveni Papyrus." In Laks and Most 1997:149–165.

———. 2003. "Sky, Sex, and Sun: The Meaning of αἰδοῖος/αἰδοῖον in the Derveni Papyrus." *Zeitschrift für Papyrologie und Epigraphik* 144:19–29.

Calame, Claude. 1997. "Figures of Sexuality and Initiatory Transition in the Derveni Theogony and Its Commentary." In Laks and Most 1997:65–80.

———. 2010. "The Authority of Orpheus, Poet and Bard: Between Tradition and Written Practice." In *Allusion, Authority, and Truth: Critical Perspectives on Greek Poetic and Rhetorical Praxis* (ed. P. Mitsis and C. Tsagalis) 13–35. Berlin.

D'Alessio, Giovan Battista. 2004. "Textual Fluctuations and Cosmic Streams: Ocean and Acheloios." *Journal of Hellenic Studies* 124:416–437.

Janko, Richard. 2001. "The Derveni Papyrus (Diagoras of Melos, *Apopyrgizontes Logoi*?): A New Translation." *Classical Philology* 96:1–32.

———. 2002. "The Derveni Papyrus: An Interim Text." *Zeitschrift für Papyrologie und Epigraphik* 141:1–62.

———. 2008. "Reconstructing (Again) the Opening of the Derveni Papyrus." *Zeitschrift für Papyrologie und Epigraphik* 166:37–51.

KPT = Theokritos Kouremenos, George M. Parássoglou, and Kyriakos Tsantsanoglou, *The Derveni Papyrus, Edited with Introduction and Commentary* (Florence, 2006).

Laks, André, and Glenn W. Most, eds. 1997. *Studies in the Derveni Papyrus*. Oxford.

Merkelbach, Reinhold. 1967. "Der orphische Papyrus des Derveni." *Zeitschrift für Papyrologie und Epigraphik* 1:21–32.

Π = the Derveni Papyrus.

Rusten, Jeffrey. 1989. "Interim Notes on the Papyrus from Derveni." *Harvard Studies in Classical Philology* 89:121–140.

Santamaría, Marco Antonio. 2012. "Critical Notes to the Orphic Poem of the Derveni Papyrus." *Zeitschrift für Papyrologie und Epigraphik* 182:55–76.

Ts. = Kyriakos Tsantsanoglou.

Tsantsanoglou, Kyriakos. 1997. "The First Columns of the Derveni Papyrus and Their Religious Significance." In Laks and Most 1997:93–128.

West, Martin. 1983. *The Orphic Poems*. Oxford.

*ZPE** = Anonymi, "Der orphische Papyrus von Derveni," *Zeitschrift für Papyrologie und Epigraphik* 47 (1982): 1*–12* (following 300).

13

The Garland of Hippolytus[1]

Richard Hunter

Trinity College, University of Cambridge

ONE OF THE MOST CELEBRATED EURIPIDEAN PASSAGES is the dedicatory address and prayer which Hippolytus offers to Artemis as he places a garland at her statue, immediately after the hymn which he and his fellow-huntsmen have sung to her as they enter.

σοὶ τόνδε πλεκτὸν στέφανον ἐξ ἀκηράτου
λειμῶνος, ὦ δέσποινα, κοσμήσας φέρω,
ἔνθ' οὔτε ποιμὴν ἀξιοῖ φέρβειν βοτὰ
οὔτ' ἦλθέ πω σίδηρος, ἀλλ' ἀκήρατον
μέλισσα λειμῶν' ἠρινὴ διέρχεται,
αἰδὼς δὲ ποταμίαισι κηπεύει δρόσοις,
ὅσοις διδακτὸν μηδὲν ἀλλ' ἐν τῆι φύσει
τὸ σωφρονεῖν εἴληχεν ἐς τὰ πάντ' ἀεί,
τούτοις δρέπεσθαι, τοῖς κακοῖσι δ' οὐ θέμις.
ἀλλ', ὦ φίλη δέσποινα, χρυσέας κόμης
ἀνάδημα δέξαι χειρὸς εὐσεβοῦς ἄπο.
μόνωι γάρ ἐστι τοῦτ' ἐμοὶ γέρας βροτῶν·
σοὶ καὶ ξύνειμι καὶ λόγοις ἀμείβομαι,
κλύων μὲν αὐδῆς, ὄμμα δ' οὐχ ὁρῶν τὸ σόν.
τέλος δὲ κάμψαιμ' ὥσπερ ἠρξάμην βίου.

Mistress, I bring you this woven garland which I have fashioned from an unravaged meadow, where no herdsman chooses to graze his animals nor has iron ever passed there, but in the springtime the bee traverses the unravaged meadow and *Aidôs* nurtures it with river waters; those who have no share in the taught, but in whose natures *sôphrosynê* has

[1] I am grateful to Hans Bernsdorff and audiences in Cambridge, Frankfurt, Ioannina, Leiden, Sydney, Thessaloniki, and Washington, DC, for helpful discussion of earlier versions. This article first appeared as "The Garland of Hippolytus" in *Trends in Classics* 1.1 (2003): 18–35.

> its place in all things for all time—these may pluck [from the meadow], but for the wicked it is not permitted. Mistress of mine, receive from a pious hand a wreath to bind your golden hair. Alone of men do I enjoy this privilege, for I keep company with you and converse with you, hearing your voice, though I do not see your face. May I end my life as I have begun it.
>
> Euripides *Hippolytus* 73–87

The extant *scholia* on these famous verses offer a compilation of detailed and rather remarkable readings, extracts from which deserve to be quoted at length:[2]

> *Scholion on line 73*: "This is a notorious problem [*zêtêma*]. Some suppose that Hippolytus garlands Artemis with a garland of flowers, but others suppose that Hippolytus is saying this about himself, namely 'Goddess, I dedicate myself as a garland to you,' that is, as the most blooming ornament [*kosmos*], for it is an ornament to the virgin to pass time with the most *sôphrôn* of the young men. Others say that the poet is not riddling [αἰνίττεσθαι] or allegorizing at all, but using words in their straightforward sense [κυρίως λέγειν] and Hippolytus is in fact carrying a garland which he derived from a meadow in which it is not holy [ὅσιον] for us to pluck flowers. 'Iron has never entered it' [line 76] indicates that the meadow has never been cropped or worked by anyone. Others say that Euripides metaphorically [τροπικώτερον] calls the hymn to Artemis a garland, for it would be remarkably strange to imagine that there was a flowery meadow where flowers were picked and it was of such a kind that those who entered were examined as to whether their *sôphrosunê* was taught or naturally acquired and the meadow was irrigated by *aidôs*. Like a philosopher he says that he is bringing a woven garland to the statue, a hymn to the god. 'From an unravaged [meadow]' means 'from my mind [διάνοια], which lacks deceit and corruption.'"
>
> *Alternatively*: "Poets quite reasonably liken their own natures to meadows or rivers or bees, and their poetry to garlands: the flowers indicate the variety and beauty of poetry, the rivers its mass and the impetus [ὁρμή] to creation, the bees its sweetness, and the garlands the honor [*kosmos*] of the subjects of song. The poet has combined all of these things and thus made the nature of his allegory more brilliant [ἐφαίδρυνε]. 'From an unravaged meadow' indicates that someone who

2 I generally follow Schwartz's text, though more work clearly needs to be done on the text of the *scholia*.

is to practice *mousikê* must have a soul which is pure and unravaged, unstained by any evil, and most of all partakes of *aidôs*. It is because of the importance of *aidôs* that they represent the Muses, who are most fertile [γονιμώταται], as virgins."

Alternatively: "... He calls the hymn a woven garland because they compose hymns by putting together words as in weaving. The unravaged meadow from where the flowers are woven into the garland and where not even a shepherd thinks it proper to graze his animals is an allegory for a virginal and undeceitful intention [ἔννοια]. The flowers of this meadow are the results of wisdom and virtue. No iron has come to cut this meadow and crop its flowers; by 'iron' he means either evil meddlesomeness [φιλοπραγμονία] and wrongdoing or the corruption of shameful pleasures, and in this way he makes clear Hippolytus' virginal and guileless character. The bee, however, is an allegory of the soul itself, for the bee is the purest of creatures (whence poets call priestesses 'bees'). He calls it[3] 'of the springtime' either because bees rejoice in the spring because of the flowers or because pure souls are always blooming, and spring is when flowers are produced."

Scholion on line 78: "This cannot be understood if one wants to understand it literally [κυρίως] as being about gardens. Therefore there is an allegory here. Poets reasonably liken their own natures to bees and rivers and meadows, and poetry itself to garlands; the flowers indicate the variety and beauty of poetry, the rivers its mass and the impetus to creation, the bees the labor [τὸ ἐπιμελές] and concentrated effort involved,[4] as well as the sweetness of the poems, and the garlands indicate that those who are praised win glory through them. Euripides has combined all of these things and thus made more brilliant the allegory through which he wished to describe his hymn to Artemis; other poets use these devices [τρόποι] in a scattered fashion. Plucking from unravaged meadows indicates that a poetic soul must be pure and unravaged, and unstained by any evil. Those who are going to practice *poiêtikê* must most of all partake of *aidôs*. For this reason some call the Muses too virgins."

3 The reference is either to the bee or to the meadow, depending on which reading is adopted.

4 Reading τὸ συντεταμένον for the transmitted τὸ συντεταγμένον, cf. LSJ s.v. συντείνω I 2.

Scholion on line 79: "A quality which does not derive from nature, but is achieved by constant practice [μελέτη], is 'learned' [διδακτόν]. Philosophers call bad things 'learned' and good things 'natural.'"

Although the whole of Hippolytus' speech here eventually comes under the scholiastic microscope, the "notorious problem" is introduced as that of the garland: is it a real or an allegorical garland? The scholars whose work lies behind the *scholia* presumably knew—and may even have been prompted to their interpretations by—the epithet Στεφανίας or Στεφανηφόρος, which was attached to this *Hippolytus* by at least the time of Aristophanes of Byzantium.[5] Our *scholia* on Euripides go back ultimately to the work of Hellenistic scholars in Alexandria, most notably Aristophanes and Aristarchus,[6] though we may find it hard to imagine either of these figures behind the metaphorical readings of the *scholia*. The very stark interpretative choice the *scholia* offer between "allegorical" or "riddling" readings on the one hand and "literal" (κυρίως) readings on the other is, of course, very familiar in ancient criticism, and these *scholia* are an excellent illustration of one turn of the scholiastic mind: interpretation begins from the question "What do the verses say?," and if the answer is "something which cannot be meant literally" (after all, *aidôs* is not "literally" a gardener), then one must seek other explanations in "troped" language and "allegory." This latter term covers a very wide range of phenomena,[7] and in this instance we are dealing with a set of interpretations which largely appeal, not—as do many ancient "allegorical" readings—to a scheme of the order of the cosmos, as for example does Porphyry in his famous discussion of Homer's "Cave of the Nymphs,"[8] but rather more simply to a metaphorical system which ancient readers tended to think of as inherent in the art of poetry itself. Before turning to the question of how, if at all, these *scholia* can help us to understand the *Hippolytos*,[9] we should investigate the intellectual affiliations of the *scholia* in rather greater detail.

The principal individual elements of the "troped," poetological interpretations (the poet as bee, the "garland" of song, the meadow of the Muses, etc.) are very familiar and appear in poetry well before Euripides.[10] Behind these *scholia* lies a very long tradition of high poetic metaphors for song; Simonides

5 See Barrett 1964:10n1.

6 See e.g. Pfeiffer 1968:222–224; Dickey 2007:32.

7 Struck 2004, Pontani 2005:26–40, and the contributions to Boys-Stones 2003 offer an excellent introduction to this subject.

8 Nauck 1886:56–81; translation and discussion in Lamberton 1983.

9 Commentators on the play have (perhaps unsurprisingly) paid these *scholia* scant attention; unless I am mistaken, Barrett's only reference to them (n. on 76–77) is to label "absurd" the "allegorisation" of the bee as really referring to the soul.

10 Cf. e.g. Steiner 1986:35–39, Nünlist 1998:60–63, 206–223.

is reported to have called Hesiod a gardener and Homer a garland-weaver because the former "planted the mythologies of gods and heroes" and the latter "wove from them the garland of the *Iliad* and the *Odyssey*" (Simonides T 47k Campbell).[11] Unsurprisingly, it is Pindar, whose victorious patrons receive both songs and (literal) garlands, who supplies our richest source of such figures (and this itself is a fact of some significance for the *Hippolytus*). When Pindar asks the eponymous nymph of Akragas to "receive this garland from Pytho" (*Pythian* 12.5), it is hard not to recall Hippolytus' prayer to Artemis. In *Nemean* 7 the song is a highly wrought and precious crown,[12]

> εἴρειν στεφάνους ἐλαφρόν, ἀναβάλεο· Μοῖσά τοι
> κολλᾶι χρυσὸν ἔν τε λευκὸν ἐλέφανθ' ἁμᾶ
> καὶ λείριον ἄνθεμον ποντίας ὑφελοῖσ' ἐέρσας.
>
> It is not difficult to weave garlands—strike up the prelude! The Muse binds together gold and white ivory with the lily flower she has removed from the sea's dew.
>
> Pindar *Nemean* 7.77–79

and at *Nemean* 8.15 the song is a "Lydian headband embroidered with resounding music,"[13] where the *scholia* note that the poet is speaking "allegorically." *Nemean* 3 offers a particularly elaborate "cocktail of song":

> ἐγὼ τόδε τοι
> πέμπω μεμιγμένον μέλι λευκῶι
> σὺν γάλακτι, κιρναμένα δ' ἔερσ' ἀμφέπει,
> πόμ' ἀοίδιμον Αἰολίσσιν ἐν πνοαῖσιν αὐλῶν κτλ.
>
> I send you this honey mingled with white milk, attended by the foam which has been stirred, a drink of song among the Aeolian breaths of pipes ...
>
> Pindar *Nemean* 3.76–79

Here the *scholia* connect milk with the natural talent, the *phusis*, needed for poetry and the honey with the πόνος of bees, and this is precisely the realm of ideas in which the Euripidean *scholia* also move.

[11] The story obviously implies the chronological priority of Hesiod, but to what extent it provides firm evidence for Simonides' view of the matter may be debated.

[12] Cf. further below p. 266.

[13] To the commentators add Kurke 1991:190–191, Ford 2002:117–118.

Poets freely used such images for their own work, but these were also the very stuff of how poetry was explained, and this intimate link with the imagery of poetry itself is fundamental for understanding the language of ancient poetic criticism; it is telling that two of Quintilian's three Latin examples of "allegory through metaphor" (*allegoria continuatis tralationibus*) are poetological images from Lucretius and Virgil (Quintilian 8.6.45). In the present case, however, what stands out is the Platonic background of the Euripidean *scholia*. Like the *scholia*, many modern critics have stressed the analogy between the "unravaged meadow" and Hippolytus' virginal soul, but crucial here is a famous passage of Plato's *Phaedrus* which was very important for later—particularly, of course, Neoplatonic—discussions of poetry:[14]

> τρίτη δὲ ἀπὸ Μουσῶν κατοκωχή τε καὶ μανία, λαβοῦσα ἁπαλὴν καὶ ἄβατον ψυχήν, ἐγείρουσα καὶ ἐκβακχεύουσα κατά τε ᾠδὰς καὶ κατὰ τὴν ἄλλην ποίησιν, μυρία τῶν παλαιῶν ἔργα κοσμοῦσα τοὺς ἐπιγιγνομένους παιδεύει· ὃς δ' ἂν ἄνευ μανίας Μουσῶν ἐπὶ ποιητικὰς θύρας ἀφίκηται, πεισθεὶς ὡς ἄρα ἐκ τέχνης ἱκανὸς ποιητὴς ἐσόμενος, ἀτελὴς αὐτός τε καὶ ἡ ποίησις ὑπὸ τῆς τῶν μαινομένων ἡ τοῦ σωφρονοῦντος ἠφανίσθη.
>
> There is a third sort of possession and madness which comes from the Muses. It takes hold of a tender and untrodden soul, and by rousing it and inducing a state of Bacchic possession in song and other forms of poetry, it educates future generations by celebrating the countless deeds of men of old. But whoever comes to the doors of poetry without madness from the Muses, in the belief that craft [*technê*] will make him a good poet, both he and his poetry, the poetry of a sane man, will be incomplete[15] and eclipsed by the poetry of the mad.
>
> Plato *Phaedrus* 245a

In his commentary on the *Phaedrus*, Proclus explains that the soul which is to receive the divine inspiration of the Muses must be clear of all other distracting influences and ideas, including (we may assume) over-subtle intellectual calculations;[16] we are here not far from the scholiastic explanation that the rejected "iron" of Hippolytus' speech stands for "evil meddlesome-

[14] It is intriguing to find part at least of this passage cited already in Satyrus' *Life of Euripides* (F 6 fr. 16 col. I Schorn), perhaps in a contrast between Euripides and truly "inspired" poetry (?Aeschylus); Schorn 2004:193–194.

[15] Commentators rightly note that ἀτελής both means "uncompleted" and also suggests "uninitiated."

[16] *Commentary on Plato's Republic* 1.181.2–17 Kroll.

ness" (φιλοπραγμονία).[17] Be that as it may, the soul which, in Proclus' words, is ἀπαθὴς καὶ ἄδεκτος καὶ ἀμιγής to everything except the "breath of the divine" (1.181.16–17 Kroll) is at least how Hippolytus sees himself, even if, of course, his Artemis is much more associated with *sôphrosynê* than with *mania*; the language of poetic inspiration and the language of mystical religious devotion are here, as so often, very close.

Plato's ἄβατος "untrodden" for a young man's soul is a word, like Hippolytus' ἀκήρατος, which can have sacral resonance—it is used for a holy place (such as a meadow) which may not be entered except under special circumstances; whereas, however, the sexual resonance of ἀκήρατος and related words is very well attested, ἄβατος in the sense "(sexually) unmounted" is only found in a humorous context in Lucian (*Lexiphanes* 19). Nevertheless, it is easy enough to see how any reader would feel this resonance in the Platonic passage, particularly when ἄβατος is put together with ἁπαλός (and particularly in the context of the ἐρωτικὸς λόγος of the *Phaedrus* as a whole), and here perhaps lies part of the origin of the scholiastic stress upon the purity of soul needed by those who wish to practice *mousikê* or *poiêtikê*. So too, although Hippolytus uses κοσμήσας (line 74) in the sense "arranging, putting together (i.e. the garland)," it is clear that the *scholiasts* felt that the word contributed importantly to the "metaphorical" sense of the passage, and the explanation that poets compare their poems to garlands to indicate "the honor (*kosmos*) of the subjects of song" (p. 13.23 Schwartz) picks up Plato's claim that possession from the Muses "celebrates [κοσμοῦσα] the countless deeds of the ancients" (*Phaedrus* 245a4).

In choosing ἄβατος Plato was also, as often, imitating in language the subject of his discourse. "Untrodden" to describe a soul is, to put it simply, the kind of "metaphor" which one might expect to find in poetry;[18] in describing the possession which comes from the Muses, Socrates speaks like one possessed in just that way. The most significant analogy here, as for the passage of the *Phaedrus* itself, is Socrates' famous account in the *Ion* of poetic inspiration and of why poetry is precisely the result of ecstatic inspiration rather than *technê* (533c8–535a2). Here too poets are like bees and the language imitates their alleged "flights":

> Poets tell us that, like bees [μέλιτται], they are bringing us songs [μέλη] which they have gathered [δρεπόμενοι] from springs flowing with honey [μελιρρύτων] in gardens and groves of the Muses, and they do this in flight. They speak the truth: for a poet is a light and winged and

[17] For scholarly and intellectual "meddlesomeness," see Hunter 2009, Struck 2004:72.

[18] The discussion of Plato's style at Dionysius of Halicarnassus *On Demosthenes* 5–7 is obviously relevant here.

> holy thing, and unable to compose before the god is inside him and he becomes out of his senses and his mind no longer resides in him.
>
> Plato *Ion* 534a7–b6

It is precisely poetic imagery and metaphor, of a kind very close to Hippolytus' imagery, which "proves" the irrational nature of poetic composition.[19] Aristotle more than once stresses that "metaphor" is the most important aspect of poetic language and that making metaphors is a natural gift:

> It is important to use each of the elements I have mentioned appropriately, including double nouns and glosses, but by far the most important aspect of diction is the metaphorical. This is the only aspect which cannot be acquired from another and it is a sign of natural gifts [εὐφυία], for to make good metaphors is to observe similarity.
>
> Aristotle *Poetics* 1459a4–8[20]

Although this is not the same point as Plato's insistence that poetry is the result of inspiration, not *technê*, these comments can clearly be seen to stand in the same tradition, particularly as it is metaphorical language which Plato uses in the *Ion* to illustrate the irrational nature of poetic composition. From the perspective of this later tradition, Hippolytus' highly metaphorical address to Artemis would illustrate the very lesson he teaches, namely the primacy of *phusis* over "taught qualities," for only someone with a very special εὐφυία, who does not in any sense rely on what he has "learned," could "make metaphor" like this. We will see that Euripides certainly had other reasons as well for making Hippolytus speak like this,[21] but it is perhaps not utterly idle to wonder whether the tradition of reflection upon the nature of poetic metaphor which we have found in Plato and Aristotle had roots already in fifth-century discussion of poetry and is reflected in Hippolytus' opening speech.

Before we proceed, it may be as well to cast a quick glance at the poetological ideas themselves which the *scholia* display. Many are, as we have noted, very familiar and not to be traced to any particular intellectual tradition, but we may suspect that much can again be traced back to Plato's *Ion*. The notion that poets and poetry are likened to rivers because of "mass [πληθύς] and the impetus [ὁρμή] to creation" might seem, on one hand, to pick up Socrates' claim that

19 We might comparepoetic inspiration to the workings of a magnet (*Ion* 533d–e), which some have seen as (pointedly) an adoption of the mode of epic simile.

20 Cf. *Rhetoric* 3 (1405a8–10).

21 Cf. below pp. 269–270.

poets and rhapsodes only perform in that one "genre" "towards which the Muse impels [ὥρμησεν] them" (*Ion* 534c1–2).[22] On the other hand, however, the reference to "mass," suggestive of epic grandeur or the raging and swollen mountain torrent which is Horace's vision of Pindar (*Odes* 4.2),[23] might seem untrue to the apparent exclusivity of the ποτάμιαι δρόσοι which water Hippolytus' garden of *Aidôs*, a source perhaps more Callimachean than epic.[24] The *scholia* are, of course, nothing if not eclectic. If rivers denote the rushing power of poetry, the bee indicates, as it does for Horace in the same poem, the *labor plurimus* involved in making *operosa … carmina*;[25] in the scholiast's τὸ ἐπιμελὲς καὶ τὸ συντεταμένον we are not far from "Callimachean" ideals, and Aratus' σύντονος ἀγρυπνίη (Callimachus *Epigram* 27.4 Pfeiffer), if that is the right reading, may particularly come to mind.

As compilations, the *scholia* are of course less concerned with a consistent poetic "program" than with the very overload of poetological imagery which they find in the Euripidean verses. For us that imagery looks both forward and back. Callimachus' famous image for his poem at the end of the *Hymn to Apollo* shares more than one element with Hippolytus' remarkable prayer:

> Δηοῖ δ' οὐκ ἀπὸ παντὸς ὕδωρ φορέουσι μέλισσαι,
> ἀλλ' ἥτις καθαρή τε καὶ ἀχράαντος ἀνέρπει
> πίδακος ἐξ ἱερῆς ὀλίγη λιβὰς ἄκρον ἄωτον.
>
> To Deo the bees do not carry water from every source, but only from that which rises up pure and untainted, a tiny trickle from a holy spring, the height of perfection.
>
> Callimachus *Hymn to Apollo* 110–112

The bee image (the Euripidean *scholia* note the usage of "bee" as "priestess," which must be part of Callimachus' image)[26] and the stress on a sacral purity and exclusivity strongly recall Hippolytus' attitudes, the metaphorical language in

22 Murray (1996:119) notes that Plato's expression here picks up the Homeric ὁρμηθεὶς θεοῦ (*Odyssey* viii 499 of Demodocus, where, though many modern editors take a different view, the *scholia* note the ὁρμή from the god); *pace* Murray, however, it is far from clear that Proclus *Commentary on Plato's Republic* 1.184.27–28 Kroll, who notes Homeric influence on Plato here, is actually thinking of this passage of the *Odyssey*.

23 On this imagery see e.g. Hunter 2003:220–223. Somewhere behind the scholiast's language is probably *Iliad* II 488 πληθὺν δ' οὐκ ἂν ἐγὼ μυθήσομαι … .

24 See below.

25 The etymological play in the *scholia* on μέλισσα and ἐπιμελές is not, to my knowledge, found elsewhere, though it might be thought that the Horatian passage implies it.

26 For discussion see Williams' note on line 110; of particular importance is *Supplementum Hellenisticum* 990.2.

which he expresses them, and the explanations of the *scholia*.[27] Modern criticism has tended to write "religion" out of Callimachus' poetry, with the result that his sacral language is seen as "purely literary," but Hippolytus' prayer should make us pause. If the *scholia* offer as one interpretation that Hippolytus' garland is in fact a song in the goddess' honor, the Callimachean *Hymn to Apollo* is indeed an offering to the god, and one which we know that he accepts.[28] Callimachus draws the sacral boundaries in much the same terms as does Hippolytus:

> ὡπόλλων οὐ παντὶ φαείνεται, ἀλλ' ὅτις ἐσθλός·
> ὅς μιν ἴδηι, μέγας οὗτος, ὃς οὐκ ἴδε, λιτὸς ἐκεῖνος.
> ὀψόμεθ', ὦ Ἑκάεργε, καὶ ἐσσόμεθ' οὔποτε λιτοί.
>
> Apollo does not appear to everyone, but to he who is good; he who sees him, this man is great, he who does not see him, that man is of no value; we shall see [you], Far-Worker, and we shall never be of no value.
>
> Callimachus *Hymn to Apollo* 9–11

If Hippolytus knows that he will never actually "see" his goddess (see 85–86, 1391–1396), it is nevertheless the κακοί—those whom Callimachus would call the ἀλιτροί (2), the οὐκ ἐσθλοί (9), and the λιτοί (10–11)—who may not enter the meadow.[29] If viewed through a Callimachean lens, the "metaphorical" interpretation of Hippolytus' speech which we find in the *scholia* becomes, if not necessarily easier to accept, at least firmly contextualized. As we have seen, there are important differences between the various elements of the pattern. Whereas Hippolytus, like Pindar before him (see e.g. *Olympian* 9.100–104), rejects "the taught" in favor of natural gifts,[30] the *scholia* seem to acknowledge both as important poetic ideas; if Callimachus does not explicitly (but cf. lines 42–46) stress *technê* in the *Hymn to Apollo* and the image of the pure spring would seem to foreground the gifts of divine nature, nevertheless, his emphasis on this elsewhere is well known, and it can be argued that the "Reply to the Telchines" precisely lays claim to both *technê* and the divine inspiration of the *Ion*.[31]

27 καθαρός is a particularly good example of the seepage between sacral and critical language, cf. e.g. "Longinus" *On the Sublime* 33.2.

28 For these ideas in Hellenistic and Roman poetry see Hunter 2006:14–15.

29 On a second-century AD inscription from Attica members of a club are to be tested to see εἴ ἐστι ἁγνὸς καὶ εὐσεβὴς καὶ ἀγαθός (Sokolowski 1969: no. 53, line 33). There is a helpful discussion of the mystical aspect of Hippolytus' language in Asper 1997:51–53.

30 Barrett calls the idea "a commonplace of old aristocratic thought" (1964:173).

31 See Hunter 1989.

Hippolytus' mode of speech looks back also. As we have seen, some of the closest parallels are to be found in Pindar, and it is in Pindar too where the sharpest lines are drawn between those who can and who cannot understand. A famous passage of Pindar's *Second Olympian* asserts the special nature of what Pindar has to say:

πολλά μοι ὑπ'
ἀγκῶνος ὠκέα βέλη
ἔνδον ἐντὶ φαρέτρας
φωνάεντα συνετοῖσιν· ἐς δὲ τὸ πὰν ἑρμανέων
χατίζει. σοφὸς ὁ πολλὰ εἰδὼς φυᾶι·
μαθόντες δὲ λάβροι
παγγλωσσίᾳ κόρακες ὣς ἄκραντα γαρυέτων
Διὸς πρὸς ὄρνιχα θεῖον·

> I have under my arm many swift arrows inside their quiver which speak to those who understand; in general, however, they require interpreters. Wise is the man who naturally knows many things. Those who have learned are unruly and their words spill out; they are like a pair of crows who caw in vain against the divine bird of Zeus.
>
> Pindar *Olympian* 2.82–89

Eustathius took this passage as programmatic of Pindar's poetry as a whole, and to ancient scholars (at least from Aristarchus on),[32] confronted—as in Euripides' *Hippolytus*—with a passage where a "non-allegorical" reading was simply not possible (Pindar does not "literally" have arrows and a quiver, any more than *Aidôs* is a market-gardener), where there is an explicit contrast between "the wise man who knows much by nature" and "those who have learned," and which followed directly on a passage of apparently mystical eschatology, it was clear that Pindar was asserting that his difficult poems required "interpreters" (i.e. commentators) for ordinary people ("common folk," the "nonspecialists," "the many"). It was then entirely "natural" to see the crows and the eagle as "riddling" references to (respectively) Simonides and Bacchylides and to Pindar himself. The text itself seemed to direct the scholars to read "riddlingly."

Such dichotomies in the potential audience either originally arose in or were confirmed by sacral or mystical contexts; Hippolytus' exclusivity suggests this, and indeed any claim to purity implies a group of the "impure," as we can

32 Aristarchus is cited by the *scholia* on line 85 (Drachmann p. 98). For Eustathius see Drachmann III.287.1–8.

see, for example, on the gold leaves of the Underworld.[33] These dichotomies soon found their way, however, into the exegesis of texts, particularly, though not exclusively, what we might call "allegorical" exegesis, for such interpretation inevitably constructs a dual readership—the "few," the "wise," the "initiated" on the one hand, and "the many," "the vulgar," the "uninitiated" on the other.[34]

This process is now most familiar from the Derveni Papyrus, where the commentator seems to distinguish (the text is unfortunately broken) between "the many" and "those pure (?) of hearing" (col. VII 10–11); given the nature of the text, the process of transition from "religious" to "literary" exegesis is here starkly exposed. "Metaphorical" and "riddling" language creates boundaries and displays them openly. On the elaborate "crown of song" at *Nemean* 7.77–79, Andrew Ford comments that this image "is a form of kenning ... but it is also a form of knowing, a mode of addressing the *sophoi*";[35] just the same could be said of Hippolytus' images.

Another, though closely related, distinction drawn within Archaic poetry is also relevant here. The language of the ἀγαθός and the κακός, and indeed of σωφροσύνη, is of course most familiar from the sociopolitical world of sympotic elegy. Theognis describes a world turned upside down:

νῦν δὲ τὰ τῶν ἀγαθῶν κακὰ γίνεται ἐσθλὰ κακοῖσιν
 ἀνδρῶν· ἡγέονται δ' ἐκτραπέλοισι νόμοις·
αἰδὼς μὲν γὰρ ὄλωλεν, ἀναιδείη δὲ καὶ ὕβρις
 νικήσασα δίκην γῆν κατὰ πᾶσαν ἔχει.

But now good men's evils have become virtues for the base; they rejoice in customs turned upside down. *Aidôs* has perished, and shamelessness and outrage have defeated justice and hold sway over the whole land.

Theognis 289–292

The term αἰδώς is as much a catchword for the self-appointed ἀγαθοί in Theognis' world of aristocratic power and values as it is in Hippolytus' dominating sense of self; elsewhere the same point is made explicitly:

ἀνδράσι τοῖσ' ἀγαθοῖσ' ἕπεται γνώμη τε καὶ αἰδώς·
 οἳ νῦν ἐν πολλοῖς ἀτρεκέως ὀλίγοι.

33 Cf. e.g. texts 5–7 and 9 in Graf and Johnston 2007.

34 Through Philodemus we can see traces of these dichotomies in Hellenistic literary criticism; Fantuzzi and Hunter 2004:452. [Plutarch], *De Homero* 92 also explicitly refers to the two classes of Homeric audience, the φιλομαθοῦντες and the ἀμαθεῖς; Pontani 2005:32–33.

35 Ford 2002:123.

> Judgment and *aidôs* attend the good; now they are really few among many.
>
> Theognis 635–636

In another well-known passage, which concludes one of the fullest early examples of the "ship of state" allegory, the now-familiar language of the ἀγαθός (or the ἐσθλός) and the κακός is combined with an appeal to the "decoding" of poetic imagery:[36]

> φορτηγοὶ δ' ἄρχουσι, κακοὶ δ' ἀγαθῶν καθύπερθεν.
> δειμαίνω, μή πως ναῦν κατὰ κῦμα πίῃ.
> ταῦτά μοι ᾐνίχθω κεκρυμμένα τοῖσ' ἀγαθοῖσιν·
> γινώσκοι δ' ἄν τις καὶ κακός, ἂν σοφὸς ᾖι.

> The cargo-carriers are in charge, and the base are above the good; I am afraid that a wave will swallow up the ship. Let these be my veiled riddles for the good; even a base man, if he is wise, would know the meaning.
>
> Theognis 679–682

If we then ask for the resonances of Hippolytus' extraordinary imagery for an Athenian audience in the late fifth century, there will of course be more than one answer, but prominent among them will be not just the sacral, but also the world of the aristocratic, perhaps now "old-fashioned," symposium and the poetry which accompanied it; this is one of the important truths to which the neglected *scholia* direct us. When at the start of the *Homeric Problems* "Heraclitus" illustrates what *allêgoria* is, the three examples he chooses are now-famous instances of Archaic poetry: Archilochus (fr. 105 W) and Alcaeus (frs. 208, 6 V) describing storms, which are "in fact" war and internal strife, and Anacreon (*PMG* 417) addressing a Thracian filly, who is really a lovely girl. The setting for all such poems was very probably a male gathering such as the symposium, i.e. a closed "reception context," a gathering of "those who know," and one in which, as we have seen, both "coded" modes of speech, such as the riddle and the *eikôn*, and (at least during the later fifth century) what we now call "poetic criticism" flourished. The gradual disappearance of this style of figured speech is a major issue of literary history; how archaic this style was already felt to be as Hippolytus spoke is a question to which the *scholia* direct us.

Hippolytus' prayer takes us, of course, in other (related) interpretative directions as well. We may wish (rightly) to set this speech within an

[36] Cf. further Ford 2002:75–76; Hunter 2010.

epistemological pattern whereby the three central characters of the tragedy are each characterized by a different form of knowledge which orders (but eventually undermines) their world: Phaedra, particularly of course in her great speech to the chorus at lines 373ff, by moral reflectiveness leading to clear ethical principles, Theseus by a straightforward reliance upon perception and inherited values, and Hippolytus by a "revealed" truth and certain sense of self (the very way he speaks shuts out "the many"). So too have critics long discussed the battle for control of language in this play, for example, for control of the meaning of σωφροσύνη or Phaedra's struggle with the semantic range of αἰδώς;[37] Hippolytus' speech, with its claims to the control of metaphor and by its juxtaposition to his exchange with the servant, who insists upon a kind of ὀρθοέπεια while also revealing the traps language sets for us (the ambiguity of σεμνός, etc.), introduces this theme to powerful effect.

The division of the world into "those who understand" and "those who do not" implied in Hippolytus' prayer and which, as we have seen, is a prominent feature not just of forms of religious worship but also of the world of Archaic poetry and its exegesis, resurfaces, as do Hippolytus' claims to σωφροσύνη (995, 1007, 1013, 1034–1035) and αἰδώς (998), in the speech of self-defense he makes to his father. He begins with a very striking *proemium:*

> ἐγὼ δ' ἄκομψος εἰς ὄχλον δοῦναι λόγον,
> ἐς ἥλικας δὲ κὠλίγους σοφώτερος·
> ἔχει δὲ μοῖραν καὶ τόδ'· οἱ γὰρ ἐν σοφοῖς
> φαῦλοι παρ' ὄχλωι μουσικώτεροι λέγειν.
> ὅμως δ' ἀνάγκη, ξυμφορᾶς ἀφιγμένης,
> γλῶσσάν μ' ἀφεῖναι.

> I am not clever at speaking to the rabble, but more skilled before my equals and a small audience. This is only reasonable. Those who fail before the wise have more success with speaking in front of the rabble. Nevertheless, in this present misfortune, I must let loose my tongue.
>
> Euripides *Hippolytus* 986–991

This "tactless ... contempt for his audience" (Barrett) might seem a truly remarkable form of the "unaccustomed as I am" topos, but much is at stake here. Barrett notes that Hippolytus' reference to the *ochlos* is "especially tactless since although there is of course a crowd gathered round ... it is only to Theseus that his arguments are addressed," but we may wonder if this is not

37 See e.g. Goldhill 1986:132–137; Gill 1990.

one of those places in tragedy where the audience may well feel itself involved, if not specifically addressed; *ochlos* is (unsurprisingly) one of the terms for the audience used in the famous account of Athenian theatrical history offered by Plato, yet another elitist (*Laws* 3.700a–1b).

It is the fact of public "performance," as well as the ignorance of the broad audience, which Hippolytus rejects. Words matter to him, and "letting loose the tongue" (991) is not a mode he favors; as we know from the violence of his reaction to the Nurse's attempt to win him over (653–655), even hearing words of a morally corrupt kind threatens to make him κακός and stains his purity (ἁγνεύειν) so that he will need to wash out his ears with "water from running streams." Here it is now very hard not to recall (again) the distinction in the Derveni commentary between "the many" and "those pure (?) of hearing" (col. VII 10–11), in a chapter precisely about the exegesis of an "allegorical" text; Tsantsanaglou's τὴ]ν ἀκοὴν [ἁγνεύο]ντας is there almost universally accepted.

As the rejected crows of Pindar's *Second Olympian* are indiscriminate in their choice of language (λάβροι παγγλωσσίαι), so the exercise of linguistic choice is the activity of the *sophos*. The Plutarchan treatise *On the Education of Children* quotes *Hippolytus* 986–989 in support of the need to expose children only to the right kind of education, and the distinctions which Plutarch draws make the passage worth quoting at length:

> I say again that parents must cling to the uncorrupted and healthy education and must take their sons as far away as possible from the rubbish of public speeches [τῶν πανηγυρικῶν λήρων], for to give pleasure to the many [οἱ πολλοί] is to displease the wise [οἱ σοφοί]. Euripides supports this ... *Hippolytus* 986–989 ... I see that those whose practice it is to speak in a manner which pleases and wins favor with the vulgar rabble [τοῖς συρφετώδεσιν ὄχλοις] turn out generally to be dissolute in their lifestyle and fond of pleasure. This is just what we would expect. If as they provide pleasure for others they neglect what is honorable [τοῦ καλοῦ], they would be slow indeed to place what is morally correct and healthy [τὸ ὀρθὸν καὶ ὑγιές] above the pursuit of their own luxurious pleasures or what is modest [τὸ σῶφρον] above the delightful [τοῦ τερπνοῦ].
>
> Plutarch *On the Education of Children* 6a–c

The context here is quite different from that of the *Hippolytus*, but Plutarch too is the spokesman for a self-appointed elite, the σοφοί, whose authority depends upon a shared body of knowledge (*paideia*) which excludes the "uninitiated"; like Hippolytus, Plutarch equates verbal excess and facility with a morally impure life and an absence of *sôphrosunê*.

From the outside such claims, whether those of a Hippolytus or of a Plutarch, are always open to charges of hypocrisy (as, for example, Lucian knew only too well). Thus Theseus famously throws in Hippolytus' face the charge of hypocritical allegiance to "Orphic" behavior:

> ἤδη νυν αὔχει καὶ δι' ἀψύχου βορᾶς
> σίτοις καπήλευ' Ὀρφέα τ' ἄνακτ' ἔχων
> βάκχευε πολλῶν γραμμάτων τιμῶν καπνούς·
> ἐπεί γ' ἐλήφθης.
>
> Now hold your high opinions and with your lifeless food make a show of your diet; with Orpheus as your leader revel on and honor writings, insubstantial as smoke. You have been found out!
>
> Euripides *Hippolytus* 952–955

What is important here is not whether Hippolytus was really an Orphic, but rather the familiar and much commented upon phenomenon of the association of "Orphics" with "books" (cf. Plato *Republic* 2.364e); here, if anywhere, were Greeks with "sacred books" to be honored (954) and, as the Derveni Papyrus has shown us, interpreted.[38] Such books offered a kind of knowledge not (to be) widely available and one which both seemed to invite and may perhaps have exploited *allegorêsis*. Texts intended for and/or taken up as privileged by particular groups are always fertile ground for "metaphorical" or "allegorical" reading, for this is precisely one of the ways in which the specialness of the text is preserved. In principle, of course, this may also apply to oral "texts," as we see not just in pre- or partially literate societies, but in, say, the "secret knowledge" of closed societies (fraternities, Masons, etc.) in highly literate contexts. Committing knowledge to writing risks its promulgation among the "profane," and if this must be done, the knowledge must therefore be "encoded" in such a way that it is of no use if it falls into the wrong hands; metaphor and "allegory" are forms of literary code. In antiquity the idea of religious "mysteries" is never far away in this context: the Platonic Socrates seems to link "allegory" with eschatological rites (*Phaedo* 69c), the critic Demetrius tells us that "the mysteries are conducted through allegory to increase their power to instill amazement and terror ... for allegorical language is like darkness and night" (*On Style* 101), and the Hippocratic "Law" concludes by noting that the holy facts of medicine are to be revealed only to those who have been initiated through knowledge (*CMG* I.i.8).[39]

[38] Cf. Henrichs 2003 for a discussion of the general phenomenon.

[39] On allegory and the mysteries see e.g. Pontani 2005:34–36.

The metaphorical and mystical mode of Hippolytus' opening speech may thus be seen to prepare us for his terrible fate. Theseus' angry words—ironically placed in the mouth of a "tyrant"—reflect the "democratic" suspicion that those who hide things in books have something (perhaps risible) to hide; metaphorical language may, by its very nature, seem antithetical to the proclaimed transparency of democratic principles.[40] Hippolytus, who of course surrounded himself with ἄριστοι φίλοι (1018), is thus damned both ways: on the one hand, his language and behavior suggest the closed circle of the aristocratic symposium, predominantly of course an oral culture, and on the other he can be assimilated to suspect sects who claimed to find revealed truth in writings. Both frames testify to the very singularity of this character and the struggle to find the appropriate categories for him. That singularity was strikingly signaled by his opening dedicatory address to Artemis, which invites "interpretation," whether we call this "allegorical" or prefer (with Barrett) to speak of "transparent symbolism."[41] It is this invitation to interpretation upon which the ancient scholiasts focused, and so should we.

The scholiasts sought to understand the intellectual structure which lay behind Hippolytus' words; we may not wish to follow the path they trod, but their curiosity is something we should ponder hard before going our own way. If there is a continuing tradition of criticism from antiquity to the present, then it is one of debate and struggle, and the authors of many of our *scholia* knew that the texts of the past mattered and were worth struggling over. Old trends are often the best.

Bibliography

Asper, M. 1997. *Onomata allotria: Zur Genese, Struktur und Funktion poetologischer Metaphern bei Kallimachos*. Stuttgart.

Barrett, W. S. 1964. Euripides, *Hippolytos*. Oxford.

Boys-Stones, G. R., ed. 2003. *Metaphor, Allegory, and the Classical Tradition: Ancient Thought and Modern Revisions*. Oxford.

Dickey, E. 2007. *Ancient Greek Scholarship: A Guide to Finding, Reading, and Understanding Scholia, Commentaries, Lexica, and Grammatical Treatises, from Their Beginnings to the Byzantine Period*. Oxford.

Fantuzzi, M., and R. Hunter. 2004. *Tradition and Innovation in Hellenistic Poetry*. Cambridge.

40 Cf. the remarks of Ford (2002:87).

41 Barrett 1964:172.

Ford, A. 2002. *The Origins of Criticism: Literary Culture and Poetic Theory in Classical Greece*. Princeton.

Gill, C. 1990. "The Articulation of the Self in Euripides' *Hippolytus*." In *Euripides, Women, and Sexuality* (ed. A. Powell) 76–107. London.

Goldhill, S. 1986. *Reading Greek Tragedy*. Cambridge.

Graf, F., and S. I. Johnston. 2007. *Ritual Texts for the Afterlife*. London.

Henrichs, A. 2003. "*Hieroi logoi* and *Hierai bibloi*: The (Un)written Margins of the Sacred in Ancient Greece." *Harvard Studies in Classical Philology* 101:207–266.

Hunter, R. 1989. "Winged Callimachus." *Zeitschrift für Papyrologie und Epigraphik* 76:1–2.

———. 2003. "Reflecting on Writing and Culture: Theocritus and the Style of Cultural Change.'" In *Written Texts and the Rise of Literate Culture in Ancient Greece* (ed. H. Yunis) 213–234. Cambridge.

———. 2006. *The Shadow of Callimachus*. Cambridge.

———. 2009. "The Curious Incident ...: Polypragmosyne and the Ancient Novel." In *Readers and Writers in the Ancient Novel* (ed. M. Paschalis, S. Panayotakis, and G. Schmeling) 51–63. Groningen.

———. 2010. "Language and Interpretation in Greek Epigram." In *Archaic and Classical Greek Epigram: Contextualisation and Literarization* (ed. M. Baumbach, A. Petrovic, and I. Petrovic) 265–288. Cambridge.

Kurke, L. 1991. *The Traffic in Praise: Pindar and the Poetics of Social Economy*. Ithaca.

Lamberton, R. 1983. *Porphyry, On the Cave of the Nymphs*. Barrytown, NY.

Murray, P. 1996. *Plato on Poetry*. Cambridge.

Nauck, A. 1886. *Porphyrii philosophi Platonici opuscula selecta*. Leipzig.

Nünlist, R. 1998. *Poetologische Bildersprache in der frühgriechischen Dichtung*. Stuttgart.

Pfeiffer, R. 1968. *History of Classical Scholarship*. Oxford.

Pontani, F. 2005. *Eraclito, Questioni omeriche sulle allegorie di Omero in merito agli dèi*. Pisa.

Schorn, S. 2004. *Satyrus aus Kallatis*. Basel.

Sokolowski, F. 1969. *Lois sacrées des cités grecques*. Paris.

Steiner, D. 1986. *The Crown of Song: Metaphor in Pindar*. London.

Struck, P. T. 2004. *Birth of the Symbol: Ancient Readers at the Limits of Their Texts*. Princeton.